HUMAN
DISEASES AND
CONDITIONS

HUMAN DISEASES AND CONDITIONS

Neil Izenberg, M.D.

Editor in Chief

Published in Association with the
Center for Children's Health Media,
The Nemours Foundation

Volume 3

Pancreatic Cancer–Zoonosis

Index

Charles Scribner's Sons
An Imprint of The Gale Group
New York

The information in *Human Diseases and Conditions* is not intended to take the place of medical care by physicians and other health care professionals. This book does not contain diagnostic, treatment, or first aid recommendations. Readers should obtain professional advice in making all health care decisions.

Library of Congress Cataloging-in-Publication Data

Human diseases and conditions / Neil Izenberg, editor in chief.
    p. cm.
  "Published in association with the Center for Children's Health Media, the Nemours Foundation."
  Contents: V. 1. Abscess-Dysrhythmia.
  Includes bibliographical references and index.
  Summary: Present articles dealing with all kinds of diseases and disorders, from acne and brain tumor to tobacco-related diseases and yellow fever.
  ISBN 0-684-80543-X (set: alk. paper) —ISBN 0-684-80541-3 (v. 1 : alk. paper)
1. Medicine, Popular—Encyclopedias Juvenile. [1. Diseases—Encyclopedias. 2. Health—Encyclopedias.] I. Izenberg, Neil.

RC81.A2 H75 2000
616'.003 —dc21

                                 99-051442

ISBN 0-684-80542-1 (vol. 2)
ISBN 0-684-80621-5 (vol. 3)

1 3 5 7 9 11 13 15 17 19 20 18 16 14 12 10 8 6 4 2

Printed in the United States of America

The paper used in this publication meets the minimum requirements of the American National Standard for Information Sciences—Permanence of Paper for Printed Library Materials, ANSI Z39.48-1992.

Contents

Contents

Contents

HUMAN
DISEASES AND
CONDITIONS

P–Q

P–Q

Pancreatic Cancer

Pancreatic (pan-kree-AT-ik) cancer is a condition in which the cells in the pancreas (PAN-kree-us), a digestive gland located behind the stomach, divide without control or order, forming tumors that frequently spread to other parts of the body. It is usually fatal.

KEYWORDS
for searching the Internet
and other reference sources

Cancer

Digestive Diseases

What Is Pancreatic Cancer?

The pancreas is a six-inch-long gland in the abdomen* that is surrounded by the stomach, intestine, and other digestive organs. It is shaped like a long, flattened pear, wide at one end and narrow at the other. This gland produces fluids that contain digestive enzymes (EN-zymes), proteins that help the body break down food for use in the body.

These fluids travel through a series of ducts, or tubes, into a main pancreatic duct that joins the common bile duct coming from the liver and gallbladder. Along with the bile, which helps the body digest fat, the pancreatic juices empty into the small intestine. The pancreas also manufactures and releases hormones that help the body store or use the energy that comes from food. One example of these is insulin, which helps control the amount of sugar in the blood. The pancreas's hormone-releasing cells are called islet (EYE-let) cells.

Cancer usually begins in the juice-carrying ducts; only rarely does it start in the islet cells. A tumor forms and eventually grows into the surrounding organs. Cancer cells may also break away from the tumor and spread to other parts of the body, such as the lymph nodes*, liver, lungs, and bones.

Finding cancer early is the key to treating it successfully, but with pancreatic cancer, symptoms usually are not noticeable until the cancer has spread to other parts of the body. By then it is usually too late for successful treatment.

What Are the Symptoms of Pancreatic Cancer?

People with cancer of the pancreas eventually develop pain in the upper abdomen that sometimes spreads to the back and may become worse after eating or lying down. They also may experience nausea, loss of appetite, weight loss, and weakness. If the tumor blocks the common bile duct so that bile cannot pass into the small intestine, they develop jaundice (JAWN-dis), a condition in which the skin and whites of the

** **abdomen** (AB-do-men), commonly called the belly, is the portion of the body between the chest or thorax (THOR-aks) and the pelvis.*

** **lymph nodes** are bean-sized round or oval masses of immune system tissue, located throughout the body, which store special cells that fight infection and other diseases. Clusters of them are found in the underarms, groin, neck, chest, and abdomen.*

eyes turn yellow. Islet cell cancer can cause the pancreas to make too much insulin or other hormones. As a result, the person may feel weak or dizzy and experience chills, muscle spasms, or diarrhea.

How Is Cancer of the Pancreas Diagnosed?

When doctors suspect pancreatic cancer, they perform x-rays and other imaging tests that produce pictures of the pancreas and the areas surrounding it. The symptoms described above can be caused by many other less serious conditions, so doctors need to rule out these possibilities.

All of these visual tests provide clues to determine whether the person has cancer of the pancreas. However, the only way to know for sure is to take a tissue sample and view it under the microscope, a procedure called biopsy (BY-op-see). Surgeons can obtain this tissue in different ways. They can get it through a needle that is inserted through the abdomen into the pancreas or through a thin flexible tube passed down the throat and into the stomach region.

How Is Pancreatic Cancer Treated?

Pancreatic cancer has the highest mortality rate of all cancers. Only about 1 out of 10 cases of pancreatic cancer can potentially be cured, usually when the tumor is confined to the pancreas and the immediate surrounding area. More commonly, treating the disease aims at lessening the pain and improving the person's quality of life.

In either case, the most common forms of treatment are surgery, radiation therapy, and chemotherapy (kee-mo-THER-a-pee), or a combination of them. Surgery involves removing part or all of the pancreas in a procedure called pancreatectomy (pan-kree-a-TEK-to-mee). Radiation therapy uses high-energy rays to damage cancer cells and stop them from growing and dividing. Chemotherapy is the use of anticancer drugs that are fed into a vein or given in pill form.

Who Develops Cancer of the Pancreas and Why?

As with most other types of cancer, pancreatic cancer is usually diagnosed in middle-aged and older people. It rarely occurs before age 40, and most people who develop it are around age 70. Cancer of the pancreas is the fourth most common kind of cancer in men and the fifth most common kind of cancer in women.

Doctors are not sure what causes this type of cancer. Research shows that people are more likely to develop it if they smoke cigarettes or they have diabetes*. Some studies suggest that a fatty diet that is low in fruits and vegetables contributes to pancreatic cancer, while others indicate that people who are exposed to certain harsh chemicals in their jobs are at higher risk. Heredity is another possible factor: people may inherit a tendency to develop tumors in the pancreas. However, more research is needed to pinpoint specific causes of pancreatic cancer. Many people get it for no apparent reason.

*** diabetes** (dy-a-BEE-teez) is an impaired ability to control the level of sugar in the blood because the body does not produce enough insulin or cannot use the insulin it makes.

Resources

Organizations

National Cancer Institute, National Institutes of Health, Bethesda, MD. This organization produces a pamphlet called *What You Need to Know about Cancer of the Pancreas.*
Telephone 800-4-CANCER
http://cancernet.nci.nih.gov/wyntk_pubs/pancreas.htm

The American Cancer Society's Pancreas Cancer Resource Center posts information on pancreatic cancer at its website.
http://www3.cancer.org/cancerinfo/specific.asp

▶ *See also*
Cancer

Pancreatitis

Pancreatitis (pan-kree-a-TY-tis) is a painful inflammation* of the pancreas.

What Is Pancreatitis?

The pancreas (PAN-kree-us) is a gland about 6 inches long that is shaped like a flattened pear and lies next to the stomach with its wider end near the

KEYWORDS
for searching the Internet
and other reference sources

Alcohol abuse

Biliary tract disease

Inflammation

***inflammation** (in-fla-MAY-shun) is the body's response to infection or irritation, usually marked by heat, swelling, redness, and pain.

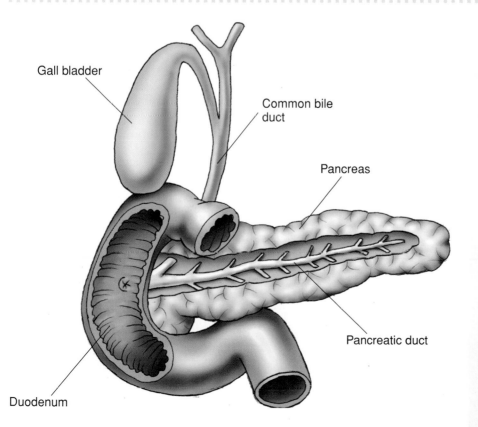

Gall bladder

Common bile duct

Pancreas

Pancreatic duct

Duodenum

◀

Pancreas, gallbladder, duodenum.

* **hormones** are chemicals that are produced by different glands in the body. Hormones are like the body's ambassadors: they are created in one place but are sent through the body to have specific regulatory effects in different places.

* **enzymes** (EN-zymz) are natural substances that speed up specific chemical reactions in the body.

* **acute** means sudden.

* **chronic** (KRON-ik) means continuing for a long period of time.

* **diabetes** (dy-a-BEE-teez) is an impaired ability to break down carbohydrates, proteins, and fats because the body does not produce enough insulin or cannot use the insulin it makes.

* **gallstones** (GAWL-stonz) are hard masses that form in the gallbladder or bile duct.

* **abdomen** (AB-do-men), commonly called the belly, is the portion of the body between the chest or thorax (THOR-aks) and the pelvis.

* **CT scans** or CAT scans are the shortened names for computerized axial tomography (to-MOG-ra-fee), which uses computers to view cross sections inside the body.

* **cancer** is an uncontrolled growth of cells or tissue the natural (untreated) course of which is often fatal.

duodenum (doo-o-DEE-num), the first part of the small intestine. The pancreas produces insulin and glucagon (GLOO-ka-gon), which are chemical messengers called hormones* that control the use of sugar in the body. The pancreas also secretes enzymes*, which are proteins that the body needs to digest other proteins, sugars, and fats. These digestive juices are carried to the small intestine by the biliary (BIL-ee-air-ee) system, which consists of a small pear-shaped organ called the gallbladder (GAWL-blad-er) and a network of ducts.

When the pancreas becomes inflamed, its powerful digestive enzymes leak out and begin to attack the pancreas itself. These enzymes cause damage that results in swelling of tissues and blood vessels. There are two forms of pancreatitis. Acute* pancreatitis occurs when the pancreas suddenly becomes inflamed but then gets better. Chronic* pancreatitis is persistent inflammation of the pancreas or a combination of persistent inflammation with repeated attacks of acute pancreatitis. Over time, the damage caused by chronic pancreatitis can lead to malabsorption (when the body cannot absorb the nutrients and calories it needs) and an abnormal secretion of insulin, that is, diabetes*.

What Causes Pancreatitis?

There are many causes of pancreatitis, but most cases of acute pancreatitis are caused by alcohol abuse or gallstones*. A patient usually feels severe pain in the upper abdomen* that may last for hours or for a few days. The abdomen may be swollen and tender. Other symptoms may include nausea, vomiting, fever, and an increased pulse rate.

How Is Pancreatitis Diagnosed?

In addition to pain, patients with chronic pancreatitis usually show signs of long-term damage such as malabsorption or diabetes. Because acute pancreatitis causes an increase in certain levels of digestive enzymes in the blood, a blood test may confirm a diagnosis of the condition. Sometimes, x-rays such as CT scans* are used to make the diagnosis.

How Is Pancreatitis Treated?

Treatment for pancreatitis depends on the type, cause, and severity of the condition. Although acute pancreatitis usually gets better on its own, patients often are hospitalized while the attack lasts. If the patient has gallstones, surgery may be needed to remove them.

Patients with chronic pancreatitis will be placed on a strict diet that limits fat and protein, which the damaged pancreas can no longer digest properly. Patients sometimes are given replacement enzymes to help digest their food, and a doctor may prescribe medication to relieve pain. Because both acute and chronic pancreatitis often are caused by alcohol, the best way to prevent the disease is to avoid drinking.

With treatment, the outlook for chronic pancreatitis often is good, but patients must stop drinking. Other less common causes of pancreatitis, such as infections, cancer*, and reactions to medicines or chemicals, need to be diagnosed properly in order to be treated the best way possible.

Resource

U.S. National Digestive Diseases Information Clearinghouse, 2 Information Way, Bethesda, MD 20892-3570. Part of the U.S. National Institutes of Health (NIH), the NDDIC publishes brochures about digestive diseases and posts a fact sheet about pancreatitis at its website. Telephone 301-654-3810

http://www.niddk.nih.gov/health/digest/pubs/pancreas/pancreas.htm

▶ *See also*
Alcoholism
Diabetes
Gallstones

Paralysis

Paralysis (pa-RAL-i-sis) is the inability to consciously control the movement of the muscles.

KEYWORDS
for searching the Internet and other reference sources

Muscular system

Nervous system

Spinal cord injury

Sang Lan's Story

As she was warming up for her routine at the July 1998 Goodwill Games, 17-year-old Chinese gymnast Sang Lan prepared to jump over the vaulting horse, a move she had performed thousands of times. But Sang flung herself too forcefully into the vault and landed on her head instead of her feet. The impact snapped the sixth and seventh vertebrae (VER-te-bray) in her neck, damaging her spinal cord and leaving her unable to move from the chest down. Sang's disability is probably permanent. This type of injury is one of the causes of the condition called paralysis.

What Is Paralysis?

Muscle is a special kind of tissue that enables our bodies to move. It is under the control of the nervous system, which processes messages to and from all parts of the body. Sometimes the nerve cells, or neurons, that control the muscles become diseased or injured. When that happens, a person loses the ability to move the muscles voluntarily, and we say that the person is paralyzed.

Paralysis of the muscles of the face, arm, and leg on one side of the body is called hemiplegia ("hemi" means "half") and usually results from damage to the opposite side of the brain. Damage to the nerves of the spinal cord affects different parts of the body, depending on the amount of damage and where it occurred. Paralysis of both lower limbs is called paraplegia, and paralysis of both arms and both legs is called quadriplegia. Paralysis may be temporary or permanent, depending on the disease or injury. Because paralysis can affect any muscle in the body, a person may lose not only the ability to move but also the ability to talk or to breathe unaided.

How Does a Person Become Paralyzed?

Physical injury—for example, sports or car accidents—poisoning, infection, blocked blood vessels, and tumors can all cause paralysis. Defects

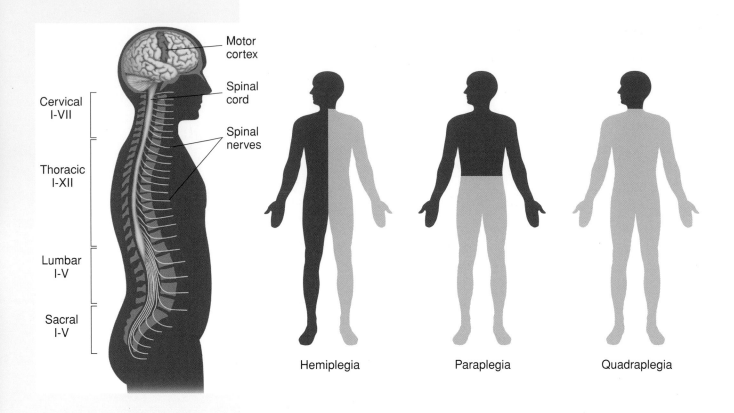

Cervical
I-VII

Thoracic
I-XII

Lumbar
I-V

Sacral
I-V

Motor cortex

Spinal cord

Spinal nerves

Hemiplegia   Paraplegia   Quadraplegia

▲

Left to right: Spinal cord showing regions (cervical, thoracic, lumbar, etc.) and nerves; hemiplegia; paraplegia; and quadriplegia.

in the developing brain of the fetus or brain injury during birth can cause a paralytic condition known as cerebral palsy. In diseases such as multiple sclerosis, inflammation scars the nerves, interrupting communication between the brain and the muscles. Sometimes the muscle tissue itself is affected. In muscular dystrophy, deterioration of the muscle tissue of the arms and legs causes increasing weakness.

Guillain-Barré (gee-YAN ba-RAY) syndrome is an autoimmune disorder in which the body's own cells attack the insulation and core of the nerve fibers, beginning in the hands and feet. In myasthenia gravis (my-es-THEE-nee-a GRA-vis), another autoimmune disorder, a chemical malfunction disrupts the communication needed for muscles to contract.

In rare cases, no physical cause for paralysis can be found. Psychologists call this condition a conversion disorder—that is, a person converts his or her psychological anxiety into physical symptoms of paralysis, but nerve and muscle function are still intact.

Signs and Symptoms

The signs and symptoms of paralysis vary. When the spinal cord is crushed, as in Sang Lan's injury, a person is immediately paralyzed and loses feeling in the affected limbs. When damage to the muscles or central nervous system is caused by a progressive disease or disorder, such as muscular dystrophy or multiple sclerosis, symptoms are gradual and often start with muscle fatigue and weakness. With poliomyelitis (PO-le-o-my-e-LY-tis) and stroke, paralysis comes on suddenly, with little or no warning.

Diagnosis

Information about symptoms and their onset helps the doctor pinpoint the cause of paralysis. With certain genetic diseases that are inherited, such as muscular dystrophy, family medical history provides important clues.

Is Paralysis Treatable?

Aside from poliomyelitis (which can be prevented by vaccination) and brain and spinal cord injuries (which in some cases can be prevented by using appropriate safety measures), it is usually not possible to prevent the conditions that cause paralysis, and most of the time there is no specific treatment. Steroid medications are sometimes given at the time of spinal cord injury to reduce inflammation in an attempt to limit the amount of damage to the spinal nerves. For people with paralysis who must use wheelchairs, treatment emphasizes exercises and special care to avoid infections and pressure sores. Patients with myasthenia gravis may be offered a drug that helps their muscles contract. Most people with Guillain-Barré syndrome recover on their own. Conversion disorder can be difficult to treat; the underlying psychological problem must be addressed.

Living with Paralysis

Many people with paralysis have normal lifespans, even when the condition is the result of progressive disease. People who are confined to wheelchairs can still drive, swim, fly planes, and even ski. But being paralyzed requires major adjustments to daily living, because the muscles a person usually relies on to do certain things no longer work. For example, for people with severe paralysis, ordinary body functions like urinating and having bowel movements may be difficult tasks. In extreme cases, a person may not even be able to breathe without assistance. Help is available to cope with most cases of paralysis, and people with this condition can often hold jobs, raise families, and participate in life's activities.

Will There Ever Be a Cure?

Ten years ago, no one would have imagined that badly injured nerves could heal. But in the future, people may be able to regain the function they have lost through injury to their motor nerves. For example, experiments with rats and cats have shown that it is possible to repair damaged nerves and that severed spinal cord tissue can be made to grow back. Of course, many questions need to be answered before these approaches can be applied to humans.

Water provides both resistance and buoyancy, which can help patients with neuromuscular diseases exercise more effectively.

▼

"Like a Mind in a Jar"

Jean-Dominique Bauby, editor of the magazine *Elle*, was 43 and had a wife and two young children when he suffered a stroke that left him with a condition called locked-in syndrome. Bauby was able to think, but he could not speak or move a single muscle in his body except for his left eye. He began to communicate by blinking his eye in a kind of code that a friend painstakingly transcribed letter by letter, first into words and then into sentences. The sentences became a book titled *The Diving Bell and the Butterfly*. The book was an instant best-seller in France and later inspired readers worldwide.

 See also

Amytrophic Lateral Sclerosis

Bedsores (Pressure Sores)

Cerebral Palsy

Incontinence

Multiple Sclerosis

Muscular Dystrophy

Poliomyelitis

Spina Bifida

Stroke

KEYWORDS
for searching the Internet and other reference sources

Cestodes

Flukes

Foodborne diseases

Infection

Infestation

Nematodes

Protozoa

Trematodes

Tropical diseases

Waterborne diseases

Tickborne diseases

Vectors

Resources

Book

Reeve, Christopher. *Still Me.* New York: Random House, 1996. A book by the actor, now paralyzed, who once played Superman.

Magazine

WE Magazine. A lifestyle magazine for people with disabilities. http://www.wemagazine.com

Organizations

National Institute of Neurological Disorders and Stroke, Office of Communications and Public Liaison, P.O. Box 5801, Bethesda, MD 20824. A U.S. government agency that is a major source of information regarding neurological disorders and stroke. http://www.ninds.nih.gov

National Spinal Cord Injury Association (NSCIA), 8300 Colesville Road, Suite 551, Silver Spring, MD 20910. http://www.erols.com/nscia/resource

Tutorial

"Paralysis Analysis." An informative tutorial on spinal-cord injuries and an update on current advances in research. http://whyfiles.news.wisc.edu/023spinal_cord/index.htm

Parasitic Diseases

Parasitic diseases are illnesses caused by infestation (infection) with parasites such as protozoa (one-celled animals), worms, or insects. These diseases are widespread in Africa, southern Asia, and Central and South America, especially among children. They include malaria and schistosomiasis, the world's most common serious infectious diseases.

Most of the world's 6 billion people are infected with parasites, which are primitive animals that live in or on the bodies of humans, animals, or insects. Often the parasites do little damage, and people may be unaware they are infected. But in any given year, more than a billion people, many of them children, fall sick with parasitic diseases, and millions of them die.

Where Do Parasitic Illnesses Occur?

Parasites live everywhere, but they particularly thrive in warm, moist climates. So they are most common in sub-Saharan Africa, the Indian subcontinent, southeastern Asia, and Central and South America. Some nations in these areas are too poor to take measures that could prevent parasitic infections—such as building water and sewage treatment plants, controlling mosquitoes, or providing adequate medical care. At the same time, in some places, parasitic diseases make so many people weak, ill, and unable to work that they slow economic development and help keep regions impoverished.

Some parasites are found worldwide, even in cooler climates and in wealthier nations, including the United States. These include pinworms, whipworms, and such protozoa as *Giardia lamblia* (which causes intestinal problems), *Babesia* (which is spread by ticks and causes fever and chills), *Trichomonas vaginalis* (which infects the genital tract of men and women), and *Cryptosporidium parvum* (which has caused outbreaks of diarrheal illness in some cities of the United States).

What Are the Most Common Parasitic Diseases?

The intestinal roundworm *Ascaris lumbricoides* causes ascariasis, estimated to infect 1 billion people, although it often does little damage. More important in its impact is malaria, which is estimated to cause 300 million to 500 million illnesses a year and about 2 million deaths. About half of those deaths occur in children under age 5. *Schistosoma* blood flukes cause schistosomiasis (shis-to-so-MY-a-sis), which is estimated to cause 120 million illnesses, 20 million of them severe.

Other parasitic diseases that are estimated to cause a million or more cases of illness are filariasis, amebiasis, Chagas' disease, leishmaniasis, and African sleeping sickness (trypanosomiasis).

Ectoparasites "Ecto-" means "outer." Ectoparasites live on the outer surface of humans. They include lice and the mites that cause scabies (SKAY-beez).

How Do Parasitic Diseases Spread?

In most cases, people get a parasitic infection by bathing in, swimming in, or drinking water that contains parasites; by eating food that has not been cooked thoroughly; or by coming into contact with untreated sewage. That commonly can happen when human waste is used to fertilize fields. It also can happen if people who handle food do not wash their hands thoroughly after a bowel movement.

Many impoverished nations are undergoing rapid urbanization, meaning many people are crowded together into fast-growing cities that may lack sewage treatment facilities. Raw (untreated) sewage may be dumped into rivers whose water is also used for drinking, bathing, washing, and cooking. Parasitic diseases spread easily in such conditions.

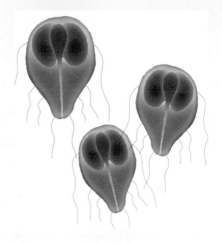

▲ The *Giardia lamblia* protozoan.

Leishmaniasis (leesh-ma-NY-a-sis) occurs in tropical and some temperate areas. Protozoa (single-celled parasites) in the genus *Leishmania* cause the disease, which is transmitted by the bite of infected sandflies. Forms of the disease include (1) cutaneous (ku-TAY-nee-us) leishmaniasis, which causes a painless but unsightly skin ulcer that often heals on its own, leaving a depressed scar; (2) mucocutaneous (myoo-ko-ku-TAY-nee-us) leishmaniasis, which eats away at the tissues inside the nose and mouth; and (3) kala-azar (ka-la-a-ZAR), which affects the lymph nodes, spleen, liver, and bone marrow and can be fatal. The *Leishmania donovani* parasite, seen here under an electron microscope, can cause the form of leishmaniasis called kala-azar. © *Manfred Kage/Peter Arnold, Inc.*

▼

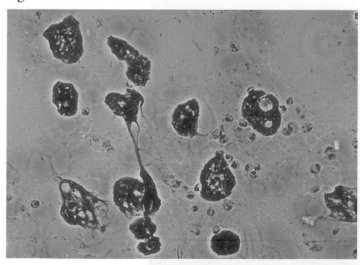

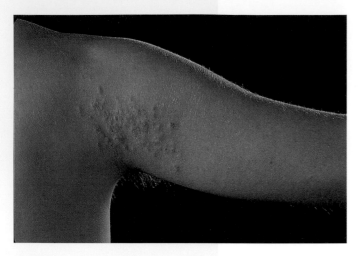

This young man has a skin rash on his upper arm caused by hookworm larvae. *St. Bartholomew's Hospital/Science Photo Library/Photo Researchers, Inc.*

Sleeping Sickness

African trypanosomiasis (tri-pan-o-so-MY-a-sis) is also called African sleeping sickness. Protozoa (single-cell animals) of the genus *Trypanosoma* cause the disease. African trypanosomiasis is found only in Africa and is transmitted by the bite of an infected Tsetse (TZEET-ze) fly. Treatment for African trypanosomiasis involves a number of drugs administered under a doctor's care over a period of weeks. Left untreated, death eventually occurs.

▶ See also
Ascariasis
Babesiosis
Chagas' Disease
Cyclosporiasis and Cryptosporidiosis
Elephantiasis
Lice
Malaria
Pinworm
Schistosomiasis
Toxoplasmosis

Insects and animals spread some parasitic diseases. Mosquitoes, for instance, spread malaria. Tsetse flies spread African trypanosomiasis (tri-pan-o-so-MY-a-sis), also called African sleeping sickness. Domestic animals spread beef and pork tapeworms.

What Happens When People Get Parasitic Diseases?

Symptoms The symptoms vary widely, but many parasitic infections cause fever, fatigue, or intestinal problems such as diarrhea or bowel obstruction (blockage of the intestines).

Diagnosis Parasitic diseases can be difficult to diagnose because many parasites do not show up on the routine blood tests that doctors perform. In addition, people with parasites are prone to get bacterial infections as well, which may fool doctors into thinking that the bacteria alone are the cause of the illness.

Special blood tests, however, sometimes help with diagnosis. In addition, parasites sometimes can be seen if samples of stool or blood are examined under a microscope.

Treatment Although most parasites can be killed by proper medication, some cannot.

How Can Parasitic Diseases Be Prevented?

Public authorities that build sewage and water treatment systems play a major part in preventing these diseases. Controlling the insects that spread some parasitic diseases also is important. So is teaching people always to wash their hands thoroughly after using the bathroom and before handling food.

Resources

The U.S. Centers for Disease Control and Prevention (CDC) has a Division of Parasitic Diseases (DPD) that posts fact sheets about many different parasitic infections at its website.
http://www.cdc.gov/ncidod/dpd/p_diseas.htm

The U.S. Food and Drug Administration's Center for Food Safety and Applied Nutrition posts a *Bad Bug Book* at its website with links to many different fact sheets about parasitic protozoa and worms.
http://www.vm.cfsan.fda.gov/~mow/intro.html

The World Health Organization (WHO) posts a fact sheet about parasitic diseases at its website.
http://www.who.int/ctd/html/intest/html

Parkinson's Disease

Parkinson's disease is a disorder of the central nervous system that causes shaking, rigid muscles, slow movements, and poor balance. The disease is progressive, meaning it tends to get worse over time.

KEYWORDS
for searching the Internet
and other reference sources

Movement disorders

Neurological disorders

Michael J. Fox's Story

Actor Michael J. Fox first noticed the twitch in his left little finger in 1991 while filming the movie *Doc Hollywood.* He remembers looking at the shaking finger and thinking, "Geez, what's that?"

Within 6 months, his whole left hand started to twitch uncontrollably, and parts of his body started to feel stiff. Fox was concerned, so he visited a doctor.

Fox was only 30 years old and appeared to be in excellent health. His roles often required physical stunts that he performed with ease. So Fox never expected to be told his shaking hand and rigid muscles meant he had Parkinson's disease, a condition that is more common among people over age 50.

What Is Parkinson's Disease?

Parkinson's disease is a movement disorder. It results from chemical imbalances in a small area deep within the middle of the brain that controls muscle movements, coordination, and balance.

The disease often is first noticed when a finger or hand starts to twitch involuntarily. The person might seem to be rolling a small ball between his fingers; a twitching motion doctors call "pill-rolling." The shaking often is barely noticeable to other people.

Slowly over months and years, the twitching gets worse. Sometimes, it affects only one part or side of the body. Although it often starts in a limb, the tremors can affect the neck, face, and head.

Muscles also become rigid and do not respond normally. The brain is lacking the ability to send the proper messages through the central nervous system to get the body to act the way a person wants. At times, the person seems to freeze in the middle of an action, such as reaching for a book or walking.

The person starts to shuffle his feet and walk slowly. The arms do not swing back and forth normally. It can become difficult to sit or walk without rolling forward and sometimes falling. As talking becomes difficult, the person speaks slowly and in a monotone.

Eventually, the symptoms become so severe the person needs help with simple activities of living, such as walking and eating. The person's ability to think also can be affected late in the disease.

Not all people develop all the symptoms. Sometimes the disease progresses quickly, from the slight tremors to incapacity within a few years.

Did You Know?

Actor Michael J. Fox is not the only famous person with Parkinson's disease who has continued to maintain an active life. Janet Reno, the U.S. Attorney General during President Bill Clinton's administration, also has the disease, as do the Rev. Billy Graham and singer Johnny Cash.

The boxer Muhammad Ali, who has the disease, created a dramatic moment at the 1996 Olympics when he carried the torch in Atlanta. In 1998, Ali joined others in promoting more research that involves people of African, Hispanic, and Asian ancestry.

Former world champion heavyweight boxer Muhammad Ali, who has Parkinson's disease. *Reuters/Corbis-Bettmann*

Often, however, especially with treatment, a person can live well for many years.

The disease affects more than 1 million Americans. About 10 percent of the cases involve people younger than age 40, like Fox. Most men and women who get the disease first show signs between ages 50 and 75.

The disease is named for a British doctor, James Parkinson, who first described the disease's symptoms in 1817. He called it "Shaking Palsy." In the 1960s, scientists began to understand how the chemical changes in the brain caused the symptoms. Eventually, research led to medications and other treatments to help control the disease.

An Imbalance Deep in the Brain

People with Parkinson's lack enough of the chemical dopamine in their brain. Dopamine (DO-pa-meen) is a neurotransmitter, which is a chemical that helps nerve cells send messages to each other. Dopamine receives assistance in sending these messages from other chemicals.

For some reason, the production of dopamine and the other chemicals is disturbed in the brains of people with Parkinson's. When that happens, the messages cannot be delivered as well between one nerve cell and the next. Shaking, rigid muscles and other problems result.

What Causes Parkinson's Disease?

No one yet knows exactly what causes the chemical imbalances. Scientists suspect there are a number of possible causes that may, in some cases, trigger the disease, such as a head injury (especially head injuries like those received during a boxing match), some medicines given for other serious conditions, abuse of certain drugs, exposure to toxic levels of carbon monoxide and other pollutants, and small strokes in the brain. Parkinson's disease is not contagious and therefore cannot be passed from one person to another, like a cold.

The disease does run in some families, which has led researchers to search for a gene that might trigger the disease. Two large European families with many Parkinson's cases appear to share a defective gene, but the abnormal gene has not been found yet in many others with the disease.

How Is Parkinson's Disease Diagnosed?

Parkinson's is a difficult disease to diagnose. There is no single test to determine if a person has it. Often, doctors rule out other causes of the shaking, such as a brain tumor or other brain disorder.

How Is Parkinson's Disease Treated?

There is hope for people with Parkinson's, because several prescription drugs can help. Most people are treated with a combination of drugs that help the brain make dopamine,

WHO WAS JAMES PARKINSON?

Parkinson's disease was first identified and named *paralysis agitans* (pa-RAL-i-sis AJ-i-tans) by the British physician James Parkinson (1755–1824). His classic description of its symptoms was described in "Essay on the Shaking Palsy." Tremors like those characteristic of Parkinson's had been noted by physicians as ancient as Galen (A.D. 138–201) and by Parkinson's contemporary Gerard van Swieton (1700–1772). Parkinson's observations of the disorder, however, were among the earliest to interpret those symptoms as a well-defined clinical syndrome. Not long after Parkinson's essay was published, the French neurologist Jean-Martin Charcot (1825–1893) began using the term "Parkinson's disease" to describe the condition.

the chemical needed to help nerve cells communicate in the brain. Other medications act like dopamine in the brain, improving the ability of the brain to control movements.

The drugs do not cure the disease, but they treat its symptoms. People are able to do many of the same things they did before the disease developed, which is why Michael J. Fox has been able to continue working.

Fox, however, also had brain surgery to destroy tiny areas of his brain that were malfunctioning. By eliminating these cells, the trembling in some people with Parkinson's can be improved.

There are experimental treatments, including transplanting brain tissue from human fetuses into the part of the brain where the dopamine is in short supply. Early results show that this might benefit some people. Because the tissue often becomes available after an abortion, the technique is controversial. Researchers are experimenting with animal cells and cells they grow in the laboratory in attempts to achieve the same results as using fetal cells.

Resources

American Parkinson's Disease Association (ADPA), 1250 Hylan Blvd., Suite 4B, Staten Island, NY 10305, (800) 223-2732. This leading support organization posts pertinent information on its website. http://www.apdaparkinson.com/

National Institute of Neurological Disorders and Stroke, Office of Communications and Public Liaison, P.O. Box 580, Bethesda, MD 20824. A U.S. government research center. Offers free publication "Parkinson's Disease: Hope Through Research" by mail or on the Internet. http://www.ninds.nih.gov/

▶ See also
Paralysis

Pelvic Inflammatory Disease (PID)

Pelvic inflammatory disease is an infection of the female reproductive system, including the cervix*, uterus*, ovaries*, and especially the fallopian tubes*. It usually is caused by a sexually transmitted disease and can reduce a woman's ability to get pregnant.

***cervix** (SER-viks) is the lower, narrow end of the uterus.

***uterus** (YOO-te-rus) in humans is the organ in females for containing and nourishing the young during development in the period before birth. Also called the womb.

***ovaries** (O-va-reez) are the sexual glands in which eggs (ova) are formed in women.

***fallopian tubes** (fa-LO-pe-an tubes) are two long slender tubes in females that connect the ovaries and the uterus. Typically, a fallopian tube is where conception (kon-SEP-shun) takes place.

***bacteria** (bak-TEER-ee-a) are round, spiral, or rod-shaped single-celled microorganisms without a distinct nucleus that commonly multiply by cell division. Some types may cause disease in humans, animals, or plants.

***vagina** (va-JY-na) In girls and women, the vagina is the canal that leads from the uterus—the womb (the organ where a baby develops)—to the outside of the body.

***sperm** are the tiny, tadpole-like cells males produce in their testicles (TES-ti-kulz) that can unite with a female's egg to result eventually in the birth of a child.

Carrie and Reg's Story

Two years after Carrie and Reg got married, they decided to start a family. Carrie began looking at the ads for strollers and baby clothes. But after a year, she had not gotten pregnant. She was sure she did not have a medical problem. After another 6 months of trying, Carrie and Reg decided to see a doctor who had experience with fertility problems.

The doctor asked if Carrie had ever had pelvic inflammatory disease (PID). She said no, she had not even heard of it. But in a series of tests, her body told a different story. Carrie's fallopian tubes (the place where egg meets sperm in conception) had been scarred by PID. After laser surgery removed the scar tissue and opened the blocked passageways, Carrie finally got pregnant.

When healthy young women have difficulty getting pregnant, damage from pelvic inflammatory disease is one of the many possible causes. In most cases, the women do not know they had the disease and never got treated. Quick treatment of PID can reduce the chances that it will cause infertility.

What Causes PID?

Most commonly, women get PID after they have had a sexually transmitted disease (chlamydial [kla-MID-e-al] infection or gonorrhea [gon-o-REE-a]) that was not treated, often because it was not noticed. The bacteria*, named *Chlamydia trachomatis* and *Neisseria gonorrhoeae*, then can move up from the vagina* to infect other parts of the reproductive system. PID often involves a wide range of other bacteria as well. In many cases, doctors cannot identify the bacteria involved.

PID also can develop after a woman gives birth or has an abortion in unsanitary conditions. In rare cases, certain medical procedures done on reproductive organs, such as injecting dye for special x-rays, can lead to PID.

What Does PID Do in the Body?

First, a quick review of conception. The ovary releases an egg into one of a woman's two fallopian tubes, where it meets with the sperm*. The newly formed embryo* travels through the tube to the uterus, an expandable sac where it will grow into a fetus*.

In PID, the bacteria usually infect the cervix and then travel upward and infect the fallopian tubes, a condition called salpingitis (sal-pin-JY-tis). Doctors sometimes use that name as a synonym for PID. But PID also can involve the uterus and the ovaries. In severe cases, a collection of pus can form in the ovaries and fallopian tubes, called a tubo-ovarian abscess, or the infection can spread to the membrane* around the reproductive organs, a condition called pelvic peritonitis (per-i-to-NY-tis).

The body usually fights off the infection. But in the struggle, tissue can be damaged and scarred, causing blockages in the delicate fallopian tubes. That means the egg and sperm may not be able to meet, or, if they do, the fertilized egg or embryo may not be able to reach the uterus.

Of women who have PID one time, about 10 percent become infertile. After three bouts of the disease, more than half may be infertile. Prompt treatment, within 3 days of symptoms, can help prevent problems.

Women who have had PID also are more likely than other women to have an ectopic (ek-TOP-ik) pregnancy. That means the embryo starts growing outside the uterus, usually in the fallopian tubes. Such a pregnancy cannot produce a baby and, if it is not ended, poses a very serious risk to the woman's safety because the growing embryo will rupture the fallopian tubes and cause life-threatening hemorrhage*.

Who Is at Risk for PID?

PID affects only women and is rare unless a woman is sexually active. Sexually active teenagers are at the highest risk by far, followed by women in their early twenties. The risk increases if a woman has many sexual partners, has sexual intercourse very frequently even with a single partner, or uses an IUD (intrauterine [in-tra-YOO-ter-in] device), a birth-control device inserted in the uterus. Frequent douching (inserting fluid into the vagina to "clean" it) may also increase the risk of PID.

What Are the Symptoms of PID?

It has been estimated that 60 percent of all cases of PID have symptoms so mild they go unnoticed. Noticeable symptoms often include:

- Pain in the lower abdomen* or pelvis
- Very sharp pain when the doctor performs a pelvic examination
- A fever of over 100 degrees Fahrenheit (38 degrees Celsius)
- A discharge of pus or irregular bleeding from the vagina
- Pain during urination or intercourse

Sometimes, long after an untreated PID infection occurs, women have chronic* (persistent) pain in the pelvis. This is sometimes called chronic PID.

How Is PID Diagnosed?

PID can be difficult to diagnose. Many conditions have similar symptoms, and no simple test can tell for sure if a woman has PID. Because it is so important to treat PID quickly, doctors usually start treatment if the symptoms even suggest PID.

To try to confirm the diagnosis, doctors do blood tests to look for general evidence of infection. They test for chlamydial infection and

*****embryo** (EM-bree-o) is, in humans, the developing organism from the end of the second week after fertilization to the end of the eighth week.

*****fetus** (FEE-tus) is, in humans, the unborn offspring in the period after it is an embryo, from 9 weeks after fertilization until birth.

*****membrane** (MEM-brayn) is a thin layer of tissue that covers a surface, lines a cavity, or divides a space or organ.

*****hemorrhage** (HEM-or-ij) means heavy and uncontrolled bleeding, often in the internal organs.

*****abdomen** (AB-do-men), commonly called the belly, is the portion of the body between the chest or thorax (THOR-aks) and the pelvis.

*****chronic** (KRON-ik) means continuing for a long period of time.

gonorrhea, and they do a pregnancy test to determine whether the symptoms are being caused by an ectopic pregnancy.

Ultrasound, a painless procedure that uses sound waves to create an image of the organs, can help doctors look for a tubo-ovarian abscess.

The most definitive test for PID is laparoscopy (la-pa-ROS-ko-pee), a surgical procedure in which a narrow device is inserted through a small incision into the abdomen so the doctor can look inside the belly. Laparoscopy usually is done only if treatment is not working or if the doctor suspects the woman may have another condition, such as appendicitis (a-pen-di-SY-tis), that requires emergency surgery.

How Is PID Treated?

Combinations of antibiotics (an-ty-by-OT-iks) that fight a wide range of bacteria are given for at least 2 weeks, usually in pills to be taken at home. If a woman is pregnant or particularly ill, she usually is hospitalized for at least a few days and given antibiotics intravenously*.

If a woman has an abscess, it may need to be drained through a tube or catheter (CATH-e-ter) inserted into the abdomen. If an abscess ruptures, or breaks open, immediate surgery is necessary.

If a woman has PID, any man who had sex with her in the previous 2 months should be treated for possible chlamydial infection and gonorrhea. Even if he has no symptoms, chances are high that he is infected and could reinfect the woman or other partners.

How Can PID Be Prevented?

Like chlamydial infections and gonorrhea, PID most surely is prevented by not having sex. A sexually active woman is most protected if she has sex only with one faithful partner, that is, a partner who has sex only with her. Short of that, a woman should limit her sexual partners. Latex condoms worn by the man during sexual activity can prevent PID if they are used correctly at all times.

A woman should seek immediate treatment if she suspects that she, or a sexual partner, has a sexually transmitted disease. Because these diseases often cause no symptoms, health officials recommend that all sexually active young women, especially teenagers, get tested routinely for chlamydial infections and gonorrhea. When chlamydial infection screening of young women was tried as an experiment, it reduced the number of cases of PID.

Resources

Book

Brodman, Michael, John Thacker, and Rachel Kranz. *Straight Talk about Sexually Transmitted Diseases*. New York: Facts on File, 1994. Focuses on prevention for young people.

---

* **intravenously** (in-tra-VEE-nus-lee) means injected directly into the veins.

The U.S. and the World

▓ In the United States, it is estimated that more than 750,000 women get PID each year. Most U.S. cases are caused by a sexually transmitted disease.

▓ With its complications of infertility and ectopic pregnancy, PID is estimated to cost the U.S. economy $4 billion a year.

▓ In developing nations of Africa and Asia, PID is far more common, with many infections caused by childbirth or abortions occurring in unsanitary settings.

Organization

U.S. Centers for Disease Control and Prevention (CDC), 1600 Clifton Road N.E., Atlanta, GA 30333. The CDC sponsors a National Sexually Transmitted Diseases Hotline. Telephone 800-227-8922

▶ *See also*
Bacterial Infections
Chlamydial Infections
Gonorrhea
Infection
Peritonitis
Sexually Transmitted Diseases

Peptic Ulcer

A peptic ulcer, sometimes called a stomach ulcer, is a sore that forms in the lining of the stomach or of the duodenum, which is the first part of the small intestine. Peptic ulcers are often the result of infection by Helicobacter pylori *bacteria.*

KEYWORDS
for searching the Internet and other reference sources

Antibiotics

Digestive system

Gastroenterology

Helicobacter pylori (H. pylori)

Infection

Enough to Give Them an Ulcer

Early in the twentieth century, peptic ulcers were thought to be caused by emotional stress and spicy foods. As a result, people were treated with bed rest and a bland diet, but they often failed to get better. Later in the century, the disease was blamed on excess stomach acid. People were treated with medicines that counteract acid or block its production, which made them feel better for a little while. The ulcers and the pain they caused, however, often came back.

Then in 1982, Australian doctors Robin Warren and Barry Marshall first discovered a link between ulcers and a bacterium known as

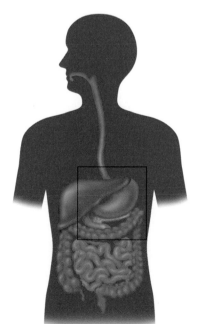

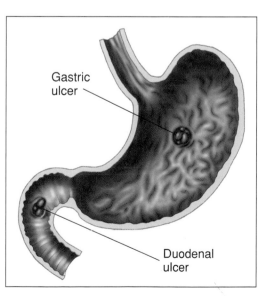

◀

Peptic ulcers may occur in the stomach (gastric ulcers) or in the first part of the small intestine (duodenal ulcers). Nearly all peptic ulcers are the result of infection with *H. pylori* bacteria.

Gut Reactions

- Over 1 million Americans are hospitalized each year because of peptic ulcers.

- The cost of health care for Americans with peptic ulcers is more than $2 billion a year.

- Recent studies have found a link between long-term infection with *H. pylori* and stomach cancer.

Helicobacter pylori (hel-i-ko-BAK-ter pi-LOR-ee). Today, doctors know that nine out of ten ulcers are caused primarily by *H. pylori*, but the public has been slow to accept this idea. In fact, a 1995 study by the American Digestive Health Foundation (ADHF) found that nearly 90 percent of Americans with ulcers still blamed their problem on stress or worry. An equally large percentage were totally unaware of *H. pylori*. But as the ADHF points out, ulcers are not caused by a boss, unless that boss is a bacterium.

What Are Peptic Ulcers?

A peptic ulcer, sometimes called a stomach ulcer, is a sore that forms in the lining of the stomach or of the duodenum (doo-o-DEE-num), which is the first part of the small intestine. This common disease can happen to people of any age and both sexes. Almost 25 million people in the United States currently have peptic ulcers, and there are about 500,000 to 850,000 new cases of the disease diagnosed each year.

What Causes Peptic Ulcers?

Doctors now know that most peptic ulcers are caused primarily by infection with *H. pylori,* a type of bacteria that lives on the lining of the stomach. In the United States, about 20 percent of people under age 40 and half of people over age 60 are infected with *H. pylori*. Most never go on to develop ulcers, however. Doctors still do not know why one person gets ulcers and another does not. They also are not sure how people catch *H. pylori*, although it may be through water or food. The bacteria also might be spread by close contact, such as kissing.

Normally, the stomach makes acid as part of the digestive process. The sensitive lining of the stomach and duodenum is protected from this acid by a mucous coating. *H. pylori* bacteria cause ulcers by weakening this mucous coating, which lets acid get through and eat holes in the lining beneath.

About 10 percent of ulcers are caused by something other than *H. pylori*. Many result from long-term use of nonsteroidal anti-inflammatory drugs (NSAIDs), which are pain relievers such as aspirin and ibuprofen. NSAIDs interfere with the stomach's ability to protect itself against acid. A few ulcers are caused by cancer of the stomach or pancreas (a gland near the stomach).

What Are the Symptoms?

The most common symptom of a peptic ulcer is a gnawing or burning pain in the stomach. This pain comes and goes over a period of days or weeks. It may occur two to three hours after a meal. It also may occur in the middle of the night, when the stomach is empty. Eating helps relieve the pain. Other possible symptoms include weight loss, poor appetite, bloating, burping, nausea, and vomiting.

If left untreated, ulcers can lead to serious problems. In some cases, the ulcer makes a hole all the way through the stomach or duodenum wall. In other cases, the ulcer or acid breaks a blood vessel and causes internal bleeding. In still other cases, the ulcer blocks the path of food trying to leave the stomach. It is important to get medical help right away for the following symptoms, which may signal a peptic ulcer or other serious problem:

- sharp, sudden, or long-lasting stomach pain

- bloody or black stools (bowel movements)

- bloody vomit or vomit that looks like coffee grounds.

How Are Ulcers Diagnosed?

To see if a person has an ulcer, the doctor may do a barium x-ray or endoscopy. In a barium x-ray, the person drinks a chalky liquid that makes the stomach, duodenum, and any ulcers show up clearly on an x-ray image. In endoscopy, the person is given medicine to relax. Then a thin, lighted tube is passed through the person's mouth and down the throat to the stomach and duodenum. This tube has a tiny camera on the end that lets the doctor view the inside of these organs.

To find out if an ulcer is caused by *H. pylori*, the doctor can check a sample of the person's blood for signs of infection. As a second option, the doctor can do a breath test, in which the person drinks a harmless solution that contains a special carbon atom. If *H. pylori* is present, it releases the carbon. The person's breath then can be tested to see if it contains the carbon. As a third option, the doctor can take a small tissue sample while doing an endoscopy. The tissue is removed through the thin viewing tube. It then can be checked for signs of infection.

How Are Ulcers Treated?

People with ulcers caused by *H. pylori* are treated with antibiotics (bacteria-fighting drugs). The most common treatment involves taking antibiotics for one or two weeks along with a medicine to reduce the amount of acid in the stomach. To be sure that all the *H. pylori* bacteria have been killed, the doctor may do another endoscopy or breath test 6 to 12 months later to check for any remaining bacteria. When antibiotics kill all the bacteria, the odds are excellent that the ulcer will completely heal.

Can Ulcers Be Prevented?

No one knows for sure how *H. pylori* bacteria spread, so ulcers are difficult to prevent. As a general precaution, however, people always should wash their hands thoroughly after going to the bathroom and before eating. They should eat food that has been properly cooked and drink water from a clean, safe source.

Resources

American Digestive Health Foundation, 7910 Woodmont Avenue, 7th Floor, Bethesda, MD 20814-3015. This organization of professional

KEYWORDS
for searching the Internet and other reference sources

Inflammation

Peritoneum

** **inflammation** (in-fla-MAY-shun) is the body's response to infection or irritation.

** **bacteria** (bak-TEER-ee-a) are round, spiral, or rod-shaped single-celled microorganisms without a distinct nucleus that commonly multiply by cell division. Some types may cause disease in humans, animals, or plants.

** **liver** is a large organ located in the upper abdomen (AB-do-man) that has many functions, including storage and filtration of blood, secretion of bile, and participation in various metabolic (met-a-BOLL-ik) processes.

societies has an Ulcer Education program that posts information about peptic ulcers at its website.
Telephone 800-NO-ULCER
http://www.gastro.org/adhf/ulcers.html

U.S. National Digestive Diseases Information Clearinghouse, 2 Information Way, Bethesda, MD 20892-3570. This service of the U.S. National Institute of Diabetes and Digestive and Kidney Diseases (NIDDK) publishes brochures and posts fact sheets about *H. pylori*, peptic ulcers, and NSAIDs at its website.
http://www.niddk.nih.gov/health/digest/pubs/hpylori/hpylori.htm

U.S. Centers for Disease Control and Prevention (CDC), *H. pylori* Education Campaign, 1600 Clifton Road, N.E., M.S. C09, Atlanta, GA 30333. CDC posts English and Spanish fact sheets about *H. pylori* and peptic ulcers at its website.
Telephone 888-MY-ULCER
http://www.cdc.gov/ncidod/dbmd/hpylori.htm

Periodontitis *See* **Gum Disease**

Peritonitis

Peritonitis (per-i-to-NY-tis) is an inflammation* of the lining of the abdominal (ab-DOM-i-nal) cavity. The slippery lining has two layers and is called the peritoneum (per-i-to-NEE-um).

What Is Peritonitis?

A number of conditions can cause peritonitis. Usually, peritonitis occurs when an infection develops in the peritoneum from a perforation (per-fo-RAY-shun), or hole, in the stomach, intestines, appendix, or one of the other organs covered by the lining. The perforation can come from a knife or gunshot wound or from a cut during surgery. People also can get peritonitis from complications of other illnesses, such as a ruptured appendix, diverticulitis (dy-ver-tik-yoo-LY-tis), a perforated ulcer, or pelvic inflammatory disease (PID). In all of these cases, bacteria* can infect the peritoneum. People with cirrhosis (si-RO-sis) of the liver* sometimes get "spontaneous bacterial peritonitis," which means they have no rupture or obvious source for the infection.

What Happens When People Get Peritonitis?

Symptoms The symptoms of peritonitis range from mild to severe pain in the stomach area. Peritonitis often causes a muscle spasm in the abdominal wall, making the abdomen* feel hard and immobile, as if it were a wooden board. A person with peritonitis usually has a fever and may feel bloated. Vomiting and diarrhea* are common.

Diagnosis   A doctor often can diagnose peritonitis through a physical examination of the patient. The diagnosis can be confirmed using abdominal x-rays or CT scans*. Occasionally, surgery is necessary to be certain that peritonitis is present.

Treatment   The treatment of peritonitis usually includes surgery and antibiotics*. Surgery is performed to repair any ruptured organs that caused the infection as well as to drain the infectious fluids from the abdominal cavity. Antibiotics are used to treat the bacterial infection. Most people who get peritonitis recover fully after treatment.

Resource

Slap, Gail B., and Martha M. Jablow. *Teenage Health Care: The First Comprehensive Family Guide for the Preteen to Young Adult Years.* New York: Pocket Books, 1994.

Pertussis *See* Whooping Cough

Pervasive Development Disorder *See* Autism

Pharyngitis *See* Strep Throat

Phenylketonuria (PKU)

Phenylketonuria (fen-il-kee-to-NU-ree-a) or PKU is an inherited metabolic disease in which the body cannot change one essential amino acid, phenylalanine (fen-il-AL-a-neen), into another needed amino acid, tyrosine (TY-ro-seen). Untreated, PKU often results in severe mental retardation, but if it is detected at birth and the children are put on a special diet, they can lead normal lives.

Children with a Strange Smell

In 1934, a mother with two children with mental retardation went to a Norwegian medical doctor, Asbjørn Følling. Dr. Følling became interested in the children's condition when the mother described the children's odd musty odor. The children, ages 4 and 6, had severe mental retardation. The younger child could not speak or walk, and still wore diapers. The older child could speak only a few words and had problems walking.

Dr. Følling examined the children's urine and found no protein or glucose in it, but he was puzzled when their urine turned a deep green, instead of staying brownish, after he added the chemical compound ferric chloride to it. Dr. Følling expanded his study to other children whose urine had the same kind of reaction and concluded that the unusual quality of the urine seemed to be connected with mental retardation. Thus, he discovered PKU, which he concluded was a genetic error in the children's metabolism*.

What Causes PKU?

PKU is a disruption in normal metabolism. Normally, an enzyme* in the body called phenylalanine hydroxylase (fen-il-AL-a-neen hy-DROK-si-lase) changes the essential amino acid* phenylalanine to another needed amino acid called tyrosine (TY-ro-seen). If phenylalanine hydroxylase is missing, as it is in PKU, phenylalanine builds up in the blood and passes out of the body in urine.

PKU affects on average one out of every 10,000–15,000 babies in the United States. Since PKU is an inherited disorder, there is a good bit of variation among different ethnic and racial groups. The condition is found less often in people of African descent (1 in every 50,000 babies) and in Ashkenazic Jews.

What Are the Signs and Symptoms of PKU?

Infants with PKU usually have lighter skin, hair, and eyes than the rest of their families, but symptoms do not appear until they are about 3 to 6 months old. These may include:

- an eczema-like rash
- seizures
- hyperactivity
- an unpleasant musty or mousy body odor (caused by phenylacetic acid in the urine and sweat)
- mental retardation

How is PKU Diagnosed?

Almost all babies born in hospitals in the United States are screened for PKU within 48 hours of birth with a blood test that measures their levels of phenylalanine. In families with a history of PKU, the disease can usually be diagnosed in the fetus during pregnancy. A pregnant woman who has untreated PKU herself has a much greater chance of having a baby with (often severe) birth defects.

Living with PKU

Jennifer is a happy 12-year-old with fair skin, blue eyes, and a very normal life except for her diet. Jennifer has PKU, which was diagnosed at birth through hospital screening. She cannot go out for pizza, drink diet

* **metabolism** (me-TAB-o-liz-um) is the process in the body that converts food into energy and waste products.

* **enzymes** (EN-zymz) are natural substances that speed up specific chemical reactions in the body.

* **amino acids** (a-MEE-no acids) are the chief building blocks of proteins. In humans, certain amino acids are required to sustain life.

sodas, or eat many of the common foods that most people take for granted.

Infants with PKU must begin treatment within days of being born to prevent their becoming mentally retarded. They must eat a special diet that restricts their intake of phenylalanine and provides the tyrosine that the body cannot make. Babies drink special formula that is low in phenylalanine. People with PKU cannot have high-protein foods such as meat, poultry, fish, milk, eggs, cheese, ice cream, and nuts; products containing regular flour; or products that contain the artificial sweetener aspartame (also known by the brand name NutraSweet). They can eat low-protein foods such as fruits, vegetables, and certain cereals.

Not adhering to the diet may cause serious problems like drops in IQ and problems with learning and behavior. Experts are not sure whether and at what age it is safe to stop treatment. Most recommend that people with PKU stay on the special diet for life.

Once destined to become mentally retarded, people like Jennifer are now growing up normally. Most people with untreated PKU, however, have severe mental retardation and are unable to live independently.

Resources

Book

Wessel, Kenneth. *A Journey into the World of PKU*. Baltimore, MD: Pediatric Genetics, 1991.

Organization

Children's PKU Network, 1520 State St., Suite 240, San Diego, CA 92111. Telephone 619-233-3202

PKU News posts information about PKU on its website. http://www.pkunews.org/

▲

Aspartame is listed as an ingredient on a packet of artificial sweetener. People with PKU are warned that the product contains phenylalanine. © *Leonard Lessin, Peter Arnold, Inc.*

▶ See also
Genetic Disorders
Mental Retardation
Metabolic Disorders

Phlebitis

Phlebitis (fle-BY-tis) is inflammation of a vein that can lead to blood clots.

KEYWORD
for searching the Internet or other reference sources

Circulatory system

Terry's Tale

Terry decided to visit her doctor because her lower left leg hurt. It also appeared swollen and red and even felt a bit warm to the touch.

As she explained her symptoms to the doctor, he looked concerned. He asked if Terry spent much time sitting. She said that as a receptionist at a busy office, she might go hours without getting up from her desk.

Because she spent a lot of time sitting down and her leg was red and swollen, the doctor suspected that Terry had phlebitis.

An Unseen Danger

Veins return blood from parts of the body to the heart. The heart beats about 100,000 times a day, driving blood through the arteries of the body and back to the heart through the veins.

Sometimes, however, the blood in veins does not flow well. It moves slowly or pools, like water sitting in a puddle. This can happen for many reasons. As in Terry's case, too much sitting at work (or on long car or plane rides) can restrict blood flow in the legs. Also, an injury, tumor, or surgery can cause damage to veins that slows blood flow. Ill people who have to spend a lot of time in bed are prone to pooling of blood in veins. Pregnant women also are at greater than normal risk, as are women who take estrogen, a female hormone in birth control pills and pills used by women after menopause*. Smoking is another major risk factor.

The pooling of blood causes the walls of the vein to stretch and become inflamed. It also can cause clotting. Clots are thick masses of blood that usually have a beneficial function, such as when they stop a cut from bleeding. But when clots form inside veins, the condition is called thrombosis. If the clot breaks free, it can cause an embolism, which occurs when a clot travels through the bloodstream and blocks the blood supply to the lungs or other organs. This can cause severe problems, including sudden death.

Phlebitis usually occurs in legs, although it can occur in other body parts. Symptoms include pain, swelling, and redness.

When phlebitis occurs in veins close to the skin, it is called superficial. When it occurs deep inside the leg, it is called deep-vein.

Diagnosis

Doctors use tests to search for clots in the veins. One involves injecting dye into a leg vein and viewing it under an x-ray to reveal clots. Doctors also can use an ultrasound machine to create an image of the leg that is similar to one from an x-ray. Or they can use a machine that measures blood pressure at various points in the leg; if it is different above and below the suspected clot, it could mean that the vein is blocked.

Treatment

The danger of phlebitis is that it will develop into thrombosis. If no clot is present, doctors treat patients with heat packs and anti-inflammatory drugs such as ibuprofen and have the person raise the affected leg to encourage better blood flow. Doctors may prescribe blood-thinning drugs such as heparin or warfarin to dissolve clots or to prevent their formation. They also monitor patients to ensure that clots do not form in the future.

*menopause (MEN-o-pawz) is the time of life when women stop menstruating (having their monthly period) and can no longer become pregnant.

Healthy vein versus vein with phlebitis.

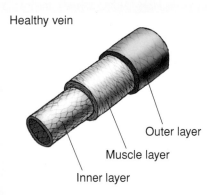

Healthy vein

Outer layer

Muscle layer

Inner layer

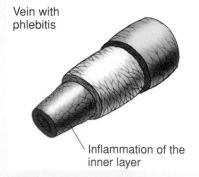

Vein with phlebitis

Inflammation of the inner layer

Prevention

The best prevention is staying active. Also, smoking and being over-weight increase the risk of phlebitis and thrombosis, so it is wise to avoid tobacco and maintain healthy weight.

▶ *See also*
Heart Disease
Thrombosis

Phobias

A phobia is a special kind of fear: an intense, persistent fear of a particular thing or situation. There are many different types of phobias. For example, social phobia is an intense, persistent fear of being painfully embarrassed in a social setting. Agoraphobia is a significant fear of being in any situation that might provoke a panic attack, or from which escape might be difficult.

KEYWORDS
for searching the Internet and other reference sources

Anxiety

Behavior

Panic

Psychology

Psychiatry

Whenever Bethani, who recently turned 15, enters a building above two stories, she checks to see if the building has stairs. She is intensely afraid of riding an elevator. Even though her friends tease her, and she herself readily admits that her fears are "silly," once an elevator door closes, she begins to sweat and her heart starts to beat uncontrollably. "It's like I'm trapped," she tells them. "As if I'll never, ever escape."

What Are Phobias?

Phobias occur in several forms. While all people, at one time or another, find themselves uncomfortable in a social situation, phobias go beyond social awkwardness. In a phobia, the exposure to the particular event provokes such enormous anxiety that it can lead to a panic attack*. The person will do almost anything to avoid the situation.

Social phobias　Social phobias can cause persistent fear of humiliation or embarrassment in certain social situations, such as walking into a classroom or even leaving the house. Individuals may feel as if everyone is looking at them. The phobia, for example, may persist to the point where the affected person spends all of his or her time at a party hiding in a corner to avoid others.

***panic attack** is a period of intense fear or discomfort with a feeling of doom and a desire to escape. The person may shake, sweat, be short of breath, and experience chest pain.

Triggers　When exposed to the trigger of the specific phobia, a person may experience high levels of anxiety, which may include a panic attack. People with specific fears, such as Bethani's fear of elevators, may know that their fear might be "silly" or "irrational," but the fear still produces significant distress. Sometimes, particularly with children, the person may not understand that their fear is excessive or unwarranted.

Trauma　Traumatic events can often lead to the development of specific phobias. Social phobias often begin in mid-teens, with the average onset

Calling All Phobias

The number of specific phobias that affect people covers the alphabet, from abluto-phobia, a fear of washing or bathing, to zoophobia, a fear of animals. Other common (and uncommon) phobias include:

- Arachibutyrophobia: fear of peanut butter sticking to the roof of the mouth

- Arithmophobia: fear of numbers

- Genuphoba: fear of knees

- Ichthyophobia: fear of fish

- Pupaphobia: fear of puppets

- Pteromerhanophobia: fear of flying

- Testophobia: fear of taking tests

▶ *See also*
Anxiety Disorders
Mental Disorders
Post-Traumatic Stress Disorder
Stress-Related Illness

between the ages of 15 and 20, although some social phobias can begin in childhood. Specific phobias can start at any age. Research has shown that many social phobias may have a hereditary component.

What Are Common Types of Phobias?

The most common type of phobia is social phobia, which is a persistent fear of humiliation or embarrassment in certain social situations. Closely connected to social phobia is agoraphobia (literally "fear of the marketplace"), which is the fear of being in a place or situations where escape might be difficult or embarrassing. People suffering from agoraphobia believe they might suddenly develop a panic attack. To cope, those with agoraphobia simply avoid any difficult situations, or endure them with anxiety.

Other specific phobias such as arachnophobia, the fear of spiders, or hydrophobia, fear of water, can lead people to avoid specific situations, where they might be confronted by frightening stimuli.

How Are Phobias Treated?

A number of prescription medications are available to treat social phobias. People with specific phobias also may benefit from counseling or psychotherapy using systemic desensitization. In this form of therapy, working with a therapist in a safe environment, people are gradually exposed to the situations or objects that cause fear. They learn techniques involving relaxation, imagery, and deep breathing that allow them an opportunity to work through their fears gradually.

Resource

The U.S. National Institute of Mental Health posts a fact sheet about phobias at its website.
http://www.nimh.gov/anxiety/anxiety/phobia/index.htm

Pink Eye *See* Conjunctivitis

Pinworm (Enterobiasis)

Pinworm, or enterobiasis (en-ter-o-BY-a-sis), is a common intestinal infection caused by the Enterobius vermicularis *parasite. It causes anal itching, and it is often spread by children to schoolmates or family members.*

KEYWORDS
*for searching the Internet
or other reference sources*

Gastrointestinal system

Infestation

Nematodes

** **contagious** means transmitable
from one person to another.*

Pinworm, or *Enterobius vermicularis* (en-ter-O-be-us ver-mik-u-LAY-ris), is a common and highly contagious* intestinal parasite. An esti-

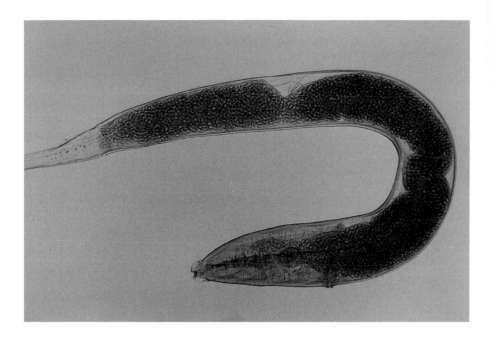

mated 200 million people worldwide, including 40 million people in North America, are infected. Pinworm is especially common in children, with a general infection rate of about 20 percent. Pinworms are small worms, usually less than 1 cm in length, and they resemble light-colored pieces of thread.

What Is the Pinworm's Life Cycle?

People become infected when they unknowingly swallow microscopic pinworm eggs. The pinworm eggs pass through the digestive tract, where they hatch in the small intestine into a larval* stage. Pinworm larvae then travel from the small intestine to the large intestine, where they attach to the intestinal wall. About two to six weeks after the eggs have been swallowed, adult female pinworms migrate from the large intestine to the rectum, where they exit from the anus to lay numerous eggs on nearby skin. The adult pinworms then return to the large intestine, where they usually die, but the new eggs become active within a few hours and remain active for up to three weeks.

Egg laying can cause itching in the infected person's anal area, and pinworm eggs can be transferred from fingers to clothing, bedding, towels, toilets, and other objects in the environment. When people handle objects that have become contaminated with pinworm eggs, they may inadvertently touch their fingers to their lips afterward and swallow the new eggs, allowing the pinworm life cycle to begin again.

** **larva** is an intermediate stage in a worm's life cycle between egg and adult.*

What Are the Signs and Symptoms of Pinworm Infection?

The most common symptom is anal itching, but most people with pinworms show no symptoms at all. Because female pinworms usually lay their eggs at night, this is when itching can be most intense, and it may interfere with sleep or may cause restless sleep. Sometimes, anal itching is so minor that it is not recognized as a symptom. In females, pinworms can migrate to the vagina, causing itching and vaginal discharge.

How Do Doctors Diagnose and Treat Pinworm Infection?

Diagnosis Pinworm infections are diagnosed if doctors find adult female worms or eggs around the anus. Doctors (or parents) place adhesive tape on the skin in the anal area, usually in the morning as egg laying occurs overnight. When the tape is removed and viewed under a microscope, eggs or worms stuck to the tape are visible.

Treatment When infection is confirmed, treatment is started. A single dose of prescription medication is given, sometimes with a follow-up dose two weeks later. Because of the contagious nature of pinworm infection, usually everyone in the household is treated. Reinfection is common and treatment may have to be repeated.

How Do People Prevent Pinworm Infection?

Proper personal hygiene can help prevent pinworm infections. It is important to wash hands after going to the bathroom and before eating. Bathing and changing underwear regularly are also useful. Despite such precautions, however, reinfection is common, particularly in children.

Resource

The U.S. National Institute of Allergy and Infectious Diseases posts a fact sheet about pinworm and other parasitic roundworm diseases at its website.
http://www.niaid.nih.gov/factsheets/roundwor.htm

▶ *See also*
Ascariasis
Trichinosis
Worms

Plague

Plague is a serious illness spread to humans by the bite of a flea carried by an infected animal, usually a wild rodent.

KEYWORDS
for searching the Internet and other reference sources

Infection

Yersinia

The Black Death

In about 1300, a massive epidemic of a deadly disease known as plague began. The epidemic, sometimes called the Black Death, started in Asia, then spread westward from the Middle East to North Africa and Europe. Between 1347 and 1350, as many as 20 million people died from plague in Europe alone. Later waves of plague continued to sweep through Europe until about 1800. At the time, people were not sure what caused the disease. They blamed it on everything from the anger of God to unhealthy vapors given off by the sick or by swamps and cesspools.

PLAGUE AND PESTILENCE

The first well-known outbreak of plague, sometimes called the Plague of Justinian, occurred during the Roman Empire. The empire reportedly lost a quarter of its population to the disease. This outbreak struck Constantinople in 542, then spread into Western Europe. Later waves of plague continued to appear around the Mediterranean Sea for the next 200 years.

A second cycle of plague, known as the Black Death, had an even greater impact. This was the greatest medical disaster of the Middle Ages. In its first wave alone, from 1347 to 1350, plague killed about a quarter of Europe's population. Once again, waves of plague continued to come and go for hundreds of years. The results were grave. Between 1350 and 1400, the average life span in Europe may have shrunk from 30 to just 20 years.

This ossuary (OSH-oo-air-ee) from Rouen in medieval France carries the bones of people who died of plague. © *Nicole Duplaix/Peter Arnold, Inc.*

The U.S and the World

- There are about 1,000 to 2,000 cases of plague each year worldwide. Today, the disease is found in Asia, extreme southeastern Europe, Africa, North America, and South America.

- During the 1980s, there were outbreaks of plague in Africa, Asia, and South America.

- In the United States from 1970 to 1995, there were about 13 cases per year.

- There is no plague in Australia or most of Europe.

- Modern outbreaks of plague usually can be traced to house rats and their fleas. Such outbreaks still crop up in some developing countries. The last such outbreak in the United States occurred in Los Angeles in 1924–1925.

What Is Plague?

In 1894, Alexandre Yersin, a French doctor studying plague in Hong Kong, first described the bacterium that causes plague. It is called *Yersinia pestis* after him. The bacteria are spread to humans by the bite of a flea carried by an infected animal, usually a wild rodent. Although plague is still a serious illness, it is now rare. During the 1980s, there was an average of 18 cases of plague a year in the United States. About one in seven of these patients died. There are sporadic outbreaks of plague each year worldwide. In the 1980s, outbreaks occurred in 17 countries, mostly in Africa, Asia, and South America.

In North America, most cases of plague in the 1990s occurred in two regions: one in northern New Mexico, northern Arizona, and southern Colorado, and another in California, southern Oregon, and far western Nevada. In the southwestern states, rock squirrels and their fleas are the most common source of human plague. In the Pacific states, California ground squirrels and their fleas are the most common source. Other rodent sources include prairie dogs, wood rats, chipmunks, and other ground squirrels, and, less frequently, wild rabbits, and pet cats.

How Is Plague Spread?

Plague usually is spread from animal to animal and from animal to human by the bite of an infected flea. Less often, it is spread by direct contact with the body fluids or tissues of a sick or dead animal. For example, a person might catch plague while skinning an infected rabbit. Plague also can be spread by tiny droplets of bacteria that get into the air from the coughing of people or cats whose infection has spread to the lungs. Other people who breathe these droplets can catch plague.

People in the western United States who come into contact with animals that might carry plague run a risk of getting the disease. Such people include campers, hikers, and hunters who visit areas with animal plague; and pet owners and animal doctors who handle infected cats.

What Are the Symptoms?

There are three main types of plague: bubonic, septicemic, and pneumonic. Bubonic plague usually starts two to six days after a person comes into contact with plague bacteria. It leads to very tender, swollen lymph nodes*, called buboes, that are often hot to the touch. Other possible symptoms of bubonic plague include fever, chills, tiredness, headache, and an overall feeling of illness.

The disease can get worse quickly if treatment is not started right away. If bacteria invade the bloodstream, the result is a severe illness known as septicemic plague. Symptoms of septicemic plague include fever, chills, tiredness, stomach pain, bleeding into the skin and other organs, and shock (a sudden drop in blood flow throughout the body that can lead to physical collapse and death). If the infection spreads to the lungs, the result is a deadly illness known as pneumonic plague. Symptoms of pneumonic plague include fever, chills, coughing, trouble breathing, and shock. Without prompt treatment, most people with pneumonic plague soon die.

What Is the Treatment?

Early diagnosis and treatment can cut the death rate for plague to less than 5 percent. The doctor may suspect plague if a person develops the telltale symptoms and has been around wild rodents, wild rabbits, or sick or dead animals that eat rodents and rabbits. To be sure, the doctor can check for signs of plague bacteria in the person's blood, mucus that is coughed up, or lymph node samples.

Antibiotic drugs are given to fight the plague bacteria. In addition, people suspected of having pneumonic plague are kept away from others to keep from spreading the disease through coughing.

How Can It Be Prevented?

People who live, work, or play in areas with animal plague can take precautions to reduce their risk, including:

■ Getting rid of rodents in and around homes, workplaces, and campsites by removing brush, rock piles, junk, pet food, and food scraps from around such areas.

*lymph nodes are bean-sized round or oval masses of immune system tissue that store special cells that fight infection and other diseases. Clusters of them are found in the underarms, groin, neck, chest, and abdomen.

- Sealing rodent entry holes in buildings.

- Using flea sprays to kill fleas during outbreaks of animal plague.

- Not touching sick or dead rodents or rabbits.

- Reporting sick or dead rodents or rabbits that may have plague to the local health department.

A vaccine for plague is available. However, it is recommended only for people whose jobs place them at very high risk, such as those who work with plague bacteria in laboratories or with wild rodents in areas with plague. Travelers to countries reporting cases of plague, and people who may have come into contact with infected animals may be given antibiotics to help ward off the disease.

Resource

U.S. Centers for Disease Control and Prevention (CDC), Division of Vector-Borne Infectious Diseases, 1600 Clifton Road N.E., Atlanta, GA 30333. CDC posts a fact sheet about plague at its website. Telephone 800-311-3435
http://www.cdc.gov/ncidod/dvbid/plagindex.htm

▶ See also
Bacterial Infections
Shock
Zoonoses

Pleurisy

Pleurisy (PLOOR-i-see) is an inflammation* of the membrane* that covers the lungs and lines the chest cavity. The lining is called the pleura (PLOOR-a).

KEYWORDS
for searching the Internet
and other reference sources

Inflammation

Pulmonary system

What Is Pleurisy?

In pleurisy, the membrane covering the lungs and lining the chest cavity becomes inflamed, and excess fluids may build up in the space. When people who have pleurisy breathe in or cough, the inflammation causes pain, which is a result of friction from the inflamed pleura. The pain is a sharp, stabbing pain that begins suddenly. There are a number of different causes of pleurisy.

What Are the Symptoms of Pleurisy?

A sharp, knifelike pain when breathing in or coughing is the primary symptom of pleurisy. People who have pleurisy tend to breathe more frequently with smaller breaths to avoid pain. Ultimately, these small breaths can lead to pneumonia*.

* **inflammation** (in-fla-MAY-shun) is the body's response to infection or irritation.

* **membrane** (MEM-brayn) is a thin layer of tissue that covers a surface, lines a cavity, or divides a space or organ.

* **pneumonia** (noo-MO-nee-a) is an inflammation of the lungs, usually caused by bacteria (bak-TEER-ee-a), viruses (VY-rus-ez), or chemical irritants.

In the play *The Glass Menagerie* by Tennessee Williams, Laura tells her mother how a boy in her high school called her "Blue Roses."

"Why did he call you such a name as that?" asks her mother, Amanda.

Laura explains that when she came back to school after she had an attack of "pleurosis," the young man, Jim, asked her what had been the matter with her. She told him she had had pleurosis, and he mistook the word for "blue roses." Thereafter, whenever Jim saw Laura, he would greet her with, "Hello, Blue Roses!"

Unfortunately, it is easier to contract pleurisy than it is to find blue roses. In the play, though, Laura does recover from her pleurosis. Her problems are of a different nature. The title of the play refers to Laura's collection of glass animals.

* **cancer** is any tumorous (TOO-mor-us) condition the natural (untreated) course of which is often fatal.

* **rheumatoid arthritis** (ROO-ma-toid ar-THRI-tis) is a chronic (KRON-ik) autoimmune disease character-ized by pain, swelling, stiffness, and deformation of the joints.

▶ *See also*
Bacterial Infections
Pneumonia
Tuberculosis

KEYWORDS
for searching the Internet and other reference sources

Asbestosis

Black lung disease

Respiratory system

Silicosis

What Causes Pleurisy?

Pleurisy may result from a number of causes. It can develop from infec-tions, such as pneumonia. It also can be a result of injury from an acci-dent or chest surgery. Sometimes, pleurisy is a complication of another disease, like lung cancer* or rheumatoid arthritis*. Another cause of pleurisy is damage to the pleura from toxic substances such as asbestos. The result in all of these cases is inflammation of the pleura that causes pain when a person coughs or breathes.

How Is Pleurisy Diagnosed and Treated?

Physicians may diagnose pleurisy when they hear a "friction rub" when the patient breathes deeply. Doctors can use several different laboratory tests to help diagnose the condition, one of which requires taking fluid out of the chest for analysis. Medicines can be given to help with the pain and inflammation. However, the underlying cause of pleurisy, such as bacte-rial pneumonia or tuberculosis (too-ber-ku-LO-sis), must be treated.

Pneumoconiosis

Pneumoconiosis (noo-mo-ko-nee-O-sis) is a disease of the lungs caused by long-term breathing of dust, especially certain mineral dusts. Forms of pneumoconiosis include black lung disease (coal worker's pneumoconiosis), silicosis, and asbestosis. The disease typically results from working in a mine for many years, but factory work and other occupations can expose people to the ill effects of breathing dusts. The term "pneumoconiosis" comes from the Greek pneumon, *meaning lung, and* konis, *meaning dust.*

What Causes Pneumoconiosis?

Only microscopic-size dust particles, about 1/5,000 of an inch across or smaller, are able to reach the tiniest air sacs (the alveoli) in the lungs. There they cannot be removed, and accumulate to cause a scarring and thickening of the lungs called fibrosis (fy-BRO-sis). Eventually, the lungs begin to lose their ability to supply oxygen to the body.

Black lung disease is caused by breathing coal dust, usually in mines. Silicosis results from inhaling silica dust from sand and rock, primarily in mines, quarries, and in occupations such as sandblasting. Asbestosis comes from breathing tiny asbestos fibers in mining, building construction, and other industries. Less commonly, other kinds of dust are continuously inhaled in work-related situations and cause pneumoconiosis.

THE WAR AGAINST BLACK LUNG

The prevalence of black lung disease did not begin to decrease until it became clear that the cause was excessively high levels of coal dust in mines. Largely due to the efforts of coal miners' unions, occupational safety conditions improved.

In 1969, the Mine Health and Safety Act set standards in the United States for maximum allowable levels of coal dust in mines. The Act also provided compensation for miners who developed black lung disease. Death rates from pneumoconiosis have been declining since the Act was passed.

Breathing coal dust was an occupational hazard for coal miners, especially those who did not wear protective masks. *Corbis-Bettman.*

What Happens When People Have Pneumoconiosis?

Symptoms   Because pneumoconiosis usually takes 20 or 30 years to develop, workers often do not notice symptoms until they are over 50. The main symptoms are coughing and difficulty in breathing, which gradually increases. Complications include emphysema (em-fe-SEE-ma) and increased risk of tuberculosis. Asbestosis patients are more likely to develop lung cancer, especially if they smoke cigarettes. Damaged lungs make the heart work harder, and heart problems can accompany severe cases of pneumoconiosis.

Diagnosis   Diagnosis is made by physical examination and through a medical history that tells the doctor which dusts patients have been exposed to. The doctor may also take chest x-rays and pulmonary (lung) function tests.

Treatment   There is no cure for pneumoconiosis, because the dust cannot be removed from the lungs. Even if it could, the damage done to the lungs from years of inflammatory reaction to the dust could not be undone. Except in a mild form called simple pneumoconiosis, the disease is progressively disabling. The only treatment is to avoid smoking and further exposure to dust, and to treat complications.

Prevention   Pneumoconiosis can be prevented by enforcing maximum allowable dust levels in mines and at other work sites, and by using protective masks. Regular medical examinations, including chest x-rays for people at risk, can detect pneumoconiosis during its earlier stages, before it becomes disabling.

▶ *See also*

Emphysema

Environmental Diseases

Lung Cancer

Tuberculosis

Resource

Derickson, Alan. *Black Lung: Anatomy of a Public Health Disaster.* Ithaca, NY: Cornell University Press, 1998. This book provides historical information on black lung disease.

Pneumonia

Pneumonia is inflammation of the lungs. It is a common illness usually caused by infection with a bacterium, virus, or fungus. It is often mild, especially in young people, and is usually curable or goes away on its own. Pneumonia may cause serious illness, especially in people who are old or already have health problems, and it remains a major cause of death.

KEYWORDS
for searching the Internet and other reference sources

Infection

Inflammation

Respiratory system

What Is Pneumonia?

Each day a person inhales large amounts of air, often laden with germs, dust, and other particles. The air is drawn deep into the lungs, two spongy air sacs in the chest where oxygen from the air is transferred to the blood. Yet despite the constant chance of inhaling germs, the lungs of a healthy person are basically sterile, meaning germ-free. How is this possible? An array of natural defenses protects these crucial organs from infection. These defenses include:

- The ability to cough deeply. This expels germs and keeps germ-trapping mucus from building up in the lungs.

- The vocal cords and the epiglottis (ep-i-GLOT-is), a flap of tissue that closes the trachea (TRAY-ke-a or windpipe) when a person swallows. These, along with the gag reflex, keep people from inhaling food, vomit, or stomach acid into their lungs.

- The cilia (SILL-ee-a), small hairs that line the inside of the windpipe, waving upward. They filter particles out of the air before they reach the lungs.

- The immune system, a complex set of organs, chemicals, and white blood cells that attack germs that may enter the body.

These defenses usually prevent pneumonia, but sometimes a person's defenses may be weakened by illness, age, or other factors. The defenses also may be overwhelmed by a particularly heavy or virulent* dose of germs.

Sometimes, the germs or chemicals that cause pneumonia are aspirated or inhaled not from the air but from a person's own throat, as when germ-bearing food or vomit is breathed into the lungs. This may cause aspiration pneumonia. Sometimes the germs are not inhaled at all but enter the lungs from the bloodstream.

How Does Pneumonia Make Breathing Difficult?

When germs or chemicals irritate lung tissue, the irritation causes inflammation, a condition that includes fever and a buildup of white blood cells and mucus in the lungs. Breathing becomes more difficult. The lungs have to work harder to transfer oxygen into the bloodstream and to remove carbon dioxide, a dangerous waste product, from the blood. Eventually, the cells of the body may not get enough oxygen, and carbon dioxide may build up in the body.

Who Is at Risk for Pneumonia?

Anyone can get pneumonia, but it tends to strike people whose natural defenses against infection are weak. A growing number of people fall into that category. They may be very old, they may have AIDS (which damages the body's immune system), they may have received organ transplants (which work only if drugs are taken to weaken the immune system), or they may be living with cancer or another serious illness.

Patients in the hospital are at special risk for developing pneumonia, especially if they have difficulty breathing deeply or coughing, as can

Streptococcal Pneumonia

The bacteria that cause streptococcal pneumonia, the most common kind of pneumonia, live in the upper respiratory systems of many healthy people without making them sick. However, if another illness reduces the immune system's ability to control these bacteria, they can reproduce rapidly to dangerous levels.

Sometimes a cold will be followed by streptococcal pneumonia, because the fluids produced by a cold's runny nose and sore throat make an excellent breeding ground for streptococcal bacteria. The majority of people recover fully after antibiotic treatment and bed rest.

*__virulent__ comes from the Latin word for poisonous, and describes a microbe that is especially well suited to countering the immune system.

Mycoplasma Pneumonia

Mycoplasma pneumonia is the most common form of atypical pneumonia. It affects mainly young people ages 5 to 35. It got the nickname "walking pneumonia" because it often has flu-like symptoms so mild that people keep walking around with it instead of getting bed rest.

One reason mycoplasma pneumonia tends to be mild is because the bacteria that cause it do not invade the deep tissue of the lungs. Instead, they grow on the mucous membranes that line the lungs. This does not cause as much swelling or lung inflammation as in other kinds of pneumonia.

happen after chest or abdominal surgery. In addition, some hospital tests and treatments require tubes to be inserted into the trachea. This can give germs a way into the lungs, making pneumonia more likely. An infection acquired in the hospital is said to be "nosocomial" (no-so-KOME-ee-al), an adjective based on the Greek word for hospital.

Other people at special risk for pneumonia are:

- Anyone who is bedridden, paralyzed, or not fully conscious, because they may lack the ability to cough or gag.
- People with chronic (long-lasting) diseases such as diabetes, heart failure, or chronic obstructive pulmonary disease, a lung disorder.
- People who smoke or abuse alcohol.
- Children who have cystic fibrosis, which causes mucus to build up in the lungs.
- Infants, because their immune systems are not fully developed.

Which Microorganisms Cause Pneumonia?

More than 75 kinds of germs can cause pneumonia. Here are some common bacterial causes:

- *Streptococcus pneumoniae* is the most common cause of adult pneumonia.
- *Staphylococcus aureus* causes many cases of pneumonia in the hospital. This is the same bacterium that produces staph infections.
- *Mycoplasma pneumoniae* is the usual cause of atypical or "walking" pneumonia, a mild form common in young people between the ages of 5 and 35.
- *Chlamydia, Legionella, Klebsiella, Pseudomonas,* and many others.

Some common viral causes that tend to affect children and the elderly are:

- respiratory syncytial (sin-SISH-al) virus. It affects mainly babies and pre-teens, usually causing mild illness that goes away after a week or so.
- Influenza A and B viruses. Very few people infected with flu virus develop pneumonia. Those who do, however, run a high risk of dying, especially if they are old or chronically ill. Sometimes, besides getting viral pneumonia, they get a "superinfection" or a bacterial infection in the lungs on top of the viral infection.
- The viruses that cause measles and chickenpox, as well as other common families of viruses.
- Epstein-Barr virus, and herpes simplex. These cause serious pneumonia most often in people with AIDS or other immune problems.

Other causes of pneumonia include:

- Fungal pneumonia, which is seen mostly in people with AIDS or other immune-system problems. The most common fungal cause is *Pneumocystic carinii* (noo-mo-SIS-tik kar-RIN-ee-i) pneumonia. PCP, as it is often called, used to be the main killer of people infected with HIV, the human immunodeficiency virus that causes AIDS. Medications now can often prevent it, but it still is a serious problem.
- Parasites, such as toxoplasma, which also can cause pneumonia.
- Reactions to certain medications.
- High doses of radiation or toxic chemicals if they are inhaled or aspirated.

What Happens When People Have Pneumonia?

Symptoms   People who have streptococcal pneumonia, the most common kind, often get a fever of 102 to 104 degrees F (39 to 40.5 degrees Centigrade) and chills that cause the body to shake. They cough, often bringing up large amounts of thick, greenish mucus, sometimes mixed with blood. They may breath more quickly, and they may have rales (pronounced "rahls"), a crackling sound that can be heard with a stethoscope. Their chests hurt, too; the stabbing pain seems to get worse the more they cough. Other symptoms include a bad headache, loss of appetite, tiredness, nausea, and vomiting.

People who are elderly or who have immune system problems often have milder symptoms in the beginning, even though their illness may be more dangerous. They might, for instance, have just a low-grade fever, tiredness, or confusion, and a sense of being ill.

People with atypical or mycoplasma pneumonia often get a dry cough, a sore throat, skin rashes, and muscle and joint pain. Because these are not the classic symptoms of pneumonia, people may think they just have a mild case of flu.

People with influenza pneumonia often have fever, a severe dry cough, rales, and severe fatigue.

Diagnosis   If a person has persistent fever and a cough, doctors will suspect pneumonia. They may be able to diagnose pneumonia by listening through a stethoscope to the person's breathing. In any case, a chest x-ray usually makes the diagnosis clear.

Finding out which germ is causing the pneumonia is often much harder. Blood samples and coughed-up mucus can be tested in the laboratory. Sometimes a lung biopsy is done. This means a sample of lung tissue is removed through surgery or extracted with a needle so it can be studied. If the pneumonia has caused excess fluid around the lung, this fluid also can be sampled with a needle. Often, however, the organism is not identified at all, or is identified too late to help with decisions about treatment.

The U.S. and the World

In the nineteenth century when few illnesses were treatable, pneumonia was called "the old man's friend." It won this grim nickname because it swiftly ended the lives of many old men and old women who had been suffering with other untreatable illnesses. It often was a sick person's last illness.

Today, medicine and good medical care usually cure pneumonia, even in the sick and elderly, and sometimes can prevent it as well. Yet pneumonia occurs in so many people that it still ranks as the sixth most common cause of death in the United States. An estimated 2 million Americans a year get it, and 40,000 to 70,000 die.

In many developing countries, pneumonia ranks first or second as a cause of death, along with diarrhea caused by infectious diseases.

Treatment If a specific type of bacteria has been identified as the cause of the pneumonia, the doctor can prescribe antibiotic drugs that target those bacteria. If the germ is not pinpointed but bacteria are suspected, the doctor may give antibiotics that are active against the most likely causes. If the cause is a virus or fungus, antibiotics will not help. Instead, some antiviral and antifungal drugs are available, although not all viruses have treatments.

When the pneumonia is severe, people often are hospitalized. They may be given oxygen or put on a ventilator (a breathing machine) to help them breathe while the medications and the immune system fight the infection.

How Is Pneumonia Prevented?

Yearly flu vaccinations can prevent pneumonia caused by certain influenza viruses, and a one-time vaccination can help protect people against pneumococcal pneumonia.

People who have the AIDS virus can reduce their chances of getting *Pneumocystic carinii* pneumonia by taking daily medication. Not smoking, or quitting the habit, and not drinking alcohol excessively also can reduce the risk of pneumonia.

To prevent pneumonia in the hospital, patients are encouraged to breathe deeply, and they are sometimes given plastic breath meters that measure how well they are doing. They also are encouraged to move around, if possible, rather than staying in bed. These practices prevent the lungs from filling with mucus and other fluids that some bacteria thrive in.

How Might Pneumonia Change a Person's Life?

Most people who are treated for pneumonia recover completely in a few weeks. Some people, especially those who are old or had lung problems to begin with, may develop permanent breathing problems from scarring of the lungs. This may limit their ability to carry out their usual activities.

Resource

The American Lung Association posts a fact sheet about pneumonia at its website.
http://www.lungusa.org/diseases/lungpneumoni.htm

▶ *See also*

AIDS and HIV
Bacterial Infections
Chlamydial Infections
Fungal Infections
Influenza
Legionnaire's Disease
Tuberculosis
Viral Infections

Poison Ivy *See* Skin Conditions

Poison Oak *See* Skin Conditions

Poison Sumac *See* Skin Conditions

Poliomyelitis

Poliomyelitis (po-lee-o-my-e-LY-tis), or polio, is a viral infection that attacks nerve cells and causes deterioration of muscles and sometimes paralysis.

KEYWORDS
for searching the Internet
or other reference sources

Muscular system

Nervous system

Paralysis

Vaccine

Iron Lungs

Remarkable photographs from the mid twentieth century show people—sometimes a large roomful—enclosed in metal tanks being attended to by nurses. The tanks were called iron lungs. In the 1940s and 1950s, these machines breathed for patients whose breathing had been either temporarily or permanently disabled by poliomyelitis. Once the most feared of childhood diseases because of its potential to cripple people for life, polio is now almost unknown in the United States. Elsewhere in the world, however, the disease still strikes thousands of people each year.

What Is Poliomyelitis?

Polio is an infection caused when a person swallows water or food contaminated with poliovirus. Poliovirus particles are found in feces, and the virus can be spread when people touch contaminated objects and then put their fingers in their mouths or handle food. It is not spread by coughing or sneezing. Once inside the body, the virus multiplies in the throat and intestines. It then either passes harmlessly from the gut or travels in the blood to all parts of the body. In a very small number of

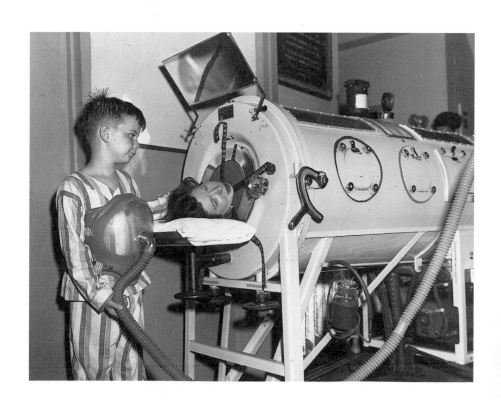

This photograph, taken in 1949, shows an 8-year-old boy with polio wearing the newly introduced one-pound portable "Monaghan" iron lung around his chest. He is standing next to an adult woman lying confined in an old-style iron lung. *Dennis Burke, Daily Mirror/Corbis-Bettman*

POLIO IN HISTORY

Polio has caused paralysis and death for most of human history. Reference to paralytic poliomyelitis can be found in Egyptian stone engravings over 3,000 years old. At the start of the twentieth century, however, few people had ever heard of the disease until epidemics of polio began to occur with regularity in the developed world. In the summer of 1916, polio became a more familiar condition in the United States when a devastating epidemic struck New York. The outbreak left 27,000 people paralyzed and 9,000 dead. Almost forty years later, on April 12, 1955, it was announced that Dr. Jonas Salk had developed the first effective vaccine against paralytic poliomyelitis. With the development of this and other later vaccines, polio has been eradicated throughout most of the industrialized world.

people, about 1 to 2 percent, the virus invades the central nervous system, that is, the brain and spinal cord, where it can cause paralysis. Depending on where the virus goes in the spinal cord, a person may also have difficulty breathing, talking, or swallowing.

Poliovirus is special in that it attacks only the nerve cells that control muscles—called motor neurons—and leaves other nearby nerve cells unaffected. Nerve cells are like roads connecting our muscles to the central nervous system, and the virus is able to travel along these roads to the spinal cord and brain. The virus infects more than 95 percent of the motor neurons in the spinal cord and many other cells in the brain. The neurons that are destroyed cannot be replaced, and paralysis is the result. But many neurons survive, and when they recover, they form new connections to the muscles. In fact, for reasons that are not clear, a nerve cell that survives the virus sprouts many more connections to muscle cells than it did originally. So even if many neurons are destroyed by the virus, often the remaining neurons are able to make up for the loss.

Signs and Symptoms

In more than 90 percent of cases, people do not know that they have caught the poliovirus. When symptoms do occur, they may be similar to those of a cold or the flu. Although paralysis is a devastating result of poliomyelitis, most people with polio do not become paralyzed. And many patients who do develop paralysis recover much of the use of their muscles weeks to months after infection. About two-thirds of patients with paralytic polio have long-lasting effects from the disease.

How Do People Know If They Have Polio?

Usually polio can be diagnosed by the kind of paralysis it causes—more on one side of the body than the other. A person cannot move his or her legs, arms, or even the muscles required for breathing. Tests identify cells in the fluid around the brain and spinal cord that are not supposed to be there. To confirm the diagnosis, samples from a throat swab and a stool culture are tested to see whether they contain poliovirus. There is an even more rapid and sensitive test, called polymerase (pol-IM-er-ase) chain reaction, that is used in some cases.

How Is Polio Prevented?

There is no treatment for polio infection, but it can be prevented by vaccination. Vaccination is a way of protecting a person from a disease by introducing the body to a harmless form of the disease-causing organism. Then if the body encounters the disease-causing germ, it is able to recognize it and fight against it. In 1952 there were 57,879 cases of poliomyelitis in the United States—the highest number of cases ever. But the introduction in 1955 of an injectable vaccine developed by Jonas Salk and in 1961 of an oral vaccine developed by Albert Sabin ultimately eradicated poliovirus in the western hemisphere. The last cases in the United States occurred in 1979, among religious groups that

FDR AND POLIO

Franklin Delano Roosevelt contracted polio at the age of 39 while vacationing on Campobello Island in New Brunswick, Canada. After a day of swimming and playing with his children, he went to bed tired and aching and awoke unable to move his legs. Two weeks later his illness was identified as polio. FDR never walked unassisted again. He had already begun a life in politics, and in 1932 he ran for president of the United States and won. Although FDR did not try to hide his bout with polio, he went to great pains to disguise the extent of his disability. The public never saw him in his wheelchair. In 1938 FDR established the March of Dimes, which funded the research and immunization effort that eliminated polio from the Americas.

In 1998 the decision was made to add a sculpture of FDR in his wheelchair to the FDR memorial in Washington. Depicting him this way was controversial. Some people felt that he would not have liked being shown in his wheelchair in the sculpture. Others argued that he would be glad to have his image encourage people with disabilities to accomplish great things.

The Franklin Delano Roosevelt Memorial in Washington, D.C. FDR's pet scotty Fala sits at the foot of the wheelchair-bound president. *UPI/Corbis-Bettmann.*

681

had declined to be vaccinated. At present, the only cases of polio reported in the United States are due to the oral vaccine itself. Five to 10 such cases are reported each year. Most of the other cases develop in close contacts of these patients who have not been properly vaccinated or who have weakened immune systems.

Of 6,241 polio cases reported from 51 countries in 1994, more than 7 of every 10 were from India, Pakistan, and Bangladesh. There are several reasons for these outbreaks: Many people live in unhealthy, crowded conditions, and they may be improperly vaccinated or not vaccinated at all.

Guidelines of the U.S. Centers for Disease Control and Prevention in Atlanta recommend giving the Salk vaccine, made from an inactivated version of the poliovirus, when an infant is 2 months old and again at 4 months. This is followed by a dose of the Sabin oral vaccine, made from an altered, live virus, at 12 to 18 months and again at 4 to 6 years of age. If only the live vaccine is used, there is a small chance of getting polio from the altered live virus itself. The substitution of the inactivated Salk vaccine for the first two doses is believed to virtually eliminate this risk.

JONAS SALK
MADE ONE VACCINE . . .

Jonas Salk was the head of the Virus Research Lab at the University of Pittsburgh when he began to study poliovirus. At first, Salk's work went slowly because it was hard to make enough virus to work with. But in 1948 researchers at Harvard University found a way of creating large quantities of virus, which enabled Salk to refine his vaccine. On July 2, 1952, he tried the vaccine on children who had had polio and recovered and found that their antibodies to the virus—proteins the body manufactures to fight against disease—had increased. Next he tried the vaccine on volunteers who had not had polio, including himself, his wife, and their children, and no one got sick. In 1954 mass inoculation of schoolchildren was begun and resulted in 60 to 70 percent prevention. Between 1955 and 1957, the annual number of new cases of polio in the United States decreased from 28,985 to 5,894.

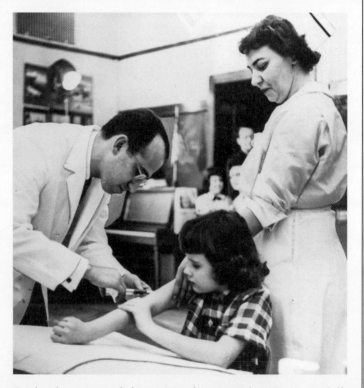

A school nurse stands by on March 10, 1954, as Dr. Jonas Salk injects an 8-year-old Pittsburgh schoolgirl with polio vaccine, still experimental. The March of Dimes helped fund the first trials in Pittsburgh, where Salk was based. *UPI/Corbis-Bettman.*

Surviving Polio

People who become paralyzed by the poliovirus have major adjustments to make. Survivors must receive physical therapy to keep their muscles from deteriorating, and they may need leg braces to walk or have to use a wheelchair. Others may need help breathing for the rest of their lives. Some people overcome early paralysis only to suffer from post-polio syndrome decades later. But most survivors of paralytic polio have normal childhoods and go on to lead fulfilling lives. The violinist Itzhak Perlman, who caught the virus at the age of 4 and wears leg braces, is one example. Franklin D. Roosevelt (see box), who got polio at age 39, went on to become one of our greatest presidents.

What Is Post-Polio Syndrome?

Neurons are constantly losing and making new connections, but in a balanced way, so that no matter how many connections are wearing out, there are always enough to keep the muscles working. But in the late 1970s, some of the people who had survived paralytic polio in the 1930s and 1940s began to complain of muscle and joint pain and of new muscle weakness. At first, physicians did not believe the complaints were real, but the number of patients kept increasing. In the 1980s, the term "post-polio syndrome" was coined to describe the condition. Post-polio syndrome is not caused by reinfection with the virus. Researchers believe that in these individuals, over time, the core, or axon, of their motor neurons may just wear out and can no longer make new connections. Or nerves may fail for other reasons. People who are affected by post-polio syndrome experience weakness, tiredness, muscle twitching, and pain. In addition, muscles affected by polio 20 to 30 years earlier begin to lose strength again. Unfortunately, no test exists to detect post-polio syndrome. The disease progresses very slowly, and treatment consists of exercise and aids such as braces or a wheelchair and assisted breathing when needed.

. . . AND ALFRED SABIN MADE ANOTHER

Another researcher, Albert Sabin, felt that using a weakened form of the live virus would provide greater protection than the killed virus used by Salk. Sabin's vaccine was cheaper to make than Salk's, and it was easier to take—people could swallow it rather than getting a shot, which meant that it did not require skilled health workers to administer it. Today children receive both vaccines as part of their immunization against polio.

Resources

Book

Kehret, Peg. *Small Steps: The Year I Got Polio.* Morton Grove, IL: Albert Whitman, 1996.

Organizations

U.S. Centers for Disease Control and Prevention (CDC), 1600 Clifton Road, N.E., Atlanta, GA 30333. The United States government authority for information about infectious and other diseases. http://www.cdc.gov

World Health Organization (WHO), Avenue Appia 20, 1211 Geneva 27, Switzerland. This group's website provides excellent information on the global polio eradication program. http://www.who.int/gpv-dvacc/research/virus1.htm

Tutorial

"A Science Odyssey: On the Edge: Paralyzing Polio." A short, entertaining introduction to the Salk and Sabin vaccines. http://www.pbs.org/wgbh/aso/ontheedge/polio

Video

Seavey, Nina Gilden. *A Paralyzing Fear: The Story of Polio in America.* PBS Home Video. (There is a companion book to this video.) http://shop.pbs.org

▶ See also
Paralysis
Viral Infections

Polyps

Polyps (POL-ips) are growths of tissue that project from the mucous membranes*. These growths normally are benign (be-NINE), which means they are not a threat to someone's health, but in some cases they can develop into cancerous tumors.

What Are Polyps?

Three of the most common types include colorectal, cervical, and nasal polyps.

Colorectal polyps These polyps grow in the colon or rectum, parts of the large intestine. They can develop into cancerous polyps. People who have colorectal polyps may notice unusual cramping, stomach pain, or bleeding when they have a bowel movement, or they may not experience any symptoms at all. Doctors usually check for polyps in people who have these symptoms, or who have relatives that were

KEYWORDS
for searching the Internet and other reference sources:

Cervical polyps

Colorectal polyps

Nasal polyps

* **mucous membranes** (MU-kus membranes) are the thin layers of tissue found inside the nose, ears, cervix (SER-viks) and uterus, stomach, colon and rectum, on the vocal cords, and in other parts of the body.

diagnosed with colorectal polyps, since sometimes polyps run in families. Most colorectal polyps develop in people over age 50.

The most common procedures for diagnosing colorectal polyps are sigmoidoscopy (sig-moyd-OS-ko-pee), an examination of the rectum and lower colon, and colonoscopy (ko-lon-OS-ko-pee), an examination of the rectum and the entire colon. The doctor inserts a flexible lighted instrument into the colon that transmits images of the inside of the colon to a monitor. If polyps are found, they are removed to prevent the development of cancer.

Cervical Polyps   These growths develop in the cervix, which is the lower part of the uterus*. Their cause is not completely understood, but they are not related to any type of sexually transmitted disease.

The most common symptom of cervical polyps is abnormal bleeding from the vagina*. Cervical polyps are relatively common and are usually found during a woman's annual pelvic examination, when the doctor checks the uterus, cervix, and vagina for any abnormalities. Most cervical polyps are benign and can be removed easily. Only rarely do they develop into cancer.

Nasal Polyps   Nasal polyps develop in the sinuses, the cavities in the skull that are located near the top of the nose and under the eyes. People who develop nasal polyps usually have a history of allergies, hay fever, sinus infections, asthma*, or cystic fibrosis*. They can cause problems with breathing and either need to be removed or treated with medications that the person inhales. Nasal polyps rarely become cancerous.

Resources

Organization

The Mayo Clinic, Rochester, MN, posts information about colorectal and nasal polyps on its website.
http://www.mayo.edu/

* **uterus** (YOO-ter-us) in humans is the organ in females for containing and nourishing the young during development in the period before birth. Also called the womb.

* The **vagina** is the canal that leads from the uterus—the womb—to the outside of the body.

* **asthma** is a lung disorder that involves attacks of breathing difficulty.

* **cystic fibrosis** (SIS-tik fy-BRO-sis) is an inherited disorder in which the body's glands release very thick mucus. This can lead to blockages and infection in the lungs.

▶ See also
   Allergies
   Colorectal Cancer
   Cystic Fibrosis

Porphyria

Porphyria (por-FEER-ee-a) refers to a group of disorders that are genetic (hereditary). Common problems in porphyria include sensitivity to light, skin rashes, abdominal (ab-DOM-i-nal) pain, and discoloration of the urine.

What Is Porphyria?

When a person inherits a defective gene* from one or both parents, he or she may develop a form of porphyria. There are six classifications of

KEYWORDS
for searching the Internet
and other reference sources

Genetic disorders

Porphyrins

* **genes** are chemicals in the body that help determine a person's characteristics, such as hair or eye color. They are inherited from a person's parents and are contained in the chromosomes found in the cells of the body.

Undated engraving of King George III (1738–1820) of England, who reigned from 1760 to 1820 and is thought to have had porphyria. *Corbis/Bettman.*

* **enzymes** (EN-zymz) are natural substances that speed up specific chemical reactions in the body.

* **liver** is a large organ located in the upper abdomen (AB-do-men) that has many functions, including storage and filtration of blood, secretion of bile, and participation in various metabolic (met-a-BOLL-ik) processes.

* **marrow** (MAR-o) is the soft tissue that fills the cavities of the bones.

* **hormones** are chemicals that are produced by different glands in the body. Hormones are like the body's ambassadors: they are created in one place but are sent through the body to have specific regulatory effects in different places.

* **acute** means sudden.

this group of disorders. Some of them are rare. While exact numbers are not available, it is estimated that one person in 10,000 to 50,000 may be affected.

All six types of porphyria are a result of a problem in the chemical process by which the body makes heme, a compound that carries oxygen and makes blood red. Making heme requires eight different enzymes*. If any one of these enzymes fails, compounds that should be turned into heme instead build up in the body, especially in the liver* and in the bone marrow*, and cause problems. Some of these compounds are called porphyrins (POR-fi-rinz), which is where the disease gets its name. The different forms of porphyria occur from the failure of different enzymes.

Acute intermittent porphyria This form of porphyria does not appear unless it is triggered by certain drugs, starvation or crash dieting, infection, and some hormones* in women. This form of porphyria is more common in women than in men. It usually occurs first during the young adult years. Symptoms include stomach pain, leg cramps, and muscle weakness. As its name indicates, it tends to occur from time to time (intermittently). In its most acute* forms, it can cause seizures*, paralysis*, depression*, and even hallucinations* or coma*. It is thought that King George III of England suffered from some form of porphyria.

Porphyria cutanea tarda (ku-TAY-ne-a TAR-da) This is the most common form of porphyria and causes blisters* on the parts of the body that are exposed to sunlight. Some people with this form also develop liver disease. Substances that can cause an attack of this type of porphyria include alcohol, heavy intake of iron (iron overload), or the use of birth control pills. Porphyria cutanea tarda usually does not affect younger women. However, the increased use of substances that can trigger an attack, such as alcohol or birth control pills, has resulted in more younger women developing the disease. This type of porphyria is not inherited. Only about 20 percent of cases have a family history of the disease.

Protoporphyria Protoporphyria (pro-to-por-FEER-ee-a) usually starts in childhood. The skin is extremely sensitive to sunlight, and painful rashes, redness, and itching may develop.

How Is Porphyria Diagnosed and Treated?

Diagnosis Porphyria is diagnosed when an excess of porphyrins (compounds involved in making heme) is found in the urine. More laboratory tests help pinpoint specific forms of porphyria.

Treatment Heme is given to treat acute intermittent porphyria. For porphyria cutanea tarda, in which there is an excess of iron in the body, the patient may be bled. A pint of blood is removed once or twice a week for several weeks, until iron levels drop to normal. Drug treatment for some forms of porphyria is available. Avoiding light and other substances that can trigger an attack is important for people who are susceptible to any form of porphyria. Sunscreens are not helpful for preventing skin eruptions. Sometimes, betacarotene (bay-ta-KAR-o-teen) is given to help with light sensitivity. Doctors recommend prevention of attacks by avoiding substances that trigger symptoms.

Resource

American Porphyria Foundation (APF), P.O. Box 22712, Houston, TX 77227.
Telephone 713-266-9617
http://www.enterprise.net/apf

Post-Traumatic Stress Disorder

Post-traumatic stress (post-traw-MAT-ik STRES) disorder is a mental disorder in which people who have survived a terrifying event relive their terror in nightmares, memories, and feelings of fear. It is severe enough to interfere with everyday living and can occur after a natural disaster, military combat, rape, mugging, or other violence.

Sara's Story

Sara felt herself trying to scream, but no sound came from her throat. Hands seemed to be gripping her. A face appeared, and Sara reached up and swung her arms wildly. She tried to fight off her attacker, but she felt defenseless.

Suddenly Sara heard her mother's voice trying to wake her, to pull her out of the nightmare. She cried as her mother hugged her tightly in the dark. Sara had experienced the same nightmare many times over the past several weeks. The details sometimes changed, but the dream always ended the same way: with someone trying to hurt her.

In reality, Sara had been attacked last month on her way home from school. Now she was showing signs of post-traumatic stress disorder.

What Is Post-Traumatic Stress Disorder?

Violent assaults are among the many events that can lead to post-traumatic stress disorder, a mental disorder that interferes with everyday living and occurs in people who survive a violent or life-threatening event. Psychological trauma* refers to an emotional shock that leads to lasting psychological damage.

* **seizures** (SEE-zhurz) are sudden attacks of disease, often referring to some type of violent spasms.

* **paralysis** (pa-RAL-i-sis) is the inability to move some part of the body.

* **depression** (de-PRESH-un) is a mental state marked by sadness and despair.

* **hallucinations** (ha-loo-si-NAY-shunz) are sensory perceptions not based in reality.

* **coma** (KO-ma) is an unconscious state, like a very deep sleep. A person in a coma cannot be awakened, and cannot move, see, speak, or hear.

▶ See also
Genetic Diseases
Metabolic Disease
Skin Conditions

KEYWORDS
for searching the Internet and other reference sources

Anxiety disorders

Crime victims

Crisis counseling

Disaster relief

Emergency services

Mental disorders

School violence

Sexual assault

Traumatic stress

Violence

* **trauma** (TRAW-ma), in the broadest sense, refers to a wound or injury, whether psychological or physical.

687

For some, such as Sara, the traumatic event involves a direct attack on them. For others, simply being a witness to a violent incident, such as a murder, can lead to post-traumatic stress disorder. The condition is a special problem for people who fight in wars or whose countries are locations for combat.

What Causes Post-Traumatic Stress Disorder?

There are many traumatic events in life. The National Center for Post-Traumatic Stress Disorder estimates that just over 60 percent of men and 50 percent of women experience at least one traumatic incident at some point. Not all go on to develop post-traumatic stress disorder, but studies show that up to 14 percent of them will.

The cause can be any event or experience that produced or threatened serious physical harm. Such events include violent personal attacks, such as rape, sexual molestation, or mugging; natural disasters, such as hurricanes, tornadoes, or earthquakes; accidents, such as fires or car crashes; terrorist attacks, such as the 1995 Oklahoma City bombing; wartime suffering; or military combat. The common element in these events is that people lived through a period when they faced great harm and felt fearful and defenseless. Their situations were life-threatening and overwhelming.

Doctors are still unsure why some people respond to such experiences by developing post-traumatic stress disorder, while others do not. However, researchers have reported finding physical changes in some people who have survived traumatic events. For example, some survivors have abnormal levels of hormones* and other chemicals that are involved in responding to stress.

What Are the Symptoms of Post-Traumatic Stress Disorder?

People with post-traumatic stress disorder can develop a wide variety of symptoms, some of which may start immediately after the event and others of which may not appear for months or years. There are several common symptoms:

- Recurring flashbacks* about the trauma. These can be nightmares, such as Sara's dream about her assault. Or they can be memories that intrude on daily events during waking hours in ways that overwhelm people. Often the memories are prompted or "triggered," such as when a combat veteran remembers his experience after hearing the crack of fireworks that sound like gunfire. These dreams or memories can be so real that people begin to act as if the trauma is occurring at that moment.

- Withdrawal from people or activities they enjoyed before their trauma. People often try to avoid situations that might cause them to remember what happened to them. They can become overwhelmed by the feeling that nothing really matters. Because they almost lost their lives in an unexpected event, they may fear that it will happen

* **hormones** are chemicals that are produced by different glands in the body. Hormones are like the body's ambassadors: they are created in one place but are sent through the body to have specific regulatory effects in different places.

* **flashbacks** are intensely vivid, recurring mental images of a past traumatic event. People may feel or act as if they were reliving the experience.

Some people develop post-traumatic stress disorder after living through terrifying events. Here, a mother comforts her son at a Red Cross shelter after the Northridge, California, earthquake of January 21, 1994. *Corbis/Reuters.*

◀

again in the future. This causes them to withdraw and become depressed. Depression, in turn, makes it hard for them to concentrate, learn, or do a job. Students may experience falling grades.

- Exaggerated displays of fear. People often overreact to ordinary situations. For example, people who were mugged might jump when someone taps them on the shoulder, while hurricane survivors might get scared during an ordinary thunderstorm.

People with post-traumatic stress disorder also may have difficulty sleeping, because they are trying to avoid nightmares. They may be too protective of themselves and loved ones and avoid situations where most people would say there is no danger. They may become easy to anger, or they may experience chest pains, rapid breathing, or dizziness for no apparent reason.

How Is Post-Traumatic Stress Disorder Diagnosed and Treated?

Many people might think about past events, especially ones that caused pain. This does not mean that they have post-traumatic stress disorder. For the disorder to be diagnosed, the symptoms must last for at least a month and lead to difficulties at school, work, home, or other social situations.

Symptoms of post-traumatic stress disorder sometimes are hidden. Often people do not want to talk about past trauma. In some cases, they may feel guilty that they survived when others died, such as in a large natural disaster. In other cases, they may blame themselves for what happened, because they think that they should have been able to fight off or escape from their attacker.

Help for Post-Traumatic Stress Disorder

Counselors and techniques for treating post-traumatic stress disorder include:

- **crisis counselor:** a professional who provides emotional support, practical help, and information to individuals or groups who recently have survived large-scale violence or disasters.

- **clinical psychologist:** a mental health professional who has earned a non-medical doctoral degree. Clinical psychologists can do psychological testing and provide mental health counseling.

- **group therapy:** mental health counseling that involves the person, a therapist, and other people with similar problems. The group talks about each other's problems.

- **psychiatrist:** a medical doctor who has completed specialized training in the diagnosis and treatment of mental illness. Psychiatrists can prescribe medications, diagnose mental illnesses, and provide mental health counseling.

- **relaxation techniques:** exercises such as meditation that help people reduce the physical symptoms of stress.

- **victim's advocate:** a professional who provides emotional support, practical help, and information to victims of a crime such as sexual assault.

School Violence

If violence occurs in a school, psychologists and social workers provide counseling for students who see or experience it. Such students are at risk for post-traumatic stress disorder. Common symptoms in children include:

- Flashbacks and disturbing memories
- Recurring nightmares and dreams of death
- Belief in omens and predictions of future disasters
- Expectation of an early death
- Avoiding any reminders of traumatic experiences
- Fear of re-experiencing trauma
- Repetitive play re-enacting trauma
- Emotional numbness or anger
- Lack of interest in activities
- Frequent stomachaches or headaches
- Frequent feelings of nervousness.

Diagnosis of post-traumatic stress disorder involves finding out what happened to the person and how it is affecting them now. Usually, this means working with a mental health specialist, such as a psychiatrist or clinical psychologist.

Counseling helps people learn how to cope with the feelings they have. The results typically are best when these discussions occur shortly after the trauma. This is one reason why specialists are brought to schools soon after a violent incident or to towns soon after a disaster. A crisis counselor is a specialist who provides short-term help to individuals or groups who recently have been through large-scale violence or disasters. Similarly, a victim's advocate is a specialist who helps crime victims find professional help.

It often is harder to treat people who show symptoms of post-traumatic stress disorder years after the traumatic event. Mental health specialists often use relaxation techniques and group therapy with others who have had similar experiences. Mental health specialists also might expose patients gradually and carefully to situations that remind them of their trauma. A car crash survivor, for example, might not want to drive again, so the person might first sit in a parked car, then drive in a deserted parking lot to overcome the fear. Prescription drugs also may be used to help a person sleep or to ease depression.

The best hope for people who experience a traumatic event is getting professional help quickly. Mental health specialists do not advise trying to hide the experience or just hoping that the feelings will go away on their own with time.

Resources

Book

Porterfield, Kay Marie. *Straight Talk about Post-Traumatic Stress Disorder: Coping with the Aftermath of Trauma*. New York: Facts on File, 1996. An informative book for young people about post-traumatic stress disorder.

Organizations

U.S. National Institute of Mental Health, 6001 Executive Boulevard, Room 8184, MSC 9663, Bethesda, MD 20892-9663. A government institute that provides information about post-traumatic stress disorder as well as other anxiety disorders.
Telephone 888-8-ANXIETY
http://www.nimh.nih.gov/publicat/reliving.cfm

American Psychiatric Association, 1400 K Street N.W., Washington, DC 20005. An organization of physicians that provides information about post-traumatic stress disorder and other anxiety disorders on its website.
http://www.psych.org

Center for Mental Health Services, P.O. Box 42490, Washington, DC 20015. A U.S. government agency. Its Emergency Services and Disaster Relief Branch offers information about mental health services after a disaster on its website, the Knowledge Exchange Network.
Telephone 800-789-CMHS
http://www.mentalhealth.org

National Center for Post-Traumatic Stress Disorder, Veterans Affairs Medical Center 116D, 215 North Main Street, White River Junction, VT 05009. A program of the U.S. Department of Veterans Affairs. Its website offers a wealth of information about how the disorder affects all kinds of people, not just veterans.
http://www.dartmouth.edu/dms/ptsd

National Center for Victims of Crime, 2111 Wilson Boulevard, Suite 300, Arlington, VA 22201. A national resource center for victims of crime. Its website provides information about post-traumatic stress disorder in crime victims.
http://www.ncvc.org

▶ See also
Anxiety Disorders
Phobias
Sleep Disorders
Trauma

Pregnancy, Complications of

Pregnancy is the period of time between conception (kun-SEP-shun) and birth. A full-term pregnancy lasts 9 months and usually does not involve major health problems. Sometimes, however, complications develop that jeopardize the health of mother and baby.

KEYWORDS
for searching the Internet and other reference sources

Childbirth

Obstetrics

What Is Pregnancy?

Pregnancy is the interval of time beginning when an egg and sperm unite and ending when a baby is born. A full-term pregnancy lasts 9 months (38 to 40 weeks). The 9 months are divided into trimester* one (the embryo* develops), two (the embryo turns into a fetus*), and three (the fetus gains weight and gets ready for birth).

What Are the Normal Discomforts of Pregnancy?

As a woman gains weight and her body changes to accommodate a growing fetus, she may experience some of the following signs or symptoms:

- Anemia*
- Backache
- Bleeding gums
- Breast tenderness
- Constipation

* **trimester** (tri-MES-ter) is any of three periods of approximately 3 months each into which a human pregnancy is divided.

* **embryo** (EM-bree-o), in humans, is the developing organism from the end of the second week after fertilization to the end of the eighth week.

* **fetus** (FEE-tus) in humans, is the unborn offspring in the period after it is an embryo, from 9 weeks after fertilization until birth.

* **anemia** (a-NEE-me-a) results when people have too few red blood cells to carry oxygen in the blood.

Anatomy of human ovum and human sperm. ▶

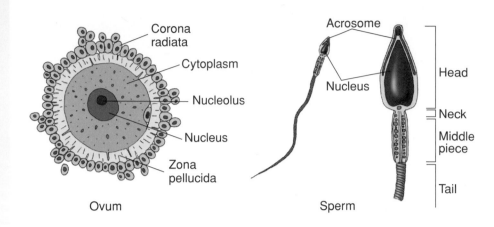

Ovum

Corona radiata
Cytoplasm
Nucleolus
Nucleus
Zona pellucida

Sperm

Acrosome
Nucleus
Head
Neck
Middle piece
Tail

* **hemorrhoids** (HEM-o-roidz) are a mass of dilated veins in swollen tissue at the margin of the anus or nearby within the rectum.

* **stretch marks** are stripes or lines on the skin (such as on the hips, abdomen, and breasts) from excessive stretching and rupture of elastic fibers, especially due to pregnancy or obesity.

* **varicose veins** (VAR-i-kose VAYNZ) are abnormally swollen or dilated veins.

Sonogram of a healthy fetus. © *Lutheran Hospital/Peter Arnold, Inc.*

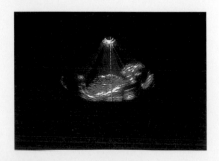

■ Edema (water retention)

■ Fatigue

■ Food aversions and cravings

■ Frequent urination

■ Heartburn

■ Hemorrhoids*

■ Nausea and vomiting

■ Stretch marks*

■ Varicose veins*

Symptoms vary from woman to woman, and even between pregnancies for an individual woman.

What Are the Common Complications of Pregnancy?

Most women get through pregnancy and giving birth without any major health problems. However, a few experience complications that threaten the health of both mother and baby. These problems can be very frightening, and they are hard to deal with when they result in the loss of a baby.

Morning sickness Morning sickness refers to nausea and vomiting, and it is misnamed. Some women have it in the morning, others at noon, and still others at night. Some women feel queasy only occasionally, whereas others feel sick all day long. Overall, about half of all pregnant women experience some degree of morning sickness, but it usually subsides on its own after about the third month of pregnancy. Only rarely does it require medical attention. No one knows what causes morning sickness, but probably it is related to the hormonal and other chemical shifts that occur in early pregnancy.

Miscarriage Miscarriage (MISS-care-ij) is also called spontaneous abortion, and it means that suddenly the pregnancy terminates on its own. Bleeding, cramping, and abdominal pain often signal a miscarriage.

Most miscarriages occur before the fourteenth week of pregnancy, which is why many women wait to tell their family and friends about a pregnancy until they have passed the 3-month mark. Occasionally, a woman will have a "late" miscarriage, which means that it occurs during the second trimester. After the twentieth week, the unexpected end of a pregnancy is called stillbirth if the baby is born dead and premature birth if the baby is alive but born before the thirty-seventh week.

Scientists estimate that as many as 40 percent of pregnancies end in miscarriage, although most of these occur so early that a woman may not even realize that she is pregnant. Early miscarriages often occur when the body naturally rejects a fetus that is not developing properly. Later miscarriages are much less common. Reasons for late miscarriages include a placenta* that is improperly attached to the uterus*, the placenta separating from the wall of the uterus for some reason, and other causes.

Gestational diabetes

Gestational* diabetes* is a type of diabetes that occurs when a woman does not produce enough insulin to handle the increased blood sugar that accompanies pregnancy. Any woman can develop this common problem, but women who are older, are overweight, and who have relatives with diabetes are at higher risk. A special diet often can control the problem without medication. Untreated diabetes during pregnancy increases the risk of certain birth defects. Such infants often have abnormally high birth weights and are prone to developing low blood sugar in the hours after birth. Most cases of gestational diabetes are temporary and disappear after the baby is born.

Ectopic pregnancy

An ectopic (ek-TOP-ik), or tubal, pregnancy is one in which the fertilized egg begins to develop outside of the uterus, usually in a fallopian tube*. Cramps, nausea, dizziness, tenderness in the

* **placenta** (pla-SEN-ta) in humans is the organ that unites the fetus to the mother's uterus.

* **uterus** (YOO-ter-us) in humans is the organ in females for containing and nourishing the young during development in the period before birth. Also called the womb.

* **gestational** (jes-TAY-shun-al) means relating to pregnancy.

* **diabetes** (dy-a-BEE-teez) is an impaired ability to break down carbohydrates, proteins, and fats because the body does not produce enough insulin or cannot use the insulin it makes.

* **fallopian tube** (fa-LO-pee-an tube) is either of the pair of long slender tubes connecting the ovaries to the uterus. Typically, a fallopian tube is where conception takes place.

CESAREAN LAW

A cesarean section is the method of delivering a child by opening the abdomen and uterus. It is performed when natural delivery presents risk to the mother or child.

The name of the procedure comes from the traditional story that the Roman ruler Julius Caesar (100-44 B.C.E.) was delivered by cesarean. More likely is the explanation that Cesarean law forbade the burial of a deceased mother before the baby was delivered.

Written accounts of the rescuing of an infant from its dead mother were recorded as early as 500 B.C.E. Cesarean sections were known to have been practiced by the ancient Romans, Indians, and Jews in the Roman era.

* **abdomen** (AB-do-men), commonly called the belly, is the portion of the body between the thorax (THOR-aks) and the pelvis.

* **ultrasound** is a painless procedure in which sound waves passing through the body create images on a computer screen.

* **ovaries** (O-va-reez) are the sexual glands from which eggs (ova) are released in women.

* **sperm** are the tiny, tadpole-like cells males produce in their testicles (TES-ti-kulz) that can unite with a female's egg to result eventually in the birth of a child.

* **umbilical cord** (um-BIL-i-kul KORD) is a cord arising from the navel that connects the fetus with the placenta.

* **cervix** (SER-viks) is the lower, narrow end of the uterus, which opens into the vagina.

* **convulsions** (kun-VUL-shunz) are violent involuntary contractions of muscles normally under voluntary control.

* **coma** (KO-ma) is an unconscious state, like a very deep sleep. A person in a coma cannot be awakened, and cannot move, see, speak, or hear.

* **cesarean section** (si-ZAR-ee-an SEK-shun) is the surgical incision of the walls of the abdomen and uterus to deliver offspring in cases where the mother cannot deliver through the vagina.

lower abdomen*, and light vaginal bleeding often accompany ectopic pregnancies. Early detection and treatment of an ectopic pregnancy are essential. If the embryo continues to grow, eventually it will burst the fallopian tube and damage it permanently. An undiagnosed ectopic pregnancy can also seriously jeopardize the health of the mother.

An ultrasound* can be used to examine the abdomen and confirm the diagnosis of an ectopic pregnancy. An ultrasound sends sound waves into the body that bounce off internal structures. A computer converts the returning sound waves into an image of the internal structures. Ectopic pregnancies usually are removed surgically.

Incompetent cervix   An incompetent cervix* is the cause of about 25 percent of late miscarriages. The cervix is the muscular opening of the uterus into the vagina (va-JY-na). An incompetent cervix means that it opens too early because of the pressure exerted by the growing fetus. An incompetent cervix can be caused by many factors, including a genetic tendency for it, stretching or tearing of the cervix during previous deliveries, and carrying multiple fetuses. An incompetent cervix can be treated by stitching the cervix closed during the second trimester or by bed rest for the last several months of pregnancy.

Preeclampsia/eclampsia and toxemia   The terms "preeclampsia/eclampsia" and "toxemia" are used interchangeably to mean the same thing: pregnancy-caused hypertension (high blood pressure). Most cases of toxemia are characterized by high blood pressure; swelling of the face, hands, and ankles; too-rapid weight gain; headaches; and protein in the urine. When left untreated, toxemia can cause nausea, vomiting, blurred vision, convulsions*, and coma*.

Toxemia most often affects young women during the last months of their first pregnancy, and the cause is unknown. Often, treatment involves hospitalization until the blood pressure returns to normal, followed by limited activity and sometimes bed rest at home.

Placenta previa   Placenta previa (PREE-vee-a) means that the placenta is lying low in the uterus. It can be dangerous if the placenta actually covers the cervix during labor and delivery. The baby still requires the blood, oxygen, and nutrients provided by the placenta during birth, and so the placenta should be the last thing out. Placenta previa can lead to premature labor, and women with this problem sometimes must limit their activity or stay in bed until the baby is born. Doctors can monitor the position of the placenta using ultrasound. When it is time to have the baby, doctors opt for a cesarean section* if the placenta is still covering or very close to the cervix.

Preterm labor and premature birth   More babies are born past their expected due date than before it, but in the United States, 7 to 10 out of 100 babies are born prematurely. A premature birth means delivery before the thirty-seventh week of pregnancy. About one-third of premature babies are born early because the mother went into labor too soon (the other cases occur because the amniotic sac* ruptures prematurely or because a health problem with the mother or baby requires early delivery).

Among the many risk factors for preterm labor are smoking, alcohol use, drug abuse, vitamin deficiencies, a job that requires standing for long time periods, infections like German measles, placenta previa or other physical causes, and poor nutrition.

Preterm labor that results in a premature birth poses serious health problems for the baby who has not finished developing inside the uterus.

Are There Risk Factors for Pregnancy Complications?

Older women (over 35) have a higher probability than younger women of experiencing high blood pressure, diabetes, and cardiovascular disease while pregnant, but these conditions are controllable with good medical care. Older women also are more prone to miscarriage, preterm labor, and postpartum (after birth) bleeding, and they have an increased risk of having a child with birth defects.

On the other end of the age spectrum, teen mothers are twice as likely to have premature babies and babies with low birth weight than are older mothers. Teenagers also are prone to premature labor, prolonged labor, toxemia, and anemia. About 1/3 of pregnant teens do not receive adequate medical care during pregnancy (as compared with about 1/4 of older women). Finally, while the chance of dying from pregnancy-related complications is very low overall, the rate is much higher in women younger than 15 than in women older than 15.

Can Pregnancy Complications Be Prevented?

Many complications of pregnancy develop in healthy mothers for unknown reasons. However, if a woman is in poor health before becoming pregnant, the likelihood of having complications is higher than usual. Regular prenatal* care, or medical care during pregnancy, is very important, because it allows doctors to detect and treat problems with mother or baby as early as possible.

Resources

Books

Chism, Denise M. *The High-Risk Pregnancy Sourcebook*. Los Angeles: Lowell House, 1998.

Eisenberg, Arlene, Sandee E. Hathaway, and Heidi E. Murkoff. *What to Expect When You're Expecting*, revised edition. New York: Workman Publishing Company, 1996.

Jovanovic-Peterson, Lois, and Morton Stone. *Managing Your Gestational Diabetes: A Guide for You and Your Baby's Good Health*. Minnetonka, MN: Chronimed, 1998.

A Primer of Pregnancy

Pregnancy begins when an egg and sperm unite and ends when a baby is born. The usual sequence of events is as follows:

- An egg is released from one of the two ovaries*.

- The egg travels down the fallopian tube toward the uterus.

- If sperm* are present during this time, the egg may be fertilized while in the fallopian tube.

- The fertilized egg continues down the fallopian tube into the uterus, where it implants into the lining of the uterus. The placenta develops, rich with blood and nutrients, and nourishes the embryo. The embryo is attached to the placenta via the umbilical (um-BIL-i-kul) cord*.

- After about 3 months, the embryo has developed the basic human structural plan and is called a fetus.

- The fetus continues to develop inside a fluid-filled sac in the uterus called the amnion (AM-nee-on).

- After 38 to 40 weeks, the baby is delivered through the vagina (the tubular structure connecting the uterus to the outside of the body) or through an incision in the abdomen and uterus (a cesarean section).

* **amniotic sac** (am-nee-OT-ik SAK) is the sac formed by the amnion, the thin but tough membrane outside the embryo, which lines the outermost embryonic membrane and contains the embryo and later the fetus, with the amniotic fluid around it.

* **prenatal** (pre-NAY-tal) means existing or occurring before birth, with reference to the fetus.

How Common Are the Common Pregnancy Complications?

The approximate percentage of pregnant women affected by the common complications of pregnancy are listed below:

- Ectopic pregnancy: 2 percent.

- Gestational diabetes: 1 to 10 percent.

- Miscarriage: as many as 40 percent of pregnancies end in miscarriage, often before a woman even knows she is pregnant. Of confirmed pregnancies, about 10 percent end in miscarriage.

- Morning sickness: 50 percent; severe nausea and vomiting that require medical care occur in less than 0.5 percent of pregnancies.

- Placenta previa: 1 percent.

- Premature birth: 7 to 10 percent of deliveries; about 1/3 of these are caused by preterm labor.

- Preeclampsia/Toxemia: 5 to 10 percent.

▶ See also

Birth Defects

Diabetes

Fetal Alcohol Syndrome

Prematurity

KEYWORDS
for searching the Internet and other reference sources

Childbirth

Neonatal intensive care

Obstetrics

Rich, Laurie A. *When Pregnancy Isn't Perfect: A Layperson's Guide to Complications in Pregnancy*, third edition. Rhinebeck, NY: Larata Press, 1996.

Sears, William, and Martha Sears. *The Birth Book: Everything You Need to Know to Have a Safe and Satisfying Birth*. New York: Little Brown, 1994.

Organizations

U.S. Centers for Disease Control and Prevention (CDC), 1600 Clifton Road N.E., Atlanta, GA 30333. The U.S. government authority for information about infectious diseases and other health disorders, the CDC posts information about the complications of pregnancy at its website. http://www.cdc.gov/health/pregnancy.htm

New York Online Access to Health (NOAH) seeks to provide high-quality full-text information for consumers that is accurate, timely, relevant, and unbiased. NOAH supports English and Spanish. NOAH was originally funded by the U.S. Department of Commerce's National Telecommunications and Information Administration and matching grants, and it brings together the assets and experience of four New York partners: City University of New York, the Metropolitan New York Library Council, the New York Academy of Medicine, and the New York Public Library. http://www.noah.cuny.edu/pregnancy/pregnancy.html

Prematurity

Premature (or preterm) babies are those born before the thirty-seventh week of pregnancy. Pregnancy is calculated from the first day of the mother's last menstrual period* before conception (kon-SEP-shun). Full-term babies are born in the thirty-eighth to forty-second week of pregnancy.

What Causes Premature Birth?

In the third trimester* of pregnancy (months 7, 8, and 9), the fetus* adds ounces of body weight and is better prepared for living outside the mother's body. Many premature babies are not ready to live on their own.

There are a variety of reasons for a mother to go into labor early. Histories of women giving premature birth show several risk factors: poverty, poor prenatal* care, poor nutrition, smoking, alcohol abuse, and drug abuse.

Physical abnormalities, such as a misshapen uterus*, may cause early labor. The cervix*, the opening to the uterus, may loosen and open too soon. If the mother has an illness (such as high blood pressure) or the baby is at risk, the doctor may induce labor. Inducing labor means the mother is given a drug to start contractions.

A Look at the Preterm Baby

Preterm infants tend to look very frail, with thin pink skin with underlying veins showing through and very little body fat. Yet they are active. Even those born 12 weeks early can open their eyes and respond to sound, light, and being touched. Their skinny arms and legs are wrinkled and covered with fine hair, called lanugo (la-NOO-go).

Small babies must be kept warm. The surface area of any baby's skin is large relative to the mass of the body. Premature babies lose heat more quickly and need a climate-controlled incubator (IN-ku-ba-tor).

Breathing Some premature babies are not ready to breathe on their own. Apnea*, when breathing stops for several seconds, is common. A special apnea mattress assists breathing, and the heartbeat is monitored. If these episodes begin to last a long time, a ventilator (VEN-ti-lay-tor) or breathing machine is used.

Premature babies may experience respiratory distress syndrome (RDS). This is because the babies' lungs do not have the slippery lubricant called surfactant (sir-FAK-tant) that allows the lungs' tiny air sacs, called alveoli (al-VEE-o-ly), to open and close smoothly. Without surfactant, babies have to struggle to transfer oxygen* and carbon dioxide*. Infants may become exhausted and may not get enough oxygen. This lack of oxygen causes major changes in the body's chemistry. Artificial surfactant and breathing assistance may be needed temporarily, until babies begin to make natural surfactant on their own.

* **menstrual period** (MEN-stroo-al PE-re-od) is the discharging through the vagina (va-JY-na) of blood, secretions, and tissue debris from the uterus (YOO-ter-us) that recurs at approximately monthly intervals in females of breeding age.

* **trimester** (tri-MES-ter) is any of three periods of approximately 3 months each into which a human pregnancy is divided.

* **fetus** (FEE-tus) in humans, is the unborn offspring in the period after it is an embryo, from 9 weeks after fertilization until birth.

* **prenatal** (pre-NAY-tul) means existing or occurring before birth, with reference to the fetus.

* **uterus** in humans is the organ in females for containing and nourishing the young during development in the period before birth. Also called the womb.

* **cervix** (SER-viks) is the lower, narrow end of the uterus.

* **apnea** (AP-nee-a) is when breathing stops for several seconds.

* **oxygen** (OK-si-jen) is an odorless, colorless gas essential for the human body. It is taken in through the lungs and delivered to the body by the bloodstream.

* **carbon dioxide** (CAR-bon dy-OK-side) is an odorless, colorless gas that is formed in the tissues and breathed out through the lungs.

◄

An infant in a hospital incubator, born 13 weeks premature. © *Simon Frazer/Princess Mary Hospital/Newcastle/SPL/Photo Researchers, Inc.*

Left to right: Embryo and fetus at 3 weeks; 7 weeks; 15 weeks; and 22 weeks ▶

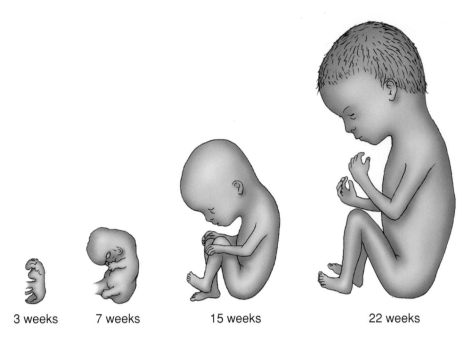

3 weeks   7 weeks   15 weeks   22 weeks

*liver is a large organ located in the upper abdomen (AB-do-men) that has many functions, including storage and filtration of blood, secretion of bile, and participation in various metabolic (met-a-BOLL-ik) processes.

*neonatal (ne-o-NAY-tal) means pertaining to the first 4 weeks after birth.

Feeding Feeding may be a problem for premature infants. Sometimes, they cannot suck adequately, and they are fed through a fine tube placed in the nose or mouth that goes into the stomach. Newborns, who even cannot tolerate tube feeding because their digestive system is too immature to handle any food, may receive nutrients through their veins.

Jaundice Preterm babies may have a yellow pigment called bilirubin (BIL-e-roo-bin) accumulate in the blood and skin, causing jaundice (JAWN-dis). The liver* is not mature enough to break down bilirubin, and high levels may causes brain damage. Treatment involves phototherapy (fo-to-THER-a-pee), exposure to fluorescent lights, which reduces the bilirubin levels.

Very Low Birth Weight Babies

A very low birth weight infant weighs less than about 3 pounds and is more than 8 weeks early. Babies this small frequently need special care, but any newborn baby who is ill or has obvious problems may be looked after in special care units called neonatal* intensive care units or NICUs.

Low birth weight is often times caused by lifestyle choices of the mother, who ignores prenatal care or does not see a physician. Smoking, alcohol, and drugs may also contribute to low weight.

Today, we are better able to help very tiny, very sick newborns survive than ever before. Specialized NICUs are available throughout the country. The cost to take care of these very sick babies is huge, and the number of premature births is increasing. About 1 out of every 10 births in the United States is premature. Many babies are surviving, but some will have lifelong problems of learning or physical development.

Resource

Luke, Barbara. *Every Pregnant Woman's Guide to Preventing Premature Birth: Reducing the 60 Proven Risks That Can Lead to Prematurity.* Middlebury, IN: Diane Publishing Company, 1998.

▶ See also
Birth Defects
Fetal Alcohol Syndrome
Jaundice
Pregnancy, Complications of

Premenstrual Syndrome (PMS) *See* Menstrual Disorders

Presbyopia

Presbyopia is a naturally occurring type of farsightedness in which the ability to see close objects clearly is reduced as people get older.

KEYWORDS
for searching the Internet
and other reference sources

Hyperopia

Ophthalmology

Optometry

Vision

As many adults pass age 40 or so, they find that it becomes harder to read newspapers and books. They start to hold these items farther away from their eyes than they had in the past, because they are trying to bring the print into focus. Eventually, as the joke goes, they find that their arms are too short. This condition is called presbyopia (pres-be-O-pe-a), which is from the Greek words meaning "old eyes." The condition causes a person to become slightly farsighted.

Normally, small muscles bend the clear lens at the front of the eyeball to focus a close image, like the words on this page. But as a person reaches his thirties and forties, the lens loses its elasticity and becomes too thick and too rigid to flex easily. This causes presbyopia.

The first sign of presbyopia usually occurs when people find that they cannot read small print as easily as they did in the past. Their eyes may feel tired more quickly, or they may develop headaches during close work. Eventually, many people need eyeglasses for reading.

People who are already farsighted will need to see their ophthalmologists* if they notice these symptoms, as they will probably need stronger prescription eyeglasses to read. For people with nearsightedess, presbyopia may seem at first to help their vision. That is because for them, the condition changes how close images are focused in a way that makes them clearer. This is sometimes called "second sight," and people with nearsightedness sometimes find for a time that they do not need their eyeglasses to read. Eventually, though, they will need eyeglasses or perhaps bifocals* to read properly.

* **ophthalmologist** is a medical doctor who specializes in treating diseases of the eye.

* **bifocals** or multifocal (progressive) lenses are prescription eyeglasses that have lenses divided into two or more sections. The bottom section allows a person to see things clearly that are close, and the top section allows a person to see things clearly that are far away.

Resource

The U.S. National Eye Institute, one of the National Institutes of Health, posts a resource list of eye health-related publications and organizations at its website.
Telephone 301-496-5248
http://www.nei.nih.gov/publications/sel-org.htm

▶ See also
Farsightedness
Nearsightedness

KEYWORDS
*for searching the Internet
and other reference sources:*

Cancer

Impotence

Proctology

PSA tests

* The **rectum** is the final portion of the large intestine, connecting the colon to the outside opening of the anus.

Prostate Cancer

Prostate cancer occurs when cells in the prostate, a male reproductive gland located between the bladder and the rectum*, take on an abnormal appearance and start dividing without control or order. These cancer cells often spread to nearby tissues and organs and sometimes to other parts of the body.

Christina's Story

Christina loved that her grandfather lived with her family. He certainly didn't act like most seventy-year-olds! He taught her everything she knew about basketball and shot baskets with her every night during the season. Lately, though, Grandpa admitted that he wasn't quite feeling up to playing with Christina. He often woke up feeling tired because he had to go to the bathroom several times each night.

Christina heard her grandfather tell her mother that he felt like his bladder was always full and that sometimes his urine even looked pinkish or reddish, like it might have blood in it. When Grandpa's doctor heard what his symptoms were, he told him to come in right away. The doctor ran some tests and confirmed his initial suspicion: Grandpa had prostate cancer.

When Christina heard the word "cancer," she was scared. She knew that people could die from this disease. Grandpa reassured her that there were treatments available that could help him. Plus, the doctor had said that his cancer was growing slowly and had not spread to other parts of the body. This was a very good sign.

What Is Prostate Cancer?

Prostate cancer is the most common kind of cancer and second most common cause of cancer deaths in men in the United States. It is found almost exclusively in men age 50 and older. With each decade of life after 50, a man's chance of developing prostate cancer increases. Each year, about 200,000 men in the United States find out that they have this disease.

Prostate cancer occurs when cells in the prostate gland divide without control or order, forming tumors*. The prostate is the walnut-sized male gland located below the bladder and in front of the rectum. The prostate surrounds the upper part of the urethra (yoo-REE-thra), the tube that empties urine from the bladder and out of the penis. This gland releases a thick fluid that helps transport sperm*.

Prostate cancer varies widely among men with the condition. Some men develop small, slow-growing tumors that remain within the prostate gland. Others develop fast-growing, aggressive tumors that spread quickly into the surrounding bone. They also can spread to nearby organs such as the bladder, rectum, and lymph nodes*. There are still other men who fit somewhere in between these two extremes. How doctors treat the disease usually depends on how rapidly the tumor is growing.

* **tumor** (TOO-mor) refers to an abnormal growth of body tissue. Tumors may or may not be cancerous.

* **sperm** are the tiny, tadpole-like cells males produce in their testicles. Sperm can unite with a female's egg to result eventually in the birth of a child.

* **lymph node** (LIMF node) is a small, round mass of tissue that contains immune cells that filter out harmful microorganisms.

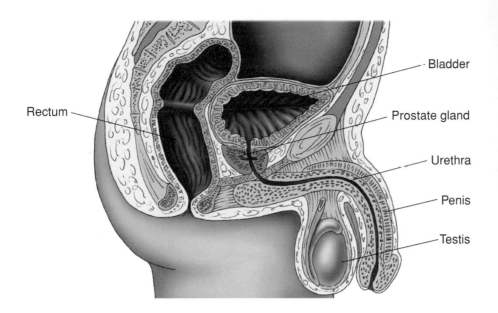

What Are the Symptoms of Prostate Cancer?

When it first starts to develop, prostate cancer usually does not cause any symptoms. That is why doctors recommend that men age 40 and older have digital rectal examinations as part of their yearly checkups. During this exam, the doctor inserts a gloved finger into the rectum and feels the prostate, which is located just on the other side of the wall of the rectum. If the gland feels hard, lumpy, or enlarged, this may be an early sign of prostate cancer.

As it continues to develop, prostate cancer may cause some of the following symptoms:

- a need to urinate frequently, especially at night

- difficulty urinating or holding back urine

- pain or burning while urinating or having sex

- blood in the urine or semen

- frequent pain or stiffness in the lower back, hips, or upper thighs.

Although these symptoms may indicate prostate cancer, they can also be caused by some other condition.

How Is Prostate Cancer Diagnosed?

Doctors usually start with a digital rectal examination. They also may take a blood sample and test it for a substance called prostate-specific antigen (AN-ti-jen), or PSA. Usually, this substance is present at abnormally high levels when a man has prostate cancer or some other problem with the prostate. Physicians may order additional laboratory tests or a urine sample to check for blood or other signs of infection.

More Men Are Talking about Prostate Cancer

Just 15 to 20 years ago, few men talked about prostate cancer, perhaps because they felt embarrassed or ashamed of the condition. After all, it affects two of men's most private activities: going to the bathroom and having sex. But in the 1990s, many famous men have stepped forward to speak about their own experiences with this disease.

Bob Dole, former U.S. senator and the 1996 Republican presidential candidate, was diagnosed with prostate cancer in 1991. He made this information public and used his fame to encourage other men to have yearly tests that might catch the disease early. He also introduced an amendment that called for increased funding for prostate cancer research.

U.S. Army General Norman Schwarzkopf is used to tough battles, having led the U.S. troops in the Gulf War. Now, as a prostate cancer survivor, he is leading efforts to promote awareness of this disease.

Professional golfers Arnold Palmer and Jim Colbert both have made their experiences with prostate cancer public. Now, they are cochairmen of the Senior PGA Tour for the Cure, which raises money to support the Association for the Cure of Cancer of the Prostate. Fans can pledge money for each birdie that their favorite players make.

The only sure way to know whether cancer is present is to do a biopsy (BY-op-see). The doctor uses a needle to remove a small amount of tissue from the prostate and has it examined under a microscope. The appearance of the cells will show whether cancer is present, and if so, how quickly it is likely to grow and spread. Cells that are slightly abnormal but still look a lot like healthy prostate cells suggest that the cancer is slow growing. Extremely abnormal-looking cells mean that the cancer is likely to grow and spread more quickly.

If cancer is diagnosed, the doctor may order additional tests to determine whether it has spread to other parts of the body.

How Is Prostate Cancer Treated?

Treatment depends on several different things: the man's age and general health, how aggressive the cancer is, and whether it has spread outside the prostate.

Sometimes, the best treatment is no treatment at all. This might sound strange at first, but for some older men and men with serious health problems, the possible risks and side effects of treatment may outweigh the benefits. Also, men whose cancer is slow growing or found at an early stage may not require treatment right away. In these cases, doctors prefer to monitor the situation carefully and wait to see how the cancer develops.

When treatment is necessary, the usual methods are surgery, radiation therapy, or hormonal (hor-MOAN-al) therapy. Some patients may receive a combination of these treatments. The surgery is called radical prostatectomy (RAD-i-kal pros-ta-TEK-to-mee), and it involves removing the entire prostate gland. Sometimes, nearby lymph nodes are removed as well.

Radiation therapy uses high-energy rays to damage cancer cells and stop them from growing and dividing. These rays might come from a machine, or they may come from radioactive material that is placed into or near the tumor. Hormonal therapy works by blocking the male hormones that the prostate cancer cells need to grow.

There are different approaches to hormonal therapy. Sometimes, surgeons might remove the testicles (TES-ti-kulz), the smooth, oval-shaped glands located behind the penis. These are the body's main source of male hormones. Doctors also might give drugs or other hormones that prevent the testicles from making testosterone (tes-TOS-ter-one).

Life after Prostate Cancer

In many men, prostate cancer can be controlled or even cured. However, the treatments often cause lasting side effects. Some men can no longer have an erection, which means that the penis no longer becomes hard during sex. Also, some men can no longer control the release of urine from the bladder. Fortunately, new treatments and surgical methods are available that may avoid these side effects. However, if these side effects occur, men may feel depressed or upset. Some men find it helpful to join a support group so they can talk to others in the same situation.

Can Prostate Cancer Be Prevented?

There is nothing a man can do to prevent prostate cancer. A diet high in fruits and vegetables and low in fat may help, but researchers have not confirmed this. Studies are under way to test certain drugs that could help to prevent prostate cancer, but no definite results are available. The best way for men to protect themselves is to see their doctors every year for checkups and report any unusual symptoms right away. Like other types of cancer, prostate cancer is easier to treat when found early.

Resources

Organizations

The American Cancer Society, 1599 Clifton Road, N.E., Atlanta, GA 30329. Information is available on prostate and other types of cancer.
Telephone 800-ACS-2345
http://www.cancer.org/

National Cancer Institute, National Institutes of Health, Rockville, MD. This organization provides an open help line during working hours.
Telephone 800-4-CANCER
http://cancernet.nci.nih.gov/

National Kidney and Urologic Diseases Information Clearinghouse, 3 Information Way, Bethesda, MD 20892-3580. This organization provides patient information.
Telephone 800-891-5388
http://www.niddk.nih.gov/

▶ See also
Cancer
Incontinence

Prostatic Enlargement

Prostatic enlargement is growth of the prostate gland that is a common result of aging in men.

What Is Prostatic Enlargement?

Prostatic (pros-TAT-ik) enlargement is more commonly known by the difficult-sounding name benign prostatic hyperplasia (be-NINE pros-TAT-ik hy-per-PLAY-zha), or BPH. Breaking this name down into parts makes it easier to understand.

"Prostatic" indicates that this is a condition that affects the prostate, the walnut-sized gland in men that is located below the bladder and in front of the rectum*. The prostate surrounds the upper part of the urethra (yoo-REE-thra), the tube that empties urine from the bladder and

KEYWORDS
for searching the Internet and other reference sources:

Benign prostatic hyperplasia

Impotence

Proctology

* **rectum** is the final portion of the large intestine, connecting the colon to the outside opening of the anus.

* sperm are the tiny, tadpole-like cells males produce in their testicles. Sperm can unite with a female's egg to result eventually in the birth of a child.

* hormones are chemicals produced by various glands in the body. A hormone is like the body's ambassador: it is created in one place but is sent through the body to have specific regulatory effects in different places.

▶ See also
Prostate cancer

out through the penis. The prostate makes a thick fluid that is important in the transportation of sperm*.

"Hyperplasia" means too much formation of cells. It indicates that this is a condition in which too much tissue grows in the prostate gland, making it larger than normal.

Finally, "benign" means that this extra tissue is not cancerous and will not spread to nearby tissues or other parts of the body.

BPH mainly affects men over the age of 50. Doctors believe that roughly half of men over age 60 and 8 out of 10 men over age 80 have this condition. Researchers are not sure what causes this condition, but they believe it may involve changes in hormone* levels related to aging.

How Is BPH Diagnosed?

Many men with an enlarged prostate have no symptoms at all. Others may have difficulty urinating. A doctor can feel whether or not the prostate is enlarged during a digital rectal examination. This involves placing a gloved finger into the rectum and feeling the prostate gland through the rectal wall.

Because an enlarged prostate is sometimes a sign of prostate cancer, the doctor often takes a blood sample and tests it for a substance called prostate-specific antigen (AN-ti-jen), or PSA. Usually, this substance is present at abnormally high levels when a man has prostate cancer. If the levels are in the normal range, that would suggest to the doctor that BPH is the more likely diagnosis. If he is uncertain at this point, the doctor may need to do further tests before ruling out cancer.

How Is BPH Treated?

BPH is rarely a threat to life but may require treatment to relieve symptoms. As the prostate enlarges, it pushes against the urethra and bladder, blocking the normal flow of urine, almost like a clamp on a garden hose. Men with this condition feel like they need to urinate more often because they cannot empty the bladder completely. Often, doctors can prescribe drugs that reduce the size of the prostate and improve the bladder's function. In some cases, surgery may be necessary.

Resources

Organization

The National Kidney and Urologic Diseases Information Clearinghouse, 3 Information Way, Bethesda, MD 20892-3560. This organization produces the pamphlet *Prostatic Enlargement: Benign Prostatic Hyperplasia.* It is also available online at http://www.niddk.nih.gov/health/urolog/pubs/prostate/index.htm

Psoriasis

Psoriasis (so-RY-a-sis) is a long-lasting skin disease that causes patches of skin to become red, thickened, and covered with silvery-looking flakes.

KEYWORD
for searching the Internet and other reference sources

Skin disorders

What Is Psoriasis?

When the American writer John Updike wrote a book about his own life, titled *Self-Consciousness,* he spent a whole chapter describing his personal battle with a long-lasting skin disease known as psoriasis. Updike called the chapter, "At War with My Skin." The word "psoriasis" comes from the Greek word for "to itch." The disease causes patches of skin to become red, thickened, itchy, and covered with silvery flakes.

What Causes Psoriasis?

Two out of every 100 people in the United States have psoriasis. In some cases, the disease is too mild to notice. In other cases, it is severe enough to cover much of the body. The cause of psoriasis is still unknown. Scientists do know that the disease cannot be passed from one person to another. In other words, it is not possible to catch psoriasis from someone else who has it.

Recent research suggests that psoriasis may be due to a problem with the immune system*. The immune system includes a type of white blood cell called a T cell. Researchers now think that people with psoriasis may have a problem with the immune system that causes it to make too many T cells in the skin.

People with psoriasis often notice that there are times when their skin gets worse, then gets better. The bad times, known as flare-ups, may be triggered by such things as climate changes, infections, stress, dry skin, and certain medicines. Flare-ups may also occur after the skin has been cut, scratched, rubbed, or sunburned. People whose relatives have psoriasis are more likely to also have it. Scientists are now studying families with psoriasis to try to find genes linked to the disease.

* **immune system** fights germs and other foreign substances that enter the body.

What Does Psoriasis Look Like?

Psoriasis causes patches of red, thickened skin with silvery flakes, most often on the scalp, elbows, knees, lower back, face, inside of the hands, and bottom of the feet. These patches are sometimes known as plaques (PLAKS). They may itch or burn, and the skin may crack. The disease also can affect the fingernails, toenails, and soft areas inside the mouth and genitals. About one out of 10 people with psoriasis gets psoriatic arthritis (so-ree-AT-ik ar-THRY-tis), a condition that causes pain, swelling, and stiffness of the joints (the places where bones meet).

How Is Psoriasis Treated?

A doctor usually identifies psoriasis by looking carefully at the skin, scalp, and nails. If the problem is psoriasis, the doctor can try various

Large red and white scaly rash on the arm of a 67-year-old man. *Dr. P. Marazzi/ Science Photo Library/Photo Reseachers, Inc.*

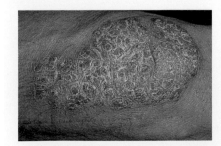

treatments that may clear up the skin for a time. The choice of treatment depends on a person's age, health, and lifestyle and the severity of the psoriasis. No one treatment works for everyone, but most people can be helped by something. These are some of the treatment choices:

- **Medicines put on the skin.** Some creams, lotions, soaps, shampoos, and bath products created to treat psoriasis may be helpful. Some bath products and lotions may help loosen flakes and control itching, but they are usually not strong enough to clear up the skin.

- **Treatments with light.** Many people with psoriasis improve if they get sunlight every day in small amounts. To better control the light that reaches the skin, doctors sometimes use special lamps that give off ultraviolet (ul-tra-VY-o-let) rays, which are a part of sunlight. In some cases, the person also takes a medicine that makes the skin more sensitive to the ultraviolet light.

- **Medicines taken by mouth.** Some people with more severe psoriasis take medicines by mouth or in a shot.

Living with Psoriasis

Many people with psoriasis find that it helps to keep the skin moist. Lotions, oils, and petroleum jelly (Vaseline) are often useful for this purpose. During the winter months, heaters can make the air inside a house quite dry, so it may help to run a humidifier (hu-MID-i-fy-er), a machine that puts moisture back into the air. It is also a good idea for people with psoriasis to avoid getting harsh soaps and chemicals on their skin. In addition, they should protect their skin from injury by taking such steps as not wearing overly tight clothes or shaving with a dull razor.

Resources

Pamphlets

American Academy of Dermatology. "Psoriasis." To order, contact the American Academy of Dermatology, P.O. Box 681069, Schaumburg, IL 60168-1069, (888) 462-DERM.
http://www.aad.org

National Institute of Arthritis and Musculoskeletal and Skin Diseases. "Questions and Answers About Psoriasis." To order, contact the NIAMS Information Clearinghouse, 1 AMS Circle, Bethesda, MD 20892-3675, (301) 495-4484.
http://www.nih.gov/niams

Organization

National Psoriasis Foundation, 6600 S.W. 92nd Avenue, Suite 300,

Portland, OR 97223-7195, (503) 244-7404. A national group for people with psoriasis. The website includes a special section for children and teenagers.
http://www.psoriasis.org

▶ See also
Arthritis
Skin Disorders

Psychosis *See* Mental Disorders

Pubertal Disorders *See* Growth Disorders

Quadriplegia *See* Paralysis

R

Rabies

Rabies is a viral infection of the central nervous system that occurs in wild and domestic mammals, particularly carnivores (flesh-eating animals). The rabies virus is contained in saliva and is transmitted to humans mainly by the bites of infected animals. Rabies is almost always fatal if the preventive vaccine is not given promptly.

KEYWORDS
for searching the Internet
and other reference sources

Central nervous system

Rhabdoviruses

Vaccines

The word "rabies" is Latin for madness or rage, referring to the extreme agitation that is a symptom of the disease. Rabies has also been called hydrophobia, which means "fear of water," because of another of its symptoms: despite extreme thirst, even the sight of water produces painful spasms of the throat in people or animals with rabies.

What Is the Incidence of Rabies in Animals and Humans?

No one can reliably estimate how many animals are infected with rabies at any given time. The incidence varies greatly from country to country and from one year to the next. Among humans, however, it has been estimated that there are about 15,000 new cases of rabies each year worldwide.

In the United States and other developed countries, human rabies is very rare owing to programs to vaccinate pets and to control stray dogs. More than half of the few cases that do occur are among immigrants and returning travelers who were exposed to dogs in other countries.

Common wild animal vectors* in North America include skunks, raccoons, foxes, and bats. Major carriers in other parts of the world include foxes in Europe, wolves in western Asia, jackals and mongooses in Africa, and bats in South America. Wild or stray dogs are major transmitters of the disease in Africa and in many countries of Asia and Latin America.

*__vectors__ are animals or insects that carry diseases and transfer them from one host to another.

How Do Rabies Infections Occur?

Rabies in humans occurs when infected animals bite people. The rabies virus is carried in the animal's saliva and may also be transmitted to humans if the saliva enters through a break in the skin, as from a lick, or onto a mucous membrane, which is the moist lining of body openings such as the mouth or nose. In rare cases, transmission of rabies can occur by exposure to air in caves occupied by swarms of rabid bats.

* **delirium** (dee-LEER-ee-um) is a condition in which a person becomes confused, is unable to think clearly, and has a reduced level of consciousness.

After the rabies virus has entered the body, it causes the disease by traveling along nerve pathways to the brain. There it produces inflammation that brings on delirium* and the other severe symptoms of the disease.

It is almost impossible for one human being to catch rabies from another. The only time this has ever happened was when one person received a transplanted cornea (a part of the eye) from someone who had rabies.

What Are the Signs and Symptoms of Rabies?

The incubation period of rabies (the time between an animal bite or other exposure and the beginning of symptoms) averages about one to two months, although symptoms may occur as soon as 10 days after a bite or as late as one year after. Bites closer to the brain, such as to the face, tend to produce symptoms sooner than bites farther away, such as arm or leg bites.

Symptoms in humans usually begin with restlessness, loss of appetite, depression, and a mild fever. These early symptoms are soon followed by uncontrollable excitement, salivation, throat spasms, delirium, and convulsions. Coma and death from paralysis and exhaustion take place in a few days to three weeks after the onset of symptoms.

In animals such as dogs, the incubation period is shorter. Signs include excitability, ferocity and biting, a hoarse bark followed by low howls, or

A DREAD DISEASE KNOWN TO THE ANCIENTS

Rabies has been known since ancient times as one of the most dreaded of all diseases. The Greek philosopher Democritus (ca. 460–370 B.C.) was the first to describe the disease, believing it to be an inflammation of the nervous system. Aristotle (384–322 B.C.) described rabies in animals. The renowned Greek physician Galen (A.D. 129–ca. 199) knew that it "follows the bite of a mad dog and is accompanied by an aversion to drinking liquids."

In modern times, the French chemist and bacteriologist Louis Pasteur (1822–1895) made medical history when, in 1885, he developed a preventive vaccine for rabies. He successfully tested his vaccine on a peasant boy, Joseph Meister, who had been bitten by a rabid dog. Although some historians have wondered whether Meister really did have rabies, this achievement made Pasteur famous and helped establish the Pasteur Institute in Paris, which conducts medical teaching and research. Joseph Meister worked at the Pasteur Institute for many years.

complete loss of voice. Wild animals that normally avoid humans may be fearless toward them and appear agitated. Normally night-active animals may be active in daylight.

How Do Doctors Diagnose Rabies?

A doctor should be contacted immediately following an animal bite, and the wound should be washed out with soap and water. Because rabies is a fatal disease if left untreated, immediate medical attention is required. Doctors can diagnose rabies by observing its most severe symptoms and signs, but there is not yet a laboratory test available to detect rabies before it reaches the central nervous system.

Diagnosis is of special importance in animals. If an animal that has bitten someone can be captured and appears rabid, it is killed and its brain tissue is examined for evidence of rabies infection. If rabies is found, the person who has been bitten must receive protective rabies vaccine.

How Do Doctors Treat and Prevent Rabies?

Preventive therapeutic measures before symptoms appear are the only reliable form of treatment. After symptoms begin, there is almost no treatment that can lead to a cure. Sedative* and painkilling drugs may be given, but only a very small number of people who were given aggressive intensive care to maintain vital functions have survived rabies infection.

> * **sedatives** are medications that calm people and reduce excitement and irritability.

Postexposure immunization   Preventive treatment is called "postexposure immunization." People who are immunized shortly after being bitten can be sure that they will be protected against rabies. Immunization consists of a series of vaccinations administered over several weeks, but it may or may not be given to a person who has been bitten by an animal. It is given if doctors and local public health authorities determine that there is a risk of rabies. For example, if a wild animal such as a fox or raccoon has bitten someone and it is found or believed to have rabies, then treatment is given. On the other hand, if the biting animal is a neighbor's dog known to be healthy and wearing a tag showing updated rabies vaccinations, then no treatment is needed.

Preexposure immunization   Preexposure immunization is given to people, such as veterinarians and forest rangers, whose work puts them at increased risk of animal bites. It is also available for campers and spelunkers (cave enthusiasts) and for people traveling in countries where rabies is a threat.

In the United States and other developed countries where there are wild animals with rabies, domestic dogs and cats are vaccinated. Control measures involving wild animals, and quarantine* of imported animals, are also important measures in rabies prevention.

Public education efforts stress the importance of vaccinating domestic animals and avoiding contact with wild animals. Young children, in particular, need to be told not to approach or pet wild animals.

> * **quarantine** is the confining of a person or animal possibly carrying a contagious disease until it is clear that there is no infection.

Resources

Books

Finley, Don. *Mad Dogs: The New Rabies Plague*. College Station: Texas A&M University Press, 1998. Describes in nontechnical language the present-day outbreaks of rabies and methods being used to combat them.

Silverstein, Alvin, Virginia B. Silverstein, and Robert A. Silverstein. *Rabies (Diseases and People)*. Hillside, NJ: Enslow Publishers, 1994. Provides general information for young adults, supplemented with many case studies.

Organizations

The U.S. National Institute of Allergy and Infectious Diseases posts a fact sheet about rabies at its website. http://www.niaid.nih.gov/factsheets/rabies.htm

Travel Health Online posts traveler information about rabies preexposure at its website. http://www.tripprep.com/travinfo/tirabi.html

▶ *See also*
Animal Bites
Viral Infections
Zoonoses

KEYWORDS
for searching the Internet and other reference sources

Environmental health

Ionizing radiation

Radionuclides

Radiation Exposure Conditions

Radiation is a naturally occurring form of energy. Everyone is exposed to small amounts of radiation, but exposure to very high doses may cause serious illness and death.

What Is Radiation and Where Is It Found?

Radiation is a form of invisible energy given off by atoms, which are the tiny particles that make up chemical elements.

Nonionizing radiation   Nonionizing radiation does not change the structure of an atom. Instead, it excites molecules and shakes them up. Natural sunlight, sun lamps, microwave ovens, radios, and televisions are sources of nonionizing radiation.

Ionizing radiation   Ionizing radiation is the more energetic form of radiation, and it can change the structure of an atom. Exposure to ionizing radiation can cause illness, because it can damage the molecules within the cells of the body, prevent the cells from functioning properly, and destroy those cells.

Naturally occurring ionizing radiation comes from distant parts of the universe and from the sun. Radon, which is a colorless, odorless, radioactive gas, provides most of the background radiation on earth.

Medical x-rays are a source of man-made ionizing radiation. Other sources of radiation are radioactive elements, which are used in medical research, nuclear power plants, and nuclear bombs.

How Does Radiation Affect the Human Body?

Radiation is a carcinogen (kar-SIN-o-jen), which means it is a cancer-causing agent. Because radiation occurs naturally from sources such as our bodies, space, rocks, soil, and radon gas, some exposure is unavoidable. The dose that the average American is exposed to during a year is considered safe, and both small and large doses of certain types of radiation are used in health care. For example, x-rays and CT scans (computerized axial tomography) are used to diagnose illnesses, and radiotherapy (high doses of radiation targeted at tumors) is used to kill cancer cells.

Exposure to very high doses of radiation, or long-term exposure to smaller amounts, however, increases the risk of injury or illness. Problems may include:

- radiation burns on parts of the body exposed to radiation

- genetic diseases or mental retardation in children whose mothers were exposed to radiation during pregnancy

- cancer of the bone marrow, thyroid, lung, breast, and kidney from long-term exposure to low levels of radiation

HIROSHIMA, NAGASAKI, AND CHERNOBYL

Much of what scientists know about the effects of exposure to high levels of radiation is based on studies of survivors of Hiroshima, Nagasaki, and Chernobyl.

In August of 1945, during World War II, American pilots dropped atomic bombs over the Japanese cities of Hiroshima and Nagasaki. The heat, which reached thousands of degrees, and the radiation released by these bombs damaged and destroyed life over millions of square miles. At Hiroshima, more than 70,000 people were killed, and over 70,000 more were injured. Many more people died of radiation poisoning in the years following the explosion of these bombs.

On April 26, 1986, in the Ukraine in Eastern Europe, the Chernobyl nuclear power plant experienced a meltdown. Because of a malfunction, the radioactive core was exposed, releasing radiation into the atmosphere. Although most of the radiation fell on Chernobyl, radioactive particles were carried by the wind all over the world. At least 29 people in Chernobyl died from radiation exposure, and several hundred others were hospitalized. Today, cancer, birth defects, thyroid disorders, and skin diseases are still affecting people exposed to the radiation from the Chernobyl accident.

▲

An ambulance worker wears protective gear against radiation exposure. In the event of a nuclear power station accident or in wartime, the suit would provide protection against radioactive fallout, and the mask and backpack would provide for air filtration. *Javier Pierini/Science Photo Library/Photo Researchers, Inc.*

▶ See also

Burns

Cancer

Environmental Diseases

Genetic Diseases

Thyroid Disease

■ lung cancer that may result from radon accumulating in basements and sticking to dust that people inhale

■ damage to blood vessels and the brain, infection, and bleeding from whole-body exposure to very high doses of radiation, which usually leads to death.

The severity of the radiation-induced condition depends on the source of the radiation, the dose, the rate of absorption into the body, and the sensitivity of the particular tissue. A large dose of radiation can lead to cell death over hours, days, or weeks. Low exposure over time causes less dramatic effects because some of the cellular damage may be repaired. Scientists have learned, however, that higher doses increase the chance of getting cancer (but do not affect the type or severity of cancer), and that most cancers do not appear for 10 to 40 years after the person was exposed.

Resources

Books

Grant, R. G. *Hiroshima and Nagasaki (New Perspectives)*. Austin, TX: Raintree/Steck-Vaughn, 1998.

Yamazaki, James N. *Children of the Atomic Bomb: An American Physician's Memoir of Nagasaki, Hiroshima, and the Marshall Islands*. Durham, NC: Duke University Press, 1995.

National Research Council. *Health Effects of Exposure to Radon: Time for Reassessment?* Washington, DC: National Academy Press, 1994.

Organizations

The U.S. National Institutes of Health (NIH) posts many fact sheets about radiation safety at its website. http://www.nih.gov

The World Health Organization has links at its website to many different organizations that focus on radiation safety, worldwide radioactivity monitoring, and protection of the human environment. http://www.who.org/peh/Radiation/radindex.htm

Rash *See* Skin Conditions

Raynaud's Disease

Raynaud's disease is a disorder in which the vessels that supply blood to the fingers and toes (the digits) contract, causing the fingers and toes to turn white, feel numb, tingle, or burn.

KEYWORD
for searching the Internet
and other reference sources

Circulatory system

What Is Raynaud's Disease?

In this condition, the arteries that supply blood to the fingers and toes respond to cold or other stimuli by going into spasm (contracting), reducing the supply of blood to the digits and turning them white. When there is no specific reason found for this contracting, the condition is called Raynaud's disease. It can appear at any age, but it occurs most often between the ages of 20 and 40 and affects females more than males.

What Is Raynaud's Phenomenon?

Raynaud's phenomenon has the same symptoms as Raynaud's disease, but its cause is known to be another disease. Diseases that can cause Raynaud's phenomenon include rheumatoid arthritis, systemic lupus, and scleroderma, which are all chronic (long-lasting) disorders of the connective tissue*. Other possible causes include atherosclerosis (in which large arteries are blocked by fat deposits) and Buerger's disease (in which small arteries in fingers and toes are blocked by inflammation).

** **connective tissue,** which helps hold the body together, is found in skin, joints and bones.*

Who Is at Risk for Raynaud's Phenomenon?

People in certain occupations are at higher risk for Raynaud's phenomenon. Anyone whose work involves the constant and repetitive use of the fingers or who uses tools that vibrate, such as a jack hammer or chain saw, are at increased risk. People with medical conditions that affect small arteries, have certain neurological conditions, or connective tissue diseases such as lupus or scleroderma, are at risk as well. Smoking may trigger or worsen spasms in blood vessels.

An elderly man has whitened fingers from Raynaud's disease. His fingertips are white because the arteries are constricted, which cuts off blood supply and causes numbness and tingling. *Dr. P. Marazzi/Science Photo Library/Custom Medical Stock Photo*

▼

What Are the Symptoms of Raynaud's Disease?

In Raynaud's disease, a person's fingers and toes first turn white or blue when they become cold because the necessary amount of blood is not reaching them. When they turn red it is a sign that blood is flowing normally again.

When people get an attack of Raynaud's disease, their fingers and toes may feel numb or tingle and burn. In severe (but rare) cases the restriction of the arteries causes the fingers to thicken, which can lead to ulcerations (loss of tissue) at the finger

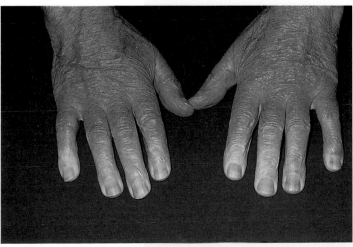

tips as well as changes in the fingernails. In the worst case, gangrene (tissue death) can occur.

What Is the Treatment for Raynaud's Disease?

Raynaud's disease can be effectively treated with medications that prevent the constriction of the blood vessels. Some ointments or creams can also be prescribed to soften the skin, though this will not help to prevent attacks. The doctor diagnoses the condition by taking a careful history from the patient. Advice on preventing flare-ups of Raynaud's can help the person avoid further episodes. In severe cases, surgery may be required to cut the nerves that control the contraction and dilation of the blood vessels.

How Can Raynaud's Disease Be Prevented?

Although Raynaud's disease may not be completely preventable in people who are susceptible to the disorder, there are some preventive measures a person can take. Some of the "do's" and "don'ts" for people who experience Raynaud's are:

- **Stop smoking.** Cigarettes constrict (close up) blood vessels.

- **Avoid high-risk activities.** Vibrating machinery, like pneumatic drills and chain saws, can trigger an attack of Raynaud's disease. Excessive typing and piano playing also involve repetitive finger motion and can trigger the disease.

- **Avoid substances that are known to trigger Raynaud's.** Polyvinyl chloride (PVC) and other substances may trigger an attack.

- **Wear layered clothing** to retain warmth, since exposing the face or forehead to cold can trigger an attack.

- **Wear gloves or mittens** to protect against cold.

▶ See also

Arthritis

Lupus

Regional Enteritis *See* Inflammatory Bowel Disease

Repetitive Stress Syndrome

Repetitive stress syndrome* occurs when doing something over and over again causes pain, muscle strain, inflammation, and possible tissue damage. Repetitive motion problems, also called repetitive stress injuries, are the most common form of occupational (workplace) illness.

Tennis Star

As a member of the high school tennis team, John served with accuracy and overwhelmed his opponents with his backhand. He worked harder

KEYWORDS
for searching the Internet and other reference sources

Cumulative trauma disorder

Ergonomics

Inflammation

Musculoskeletal disorders

Occupational health

Overuse injuries

Repetitive motion syndromes

Repetitive strain injuries

and practiced more than any other team member. Major college scouts were looking him over. During a major tournament, however, John felt pain and swelling where the tendons join the bones at the elbow. His repeated practice of straightening elbow and extending wrist—especially with his mean back swing—had caused small tears in the tendon and muscle. The doctor diagnosed epicondylitis (ep-i-kon-di-LY-tis), a classic case of "tennis elbow."

What Is Repetitive Stress Injury (RSI)?

Tennis elbow, runner's knee, and writer's cramp are common names for repetitive stress injuries (RSIs), which result from repeated movements that stress the tendons, ligaments, joint capsules, fascia (FASH-ee-a), and other soft tissues that surround or attach to muscles and bones. Repetitive stress injuries can cause inflammation* of the neck, shoulders, arms, wrists, hips, legs, and ankles.

People at highest risk include office workers using computer keyboards, factory workers using sewing machines or working on assembly

> * **syndrome** means a group or pattern of symptoms and/or signs that occur together.

> * **inflammation** (in-fla-MAY-shun) is the body's reaction to irritation, infection, or injury that often involves swelling, pain, redness, and warmth.

LEON FLEISHER: LEFT-HANDED CONCERTS

In 1964, at age 36, Leon Fleisher was one of the world's great pianists. When he noticed a weakness in the little finger of his right hand, he practiced harder to overcome it. During the following 10 months, however, the other fingers in his right hand curled under until he was unable to play piano at all.

At that time, not much was known about how repetitive movements caused carpal tunnel syndrome and other overuse injuries. Fleisher tried many different medications and therapies, but finally had to switch his performance repertoire to concertos written for the left hand alone.

In 1995, Fleisher began physical therapy and deep tissue massage, which taught him how to "de-contract" the overused muscles in his right hand. In 1996, he was able to resume playing concerts with both hands.

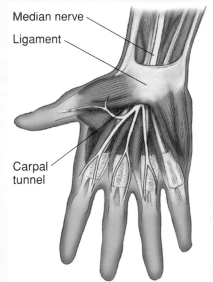

Median nerve
Ligament
Carpal tunnel

Carpal tunnel syndrome affects people who overuse their hands on piano or computer keyboards.

lines, tennis players working with tennis rackets, football players, and dancers who damage ankles and hips. Common RSIs include:

■ Carpal tunnel syndrome, which affects the hands and wrists.

■ Tendinitis, which affects the connective tissue that attaches muscles to bones, for example, Achilles tendinitis or shoulder (rotator cuff) tendinitis.

■ Bursitis, which affects the fluid-filled sacs between muscles and bones that cushion the joints.

■ Fasciitis, which affects the connective tissue that surrounds the muscles.

■ Shin splints, which affect the front of the lower leg.

Although most RSIs occur in adults, young people who spend too much time on computer keyboards, playing sports, or practicing on musical instruments also are at risk.

What Happens When People Have Repetitive Stress Syndrome?

Symptoms Warning signs of repetitive stress injuries include:

■ Electricity-like tingling in hands or fingertips

■ Soreness or weakness in hands and arms

■ Aching neck or shoulders

■ Frequent headaches

■ Pain that wakes the person up at night

■ Pain that lasts more than 24 hours.

Office workers who overuse computer keyboards are at risk for repetitive strain injury. © 1994 T. Buck/Custom Medical Stock Photo.

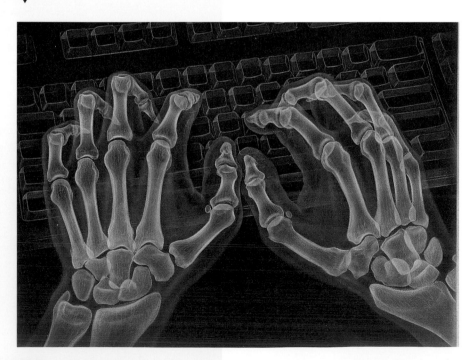

Diagnosis The doctor's physical examination and medical history usually will reveal the repetitive motion that has stressed the soft tissue and caused the injury. The doctor may recommend x-rays or blood tests to rule out other causes.

Treatment Treatment begins with rest. Temporarily, the person must give up the activity that caused the problem, or must adjust the repeated motions that caused the injury. Retraining and physical therapy may be required before the person can resume the activity. The doctor also may recommend putting a wrist or elbow in a splint to keep it from repeated bending. Other treatments include medication to relieve pain and inflammation, massage, or surgery in cases of severe injury.

Prevention   Prevention always works better than treatment. Proper warm-ups and cool-downs, frequent rests, and improved ergonomic rules for the workplace are important preventive measures. Ergonomics is the science of adapting tools and equipment to the human body—for example, chairs and desks that can be adjusted to fit the body of the user may help to prevent repetitive strain injuries. The U.S. National Institute of Occupational Safety and Health (NIOSH) is creating new standards for workplace safety to reduce the number of cases of repetitive stress syndrome.

Resources

Book

Peddie, Sandra. *The Repetitive Strain Injury Guidebook*. Los Angeles: Lowell House, 1997.

Organizations

U.S. Centers for Disease Control and Prevention (CDC), 1600 Clifton Road N.E., Atlanta, GA 30333. CDC posts an *Occupational Health* fact sheet at its website and provides a link to NIOSH.
http://www.cdc.gov/health/diseases.htm

U.S. National Institute of Arthritis and Musculoskeletal and Skin Diseases (NIAMS), Building 31, Room 4C05, Bethesda, MD 20892-2350. NIAMS posts information about shoulder problems at its website. Telephone 301-496-8188
http://www.nih.gov/niams/healthinfo/shoulderprobs/shoulderqa.htm

U.S. National Institute of Neurological Disorders and Stroke (NINDS) posts information about repetitive motion syndromes and carpal tunnel syndrome at its website.
http://www.ninds.nih.gov/patients/Disorder/repetitivemotion/repetitivemotion.htm

American Academy of Orthopaedic Surgeons (AAOS), 6300 North River Road, Rosemont, IL 60018-4262. AAOS posts patient education fact sheets about shoulder pain and carpal tunnel syndrome at its website. Telephone 800-346-AAOS
http://www.aaos.org

Arthritis Foundation, 1330 West Peachtree Street, Atlanta, GA 30309. The Arthritis Foundation publishes brochures and posts fact sheets about many different kinds of soft tissue rheumatism at its website. Telephone 800-283-7800
http://www.arthritis.org

American College of Rheumatology, 60 Executive Park South, Suite 150, Atlanta, GA 30329. ACR posts a fact sheet about tendinitis/bursitis at its website.
Telephone 404-633-3777
http://www.rheumatology.org/patients/factsheet/tendin.html

American Physical Therapy Association (APTA), 1111 North Fairfax Street, Alexandria, VA 22314-1488.
Telephone 703-684-2782
http://www.apta.org

Association for Repetitive Motion Syndromes (ARMS), P.O. Box 471973, Aurora, CO 80047-1973.
Telephone 303-369-0803

▶ *See also*
Arthritis
Carpal Tunnel Syndrome
Fibromyalgia
Strains and Sprains

KEYWORDS
for searching the Internet and other reference sources

Aspirin

Viral infection

Reye's Syndrome warning on aspirin box.
© *Leonard Lessin, Peter Arnold, Inc.*

■ 100% pure BAYER® Aspirin is caffeine free and sodium free.
■ Starts to work in minutes.
INDICATIONS: Fast acting BAYER® Aspirin is recommended for temporary relief of: headache, pain and fever of colds, muscle aches and pains, menstrual pain, toothache pain, minor aches and pains of arthritis.
DIREC... 2 years and over, take 1 ... 4 hours, as needed, up to a ... 24 hours or as directe ... children under 12 unless ...
WARNINGS: Children and teenagers should not use this medicine for chicken pox or flu symptoms before a doctor is consulted about Reye Syndrome, a rare but serious illness reported to be associated with aspirin.

occur or if redu... doctor because condition. Do n... to aspirin, have... as heartburn, u... persist or recu... unless directed... loss of hearing... any more of thi... of the reach of... seek professio... control center i... are pregnant o... health professi... IT IS ESPECIAL... DURING THE L... SPECIFICALLY... BECAUSE IT M/... CHILD OR COM...

Reye's Syndrome

Reye's (RIZE) syndrome is a rare and potentially fatal disorder in children that affects the liver, brain, and other organs. It may appear shortly after a viral infection such as chickenpox or influenza.

The children always arrived at the Australian hospital on the verge of death. They often would be unconscious or in a coma. Sometimes their bodies suffered uncontrollable spasms, and the children seemed to be slipping into insanity.

It was a tragic—and puzzling—situation. Only a week or so earlier, the children had been experiencing the typical childhood infections such as earaches, chest colds, or sore throats. Then things took a turn for the worse.

Dr. Douglas Reye was the director of pathology at that Australian hospital when these children died in the 1950s and early 1960s. He discovered odd things, such as swollen brains, discolored livers, and damaged kidneys in the children. He realized that they were dealing with an as yet unnamed disease.

In 1963, a doctor in North Carolina named George Johnson saw a link between the disease Reye had discovered and one he was seeing in children after an outbreak of influenza. The disease was initially called Reye-Johnson syndrome and is now simply Reye's syndrome.

Today, Reye's syndrome is rare because doctors have learned ways to lower people's risk of getting it as well as better ways of identifying and treating people with the illness. The syndrome is not contagious, although the viral infections that often precede it can be.

A Sudden Change

Typically, Reye's syndrome begins after a viral infection, such as a cold, influenza, or chickenpox. Most such infections do not lead to Reye's syndrome, and some cases are so mild that no one notices. Other cases are more serious.

Although adults and babies can develop Reye's syndrome, it usually occurs in children between the ages of 2 and 16.

Symptoms include vomiting, nausea, and drowsiness. There is also a change in behavior, and patients may act irrationally and seem to have lost touch with reality. If untreated, Reye's syndrome can cause loss of consciousness, coma, and death.

Reye's syndrome causes the brain and liver to swell and the liver to develop fatty deposits. The chemistry of the blood and other body fluids becomes abnormal.

No one is sure how some viral infections develop into Reye's syndrome. Some doctors suspect that an unidentified virus causes Reye's syndrome. Others theorize that people with certain genes* are more likely to get it. Some studies in the 1980s linked aspirin to the development of Reye's syndrome (see sidebar).

Treatment for Reye's syndrome occurs in a hospital. Various medications and fluids are used to bring the patient's body back into balance. The patient's condition must be closely monitored, and sometimes the use of a breathing machine may be necessary to support an unconscious patient's respiration until the illness resolves.

Resource

National Reye's Syndrome Foundation, P.O. Box 829, Bryan, OH 43506-0829, (800) 233-7393. The website has helpful information, including a list of products that contain aspirin and similar substances. http://www.bright.net/~reyessyn

Aspirin and Reye's Syndrome

Although the link between aspirin and Reye's syndrome is not conclusive, doctors and the U.S. government recommend that no child under age 16 take aspirin or products with aspirin during a viral infection. In fact, no child under age 12 with almost *any* illness should take aspirin. Aspirin substitutes, such as acetaminophen, are not linked with Reye's syndrome.

* **genes** are chemicals in the body that help determine a person's characteristics, such as hair or eye color. They are inherited from a person's parents and are contained in the chromosomes found in the cels of the body.

◄ *See also*
Chickenpox
Influenza
Viral Infections

Rheumatic Fever

Rheumatic (roo-MA-tik) fever is a complication of a strep throat infection that can lead to permanent heart damage and death. It is most common in children.

Until recently, doctors thought rheumatic fever had almost disappeared from the United States. In 1950, before the widespread use of antibiotics to fight strep* infections, more than 22,000 people died of rheumatic fever and the heart disease it caused. During the 1950s, almost 25 of every 100,000

KEYWORDS
for searching the Internet and other reference sources

Heart disease

Streptococcal infection

Sydenham's chorea

* **strep throat** is a contagious sore throat caused by a strain of bacteria known as *Streptococcus*.

THE DISCOVERY OF ASPIRIN

In the mid-nineteenth century, the Reverend Edmund Stone unwittingly discovered the earliest known effective treatment for rheumatic fever and other conditions characterized by rheumatism. Stone, like many physicians of his time, believed that God grew healing herbs for specific diseases in the localities where they naturally ocurred. Willing to put his idea to the test, he administered willow bark, which he himself sampled, to some 50 persons suffering with rheumatic fever. He reported effective results in each case. The bark was later found to contain an active ingredient of salicin (SAL-i-sin), first extracted and analyzed by Dr. Thomas MacLagan in 1839. Other chemists later produced the salicylate (sal-i-SY-late) group of drugs, which yielded sodium salicylate in 1899. This drug came to be known as aspirin and became useful for remedying symptoms associated with rheumatic fever as well as a general pain reliever.

Americans got rheumatic fever each year. But as use of antibiotics such as penicillin became more common in the 1960s, and as more poor children had access to better medical care, rheumatic fever became rare.

By the early 1980s, only about 1 in every 100,000 Americans developed it. But by 1985, the disorder had re-emerged as a significant problem in some communities. There were outbreaks in Salt Lake City, New York, Dallas, San Diego, Akron, and Columbus.

Doctors were puzzled and have renewed their interest in fighting rheumatic fever. The number of cases remains small in the United States, although in poor, less developed countries, rheumatic fever is a significant problem. Doctors are not sure if the fever's comeback in the United States is temporary, but it has shown that everyone needs to be watchful for the effects of strep infections.

From a Sore Throat to a Damaged Heart

Rheumatic fever sometimes results when the body's immune system reacts to infection by a bacterium known as Group A *Streptococcus,* commonly called strep. The same bacteria that cause strep throat can lead to other disorders, such as scarlet fever.

When the body becomes infected with the strep bacteria, the immune system produces antibodies to fight the infection. Rheumatic fever results when these antibodies begin to affect other parts of the body instead of just fighting the infection. The antibodies react to organs such as the heart as if they were the strep bacteria, perhaps because parts of these organs are chemically similar to strep.

Doctors are not sure exactly why some strep infections develop into rheumatic fever and others do not. The disorder occurs most often in children between ages 5 and 15, although it can strike younger children and adults, too.

A Turn for the Worse

The first signs of rheumatic fever usually occur within several weeks after a strep throat infection. Sometimes, people appear to have recovered from the sore throat but suddenly begin to show other symptoms:

- Muscle aches and joint pain and swelling resembling arthritis. The pain usually moves from one joint to another.

- Fever, vomiting, and sometimes nosebleeds.

- A red rash, especially on the chest, arms, and legs, which might disappear in a few hours. Lumps below the skin also may occur.

- Fatigue and problems breathing, because the heart is affected. The heartbeat also may be abnormal.

- Sydenham's chorea (see sidebar), which is uncontrollable twitching and body movements.

The most dangerous consequence of rheumatic fever is inflammation and weakening of the heart muscle. The valves that control passage of blood in and out of the heart can be damaged so that they fail to open and close properly. This condition is called rheumatic heart disease.

SYDENHAM'S CHOREA

Sydenham's chorea is the name for the involuntary movements and twitching that some rheumatic fever patients display.

"Chorea" (pronounced like the country Korea) comes from the Greek word for "dance." During the Middle Ages, chorea was the term used to describe people who traveled to the shrine of St. Vitus in what is now Germany. Some of the people apparently suffered from conditions involving abnormal body movements, such as epilepsy, and hoped to be healed at the shrine. (Catholics consider St. Vitus the patron saint of those with epilepsy, as well as of dancers and actors.)

Dr. Thomas Sydenham, a prominent physician in England during the 1600s, used the term "chorea" in connection with infectious diseases such as scarlet fever. Later, when rheumatic fever also was connected with strep infection, Sydenham's chorea was the term used to describe the shaking of the upper limbs and face caused by swelling of the brain.

Sydenham's chorea is sometimes called St. Vitus' dance.

The Importance of Antibiotics

A doctor may suspect a strep infection if a patient with a sore throat also has a fever and severe headache. However, the symptoms and physical exam findings in people with strep throat are very similar to those in people with sore throat due to a virus infection or other cause. Therefore, strep infections must be confirmed with laboratory tests. Doctors use a cotton swab to wipe the throat to test for the strep bacteria.

If the infection is caused by strep, the doctor will usually prescribe an antibiotic such as penicillin for 10 days. Doctors say that it is important to take all the antibiotic prescribed, even if the symptoms of the strep infection disappear.

Not all untreated strep infections lead to complications like rheumatic fever. For people who get rheumatic fever, doctors use antibiotics as well as other drugs that reduce swelling and relieve pain. They also closely watch the heart, to ensure that there are no problems with blood flowing through it. If the heart valves are damaged, surgery might be necessary to fix one or more valves.

The best way to avoid rheumatic fever is to treat strep infection promptly with antibiotics. Doctors, however, are worried that some bacteria are becoming resistant to traditional antibiotics. Research is ongoing into the best ways to use antibiotics and to develop new drugs to fight infections also.

▶ *See also*
Arthritis
Fever
Heart Disease
Strep Throat

Rheumatism *See* Arthritis

Rheumatoid Arthritis *See* Arthritis

Rickets

Rickets is a disease of bone most commonly caused worldwide by a deficiency of vitamin D. The deficiency may be caused by a lack of vitamin D in the diet, a lack of exposure to sunlight, or a problem the body has with absorbing or using vitamin D. If left untreated, rickets results in skeletal (bone) deformities.

KEYWORDS
for searching the Internet
and other reference sources

Hypophosphatemia

Malnutrition

Osteomalacia

What Is Vitamin D?

Vitamin D is a nutrient essential for proper bone formation. It helps regulate the amount of calcium and phosphorus in the blood, and these minerals are important components of bone formation. Vitamin D is called the "sunshine vitamin" because it is formed naturally in the skin in the presence of the ultraviolet (UV) rays found in sunlight. Vitamin

D also can be obtained from food. Vitamin D is added to milk and infant formulas, and egg yolks, liver, cod-liver oil, and other fish oils are good dietary sources of vitamin D.

What Is Rickets?

Rickets is characterized by improper hardening of the bones, resulting in skeletal deformities if left untreated. Rickets affects primarily infants and children because bone growth occurs during childhood. Rickets can occur for a number of reasons.

Nutritional Childhood Rickets   Rickets can occur because of a nutritional deficiency in vitamin D. Today this type of rickets is rare in developed countries. Children growing up in poor communities where vitamin D–rich foods may be scarce are the most susceptible to rickets. Children living in areas where there is a lack of sunshine, such as in the Northern Hemisphere in the winter, also are susceptible. Overcast and polluted atmospheres that block out the sun can also deprive children of vitamin D. Another form of nutritional rickets is seen in extremely premature babies if they are fed a vitamin D–poor formula or if their diet contains inadequate amounts of phosphorus and calcium.

Genetic Childhood Rickets   Rickets also can occur because of inherited genetic disorders that result in improper absorption or utilization of vitamin D, calcium, or phosphorus. In the United States, the most common cause of rickets is a disease called familial hypophosphatemia (hy-po-fos-fa-TEE-me-a), which means too little phosphorus in the blood. This is a genetic disease in which phosphorus "leaks" out of the body through the kidneys. However, fewer than 10 out of every 1 million babies are affected by this disease.

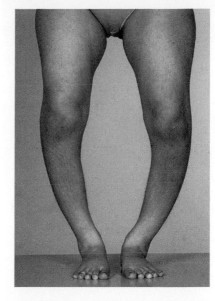

Rickets can cause bone deformities. If it begins before a child learns to walk, the spine may become abnormally curved. If it begins or continues after the child starts to walk, the legs may become bowed by the weight of the body as shown here. © *Biophoto Associates/Photo Researchers, Inc.*

A VITAMIN D TIME-LINE

- During the 1700s, cod-liver oil and sunlight were recognized as effective treatments for rickets.
- By 1918, scientists had discovered vitamins. Experiments on animals showed that cod-liver oil had a vitamin that helped prevent rickets.
- By 1924, ultraviolet (UV) light was used for treating rickets. The process was called irradiation. Researchers understood that vitamin D was formed by the effects of ultraviolet rays on the skin.
- Between 1930 and 1931, scientists in England and Germany were able to produce pure vitamin D for the first time.

Other Types of Rickets Adult rickets, or osteomalacia (os-te-o-ma-LAY-sha), causes bone problems similar to those found in childhood rickets. Osteomalacia can be caused by a nutritional deficiency of vitamin D, but it most commonly occurs when the body has problems absorbing phosphorus and calcium because of other illnesses (such as liver and kidney disease). In some instances, drugs that interfere with absorption of vitamin D cause rickets and osteomalacia.

What Are the Symptoms of Rickets?

Children with rickets may not have any symptoms, or they may feel pain and develop bone deformities. A child who has or is developing rickets may experience muscle cramps, twitches, and abnormal contractions of the hands and feet due to low levels of calcium in the blood. The muscles, limbs, and abdomen grow weak and the bones of the skull remain soft. An infant with rickets may have difficulty developing such basic movements as sitting, crawling, and walking due to weakness and pain.

The type of bone deformity caused by rickets depends on the age at which the disease develops. If it begins before the walking stage, the spine may be abnormally curved. If it begins or continues after the child starts to walk, the legs may become bowed by the weight of the body. For children with rickets, the teeth take more time to grow in, and often the wrists and ankles are thickened. Because of weak bones, children with rickets also are susceptible to fractures.

Osteomalacia can cause similar effects: soft bones, skeletal pain, muscular weakness, and susceptibility to fractures.

How Is Rickets Diagnosed and Treated?

Rickets can be diagnosed with blood tests, in which the amounts of calcium, phosphorus, and vitamin D are measured, and with x-rays. Nutritional rickets is treated with dietary supplements of vitamin D and calcium. If treated early enough, there will be no long-lasting effects. If untreated, a child may develop permanent bone deformities. Dietary supplements of vitamin D, calcium, and phosphate also may be prescribed for people with rickets caused by other diseases or by genetic defects.

How Is Rickets Prevented?

Rickets can be prevented by eating a diet rich in vitamin D as well as by spending time in the sun. A good source of vitamin D is vitamin D–fortified milk.

Resources

Mavarra, Tova. *Encyclopedia of Vitamins, Minerals, and Supplements.* New York: Facts on File, 1996.

Tamborlane, William. *Yale Guide to Children's Nutrition.* New Haven: Yale University Press, 1997.

▶ *See also*
Broken Bones and Fractures
Dietary Deficiencies
Growth Disorders

Ringworm

Ringworm is a fungal infection of the skin, scalp, or nails.

KEYWORD
for searching the Internet
and other reference sources

Tinea

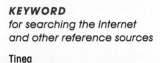

Ringworm is not caused by a worm! Ringworm is a common fungal infection that can occur on any part of the body. The name comes from the appearance of the infection on the skin, which is usually ring shaped with a raised reddish border. Ringworm is caused by both direct and indirect contact with infected people, animals, or soil. The medical term for ringworm is tinea.

What Are the Signs and Symptoms of Ringworm?

Ringworm of the skin appears as a flat, spreading, circular, or sometimes oval ring or patch. The patch may contain fluid or pus, but usually it is dry and scaly or moist and crusty. Sometimes multiple rings appear in a single patch. There are several common forms and names for ringworm:

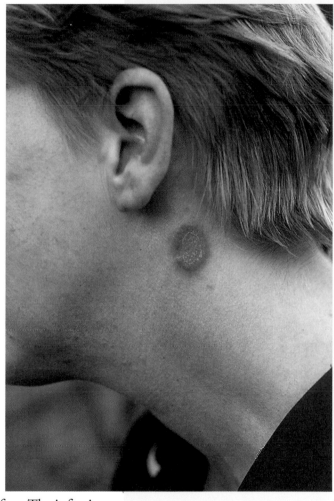

- Ringworm of the foot is called "athlete's foot" or "tinea pedis."
- Ringworm of the groin is called "jock itch" or "tinea cruris."
- Ringworm of the scalp is called "tinea capitis." It usually starts as a small pimple-like sore before spreading as a fine, scaly, bald patch. It may cause hair to become brittle and to break off, and it may be spread by sharing hats or combs.
- Ringworm of the nails is called "tinea unguium." It usually affects one or more nails of the hands or feet. The infection causes the nail to thicken and to become discolored and brittle.
- Ringworm of the body is generally called "tinea corporis."

▲

The red circular rash behind the ear is an example of ringworm of the body, or tinea corporis. *John Hadfield, Science Photo Library/Photo Researchers, Inc.*

How Do Doctors Diagnose and Treat Ringworm?

Ringworm is relatively easy to diagnose and cure. The doctor may perform a simple test for the presence of a fungus. Treatment usually consists of applying an antifungal cream for about two weeks or taking prescription medication by mouth for two to four weeks. Treatment of nail infections is usually more difficult and takes longer.

Ringworm is easily spread from one person to another, so it is important to follow the doctor's instructions, to launder clothes and bedding frequently, and to maintain good personal hygiene.

▶ See also

Athlete's Foot

Fungal Infections

Skin Conditions

Rocky Mountain Spotted Fever

Rocky Mountain Spotted Fever is a disease caused by the bacterium Rickettsia rickettsia, *when it infects a person through the bite of an infected tick. Despite its name, this disease is not limited to the Rocky Mountain area.*

KEYWORDS
for searching the Internet and other reference sources

Infection

Rickettsial diseases

Tick-borne diseases

Ken Takes a Hike

One June day, Ken took his dogs and hiked up to the top of Bitternut Mountain. The next morning when he was taking a shower, he found a tick attached to his neck at the hairline. He got his dad to remove the tick.

About 10 days later, seemingly out of nowhere, Ken developed a fever of more than 102 degrees Fahrenheit. His muscles ached, and he complained of having the worst headache of his life. Two days later, Ken's ankles and wrists were covered with a spotted rash. By the next day, the rash had spread to his whole body. Ken's parents took him to the emergency room, and he was given antibiotics to take for the next seven days. Gradually his fever, rash, and headache disappeared. Ken had had Rocky Mountain Spotted Fever.

What Are Rickettsial Diseases?

Rickettsial diseases are caused by a group of bacteria called *Rickettsia*. Lice, fleas, ticks, and mites can carry *Rickettsia* in their bodies, and can infect humans and other animals by biting them and injecting the bacteria into the bloodstream. Typhus, Q fever, trench fever, and the spotted fevers are all rickettsial diseases.

Rocky Mountain spotted fever (RMSF) is the best known of the rickettsial diseases. It occurs when a person is bitten by a tick (American dog tick, wood tick, or lone-star tick, depending on the geographic location) infected with *Rickettsia rickettsia*.

Ticks are eight-legged animals related to spiders and mites that live on the blood of humans and other animals. A person also can get RMSF when liquid from a crushed tick gets into a cut or scrape, so it is important never to squeeze ticks with bare fingers.

What Happens When People Get RMSF?

The classic symptoms of RMSF are a history of tick bite, fever, headache, and a rash. However, symptoms of RMSF vary greatly from person to person; some people never get a rash, others do not get headaches, and only about 70 percent of people know a tick has bitten them.

In addition to the physical symptoms, doctors suspect RMSF and begin drug treatment if it is the right season and the right geographic location for ticks, and if the person was outdoors in areas where ticks live. Blood tests are done to confirm RMSF, but results can take days to weeks.

Today, only 3 to 5 percent of people with RMSF die, but in the 1950s, 13 to 25 percent died. Diagnosing the disease quickly and starting treatment with antibiotics is the key to surviving RMSF.

Wood ticks carrying *Rickettsia rickettsia* are vectors for Rocky Mountain Spotted Fever. © *S.J. Krasemann/Peter Arnold, Inc.*

How Can RMSF Be Prevented?

Although avoiding places where ticks live during tick season (woods and fields) might prevent RMSF, this is not practical for many people. A person venturing into such places should wear protective clothing, such as long sleeves and pants with tight-fitting wrists and ankles, and should use tick-repellent chemicals.

It takes about six hours after a tick attaches to the skin before it passes *Rickettsia* into a person's bloodstream, so people should check their bodies for ticks promptly after they have been outdoors in areas where ticks are found.

Ticks should be removed using tweezers or fingers covered with paper, not bare fingers. The tick is grabbed as close as possible to the skin and pulled out. The area is then washed with soap and water. Camping stores also sell special devices for extracting ticks without crushing or touching them.

Resource

The U.S. National Center for Infectious Diseases (NCIDOD) is part of the Centers for Disease Control and Prevention (CDC). It posts information about Rocky Mountain Spotted Fever at its website. http://www.cdc.gov/ncidod/diseases/rmsf/rmtnsfvr.htm

---

Roundworm *See* Ascariasis; Hookworm; Worms

Rubella *See* German Measles

The U.S. and the World

- About 800 people per year are diagnosed with Rocky Mountain spotted fever in the United States.

- Children aged 5 to 9 are most frequently infected, followed by men over age 60. RMSF is most common in white males.

- Approximately 90 percent of cases occur between April and September, because ticks become active in warm weather.

- The first case of RMSF was described in the Snake River Valley of Idaho in 1899, but the name comes from cases later reported throughout the Rocky Mountains.

- RMSF can be found throughout North, Central, and South America.

- RMSF occurs mostly in the southeastern and south central United States.

▶ See also
Bacterial Infections
Lyme Disease

S

Salmonellosis

Salmonellosis (sal-mo-nel-O-sis) is a gastrointestinal disease caused by bacteria called Salmonella. This type of bacterium usually is found in foods such as poultry, milk, and eggs from infected animals.

KEYWORDS
for searching the Internet and other reference sources:

Foodborne illness

Food poisoning

Salmonella

* **immune system** is the system that defends the body against disease.

What Is Salmonellosis?

Salmonellosis is an illness caused by *Salmonella* bacteria that affects the intestine, usually resulting in diarrhea. In some people, the infection spreads to the bloodstream and other areas of the body and can be life-threatening unless they receive prompt treatment.

Salmonellosis, named after the American scientist Daniel Salmon, is one of the most common causes of food poisoning in the United States. Each year, about 40,000 cases of salmonellosis are reported to the U.S. Centers for Disease Control and Prevention, and up to 4 million additional cases may go unreported. About 1,000 people die each year of complications related to salmonellosis. Infants, the elderly, and people whose immune systems* are weakened are most vulnerable to severe infection.

The structure of a *Salmonella* bacterium. The DNA (inside the nucleus) is yellow. The cytoplasm is green. The part of the cell wall shown in brown secretes the toxins that cause symptoms in salmonellosis. © *1992 Custom Medical Stock Photo.*

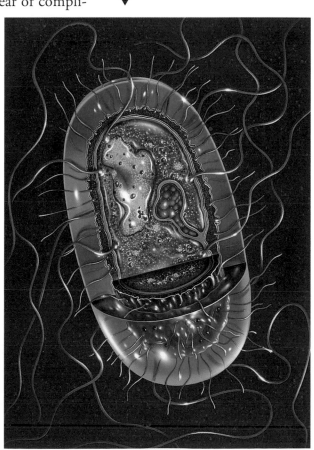

How Do People Get Salmonellosis?

In the United States, people usually get salmonellosis from eating or drinking contaminated food, most often raw milk or undercooked poultry and poultry products such as eggs. Undercooked ground beef or other meat can also cause salmonellosis. In some cases, food can be contaminated by the people handling it. Salmonellosis can also be spread through the stools of some pets, especially reptiles and pets with diarrhea.

A different species of *Salmonella* bacteria causes typhoid fever, a serious disease common in developing countries in Latin America, Africa, and Asia. Typhoid fever is spread by food and water contaminated with the bacteria. Clean water, treated (pasteurized) milk, and effective sewage systems have made typhoid fever rare in the United States and other developed countries.

What Are the Symptoms of Salmonellosis?

The symptoms of salmonellosis include diarrhea, stomach cramps, pain, fever, headache, nausea, and vomiting. They occur within 12 to 48 hours of eating or drinking contaminated food.

How Is Salmonellosis Diagnosed and Treated?

Salmonellosis is diagnosed through stool cultures from people with symptoms of the infection. *Salmonella* infections usually run their course without treatment in a few days to a week after an unpleasant period of vomiting and diarrhea. Health care professionals suggest that people drink lots of fluids and eat a bland diet while they recover from salmonellosis. Sometimes the symptoms create other problems, such as dehydration*. In those cases, people may need to go to the hospital to receive replacement fluids through their veins (an "IV"). Antibiotics may be used if the infection spreads beyond the intestine, but salmonellosis is often resistant to drugs.

How Can Salmonellosis Be Prevented?

Thorough cooking (until poultry or meat, especially ground beef, is no longer pink and eggs are no longer runny) and regular hand washing (after using the bathroom, and between handling raw meat and other foods) are the main ways to prevent salmonellosis. Only pasteurized dairy products that have been kept refrigerated should be used. Raw meat or eggs should especially be avoided.

Resources

Organizations

U.S. Centers for Disease Control and Prevention, 1600 Clifton Road N.E., Atlanta, GA 30333. This U.S. agency helps control communicable, carrier-borne, and occupational diseases and prevent disease, injury, and disability. A fact sheet on salmonellosis is available on its website. Telephone 404-639-3534
http://www.cdc.gov/ncidod/dbmd/diseaseinfo/salmonellosis_g.htm

U.S. National Institute of Allergy and Infectious Diseases, Office of Communications and Public Liaison, National Institutes of Health, Building 31, Room 7A-50, 31 Center Drive, MSC 2520, Bethesda, MD 20892-2520. This government biomedical research center posts a fact sheet on salmonellosis and other foodborne diseases on its website. Telephone 301-496-4000
http://www.niaid.nih.gov/factsheets/foodbornedis.htm

* **dehydration** is the loss of fluid from the body faster than it can be replaced.

▶ See also
Diarrhea
Food Poisoning
Gastroenteritis
Typhoid Fever

KEYWORD
for searching the Internet and other reference sources

Dermatology

Scabies

Scabies (SKAY-beez) is an itchy skin condition caused by mites that burrow under the skin.

Memories of Camp

Kelly returned from summer camp with many stories and a red, itchy rash. The skin on her wrists and thighs and between her fingers was covered with pimple-like bumps and she could see small S-shaped burrows under her skin. Kelly's neighbor, who was a dermatologist (der-ma-TOL-o-jist), or skin doctor, took one look and suspected scabies. When Kelly found out, she was embarrassed. She felt dirty and unclean even though she took a shower every day. She felt better when her neighbor told her that scabies does not discriminate. It affects young and old, boys and girls, and those who shower once a week or every day. He told her she must have picked it up at camp but that it was easy to get rid of.

What Causes Scabies?

Scabies is a skin condition caused by mites that dig under the skin. Mites are eight-legged animals related to spiders, scorpions, and ticks. They are so tiny that they require a microscope to be seen. The scientific name for the scabies mite, or "itch mite," is *Sarcoptes scabiei*. Its relatives cause mange (MAYNJ), an inflammation of the skin that results in hair loss, in dogs, pigs, horses, and cows.

Scabies is a common, contagious* skin condition that passes easily from person to person. Outbreaks of scabies, in which many people get infested at once, can occur in places like nursing homes, childcare centers, and dormitories. The scabies mite cannot live very long away from the body. It can be spread by skin-to-skin contact or by clothing or bedding that has been used very recently by an infested person. Kelly acquired scabies from someone at camp, perhaps from borrowing a towel.

When Kelly first came into contact with the mites, females full of eggs burrowed under her skin and laid eggs. For a person who has never had scabies, it usually takes two to six weeks to develop symptoms, meaning itching and a rash, which is an allergic reaction to the mites. People who have had scabies before usually react within days.

* **contagious** (kon-TAY-jes) means transmittable from one person to another.

How Is Scabies Diagnosed and Treated?

Kelly's neighbor, the dermatologist, suspected she had scabies based on her intense itching, where the rash was located on her body, and how the rash looked. To make sure, he scraped at the skin between her fingers. He put the scrapings on a slide and when he looked at them with a microscope, he saw several mites and eggs.

Prescription drugs called scabicides (SKAY-bi-sydz), such as permethrin (per-METH-rin) and lindane (LIN-dayn), are usually used to kill scabies mites and eggs. Because scabies is so contagious, Kelly's neighbor instructed the whole family to bathe, then apply the scabicide lotion all over the body from the chin to the toes, and to wash all the recently used clothes, bedding, and towels in hot water. They were instructed to repeat the process in a week. The dermatologist also gave Kelly

The itch mite *Sarcoptes scabiei* responsible for scabies. © *Arthur M. Siegelman, Visuals Unlimited.*

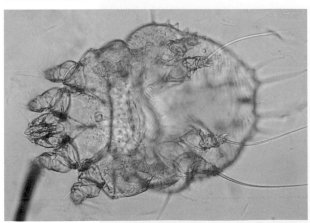

733

*__antibiotics__ (an-ty-by-OT-iks) are drugs that kill bacteria.

an antibiotic* ointment because she had some skin infections caused by scratching. Four weeks later, Kelly's skin was back to normal.

Resources

Organization

Centers for Disease Control and Prevention, 100 Clifton Road N.E., Bldg. 1, SSB249, MS A34, Atlanta, GA 30333. This U.S. agency helps control communicable, carrier-borne, and occupational diseases and prevent disease, injury, and disability. A fact sheet about scabies is available on its website.
Telephone 404-639-3534
http://www.cdc.gov/incidod/hip/abc/facts37.htm

▶ See also
Parasitic Diseases
Skin Conditions

Scarlet Fever

Scarlet fever is a bacterial infection that causes a sore throat, rash, and chills.

KEYWORDS
for searching the Internet and other reference sources

Rash

Streptococcal infection

The words "scarlet fever" once struck fear in the hearts of people. The bacteria that cause scarlet fever are easy to spread, and in the 1800s there were epidemics. Children younger than 10 years old were especially at

POOR BETH

" How dark the days seemed now, how sad and lonely the house, and how heavy were the hearts of the sisters as they worked and waited, while the shadow of death hovered over the once happy home." With these words, author Louisa May Alcott captures the fear and tragedy that scarlet fever spread in the 1800s.

Based on Alcott's own growing-up years, *Little Women* is the tale of Jo March and her sisters, Meg, Amy, and Beth. Immensely popular since its publication in 1869, it has been made into a movie at least four times. Beth, beloved by family and friends for her sweet nature and musical talent, develops scarlet fever when the girls' mother is away caring for their father, who has been injured in the Civil War. This sad part of the story never fails to bring tears to readers and movie audiences.

SCARLET FEVER IN HISTORY

The earliest concise description of scarlet fever and its symptoms was given by the German physiologist Daniel Sennert. In 1619 Sennert accurately observed and recorded the sequence of the disease's symptoms: the appearance of the associated rash, its decline, and scaling of the skin. In the eighteenth century, epidemics of scarlet fever were reported throughout Europe and America. During this time, physicians developed a clear clinical understanding of the disease. The first clinical standards for differentiating scarlet fever from similar diseases were established by Armand Trousseau. In 1887 the English physician Edmund Emmanuel Klein identified scarlet fever as being caused by Streptococcus bacteria that were observed to grow on the tonsils and secrete a rash-producing toxin. The American physician George F. Dick and his wife Gladys R. H. Dick isolated the toxin in the 1920s. After World War II, penicillin became available as an effective means of curing the disease.

risk of death or serious complications, such as rheumatic fever. Scarlet fever also was a mysterious disease, because it would infect only some members of a family and not others. A good example of scarlet fever's effect can be found in the 1869 book *Little Women* (see sidebar).

Today, scarlet fever is not as deadly, because antibiotics are available to fight the streptococcal bacteria that cause the infection.

A Sore Throat That Gets Worse

Scarlet fever is caused by exposure to someone who is infected with streptococcal bacteria. People with the strep infection can spread it by sneezing or coughing. It also can be spread by sharing drinking glasses or eating utensils with people who are infected.

The first signs of scarlet fever usually start within a week of exposure to the strep bacteria. A sore throat develops, which is known as strep throat. But in some people, the particular kind of strep bacteria, known as Group A Streptococcus, causes a toxic reaction. A skin rash appears within 1 or 2 days of the sore throat. It looks like a sunburn on the neck, chest, and underarms. Less often the rash can appear on the face or the groin. The skin feels rough, like sandpaper. Within a week, the rash usually starts to fade, and flaking and peeling of the skin occur.

Scarlet fever also causes a fever with temperatures over 101 degrees Fahrenheit. Glands around the jaw and neck swell and are painful. Chills, nausea, and vomiting can result.

In rare cases, scarlet fever also can result from a skin infection known as impetigo.

Scarlet fever body rash. © Biophoto Associates/Photo Researchers, Inc.

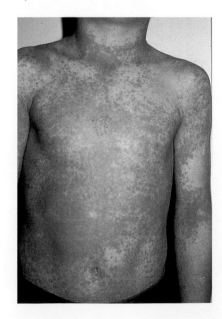

▶ *See also*
Rheumatic Fever
Strep Throat

KEYWORDS
for searching the Internet
and other reference sources

Bilharzia

Parasites

* **parasitic** means caused by
creatures that live in and feed on
the bodies of other organisms. The
animal or plant carrying the
parasite is called its host.

Strep throat and scarlet fever can be serious without treatment from a physician. A doctor who suspects a strep infection will use a cotton swab to get a bit of the bacteria from the throat for laboratory testing to confirm that it is streptococcal bacteria. Treatment with antibiotics for 10 days usually kills the bacteria.

Schistosomiasis

Schistosomiasis (shis-to-so-MY-a-sis), also known as bilharzia (bil-HAR-zee-a), is a disease caused by parasitic worms that affects more than 200 million people worldwide.

Schistosomiasis is caused by parasitic* worms called blood flukes of the genus *Schistosoma*. Three species within the genus (*Schistosoma mansoni, S. japonicum,* and *S. haematobium*) are responsible for most infections. Blood flukes live in water in tropical areas of the world and are common in Africa, South America (Brazil, Venezuela, and Surinam), parts of the Caribbean (Saint Lucia, Antigua, Montserrat, Martinique, Guadeloupe, the Dominican Republic, and Puerto Rico), some Middle Eastern countries, parts of China, the Philippines, and Southeast Asia. Contact with contaminated water through bathing, swimming, or wading is the most common method of infection.

What Is the Life Cycle of *Schistosoma*?

Freshwater rivers, lakes, and streams become contaminated when people who have schistosomiasis urinate or defecate in the water, leaving behind

A woman and children wash clothes in a pond that contains snails carrying fluke worms in Morogoro, Tanzania. The snails release infective larvae into fresh water. *Andy Crump, TDR, WHO/Science Photo Library/Photo Researchers, Inc.* ▶

blood fluke eggs. After the eggs hatch, the *Schistosoma* larvae* attack a certain species of snail (if the snail is not present, the larvae will die). After the snail is infected, the larvae grow and develop in the snail. When the larvae leave the snail, if they come in contact with a human within 48 hours they burrow into the skin and enter blood vessels. The parasites then grow in the bloodstream, where they produce eggs. Some of the eggs travel to the liver. Others enter the intestine or the urinary bladder, where they pass out of the body through urine or stool. If the eggs reach a freshwater supply, the cycle begins again.

What Are the Signs and Symptoms of Schistosomiasis?

Initially, skin may be itchy and a rash may appear where the *Schistosoma* burrow into the skin. As the worms develop in the liver, fever, chills, cough, and muscle aches may develop. There may be liver enlargement or malfunction, diarrhea, abdominal pain, and vomiting. The kidneys may be also affected. In rare cases, eggs can reach the brain or spinal cord and cause seizures. Even without treatment, most cases do not result in permanent damage to organs, though there may be significant long-term health effects.

Sometimes, however, the infection scars the liver so much that blood flow through the liver is partially blocked. This causes a condition called portal hypertension (POR-tal HY-per-ten-shun), which may cause sometimes fatal bleeding from swollen veins in the stomach and esophagus*.

How Is Schistosomiasis Diagnosed and Treated?

Schistosomiasis is diagnosed by identifying eggs in stool or urine samples. Repeated samples may be required to identify the parasite. Blood tests may be used to identify the need to search for eggs but are not usually enough to make decisions about treatment. Treatment depends on the severity of the infection. A drug called praziquantel (pra-zi-KWAN-tel) is used to treat the infection.

How Is Schistosomiasis Prevented?

In many parts of the world, there is no way of knowing whether water is contaminated with blood fluke larvae. It is best to avoid any contact with fresh water in areas where *Schistosoma* are known to occur. Swimming in ocean water and chlorinated pools is generally considered safe.

Resources

Organizations

Centers for Disease Control and Prevention, 100 Clifton Road N.E., Bldg. 1, SSB249, MS A34, Atlanta, GA 30333. This U.S. agency helps control communicable, carrier-borne, and occupational diseases and prevent disease, injury, and disability. A fact sheet on schistosomiasis is available on its website.
Telephone 404-639-3534
http://www.cdc.gov/ncidod/dpd/schisto.htm

* **larvae** are worms at an intermediate stage of the life cycle between eggs and adulthood.

* **esophagus** (e-SOF-a-gus) is the tube connecting the stomach and the throat.

The U.S. and the World

Schistosomiasis is a leading cause of illness in tropical areas of the world. According to the World Health Organization (WHO), only malaria is considered more widespread among tropical illnesses. More than 20 million people worldwide suffer severe consequences of schistosomiasis, and about 120 million show symptoms. Overall, about 200 million people are infected and 600 million are at risk. WHO estimates that more than 80 percent of all the people infected with schistosomiasis live in sub-Saharan Africa. The infection leads to an estimated 20,000 deaths each year. United States residents can get schistosomiasis when traveling to other parts of the world where the disease occurs; schistosomiasis has even struck some Americans who were on African river-rafting trips.

▶ See also
Parasitic Diseases

KEYWORDS
*for searching the Internet
and other reference sources*

Catatonia

Mental disorders

Paranoia

Psychosis

World Health Organization, 2 United Nations Plaza, 2 Building, Rooms 0956-0976, New York, NY 10017. A United Nations agency dedicated to achieving the best health possible for people worldwide. Public health information is available on its website. Telephone 212-963-4388
http://www.who.int/

Schizophrenia

Schizophrenia (skit-so-FRE-ne-a) is a serious mental disorder that causes people to experience hallucinations, delusions, and other confusing thoughts and behaviors, which distort their view of reality.

> "... why will you say I am mad? The disease had sharpened my senses—not destroyed—not dulled them. Above all was the sense of hearing acute. I heard all things in the heaven and in the earth. I heard many things in hell. How, then, am I mad? Harken! and observe how healthily—how calmly—I can tell you the whole story."
>
> *From* The Tell-Tale Heart *by Edgar Allan Poe (1843)*

Poe's short story features a narrator who deals with the symptoms of a serious mental disorder called schizophrenia. He hears things (in the end, the beating of a dead man's heart) that others do not hear, and he believes that people are out to get him. His thinking is distorted, and he has lost touch with reality.

What Is Schizophrenia?

Schizophrenia is one of the most severe and disabling of all mental disorders. People with this complex and often-misunderstood condition experience hallucinations*, delusions*, and other confusing thoughts and behaviors, which distort their view of reality. About 1.5 million people in the United States have the disorder.

The term schizophrenia comes from Latin and means "split mind." The minds of people with schizophrenia cause them to have periods when they are unable to separate the unreal things they see, hear, and think from the real world as it exists for most people.

Many people incorrectly believe that having schizophrenia means that a person has many personalities. However, there actually is a separate mental disorder, called multiple personality disorder*, in which a person goes back and forth between two or more distinct identities. Schizophrenia is a different condition.

With proper treatment and the support of family, friends, and mental health professionals, people with schizophrenia have a better outlook

* **hallucinations** are false perceptions. People hear voices, see visions, or otherwise sense things that are not really there.

* **delusions** are false beliefs that a person clings to, despite their lack of basis in reality.

* **multiple personality disorder** (MUL-ti-pul per-so-NAL-i-tee dis-OR-der), also known as dissociative identity disorder, is a mental disorder in which a person displays two or more distinct identities that take control of behavior in turn.

today than in the past, when many were condemned to mental hospitals where they often were mistreated.

What Causes Schizophrenia?

No one is sure what causes schizophrenia. It runs in some families, and a person whose parent has the disorder has a 10 to 15 percent chance of developing schizophrenia. This suggests that genes* play a role, but one identical twin may develop schizophrenia, while the other who shares the same genetic makeup may not. Many scientists think that genes put some people at risk for schizophrenia, but that other factors in the person's life trigger the symptoms. Other studies suggest that neurotransmitters* in the brains of people with schizophrenia are not working properly. Neurotransmitters are chemical substances that help nerve cells communicate. An imbalance of neurotransmitters seems to cause the nerve cells to send the wrong signals. This might explain the hallucinations and distorted views of reality that people with schizophrenia have.

*genes are the hereditary material that helps determine many physical and mental characteristics.

*neurotransmitters are chemicals that carry messages from the brain to other parts of the body.

What Are the Symptoms of Schizophrenia?

Schizophrenia often begins in the late teens and early twenties for males, and the twenties and thirties for females. Children as young as five can develop schizophrenia, as can older men and women, although such cases are rarer.

The first signs often are hard to recognize. People might withdraw and experience trouble with school, work, or social relationships. Attention to personal hygiene drops. Thinking and talking become disorganized. People might start displaying inappropriate facial expressions or emotions, such as laughing at a tragedy. Of course, just because people act this way does not always mean that they are developing schizophrenia.

People with schizophrenia develop other symptoms as well. One of the clearest symptoms of the disorder is having hallucinations. The most common hallucination involves hearing one or more voices that are not

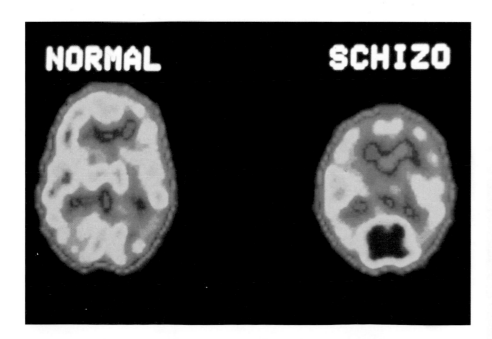

These positron emission tomography (PET) scans are computer-generated images that show how the brain is functioning. Compare the brain activity in a healthy person (left) to that in a person with schizophrenia (right). The red area in the brain on the right shows intense activity by tiny particles with a positive electric charge, called positrons. *NIH, Science Source/Photo Researchers, Inc.*

paranoid (PARE-a-noyd) refers to behavior that is based on delusions of persecution or grandeur. People with persecution delusions falsely believe that other people are out to get them. People with delusions of grandeur falsely believe that they have great importance, power, wealth, intelligence, or ability.

really there. Sometimes the voice comments on the world or the person's thoughts. Other times, the person hears two voices arguing or someone saying to do certain things.

In addition, people with schizophrenia often hold irrational beliefs. Some become paranoid*, which means that they falsely believe that other people are out to get them or that they are very important. Paranoid people may think that the police are against them, that outside forces are controlling their actions, or that people are always talking about them. Other people with schizophrenia become catatonic*, which means that they show extreme disturbances in movement. Catatonic people may sit rigidly, staring at nothing, and not reacting to things around them. In some cases, they may engage in pointless motions.

How Is Schizophrenia Diagnosed and Treated?

By the time a person with schizophrenia experiences hallucinations, it is obvious to family members and friends that something is very wrong. Even the person with schizophrenia might sense during clear moments that there

SCHIZOPHRENIA IN HISTORY

Psychiatry is the field of medicine that deals with the study, treatment, and prevention of mental disorders. The field was still in its infancy during the nineteenth century, but it underwent a revolution around the turn of the twentieth century. Progress in other areas of science, such as the study of the brain and nervous system, increased scientific interest in how physiological problems might be related to psychological states.

One scientist who was drawn to this question was German psychiatrist Emil Kraepelin (1856–1926). While developing a classification system for mental illnesses, Kraepelin defined dementia praecox as a major form of psychosis, a serious mental illness that leads to thoughts and behaviors that are out of touch with reality. The Swiss psychiatrist Paul Eugene Bleuler (1857–1893) later refined the concept of dementia praecox and renamed it schizophrenia.

Throughout history, mental patients often were treated as prisoners. This drawing was made in 1812 in Bedlam, the popular name for the Hospital of St. Mary of Bethlehem, a famous "insane asylum" in London. Today the word "bedlam" is used to describe any place that is the scene of uproar and confusion. *Mary Evans Picture Library/Photo Researchers, Inc.*

is a serious problem. Before diagnosing the disorder, a physician first makes sure that nothing else is causing the symptoms. Some viruses, drugs, and poisons can cause a person to experience schizophrenia-like symptoms.

Hospitalization often is necessary, at least at first. Antipsychotic drugs* can reduce or stop the hallucinations and disorganized thoughts and speech. Psychotherapy* can help people with schizophrenia and their family members cope with the disorder. With proper treatment, one third of schizophrenia patients can expect a significant and lasting improvement, one third will improve but will have some lasting symptoms and periods of relapse, and one third will remain severely and permanently affected.

Resources

Book

Torrey, E. Fuller, M.D. *Surviving Schizophrenia*, third edition. New York: HarperPerennial, 1995. A comprehensive and understandable overview of the disorder.

Organizations

U.S. National Institute of Mental Health, 6001 Executive Boulevard, Room 8184, MSC 9663, Bethesda, MD 20892-9663. A government institute that provides information about schizophrenia.
http://www.nimh.nih.gov

American Psychiatric Association, 1400 K Street Northwest, Washington, DC 20005. An organization of physicians that provides information about schizophrenia.
http://www.psych.org

National Alliance for the Mentally Ill, 200 North Glebe Road, Suite 1015, Arlington, VA 22203-3754. A self-help organization for people with serious mental illness and their family and friends.
Telephone 800-950-NAMI
http://www.nami.org

*catatonic (kat-a-TON-ik) refers to an extreme disturbance in movement that has a psychological cause. Catatonic people can develop a wide range of symptoms, including becoming very inactive and withdrawn, displaying excessive activity with no purpose, refusing to talk or follow instructions, becoming rigid if others try to move them, adopting strange gestures and facial expressions, and repeating the words or copying the movements of others.

*antipsychotic drugs are medications that counteract or reduce the symptoms of a severe mental disorder such as schizophrenia.

*psychotherapy involves talking about feelings with a mental health professional. The therapist can help the person change thoughts, actions, or relationships that play a part in the mental disorder.

▶ See also
Mental Disorders
Multiple Personality Disorder

Sciatica

Sciatica (sy-AT-i-ka) is a form of lower back pain that usually moves from the buttocks down the back of the leg.

What Is Sciatica?

When something squeezes the sciatic nerve, the main nerve in the leg, people feel pain in the back of the lower body. That pain, called sciatica,

KEYWORDS
for searching the Internet and other reference sources

Herniated disk

Lower back pain

Sciatic nerve

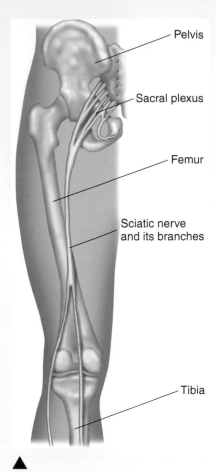

The sciatic nerve is the main nerve in the leg. It branches into the tibial and peroneal nerves.

*osteoarthritis (os-tee-o-ar-THRY-tis) is a painful joint disease.

*spondylolisthesis (spon-di-lo-lis-THEE-sis) is a condition in which one vertebra slips over the other.

*spinal stenosis (SPY-nal ste-NO-sis) is the narrowing of the spinal canal.

*chronic (KRON-ik) means continuing for a long period of time.

usually moves down the buttocks to the leg below the knee, but it can go all the way down to the foot. Sciatica varies from mild, tingling pain to severe pain that leaves people unable to move. Some people with sciatica feel sharp pain in one part of the leg or hip and numbness in other parts. This pain gets worse after standing or sitting for a long time.

Sciatica is most common in people who are ages 30 to 70, and it affects about three times as many men as women. At risk are:

- people who are sedentary (not very active)
- people who exercise improperly
- people who smoke
- athletes
- people who lift, bend, and twist in awkward positions in their jobs
- pregnant women
- tall people.

What Causes Sciatica?

There are many ways the sciatic nerve can become compressed, but the exact cause is often unknown. The most common causes of sciatica are a herniated disc or a tumor within the spine. Discs are the pads between the bones (called vertebrae) of the spine. They are filled with a gelatin-like substance that cushions the vertebrae from the impact of walking, running, lifting, and similar activities.

A disc that has torn and has this gelatin-like material oozing out of it is said to be herniated. Other common causes of sciatica include bony irregularities of the vertebrae such as osteoarthritis* or spondylolisthesis*. Spinal stenosis* is a less common cause. In some cases, diabetes or alcoholism can cause sciatica.

How Is Sciatica Diagnosed and Treated?

Sciatica is diagnosed through a medical history and a physical examination. Sciatica often clears up within several days to a week. It is usually treated with bed rest for a day or two (only if people cannot bear the pain), local heat, massage, pain relievers, and muscle relaxants. Sciatica tends to return and can become chronic*. Chronic sciatica is treated by trying to alleviate the cause of the pain by advising people to lose weight, improve muscle tone and strength, and improve posture. Surgery may be necessary in cases where there is no relief from pain, disc disease, or spinal stenosis. The goal of surgery is to eliminate the source of pressure on the sciatic nerve.

Can Sciatica Be Prevented?

Sciatica or recurrence of sciatica can sometimes be prevented by standing, sitting, and lifting properly; exercising; and working in a safe environment. That means using chairs, desks, and equipment that support the back or help maintain good posture, and taking precautions when lifting and bending.

Resources

Book

Tollison, David. *Handbook of Pain Management.* Baltimore: Williams and Wilkins, 1994.

Organization

National Arthritis and Musculoskeletal and Skin Diseases, National Institutes of Health. Office of Communications and Public Liaison, Building 31,Room 7A-50, 31 Center Drive, MSC 2520, Bethesda, MD 20892-2520. Consumer health information is available on its website. Telephone 301-496-4000
http://www.nih.gov

▶ *See also*
Slipped Disk

Scoliosis

Scoliosis (sko-lee-O-sis) is a lateral, or side-to-side, curvature of the spine that most often occurs gradually during childhood or adolescence.

KEYWORDS
for searching the Internet and other reference sources

Back pain

Orthopedics

Skeletal system

Spine

Vertebrae

What Is Scoliosis?

The name "scoliosis" comes from the Greek word meaning curvature. Everyone's backbone curves to some degree from front to back, which is necessary for proper movement and walking. In scoliosis, however, the spine curves in a side-to-side direction too, or the curve may be S-shaped when another part of the spine develops a counterbalancing secondary curve. Depending on the degree of curvature, this may cause other physical problems, such as pain and breathing difficulties. The parts of the spine most commonly involved are the thoracic (tho-RAS-ik), or chest region, and the lumbar (LUM-bar), or lower back region.

Scoliosis is a fairly common condition. It has been estimated that about 3 out of every 100 people have this disorder to some degree. Girls are about 5 times more likely than boys to develop scoliosis.

Causes, Known and Unknown

The most common form of scoliosis is called idiopathic (id-ee-o-PATH-ik), which means that the cause is unknown. Usually, scoliosis becomes apparent just prior to or during adolescence, when the body's rate of growth speeds up markedly. The curvature stops increasing after people have reached their mature height.

Rarely, scoliosis is a congenital (present at birth) abnormality of the vertebrae (VER-te-bray), or spinal bones, and continues to develop throughout childhood. Poliomyelitis (po-le-o-my-e-LY-tis) has caused

* **ligament** (LIG-a-ment) is a fibrous band of tissue that connects bones or cartilages (CAR-ti-lij-ez), serving to support or strengthen joints.

* **sciatica** (sy-AT-i-ka) is pain along the course of either of the sciatic (sy-AT-ik) nerves, which run through the pelvis and down the backs of the thighs.

* **chronic** (KRON-ik) means continuing for a long period of time.

scoliosis in some people by paralyzing or weakening the spinal muscles on one side of the body.

Occasionally, an injury such as a disk prolapse (slipped disk) or a sprained ligament* in the backbone can cause temporary scoliosis. When this happens, the curvature may be accompanied by back pain and sciatica*.

People who have scoliosis often have family members with the same condition. This suggests that heredity also is a causal factor in some cases of scoliosis.

What Are the Signs and Symptoms of Scoliosis?

Because scoliosis can develop very gradually, there may be no observed signs or symptoms in its early stages. Often, the curvature is first noticed in a teenager indirectly: one shoulder may become noticeably higher than the other, or a dress or jacket may not hang straight.

Early symptoms of scoliosis may include an unusually tired or achy feeling in the lower back after standing or sitting for a long time.

For some, the curvature eventually may become more severe and easier to recognize. Severe scoliosis can cause chronic* back pain. If the curvature exceeds an angle of about 40 or 45 degrees, it can interfere with breathing and affect heart function.

Spinal column and pelvis in an adolescent girl with scoliosis. ▶

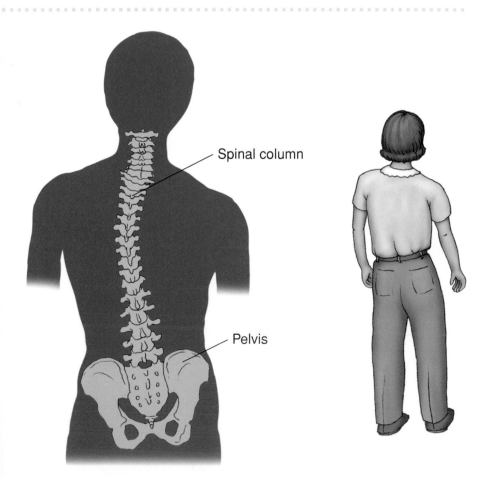

Spinal column

Pelvis

How Do Doctors Diagnose and Treat Scoliosis?

Diagnosis   Scoliosis is not always easy to diagnose, especially if it does not hurt or have visible signs. A physical examination of the spine, hips, and legs is the first step, followed by an x-ray if needed.

In the United States, public schools often do a simple test for scoliosis called the forward-bending test. The school nurse or another staff member has students bend over parallel to the floor with their shirts off to check for curvature. If scoliosis is suspected, the student is referred to a family doctor for further evaluation. The doctor might want to have an x-ray taken for a clearer view of the spine.

The severity of scoliosis is diagnosed by determining the extent of curvature of the spine. The curvature is the angle of slant of the spinal bones measured in degrees.

Treatment choices   If the cause of scoliosis is known, such as an injury or unequal leg length, the treatment is designed to address the cause. For example, wearing a shoe with a raised heel can correct scoliosis caused by unequal leg length.

In idiopathic scoliosis, however, the choice of treatment depends largely on the severity of the condition. If the angle of curvature is slight (say, 10 to 15 degrees) nothing may need to be done other than having regular checkups to make sure the curvature does not worsen. Somewhat greater curvature can be treated by wearing any of several types of back braces. An angle of curvature of 40 degrees or more may mean that a corrective operation will be needed.

Living with Scoliosis

Fortunately, much of the deformity of scoliosis can be prevented if the condition is detected early. In most instances, no lifestyle changes are needed, and people can carry on with their normal activities.

Resources

The National Institute of Arthritis and Musculoskeletal and Skin Diseases (NIAMS), part of the U.S. National Institutes of Health (NIH), posts information about scoliosis on its website.
http://www.nih.gov/niams/healthinfo/scochild.htm

The Nemours Foundation posts a fact sheet about scoliosis at its website.
http://kidshealth.org/teen/bodymind/scoliosis.html

The Southern California Orthopedic Institute also has a helpful website.
http://www.scoi.com/scoilio.htm

Back Braces, Past and Present

A hundred years ago, teenagers who had to wear back braces for scoliosis faced some very uncomfortable choices. As if being tortured, they were strapped to racks in an attempt to straighten their backs. Later on, metal jackets that weighed up to 30 pounds were worn to try to reduce the curvature. Lighter jackets, made of plaster of paris, came next, but often they were hot and itchy.

Today's back braces are big improvements. Many are made of lightweight materials and do not have to be worn all the time. There are several different types to choose from to suit the teenager's particular requirements. Some are worn only while sleeping; others can be worn under clothing, so that they are not visible. Still others are of a low-profile type that comes up under the arms and are quite comfortable.

Wearing a back brace sometimes causes emotional problems. Some teenagers may resist the idea of wearing a back brace, because they fear their friends or classmates may reject or ridicule them. Counseling or support groups often are helpful in sharing experiences and problems and should be considered as part of the treatment.

Tomorrow's back braces undoubtedly will be even more adaptable, as medical engineers are constantly making improvements.

▶ *See also*
Poliomyelitis
Sciatica
Slipped Disk

Scurvy

KEYWORD
for searching the Internet
and other reference sources

Ascorbic acid

Scurvy is a disease that results when people do not get enough vitamin C (also called ascorbic acid) in the diet over a period of weeks or months. Some of the effects of scurvy are spongy gums, loose teeth, weakened blood vessels that cause bleeding under the skin, and damage to bones and cartilage, which results in arthritis-like pain.

What Is Scurvy?

Scurvy was one of the first recognized dietary deficiency diseases. During the sea voyages of the fifteenth to eighteenth centuries, many sailors suffered from scurvy. The Portuguese navigator Vasco da Gama (ca 1460–1524) lost half his crew to the disease during their voyage around the Cape of Good Hope, and the British admiral Sir Richard Hawkins (1532–1595) lost 10,000 sailors to scurvy. In 1747, the British naval physician James Lind conducted experiments to see which food or liquids might be able to prevent scurvy. He found that lemons and oranges enabled sailors to recover from scurvy. Both of these citrus fruits are rich sources of vitamin C.

What Is the Role of Vitamin C in the Body?

Vitamin C is necessary for strong blood vessels, healthy skin, gums, and connective tissue, formation of red blood cells, wound healing, and the absorption of iron from food.

What Are the Symptoms of Scurvy?

The main symptom of scurvy is bleeding (hemorrhaging). Bleeding within the skin appears as spots or bruises. Wounds heal slowly. The gums become swollen, and gingivitis (jin-ji-VY-tis), which means inflamma-

---

HAVE YOU EVER HEARD ANYONE CALLED A "LIMEY"?

In *Treatise of the Scurvy*, published in 1753, James Lind wrote about the first example of a research experiment set up as a controlled clinical trial. To study the treatment of scurvy, Lind divided sailors who had it into several groups and then fed each group different liquids and foods. He discovered that the group fed lemons and oranges was able to recover from scurvy.

By the end of the eighteenth century, the British navy had its sailors drink a daily portion of lime or lemon juice to prevent scurvy. The American slang term for the English, "limeys," originated from that practice.

tion of the gums, usually occurs. Bleeding can take place in the membranes covering the large bones. It can also occur in the membranes of the heart and brain. Bleeding in or around vital organs can be fatal.

Scurvy develops slowly. In the beginning, a person usually feels tired, irritable, and depressed. In the advanced stages of scurvy, laboratory tests show a complete absence of vitamin C in the body.

Who Is at Risk for Scurvy?

Scurvy is less prevalent today than it was in the time of Vasco da Gama and Richard Hawkins, but people who are on diets that lack a diversity of foods may develop scurvy or scurvy-like conditions. Infants who depend solely on processed cow's milk for nutrition and are not given vitamin C supplements are at risk for scurvy. Elderly people, whose diets often lack citrus fruits or vegetables that contain vitamin C, represent another at-risk group. People who follow diets that limit them to very few food choices also may be susceptible to developing scurvy.

How Is Scurvy Treated?

To treat scurvy, people take vitamin C supplements (vitamin pills) and eat foods rich in vitamin C. In addition to citrus fruits like oranges and grapefruits, good sources of vitamin C include broccoli, strawberries, cantaloupe, and other fruits and vegetables.

▲

A British sailing ship. *Visuals Unlimited.*

Resources

Books

Mavarra, Tova. *Encyclopedia of Vitamins, Minerals, and Supplements.* New York: Facts on File, 1996.

Slap, Gail B. *Teenage Health Care.* New York: Pocket Books, 1994.

Organization

The U.S. National Institutes of Health (NIH) has a search engine at its website that locates information about scurvy and about vitamin C research. http://www.nih.gov

▶ See also
Dietary Deficiencies
Gum Disease

Seasickness *See* **Motion Sickness**

Seizures

Seizures (SEE-zhers) occur when the electrical patterns of the brain are interrupted by powerful, rapid bursts of electrical energy. A

KEYWORDS
for searching the Internet and other reference sources

Brain Function

Epilepsy

Neurology

seizure may cause a person to lose consciousness, to fall down, to jerk or convulse, or simply to blank out for a few seconds. Infection, injury or medical problems can cause a seizure. Epilepsy is a disease of the nervous system characterized by recurring seizures.

Two Stories

Eric's story   As part of his sixth grade study of self-awareness, Eric was assigned to draw the frames of a film that would show the world as he saw it. Teachers were puzzled by what Eric drew. One frame showed him pouring milk, the next frame was completely black, and the next frame showed spilled milk. In another sequence, Eric drew a teacher calling on him to answer a math problem, followed by another black frame, and then a picture of the teacher complaining that Eric was not paying attention. The teachers realized that Eric's project did show the world as he saw it. The mysterious black frames were blackouts. Doctors determined that Eric had absence seizures, a type of seizure that causes a brief loss of consciousness. Medication successfully controlled Eric's seizures.

Carol's story   All the students in Carol's art class were preparing work for an art show when Carol stood up and began walking around the room. Looking like she was in a trance, Carol smacked her lips and tugged at the sleeve of her dress. About two minutes later, Carol became aware of her surroundings, only to discover that her classmates were laughing at her strange behavior. Embarrassed, she ran from the room. Carol had experienced a complex partial seizure.

What Is a Seizure?

Whether a person is sleeping or awake, millions of tiny electrical charges pass between neurons* in the brain and to all parts of body. These cells "fire," or transmit electrical impulses, in an orderly and controlled manner. Seizures occur when overactive nerve cells send out powerful, rapid electrical charges that disrupt the brain's normal function. The disruption can temporarily affect how a person behaves, moves, thinks, or feels.

Symptoms of a seizure can include combinations of the following:

- twitching and tingling in part of the body (for example, fingers and toes)
- muscle spasms spreading to arms and legs
- hallucinations
- intense feeling of fear or of familiarity (sometimes called déjà vu)
- a peculiar sensation, sometimes called an aura, immediately before the seizure (for example, seeing a flashing light or sensing strange odors)
- loss of consciousness.

*neurons are nerve cells. Most neurons have extensions called axons and dendrites through which they send and receive signals from other neurons.

How Do Seizures Differ?

There are two kinds of seizure disorders: an isolated seizure that occurs only once, and epilepsy (EP-i-lep-see). Epileptic seizures occur more than once, and they occur over a period of time. In both epilepsy and isolated seizures, the seizure may have different symptoms or characteristics depending on where it begins in the brain and how the electrical discharge spreads across the brain. Seizures can be generalized or partial.

Generalized seizures   Generalized seizures affect nerve cells throughout the cerebral cortex (the cauliflower-like outer portion of the brain), or all of the brain. Generalized seizures often are hereditary, which means they run in families. They may also be caused by imbalances in a person's kidney or liver function, or in their blood sugar.

The most common generalized seizures are:

- **Generalized tonic-clonic seizure (formerly called grand mal seizure):** In the tonic phase of this seizure, people often lose consciousness, drop to the ground, and emit a loud cry as air is forced over their vocal cords. In the clonic phase, body muscles contract all at once or in a series of shorter rhythmic contractions, causing thrashing motions. Usually, this kind of seizure lasts for about one or two minutes and is followed by a period of relaxation, sleepiness, and possibly a headache.

- **Absence seizure (formerly called petit mal seizure):** Loss of consciousness in this seizure is often so brief (usually 10 to 30 seconds) that a person does not even change positions. The person may display a blank stare, rapid blinking, or chewing movements. Facial or eyelid muscles may jerk rhythmically. Absence seizures may be inherited and usually are seen for the first time in children between the ages of 6 and 12.

- **Infantile spasms:** This type of seizure occurs before age 4 and may cause a child to suddenly flex the arms, thrust the trunk forward, and extend the legs. The seizure lasts only a few seconds, but can recur several times a day.

- **Atonic seizures:** Also seen primarily in children, these seizures cause a complete loss of muscle tone and consciousness, which means they pose a serious risk of injury due to falling.

- **Myoclonic seizures:** Brief seizures characterized by quick jerking movements of one limb or several limbs. The person experiencing the seizure does not lose consciousness.

- **Febrile seizures:** These seizures occur in infancy or childhood and cause a child to lose consciousness and convulse. The seizures are accompanied by a high fever and they are described as either simple or complex. Simple febrile seizures account for about 85 percent of febrile seizures. They occur once in 24 hours and last less than 15 minutes. Complex febrile seizures last more than 15 minutes or occur more than twice in 24 hours.

Partial seizures Partial seizures affect nerve cells contained within one region of the cerebral cortex. Types of partial seizures include:

- **Simple partial:** The seizure-related brain messages remain very localized, and the patient is awake and alert. Symptoms vary depending on what area of the brain is involved. They may include jerking movements in one part of the body, emotional symptoms such as unexplained fear, an experience of peculiar smells, or nausea.

- **Complex partial:** A person loses awareness of surroundings and is unresponsive or only partially responsive. There may be a blank stare, chewing movements, repeated swallowing, or other random activity. After the seizure, the person has no memory of the experience. In some cases, the person may become confused, begin to fumble, to wander, or to repeat inappropriate words or phrases.

What Causes A Seizure?

A seizure generally is easy to recognize, but finding the cause can be extremely difficult. Doctors begin with a thorough physical examination. They try to determine if the person has experienced other seizures or has a family history of seizures. Physicians also want to know if the patient has experienced an aura*, because that can help establish the location in the brain of the seizure. They also will note the person's age and the nature of the movements the person made during the seizure.

An electroencephalogram (e-LEK-tro-en-SEF-a-lo-gram), commonly known as an EEG, records electric currents in the brain and can track abnormal electrical activity. Doctors may also look for structural brain abnormalities using other types of scans, including computerized tomography (CT) and magnetic resonance imaging (MRI). In some research centers, positron emission tomography (PET) is used to identify areas of the brain that are producing seizures.

A lumbar puncture, sometimes called a spinal tap, can detect infection. The procedure requires that a physician carefully insert a thin needle between two vertebrae (bones) in the patient's spine and draw out a small amount of cerebrospinal fluid (CSF). The fluid is analyzed for the presence of bacterial or viral infections, tumors, or blood disorders that might provide a clue to the cause of the seizure.

Seizures are associated with the following diseases and conditions:

- Epilepsy, a disorder of the nervous system characterized by seizures that occur more than once and over a period of time.

- Head trauma that damages the brain.

- Loss of oxygen caused by birth trauma, carbon monoxide poisoning, or near drowning.

- Brain infections, such as meningitis or encephalitis.

- Brain tumor.

- Stroke.

* **aura** is a warning sensation that precedes a seizure or other neurologic disorder.

- Toxic (poisonous) agents, including drug abuse or ingestion of poisons such as lead, alcohol, or strychnine.

- Withdrawal from alcohol and drugs.

- Metabolic imbalances such as hypoglycemia (very low blood sugar), uremia (kidney failure), or liver problems.

- Eclampsia or toxemia, which may occur during pregnancy and is characterized by high blood pressure, protein in the urine, and fluid retention.

It is important to remain calm and not to panic when someone has a seizure. An adult usually will ask if the person has epilepsy. If the person is unable to communicate, an adult will check for a medical identification bracelet or tag that carries information about the underlying cause of the seizure.

Resources

Books

Orrin, Devinsky, M.D. *A Guide to Understanding and Living With Epilepsy*. Philadelphia: F.A. Davis, 1994. An easy-to-read guide with a glossary of terms and antiepileptic drugs.

Wilner, Andrew N. *Epilepsy: 199 Answers. A Doctor Responds to His Patients' Questions*. New York: Demos Vermande, 1996.

Organization

The Epilepsy Foundation, 4351 Garden Drive, Landover, MD 20785. Formerly the Epilepsy Foundation of America, this national organization offers information on seizures and epilepsy. The website provides general information on diagnosis and treatment, plus web links and a chat room for teenagers.
Telephone 800-332-1000
http://www.efa.org

▶ See also
Brain Tumor
Diabetes
Encephalitis
Fever
Hypoglycemia
Incontinence
Infection
Kidney Disease
Lead Poisoning
Lupus
Meningitis
Stroke
Substance Abuse

Senile Dementia *See* Alzheimer's Disease

Sexually Transmitted Diseases (STDs)

Sexually transmitted diseases (or STDs) are a varied group of infections that usually are passed from person to person by sexual contact. Some also spread from mother to child during pregnancy or childbirth. Widespread around the world, STDs are particularly common among

KEYWORDS
for searching the Internet and other reference sources

Infection

Public health

Venereal disease

people in their teens and early twenties. STDs range in severity from pubic lice, which usually cause only discomfort, to AIDS, which has caused millions of deaths in a worldwide epidemic.

Sexual contact between people is one important way that many disease-causing organisms spread. More than 30 bacterial, viral, and parasitic diseases can pass from person to person in this way. For some of these, sexual contact is the main route of transmission. These are the illnesses we generally call sexually transmitted diseases (STDs).

Most STDs primarily affect only the sexual organs and other parts of the reproductive system. That is true of chlamydial (kla-MID-i-al) infections, gonorrhea (gon-o-REE-a), genital herpes, genital warts, and trichomoniasis (trik-o-mo-NY-a-sis). Other STDs may enter through the sexual organs but affect other parts of the body. That is what happens in AIDS and syphilis.

Besides AIDS, some STDs can have serious complications, especially for women. Chlamydia and gonorrhea often cause no symptoms in women (and sometimes in men), which means they can easily go untreated. But

Sexually transmitted diseases affect many different parts of the body.

▶

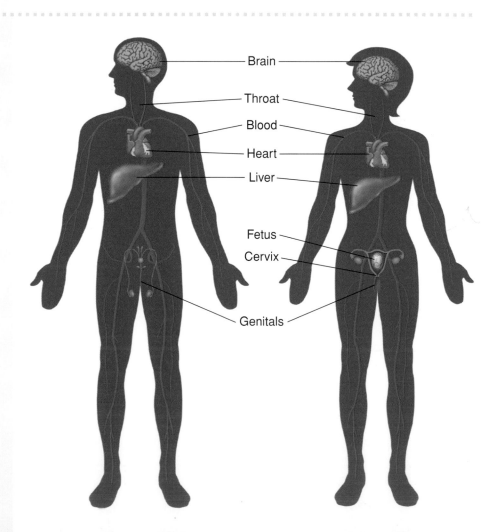

Brain

Throat

Blood

Heart

Liver

Fetus

Cervix

Genitals

if that happens, these infections sometimes develop into pelvic inflammatory disease. That can lead to infertility, meaning a woman finds it difficult or impossible to get pregnant. In addition, if women are infected with certain strains of the human papillomavirus, a sexually transmitted virus, they may run a higher risk of getting cancer of the cervix, part of the female reproductive system.

If syphilis goes untreated in men or women, it can cause fatal heart problems, as well as blindness, deafness, and insanity, many years later.

Are All Infections of the Genital Tract Spread by Sexual Contact?

No. For instance, yeast infections of the genital tract usually do not involve sexual contact. Most often, the yeast (a kind of fungus) spreads from a person's own skin or intestinal tract, where it does no harm, into the person's genital tract, where it can cause symptoms. So a person could get such an infection even if he or she had never engaged in sexual activity. The most common of these yeast infections is called candidiasis (can-di-DI-a-sis).

Who Is at Risk for STDs?

Just about anyone who has sexual contact with another person can get an STD. People who are infected with one STD are likely to have other STDs as well. Once cured, they also are at higher risk of getting infected again.

STDs are particularly common among young people, aged 15 to 24. Experts see several reasons for this: Young people are less likely to be married, so if they engage in sex, they may tend to have more sexual partners than older people. Young people more often fail to use condoms during sexual activity, even though condoms can protect a person from most sexually transmitted diseases. Young people may be too embarrassed, too short of money, or too worried about privacy to get regular checkups or to get prompt medical treatment for STDs. As a result, they may stay infected—and may be able to infect others—for longer than necessary.

In general, people run a higher than usual risk of getting infected if they begin sexual activity at an early age, have a number of sexual partners, do not always use condoms, and do not get regular medical checkups. But even a person who has sex only one time, with only one partner, can get an STD if his or her partner is infected. The only clear way to prevent getting an STD is to abstain from sexual activity.

How Do STDs Spread?

People with STDs often do not realize they are infected, and so they spread the disease to others, including people they love most—wives, husbands, and children.

Sexual contacts These diseases can spread through sexual contact between people of the opposite sex (heterosexual sex) or between people of the same sex (homosexual sex). Sexual activities that can spread STDs include sexual intercourse, anal sex, and oral-genital sex.

chancroid (SHANG-kroid) is a bacterial infection that causes painful sores in the genital region. Relatively rare in the United States, it mostly occurs in tropical and subtropical areas.

Non-STDs: A Matter of Definition

Many infections *can* spread through sexual contact but *usually* spread in other ways. These illnesses generally are not classified as sexually transmitted diseases. They include:

- Hepatitis B and cytomegalovirus, viruses that usually spread through blood

- Bacteria like salmonella, parasites like amebas, and the virus Hepatitis A, all of which usually spread through water or food that has been contaminated with feces from an infected person

Other routes of transmission STDs also sometimes spread in nonsexual ways. Many of them—including HIV, gonorrhea, chlamydia, syphilis, and genital herpes—can be spread from mother to baby during pregnancy or childbirth. HIV can also spread through breastfeeding.

HIV, the virus that causes AIDS, can spread if an infected person shares needles, or if contaminated blood is given in a blood transfusion. In the United States, strict testing has made blood transfusions extremely safe, but the risk may be higher in some other countries.

STDs that cause sores on the skin, such as genital herpes, syphilis, and chancroid*, can spread sometimes if the sores touch another person's skin. The sores also can serve as a way for HIV to enter the body, making infection with the AIDS virus more likely. Preventing or treating these sores is important in the prevention of AIDS.

Most STDs cannot be spread by contact with an object, such as a toilet seat. One exception is trichomoniasis, which is thought to spread sometimes through towels or bathing suits recently used by an infected person.

What Happens When People Get STDs?

Symptoms Several of the most common of these diseases—chlamydia, gonorrhea, and trichomoniasis—can cause pain during urination and a pus-like discharge from the sexual organs. In many cases, however, there are no symptoms in these illnesses. Several other STDs cause sores or blisters in the genital region. These include syphilis, genital herpes, and chancroid. The symptoms of HIV/AIDS include getting frequent fungal and parasitic infections.

Diagnosis From the symptoms and a look at any skin sores that may be present, a doctor may suspect an STD. Tests of various kinds can usually tell for sure which infection, if any, a person has.

Because chlamydia and gonorrhea are very common in young women, but often cause no symptoms and can lead to infertility, doctors recommend that young women who engage in sexual activity get tested routinely for these illnesses so they can be treated.

In addition, anyone whose sexual partner has been diagnosed with an STD, or whose partner has symptoms of an STD, should be tested and treated if they are also infected.

How Are STDs Treated?

STDs can be divided into curable illnesses and illnesses that can be treated but not cured.

Curable illnesses Curable illnesses usually are caused by bacteria or parasites. These include chlamydia, gonorrhea, syphilis, and chancroid, all caused by bacteria, and trichomoniasis, caused by a parasite. These can be cured with medication. Syphilis and gonorrhea, in fact, often can be cured by a single swallow or shot of medicine.

Treatable illnesses Ilnesses that are treatable, but not curable, usually are caused by viruses. These include HIV/AIDS, genital herpes, and genital warts. These cannot be cured with drugs, because the viruses remain in the body. But, in most cases, medication or other treatment can reduce symptoms. In the case of people with HIV infection, medication can increase the life span and the quality of life.

How Can STDs Be Prevented?

Abstinence and safer sex The only sure way to avoid getting an STD is not to have sexual contact with anyone (called abstention or abstinence).

For people who do engage in sex, the safest relationship is when two people who are not infected have sexual contact only with each other. The problem is that it is impossible to know for sure whether someone is infected or not. People may not always tell the truth about their sexual behavior in the past—or they may mistakenly think they were protected in the past. Many people with an STD do not know or believe they have one.

That is one reason why health officials recommend that people who engage in sex always use latex condoms unless they are trying to get pregnant. Using latex condoms can lower the risk of getting an STD, but the condoms must be used properly, and they must be used every time a person engages in sexual activity.

Education and awareness At the public health level, education is an important part of preventing STDs. Awareness about the need to prevent STDs has greatly increased in recent decades, largely because of the emergence of AIDS. Information about how to prevent STDs is now widely published in the media and taught in schools. Young people are being urged to abstain from sex or to use condoms if they are sexually active.

Contact tracing In addition, when a person is diagnosed with an STD, doctors or health officials try to locate the person's sexual partners so they can be tested and treated. This kind of confidential "contact tracing" is done without revealing the infected person's name. It prevents the person's sexual contacts from unknowingly spreading the disease.

But the only sure way to prevent getting an STD is to abstain from sex.

Resources

Book

Brodman, Michael, M.D., John Thacker, and Rachel Kranz. *Straight Talk About Sexually Transmitted Diseases*. New York: Facts on File, 1998. This book focuses on prevention for young people and includes explicit discussion of more and less risky sexual activity.

Organizations

The National Institutes of Health posts information about sexually transmitted diseases on its website.
http://www.nih.gov/factsheets/stdinfo.htm

The U.S. and the World

Sexually transmitted diseases take a heavy toll throughout the world. By the end of 1998, AIDS had killed almost 14 million people worldwide, including more than 400,000 people in the United States. More than 33 million people were living with HIV infection, mostly in under-developed countries in Africa and Asia.

While other sexually transmitted diseases seldom cause death, they do cause a heavy burden of illness. In 1995, the World Health Organization estimated that 333 million new cases of curable STDs occurred. That included:

- 89 million cases of chlamydial infection

- 62 million cases of gonorrhea

- 12 million cases of syphilis

- 170 million cases of trichomaniasis

Throughout the world, including the United States, STDs tend to be more common in urban, unmarried teenagers and in young adults.

In the United States, it is estimated that most adults will be infected with a sexually transmitted disease at some time, although they may not know it. Some form of the human papillomavirus, for instance, infects most Americans. Some strains of human papillomavirus cause genital warts; others can promote cervical cancer. And more than 1 in 5 Americans is thought to be infected with the virus that causes genital herpes.

Of the bacterial STDs, chlamydia is the most common. It is estimated to cause about 4 million cases a year in the United States, although only about 10 percent of those get reported to health agencies. It is thought that 1 in 10 adolescent women and 1 in 20 adult women of child-bearing age are infected.

The U.S. Centers for Disease Control and Prevention (CDC), 1600 Clifton Road, N.E., Atlanta, GA 30333, has a National STD Hotline that is open from 8:00 AM to 11:00 PM EST.
Telephone: 800-227-8922.

The CDC also posts information about sexually transmitted diseases at its website.
http://cdc.gov/od/owh/whstd.htm

The American Social Health Association posts a *Sexual Health Glossary* and fact sheets about STDs at its website.
http://www.ashastd.org/main/main.html

KidsHealth.org, the website of The Nemours Foundation, has information for teens and others about STDs.
http://kidshealth.org

Shin Splints *See* Strains and Sprains

Shingles

Shingles is caused by a viral infection of the sensory nerves of the skin and causes a painful rash on the skin. The medical name for shingles is "herpes zoster." The virus that causes herpes zoster is the same virus that causes chickenpox (varicella).

KEYWORDS
for searching the Internet
and other reference sources

Dermatology

Infectious diseases

Viruses

Zoster

What Is Shingles?

A person cannot develop shingles unless he or she has had chickenpox. Shingles is caused by the same virus that causes chickenpox, the herpes zoster virus. Whereas chickenpox is a highly contagious disease, shingles usually is not transmitted from one person to another. However, a person can develop chickenpox from coming in direct contact with the blisters on a person with shingles. After recovering from chickenpox, the herpes zoster virus may remain in part of the nervous system for years without causing any illness. Shingles may be brought on as a side effect of another disease, such as Hodgkin's disease (a cancer of the lymph system), or from treatments that suppress the immune system*. However, most of the time, there is no known cause for the virus to become active and cause shingles.

* **immune system** fights germs and other foreign substances that enter the body.

What Are the Symptoms of Shingles?

The affected skin area first feels sensitive, and then becomes painful. Before blisters from shingles develop, a person may have chills and fever, feel tired, and have an upset stomach. These symptoms may last for 3 or 4 days. By the fourth or fifth day, a rash made up of small red spots appears. The small red spots turn into blisters that are filled with the herpes zoster virus. After another few days, the blisters become yellow and dry out. Crusts develop over the dried-out blisters. When they drop off after several weeks, they sometimes leave small scars.

Usually, the rash and blisters involve a limited area of skin, most often on one side of the chest, abdomen, or face.

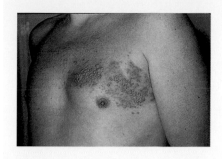

Shingles rash. © *Biophoto Associates/Photo Researchers, Inc.*

What Is the Treatment for Shingles?

Treatment for shingles is directed mainly at reducing the pain involved. Medications are also used to attack the viruses. Wet compresses applied to the affected areas can sometimes soothe the pain. Mild pain relievers such as acetaminophen can be used.

Who Is at Risk for Shingles?

Shingles occur mostly in older people whose immune systems are no longer able to keep the virus in the nervous system inactive. This age group develops shingles more often, although shingles can develop at any age. After an attack of shingles, a person may be immune for the rest of his or her life.

Most people recover from the disease without any problems. However, in older patients, the pain may last for months or years after the blisters have healed. This is called postherpetic neuralgia (post-her-PET-ik noo-RAL-je-ah).

What Other Diseases Can Herpes Zoster Cause?

The herpes zoster virus can cause several other diseases:

- **Chickenpox** is usually a mild disease that causes a rash and fever. It is very contagious.

- **Herpes zoster oticus,** also called Ramsay Hunt syndrome and viral neuronitis, causes ear pain, hearing loss, vertigo (a spinning sensation), and may paralyze a part of the face.

- **Ophthalmic herpes zoster** involves the eyelid and sometimes the eye itself. It can be serious if the eye is involved.

Resources

Oldstone, Michael. *Viruses, Plagues, and History.* New York: Oxford University Press, 1998.

Schwarz, Richard H. "When You Get a Childhood Illness." *American Baby,* February 1999, p. 22.

The U.S. Centers for Disease Control and Prevention (CDC), 1600 Clifton Road, N.E., Atlanta, GA 30333. The United States government authority for information about infectious and other diseases, the CDC posts information about shingles at its website. http://cdc.gov/ncidod/srp/varicella.htm

▶ *See also*
Chickenpox

KEYWORD
for searching the Internet
and other reference sources

Circulatory system

Shock

Shock is a dangerous physical condition in which the flow of blood throughout the body is drastically reduced, causing weakness, confusion, or loss of consciousness. It can result from many kinds of serious injuries and illnesses. If shock is not treated quickly, a person can suffer permanent organ damage and die.

What Is Shock?

"I studied for days, but I failed the test. I'm in shock," says one teenager to another.

In everyday speech, "shock" is common and sometimes even fun. People line up to get shocked by horror movies. They want to feel an emotional jolt from seeing something sudden, surprising, and scary. Their hearts may beat a little faster for a moment, but when the movie ends they're as healthy as before.

This kind of emotional shock has nothing to do with medical shock. "Shock" in the medical sense also can be sudden, surprising, and scary. But it is a very specific physical condition that is extremely serious.

Shock occurs when the amount of blood reaching the brain and other parts of the body is reduced drastically; in other words, when the blood pressure falls very low. Since the blood carries oxygen needed by every cell in the body, the drop in blood flow deprives the cells of oxygen. The brain, the biggest user of oxygen, is affected, making the person confused, dazed, or unconscious. As cells struggle to function without enough oxygen, many chemical processes in the body are disrupted. Organs, including the lungs, kidneys, liver, and heart, start to fail. Unless the blood flow is restored quickly, the damage may be fatal.

What Causes Shock?

There are several underlying causes of shock. Often, a case of shock involves two or all three of these types of underlying problems. These include:

■ There is not enough fluid in the bloodstream. This kind of shock is called hypovolemic (hy-po-vo-LEEM-ik) shock. It can be caused by heavy bleeding from an injury, such as a gunshot wound or wounds suffered in a car crash. It also can be caused by severe bleeding from a medical condition, such as an aortic aneurysm* or bleeding stomach ulcers. It can also occur if a person loses large amounts of fluids other than blood. That can happen, for instance, if a person has severe vomiting and diarrhea or has been badly burned over a large part of the body.

■ The blood vessels dilate (expand) too much. If this happens, blood pressure (the pressure within the blood vessels) can become so low that not enough blood is pushed out to reach vital tissues. The most

*aortic aneurysm (ay-OR-tik AN-yoo-rizm) is a weak spot in the aorta, the body's largest blood vessel. The weak spot can rupture or break, causing massive internal bleeding.

common example of this kind of shock is septic (SEP-tik) shock, which is caused by a severe bacterial infection.

- The heart fails to pump the blood strongly enough. This is called cardiogenic (kar-dee-o-GEN-ik) shock. It can be caused by many heart problems including a heart attack, an abnormal heart rhythm, a blood clot in the heart, or a buildup of fluid around the heart that presses on the organ, or by severe damage to a heart valve.

What Is Septic Shock?

Septic shock occurs when a person is infected with bacteria that get into the bloodstream and produce a dangerous level of toxins (poisons). Even when treated, it is sometimes fatal.

It is most likely to occur in hospitalized people who have recently had surgery or who have had drainage tubes, breathing tubes, or other devices inserted into their body. Such devices increase the chances that bacteria will get into the bloodstream.

Other people at risk for septic shock are those with weakened immune systems, including those who have diabetes, cirrhosis, leukemia, or AIDS. Newborns and pregnant women are also at risk.

Toxic shock syndrome is a form of septic shock that originally was linked to use of certain tampons.

What Is Anaphylactic Shock?

Anaphylactic (an-a-fi-LAK-tik) shock is a severe allergic reaction in which fluid leaks out from the blood vessels and the blood vessels dilate as well. In certain people, it can occur as a reaction to medication, blood transfusions, bee stings, or peanuts or other foods. It can be fatal.

What Are the Symptoms of Shock?

Whatever its cause, people with shock have rapid and shallow breathing, cold and clammy skin, a weak but rapid pulse, low blood pressure, and weakness all over the body. They are dizzy, confused, and may become unconscious.

How Is Shock Treated?

People in shock should be taken by ambulance to a hospital as quickly as possible. Until then, they should be kept lying down on their back with their feet raised about a foot higher than their head. This helps get the blood flowing to the brain and heart. They should be covered with a coat or blankets to keep them warm.

Medical workers will try to raise the blood pressure by giving fluids intravenously (through a needle into a vein). If the shock was caused by blood loss, a blood transfusion may be necessary as well. If the blood pressure still remains dangerously low, drugs known as pressors may be used to raise the blood pressure. For anaphylactic shock, doctors give the drug epinephrine (ep-i-NEF-rin), also called adrenaline, to constrict (narrow) the blood vessels.

Oxygen is routinely given, and some people need to be put on a ventilator (a breathing machine) to increase the amount of oxygen getting to their cells. If septic shock is suspected, antibiotics are given intravenously.

Electrical Shock

An electric current that passes through the body is called a shock. Although it can also be dangerous (electrical accidents kill about 1,000 people a year in the United States), electrical shock is different from the medical shock discussed in this article.

Medical shock is a reduction in blood flow. Electrical shock primarily causes internal burns and disruption of heart rhythms. Sometimes, however, an electrical shock can cause medical shock. This can happen if the burns lead to rapid loss of fluid and the heart problems prevent adequate pumping of blood.

Once the person is out of immediate danger, doctors can try to treat the underlying causes.

How Can Shock Be Prevented?

Following safety rules to prevent fires and serious accidents, including car crashes, would prevent many cases of shock. To prevent bacterial infections that can cause septic shock, hospitals have rules about sterilizing equipment and washing hands. To prevent anaphylactic shock, people with allergies need to carefully avoid the substances that trigger them.

Resource

Organization

The Virtual Hospital posts information on shock based on the *University of Iowa Family Practice Handbook,* 3rd edition, at http://www.vh.org/Providers/ClinRef/FPHandbook/Chapter01/18-html.

▶ *See also*

Allergies

Burns

Heart Disease

Toxic Shock Syndrome

Sickle-cell Anemia

Sickle-cell anemia, also called sickle-cell disease, is a hereditary disorder in which abnormal hemoglobin* within the red blood cells (RBCs) causes the cells to take on abnormal sickle (crescent) shapes. This decreases the ability of the hemoglobin to transport oxygen throughout the body. The sickled cells tend to bunch up and clog the blood vessels, and they tend to break apart more easily than normal RBCs. This may cause inflammation, pain, tissue damage, and anemia*.

What Are the Sickle-Cell Trait and Sickle-Cell Disease?

Normally, red blood cells (RBCs) are rounded and flattish, like a saucer. They pass easily through the tiniest blood vessels. Red blood cells sickle or take on the crescent shape when they carry an abnormal form of hemoglobin called hemoglobin S. The abnormality in hemoglobin S occurs because of the presence of a faulty gene*.

People inherit one set of genes from each parent. They can inherit either two normal hemoglobin genes (HbA), one normal hemoglobin gene and one gene for the abnormal hemoglobin gene (HbS), or two abnormal HbS genes, depending on the composition of their parents' genes.

When a person carries one HbS and one HbA gene, the presence of the normal gene is sufficient to override the effects of the HbS gene so

KEYWORD
for searching the Internet and other reference sources

Inherited diseases

***hemoglobin** (HEE-mo-glo-bin) is a protein found in red cells. It binds to oxygen so that oxygen can be carried by way of the circulatory system throughout the body for use by other cells.

***anemia** (a-NEE-mee-a) is a condition in which the amount of oxygen transported by the blood is reduced either because of a reduced number of RBCs or because there is too little hemoglobin in the RBCs.

***genes** are chemicals inherited from both parents that help determine physical characteristics, such as whether a person has brown hair or blue eyes, or in this case, normal or abnormal hemoglobin.

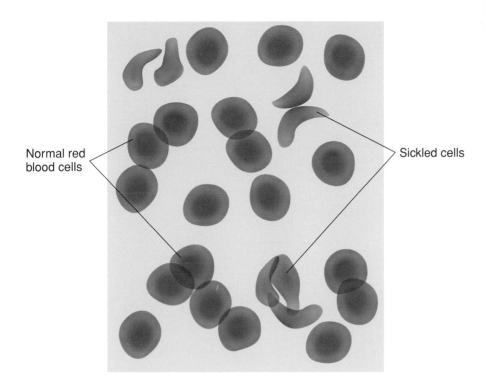

Normal red blood cells

Sickled cells

The shape of sickled red blood cells compared to normal red blood cells.

the symptoms of sickle-cell disease do not develop. These people, however, are said to have the sickle-cell trait or to be carriers of the sickle-cell trait, and they may pass it on to their children. Prospective parents who are likely to carry the HbS gene may wish to be tested for its presence and receive genetic counseling before having children.

When people inherit two abnormal HbS genes, one from each parent, they have sickle-cell disease, and they show symptoms of that disease. They have only abnormal HbS genes to pass on to their children.

Since sickle-cell disease is a genetic disorder, its frequency varies in different populations worldwide. It is found most frequently in Africa, where in some locations up to 40 percent of the population has at least one HbS gene. The gene is also found in people in Mediterranean and Middle Eastern countries, such as Italy, Greece, and Saudi Arabia. There are groups of people in India, Latin America, the Caribbean, and the United States where the HbS gene is also found.

Among people of African ancestry in the United States, about 8 in every 100 individuals carries at least one HbS gene (has the sickle-cell trait) and about 40,000 people carry two copies of the HbS gene and have sickle-cell disease.

What Are the Effects of Sickle-Cell Disease?

People who have sickle-cell disease get infections more frequently than other people. In 1987 the National Institutes of Health recommended that all babies, regardless of ethnic background, be tested for the presence of the HbS at birth. Babies with sickle-cell disease are often given antibiotics* to prevent infections. Before this screening became common,

*antibiotics (an-ty-by-OT-Iks) are drugs that fight bacterial infection.

One normal and one sickled red blood cell side by side under the electron microscope, photographed at 18,000 times actual size. © *Stanley Flegler, Visuals Unlimited.* ▶

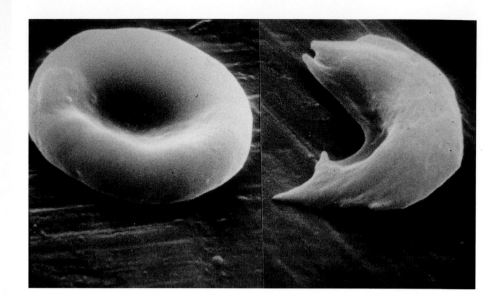

many babies born with sickle-cell disease died in infancy. Today the use of preventive antibiotics has significantly reduced the number of babies who die.

Infants, older children, and adults with sickle-cell disease also periodically experience bouts of critical illness called crises. They also suffer from complications of anemia.

Because sickle-cell disease is hereditary, people are born with it and will have it all their lives. There is no way one person can catch sickle-cell disease or sickle-cell trait from another, and there is no way the disease can be cured.

Crises   Sickle-shaped red blood cells clump more easily than normal RBCs. Sickle-cell crises start suddenly when clumping of sickled RBCs in the blood vessels obstructs the normal flow of blood, depriving various tissues and organs of oxygen. The first crises usually appear in early childhood.

The inheritance pattern for the sickle-cell gene HbS. ▶

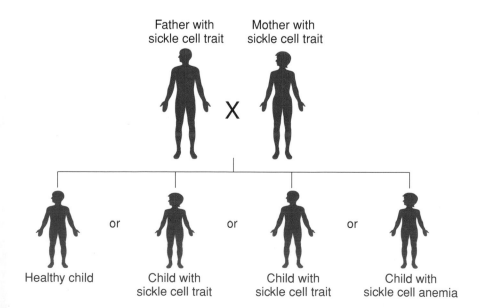

Father with sickle cell trait   Mother with sickle cell trait

X

Healthy child   or   Child with sickle cell trait   or   Child with sickle cell trait   or   Child with sickle cell anemia

Crises may be brought on by respiratory infection, by a loss of body fluids from vomiting or diarrhea, by situations where the body's need for oxygen is increased, or they may occur for no obvious reason. They may last for several days, and cause fever and sharp, intense pain in the back, abdomen, chest, arms and legs. In infants, the hands and feet may become swollen and painful.

Crises may damage nearly any part of the body, but especially the bones, kidneys, intestines, lungs, liver, spleen, and the central nervous system*, including the brain. There may also be eye damage, stroke, convulsions, or paralysis. The damage is caused because the clumping of RBCs in a blood vessel deprives tissues of oxygen.

* **central nervous system** refers to the brain and the spinal cord, which coordinate the activity of the entire nervous system.

Many people with sickle-cell disease go for long periods during which they may feel relatively well and engage in most normal activities and are free of crises (in remission). Others may experience pain on a daily basis, and some need to be hospitalized as a result of crises several times a year.

Anemia   Sickle cells are more easily broken down and destroyed than normal RBCs. Sickle cells have a lifespan of 10 to 20 days compared to 90 to 120 days for a normal RBC. People with sickle-cell anemia thus cannot keep up a normal level of oxygen-carrying hemoglobin in their blood. This is so despite the fact that they make red blood cells faster than people without the disease. The result is that they are anemic.

The anemia may become so severe that a person will need to have a blood transfusion. The long-term effect of anemia is that the heart has to work harder to pump more blood through the body. Over time the heart enlarges, increasing the risk of heart attack and heart failure.

Other complications of sickle-cell disease   People who have sickle-cell disease are more susceptible to all kinds of bacterial and fungal infections. They are more likely to have strokes* and to experience kidney failure. In some people, the liver enlarges, and by age 30, 70 percent of people with sickle-cell disease have developed gallstones.

* **stroke** is a blocked or ruptured blood vessel within the brain, which deprives some brain cells of oxygen and thereby kills or damages these cells. Also called apoplexy (AP-o-plek-see).

Modern medicine has increased the survival of people with sickle-cell disease. About half the people with sickle-cell disease live beyond 50 years. Still, living with the pain and complications of this condition can cause emotional stress on both the person with the disease and the family.

How Is Sickle-Cell Disease Diagnosed?

Sickle-cell disease and sickle-cell trait can be diagnosed by a test that is much simpler than its name: hemoglobin electrophoresis (e-lek-tro-fo-REE-sis). This test detects the presence of HbS and other abnormal hemoglobins. A complete blood count (CBC) counts the number of RBCs and checks for abnormal shapes.

How Is Sickle-Cell Disease Treated?

There is no cure for sickle-cell anemia. Much treatment is preventive and directed toward symptoms. Antibiotics may be given to prevent infections. Fluid intake is important to prevent dehydration*, a major

* **dehydration** (dee-hy-DRAY-shun) is loss of fluid from the body.

A Possible Benefit of the Sickle-Cell Trait

Sickle-cell disease is especially prevalent among people of African or African American descent. No one knows for sure why this is so. However, it is believed that the gene that causes sickle-cell disease also provides natural resistance to malaria, an often-fatal disease. The parts of Africa where malaria is most prevalent, such as Ghana and Nigeria, are also the areas where the incidence of sickle-cell anemia and sickle-cell trait is greatest. It is believed that the gene that causes the sickle-cell trait also gives these people some advantage in surviving malaria. This allows them to live and reproduce, thereby passing the gene along to later generations. However, people with sickle-cell disease (two copies of the HbS sickle-cell gene) do not have this advantage and are more likely to die of malaria.

cause of sickling. Folic acid may be given daily to lessen the anemia by helping to make new red cells. Children are given a complete set of immunizations. Lifestyle habits that can help sickle-cell patients stay healthy and have fewer crises include drinking plenty of water, avoiding extremes of heat and cold, avoiding stress and overexertion, getting enough sleep, and having regular medical check-ups.

Treatment in a sickle-cell crisis may require oxygen therapy, pain relieving medications, antibiotics, and intravenous fluids to offset dehydration. Blood transfusions may also have to be performed. Treatment of pain is a major concern for physicians whose patients have sickle-cell disease. The benefits of different pain relievers and their unwanted side effects must be balanced for each patient.

Research is ongoing to find better ways to treat people with sickle-cell disease. Some of these research efforts are directed at stimulating the production of fetal hemoglobin, a form of hemoglobin found in infants, even those with sickle-cell disease. Other research is directed toward the development of drugs that block dehydration in cells. Gene therapy and the transplantation of healthy bone marrow that makes normal red blood cells are also under investigation.

Resources

Organizations

The NIH National Heart, Lung, and Blood Institute Information Center, P.O. Box 30105, Bethesda, MD 20824-0105. Posts information about sickle-cell disease on its website.
Telephone 301-592-8573
http://www.nhlbi.nih.gov/health/public/blood/sickle/sca_fact.txt

Sickle-Cell Disease Association of America, Inc., 200 Corporate Pointe, Suite 495, Culver City, CA 90230-7633. This association has a hotline staffed by counselors and provides free education materials.
Telephone 800-421-8453

SIDS *See* **Sudden Infant Death Syndrome**

Silicosis *See* **Pneumonoconiosis**

Sinusitis

Sinusitis is an infection within the paranasal sinuses, which are spaces in the bones of the face and the skull located around the nose, under the cheekbones, and near the eyes.

KEYWORDS
for searching the Internet and other reference sources

Allergies

Bacterial infection

Viral infection

What Is Sinusitis?

Sinusitis is one of the most common health problems. It affects more than 35 million Americans each year, often because they catch a cold or have allergies.

Openings in the nose connect to pairs of sinuses in the bones of the face and skull. The sinuses are air-filled spaces with linings that produce mucus. This mucus normally drains into the nose. The linings of the sinuses become infected in sinusitis, which causes them to swell. The swelling prevents the normal drainage of fluid from the sinus areas. This blockage causes a pressure buildup and pain. The areas under the cheekbones, and around the eyes, or near the involved sinuses hurt and become tender to the touch.

Sinusitis can come and go in a week or so, like a cold. It also can be chronic, which means it lasts many weeks or months.

What Causes Sinusitis?

Bacteria and viruses usually cause the infection in sinusitis. It most commonly occurs during a cold. Allergies to dust, grass, and other substances can also cause sinusitis. Even swimming underwater and flying in an airplane can contribute to sinusitis.

What Are the Symptoms of Sinusitis?

The first sign usually is a stuffy nose. The mucus that comes out is thick and appears yellow and green. Sometimes, the mucus contains small amounts of blood.

The clogged sinuses and swelling cause pain around the nose and eyes. The pain feels worse when the person bends forward. Headaches are common, and it even can feel as if there is a toothache, because sinus pressure can push on nerves under the teeth. A fever may also be present as well as a cough.

How Is Sinusitis Treated?

If the sinusitis is part of a cold or flu, the symptoms usually go away on their own. Doctors may prescribe antibiotics if the sinusitis is thought to

Locations of the paranasal sinuses.

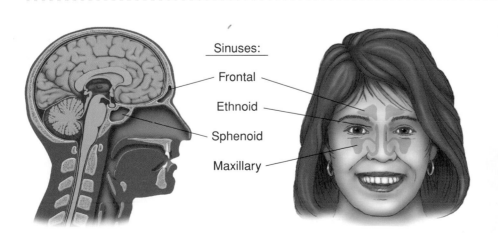

Sinuses:

Frontal

Ethnoid

Sphenoid

Maxillary

be caused by a bacterial infection. Otherwise, rest, decongestants, warm pads on the face, and lots of liquids are the treatment. A humidifier with a cool mist can also help.

If the symptoms last more than a month, the sinusitis is chronic and may be triggered by allergies to such things as dust, trees, and animal dander. Doctors advise people with chronic sinusitis to try to avoid the things that cause their allergies. Special filters are available for air-conditioning and heating systems. Allergy medicines may help to prevent further attacks of sinusitis.

Surgery is available for people with chronic sinusitis. A nasal passage is opened with a small cutting tool, which helps to open the sinus, allowing it to drain better.

Resource

The American Academy of Otolaryngology—Head and Neck Surgery Inc. This organization's website includes information on sinusitis, including an interactive test to see whether you just have a cold or have sinusitis.
http:/www.entnet.org

Skin Cancer

Skin cancer is a disease in which rapidly multiplying, abnormal cells (cancer cells) are found in the outer layers of the skin.

KEYWORD
for searching the Internet
and other reference sources

Dermatology

Melanoma

Moles

Oncology

The Most Common Cancer

In 1985, former president Ronald Reagan had a growth called a basal (BAY-zuhl) cell carcinoma removed from the side of his nose. The president had often been described as looking tanned and healthy, and when the news broke, it raised public awareness of skin cancer and the dangers of overexposure to the sun. Each year, about one million Americans will be diagnosed with skin cancer.

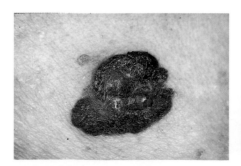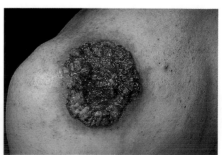

Melanoma (left) is less common than basal cell carcinoma (right) but it is far more aggressive. *Left: © James Stevenson, Science Photo Library/Photo Researchers, Inc. Right: © M. Abbey/Photo Researchers, Inc.*

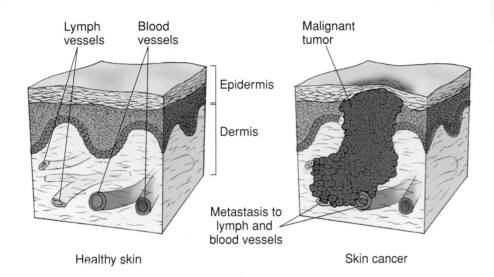

Lymph vessels · Blood vessels · Malignant tumor · Epidermis · Dermis · Metastasis to lymph and blood vessels · Healthy skin · Skin cancer

Healthy skin cells protect the body (left), but cancer cells grow and divide uncontrollably (right), crowding out the healthy cells nearby. Melanoma is particularly dangerous because it can spread throughout the body.

What Is Skin Cancer?

The skin often is called the largest organ of the body. It protects people by keeping water and other fluids inside the body, by helping to regulate body temperature, by manufacturing Vitamin D, and by performing a range of other complex functions. The skin also is a critically important barrier between people and such foreign invaders as bacteria. The skin is very personal: it is the first part of the body that people present to the world.

Types of skin cancer   Skin cancer is the most common of all cancers. It accounts for 50 percent of all cases of cancer. Cancers of the skin are divided into two general types: melanoma (mel-a-NO-ma) and nonmelanoma skin cancers. Nonmelanoma skin cancers are the most common cancers of the skin. They are also the most curable. Melanoma is much less common than nonmelanoma skin cancers, but it is far more aggressive and it is often lethal.

Melanoma   The outer layer of the skin is called the epidermis (ep-i-DER-mis). It consists of layers of flat, scaly cells called squamous (SQUAY-muss) cells, under which are round cells called basal cells. The deepest part of the epidermis consists of melanocytes (MEL-a-no-sites), which are the cells that give skin its color. Melanoma begins in the melanocytes.

Nonmelanoma skin cancers   The two main types of nonmelanoma skin cancers are basal cell carcinoma and squamous cell carcinoma. These cancers develop in different layers of the skin, but they both appear more commonly on sun-exposed areas of the body. Squamous cell carcinomas grow more quickly than basal cell carcinomas.

How skin cancer develops   Skin cancer begins with damage to the DNA of the cells in skin. DNA is information we inherit from our parents that tells the cells of the body how to perform all the activities

ABCDs of Melanoma Screening

The American Academy of Dermatology recommends checking the skin on a regular basis for changes in moles, freckles, and beauty marks. Their ABCD system for recognizing changes:

- **A:** asymmetrical shape.

- **B:** border with ragged, blurred, or irregular shape.

- **C:** color variations.

- **D:** diameter greater than 6 millimeters (size of a pencil eraser).

Moles that match any of the ABCDs should be seen by a doctor.

needed for life. DNA is contained in genes, and each cell has an identical set of genes. Some of these genes carefully control when cells grow, divide, and die. If a gene is damaged, the cell receives the wrong instructions, or no instructions at all. When that happens, the cell can begin to grow and divide uncontrollably, forming an unruly cluster that crowds out its neighbors and forms a cancerous growth, or tumor. Melanoma is potentially a serious cancer because it has the ability to spread to other places in the body. Nonmelanoma skin cancers, however, tend to stay put and are less likely to spread.

What Causes Skin Cancer?

Certain kinds of risk factors suggest who might be likely to develop cancer. A risk factor is anything that increases a person's chances of getting a disease like skin cancer.

Melanoma One risk factor is having certain types of moles. Another risk factor is having fair skin. The risk of melanoma is about 20 times higher for light-skinned people than it is for dark-skinned people. But dark-skinned people still can get melanoma. A person's chances of getting melanoma are greater if one or more close relatives have gotten it. People who have been treated with medicines that suppress the immune system (the body's defenses against infection) have an increased risk of developing melanoma. Exposure to ultraviolet radiation—for example, sunlight, tanning lamps, and tanning booths—also is a risk factor for melanoma.

Nonmelanoma skin cancers Most nonmelanoma skin cancers are caused by unprotected exposure of the area that has the cancer to ultraviolet radiation. Most of this radiation comes from sunlight, but it may also come from artificial sources. Although children and young adults usually do not get skin cancer, they may get a lot of exposure to the sun that could result in cancer later on. Other risk factors for nonmelanoma skin cancers include having fair skin, and having a weakened immune system as a result of medical treatment for other conditions. In addition, exposure to certain kinds of chemicals increases a person's risk of getting nonmelanoma skin cancers.

Skin Cancer Is Not Always Easy to Detect

Melanoma may show up as a change in the size, color, texture, or shape of a mole or other darkly pigmented area. Bleeding from a mole that is not the result of a scratch or other injury may also be a warning sign of cancer. Nonmelanoma skin cancers can be hard to tell from normal skin. The most important warning signs are a new growth, a spot or bump that seems to be growing larger (over a few months or a year or two), or a sore that does not heal within three months.

Diagnosis When either a melanoma or a nonmelanoma skin cancer is suspected, the doctor will take a special sample of skin (a biopsy) from the abnormal area for examination under the microscope.

How Is Skin Cancer Treated?

The first step in treating skin cancer is to stage it, that is, to decide whether and how far it might have spread. Staging a cancer is an important step in deciding what the best treatment for the patient is. It also helps to determine the patient's prognosis (outlook for survival). The most common system used to stage skin cancers assigns a Roman numeral from 0 to IV to the cancer. So, for example, stage 0 means the cancer has not spread beyond the tissue beneath the skin; stage IV means that the cancer has spread to other organs such as the lung, liver, or brain, and is less likely to be curable.

Fortunately, most nonmelanoma skin cancers can be completely cured by a variety of types of surgery depending on the size of the cancer and where it is. If a squamous cell cancer appears to have a high risk of spreading, surgery may sometimes be followed by radiation or chemotherapy (kee-mo-THER-a-pee). Chemotherapy refers to the use of anticancer drugs that can be injected into a vein in the arm or taken as tablets. In some precancerous conditions, chemotherapy may simply be placed directly on the skin as a cream.

Treatment for melanoma includes surgery and chemotherapy. Radiation therapy (which uses high-energy rays to kill cancer cells) is not usually used to treat the original melanoma that developed on the skin.

To Prevent Skin Cancer, Slip! Slap! Slop!

A popular anti-skin cancer slogan in Australia goes, "Slip on a shirt! Slap on a hat! Slop on some sunscreen! Seek shade!" The most important way of lowering the risk of nonmelanoma skin cancer is to stay out of the sun. This is especially important in the middle of the day, when sunlight is the most intense. Because no one wants to stay indoors all day, children and adults can protect their skin by covering it with clothing and by using a sunscreen with an SPF factor of 15 or more on areas of the skin exposed to the sun. Wide-brimmed hats and wrap-around sunglasses with 99 to 100 percent ultraviolet absorption help to protect the eyes. Tanning booths should be avoided.

What Is New in Skin Cancer Research?

Scientists have made enormous progress in understanding how ultraviolet light damages DNA and how DNA changes cause normal skin cells to become cancerous. In addition, researchers are looking into ways of treating skin cancers by enlisting the patient's immune system (the body's defenses against tumors and infection) to fight cancer cells.

A new type of treatment being studied called photodynamic (fo-to-dy-NAM-ik) therapy treats tumor cells with a special chemical that makes them sensitive and then shines a laser light on them, which kills them. Drugs related to vitamin A are being studied for use with some skin cancers. But the treatment has side effects, and its benefits have not been conclusively demonstrated. Researchers studying melanoma in particular are experimenting with adding genes to cancer cells to make

Sunshine and Skin Cancer

Cumulative Effects of Tanning

Long-term exposure to the ultraviolet (UV) rays of the sun damages the body's skin cells and can lead to cancer. For example, repeated sunburn and tanning cause the skin to wrinkle and to lose its ability to hold its shape. Dark patches called lentigos (len-TEE-goes) (age spots or liver spots) may appear, along with scaly precancerous growths and actual skin cancers. The sun's UV radiation also increases a person's risk of developing eye problems, including cataracts, which can cause blindness.

Burning and Peeling

Burning and peeling are signs that a person's skin has been damaged. The sun can also damage the DNA of cells, and if a person is exposed to the sun (or other forms of UV light) over many years, skin cancer may result.

Sunglasses

Sunglasses are an effective way of preventing sun damage to the eyes. But not just any sunglasses will do. The right kind of sunglasses are wrap-around UV-absorbant sunglasses, which block 99 to 100 percent of ultraviolet radiation. If the label on the glasses reads

- UV absorption up to 400 nm, or
- special purpose, or
- meets ANSI UV requirements

it means the glasses block at least 99 percent of UV rays. Whether the glasses are dark or light does not matter. The protection comes from an invisible chemical that is applied to the lenses. Any type of eyewear can be treated to make it UV-absorbant.

them more sensitive to drugs, to replace damaged genes, or to encourage the immune system to attack the abnormal cells.

Living with Skin Cancer

The most important thing to remember about skin cancer is that most of it is preventable. It is never too late for people to begin to protect their skin. Because a person who has had one skin cancer is at risk for another one, monthly self-examinations should become part of a routine. Cancer is most likely to recur (that is, to come back) in the first five years after treatment. A person who loves being in the sun will have to adjust to a life without sun worshipping. But except for staying out of the sun, almost everyone with skin cancer can go back to the life they had before they got cancer.

Resources

Books

Murphy, Gerald P., et al. *Informed Decisions: The Complete Book of Cancer Diagnosis, Treatment, and Recovery.* New York: Viking, 1997.

Poole, Catherine M., and Guerry DuPont IV. *Melanoma: Prevention, Detection, and Treatment.* New Haven, CT: Yale University Press, 1998.

Organizations

U.S. National Cancer Institute (NCI), Bethesda, MD 20892. NCI coordinates the government's cancer research programs and clinical trials. Its website posts *What You Need to Know About* fact sheets for skin cancer, melanoma, and moles and dysplastic nevi.
http://cancernet.nci.nih.gov/wyntk_pubs

American Academy of Dermatology, 930 N. Meacham Road, Schaumberg, IL 60173. Provides information about the science and medicine of the skin.
Telephone 888-462-DERM
http://www.aad.org

American Cancer Society (ACS), 1599 Clifton Road N.E., Atlanta, GA 30329-4251. ACS has resource centers at its website for melanoma and nonmelanoma skin cancer.
Telephone 800-ACS-2345
http://www3.cancer.org

OncoLink. The University of Pennsylvania's Cancer Center Web site. A valuable store of information for patients about all aspects of cancer.
http://www.cancer.med.upenn.edu

▶ See also
Cancer
Skin Conditions
Tumor

Skin Conditions

Skin conditions include various rashes, diseases, infections, injuries, growths, and cancers that affect the skin.

Leaves of Three, Let Them Be

Alison loved to take long walks in the woods in the summer, but one day she developed a streaky rash two days after she had gone on a hike. At first, her skin was red and swollen in spots. Soon, however, little blisters formed and began to itch intensely. Alison had developed a rash from poison ivy. Her mother warned her not to scratch, because her fingernails might carry germs that could cause an infection. It was hard to resist, but cool showers and a soothing lotion helped. Within a few days, the blisters began to scab over. It took about 10 days for the rash to heal completely. Afterward, Alison was careful to wear long-sleeved shirts and long pants when walking in the woods and to stay away from poison ivy, identifiable by its clusters of three leaves.

What Does the Skin Do?

The skin is the largest and most visible organ of the body. It also is one of the most complex, because it has so much to do. The main job of the skin is to protect a person's inside parts from the outside world. It acts as

Anatomy of the skin.

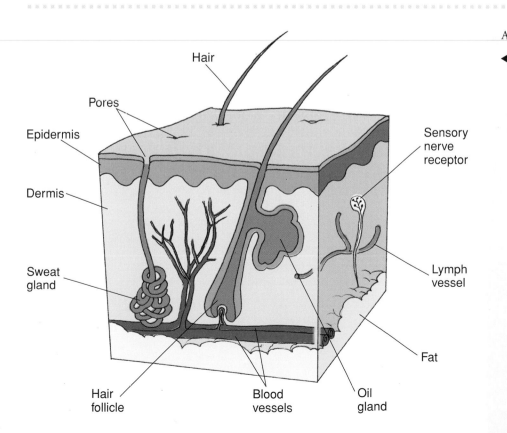

771

a shield against sun, wind, heat, cold, dryness, pollution, and cigarette smoke. All of these things can injure the skin over time. In addition, the skin comes into contact with and helps protect the body from germs; allergens (AL-er-jens), which are substances that can cause allergic reactions; and irritants, which are harsh chemicals that can hurt the skin. In addition, special nerve endings in the skin alert the brain to heat, cold, and pain.

What Can Go Wrong?

It is not surprising that many things can go wrong with an organ so big and complicated. Allergens and irritants can make the skin break out in a rash. Dermatitis (der-ma-TY-tis) is a general term for red, inflamed skin from a variety of causes.

There also can be glitches in the way the skin works. For example, it can make too much oil, leading to acne (AK-nee). If the skin makes too many new cells, the result can be psoriasis (so-RY-a-sis). If the skin makes too little or too much coloring matter, called pigment, the result can be patches of abnormally light skin (hypopigmentation) or dark skin (hyperpigmentation).

The skin also can be affected by injuries, such as sunburn, and by viral infections, such as cold sores. Other kinds of skin infections are caused by bacteria and fungi. In addition, the skin can be affected by both non-cancerous growths, such as birthmarks, and skin cancers.

What Are Some Common Skin Problems?

These are some of the most common skin problems seen by dermatologists (der-ma-TOL-o-jists), doctors who specialize in treating skin problems:

- **Acne**: pimples, blackheads, whiteheads, and deeper lumps. Almost all teenagers have at least a little acne, and some adults have the problem as well. Acne develops when the skin makes too much oil and sheds dead cells too fast. Bacteria also plays a role.

- **Athlete's foot**: a fungal infection that may cause the skin on the foot to look red and peel, crack, flake, or even blister. Sweaty feet and tight shoes provide the perfect setting for a fungus to grow. Athlete's foot is most common among teenagers and adult men.

- **Atopic (ay-TOP-ik) dermatitis, also called eczema (EK-zem-ah)**: a red, itchy rash that often runs in families and accompanies allergies. In babies, it typically leads to itching, oozing patches with scabs, mainly on the face. In older children, the patches tend to be dry, and the affected skin may flake and thicken. In teenagers, the patches usually occur inside the elbow bends, backs of knees, ankles, wrists, face, neck, and upper chest.

- **Birthmarks**: a skin mark that develops before or shortly after birth. Several kinds of common birthmarks are caused by overgrowth of blood vessels. Such marks are usually painless.

- **Cold sores**: an infection caused by the herpes (HER-peez) simplex

Skin Deep

- The average adult body has two square yards of skin, which make up about 15 percent of the body's total weight.

- A one-inch square of skin contains millions of cells as well as many special nerve endings for sensing heat, cold, and pain.

- The average thickness of skin is one-tenth of an inch, but it ranges from very thin on the eyelids to thick on the soles of the feet.

virus that leads to sores, usually around the mouth and nose. Some sores are barely noticeable, but others hurt. Cold sores are common among children and arc easily spread from person to person by kissing or sharing dishes or towels.

- **Contact dermatitis:** a red, itchy rash that occurs when the skin comes into contact with an allergen or something else to which the skin is sensitive. Examples include poison ivy and sensitivities to nickel, rubber, and skin care products.

- **Dandruff:** flaking of the skin on the scalp. Some flaking is part of the normal process by which the outer layer of skin cells is regularly shed. If the flaking becomes obvious on a person's hair and clothes, it is called dandruff. If the scalp is red or if there are large flakes along with flaking elsewhere, the problem may be something else.

- **Hives:** pale red, swollen bumps that occur in groups on the skin. Hives are usually itchy, but they may also burn or sting. They are caused when the body releases a chemical called histamine (HIS-ta-meen) as part of a reaction to such things as foods, medications, insect bites, infections, cold, or scratching of the skin.

- **Irritant dermatitis:** a red, itchy rash that occurs when the skin comes into contact with a harsh chemical. Examples of irritants include strong soaps or detergents and industrial chemicals.

- **Moles:** growths that can appear anywhere on the skin, alone or in groups. They are usually brown and can have various shapes and sizes. Everyone has at least a few moles, and some people have forty or more. Most moles are not cancerous, but some may turn into a serious form of skin cancer called malignant melanoma (mel-a-NO-ma).

- **Poison ivy:** a common type of contact dermatitis that occurs when a sensitive person comes into contact with a substance found in the sap of poison ivy plants. Poison oak and poison sumac (SOO-mak) plants can have the same effect. The result is a streaky rash with redness and swelling, followed by blisters and itching. About 85 percent of all people will have this kind of allergic reaction to poison ivy.

- **Psoriasis:** a long-lasting skin disease caused when too many new cells are made, resulting in patches of red, thickened skin covered with silvery flakes. Four to 5 million Americans have psoriasis. It may result from a problem with the immune system, which normally fights germs and other foreign substances in the body.

BoTox and Wrinkle Relief

One of the drugs in the fight against wrinkles is called BoTox. BoTox, short for Botulism Toxin type A, is a byproduct produced by the bacterium *Clostridium botulinum*. In food, the bacterium causes a potentially fatal type of food poisoning known as botulism. To remove wrinkles, a small amount of BoTox is injected into the muscles under the wrinkled skin. The BoTox temporarily paralyzes the muscles and restricts their movement. The result, after 3 to 5 days, is that the wrinkles temporarily disappear. This is not a permanent treatment—it must be repeated every 3 months.

Poison ivy plant (*Rhus radicanus*). Its green leaves turn red in the fall.
© C. Allan Morgan, Peter Arnold, Inc.

Rash Thoughts

These are the medical terms for some common skin spots and bumps:

- **Comedo** (KOM-ee-do): a blackhead, whitehead, or pimple. Example: acne.

- **Macule** (MAK-yool): a small, flat, colored spot. Example: freckles.

- **Papule** (PAP-yool): a small, hard bump. Example: warts.

- **Plaque** (PLAK): a large, raised patch of skin. Example: psoriasis.

- **Pustule** (PUS-tyool): a pimple filled with pus. Example: acne.

- **Wheal** (WEEL): a short-lasting, swollen bump. Example: hives.

- **Ringworm:** a skin infection caused by a fungus (not a worm). Ringworm is marked by red, itchy, ring-shaped patches that may flake or blister. It commonly affects the feet, scalp, trunk, nails, and groin.

- **Rosacea (ro-ZAY-she-a):** a skin disease that causes redness and swelling on the face that may gradually spread to the cheeks and chin. Small blood vessels and tiny pimples may appear on or around the red area. Fair-skinned adults, especially women, are most likely to get rosacea.

- **Seborrheic (seb-o-REE-ik) dermatitis:** a common condition that causes red skin and greasy-looking flakes, mainly on the scalp, on the sides of the nose, between the eyebrows, on the eyelids, behind the ears, or on the chest. In babies, this condition is called cradle cap. In adults, it often occurs in people with oily skin and hair, and it may occur in those with acne or psoriasis.

- **Shingles:** a skin eruption caused by the same virus that causes chickenpox. It starts with pain or tingling on one side of the body or face, followed by a red rash with small blisters. After a person has chickenpox, the virus may live on in the nerve cells and come out years later as shingles. An episode of shingles may last weeks.

- **Skin cancer:** the most common of all types of cancer, including various kinds of growths on the skin. About 700,000 Americans get skin cancer each year. The main cause is the sun's harmful rays.

- **Sunburn:** the immediate result of getting too much sun. The skin is injured, just as if it had been burned by heat, and turns red and painful. If the sunburn is severe, blisters may form. The long-term effects of sun damage include wrinkles, certain skin bumps and spots, and skin cancer.

- **Vitiligo (vit-i-LY-go):** a condition that causes white patches of skin due to a loss of pigment in the cells and tissues. It affects 1 or 2 out of every 100 people. Although vitiligo strikes people of all races, it is particularly noticeable in those with dark skin.

- **Warts:** small, hard bumps on the skin or inner linings of the body that are caused by a virus. Most are skin-colored, raised, and rough, but some are dark, flat, or smooth. Warts are common on the fingers, hands, arms, and feet. Some warts occur on the genitals and can be spread during sex.

- **Wrinkles:** a common sign of skin aging. The main cause of wrinkles is getting too much sun over a lifetime. Cigarette smoking also plays a major role.

How Are Skin Conditions Diagnosed?

Nearly everyone has a skin problem at some point in life. Such problems can affect anyone, from newborns to older adults. A doctor can identify many skin problems just by looking closely at the skin. The doctor may also ask about the person's current symptoms, past illnesses, and family history.

In some cases, the doctor may need to do a biopsy (BY-op-see). This involves removing a small bit of skin so that it can be looked at under a microscope. If an infection caused by a fungus is suspected, the doctor may scrape off some skin flakes, which can be checked at a lab for signs of fungus. Another way to check for an infection caused by bacteria or a fungus is with a culture. This involves taking a sample from the site of possible infection and placing it in a nourishing substance called a medium to see what kind of bacteria or fungi grow.

If contact or allergic dermatitis is suspected, the doctor may do patch testing to find out what allergens are to blame. This involves putting tiny amounts of different substances on the skin under a patch. The skin is checked 2 days later to see which substances, if any, caused a reaction.

How Are Skin Conditions Treated?

- **Medicines**: Many medicines used to treat mild skin conditions are sold without a prescription in creams, lotions, gels, pads, and shampoos. Stronger medicines that are put on the skin, taken by mouth, or given in a shot are available only from a doctor or with a doctor's prescription.

- **Surgery**: Doctors use several kinds of surgery to remove or destroy abnormal skin tissue. Excision involves removing a skin growth by cutting. Cryosurgery involves destroying a skin growth by freezing it with an extremely cold liquid such as liquid nitrogen. Electrosurgery involves destroying a skin growth by burning it with electricity. Laser surgery involves destroying skin tissue with a laser—a tool that produces a very narrow and intense beam of light. Surgery is used for such things as warts, skin cancer, moles, and birthmarks.

- **Light therapy**: Doctors treat certain skin problems with lamps that give off ultraviolet rays. In some cases, the person also takes a drug that makes the skin more sensitive to ultraviolet light. This therapy is used for such things as psoriasis and vitiligo.

The Skinny on Skin Care

These tips can help keep a person's skin feeling healthy and looking its best:

- Protect the skin from the sun's harmful rays. Avoid the midday sun, cover up with clothing, and use a good sunscreen with an SPF of 15 or higher.

- Wash the face gently with lukewarm water, a mild soap, and a washcloth or sponge to remove dead cells.

- Reduce dry skin by keeping baths short and using warm water. Use soap only as needed on the face, underarms, genitals, hands, and feet.

- Dry off the skin after bathing by brushing it lightly with the hands or patting it with a towel.

KEYWORDS
*for searching the Internet
and other reference sources*

Breathing disorders

Obstructive sleep apnea

Respiratory system

Snoring

***oxygen** (OK-si-jen) is an odorless, colorless gas essential for the human body. It is taken in through the lungs and delivered to the body by the bloodstream.

Resources

Book Chapter

"Chapter 30. Your Skin." In: David E. Larson, editor. *Mayo Clinic Family Health Book,* 2nd edition. New York: William Morrow, 1996.

Organizations

American Academy of Dermatology, P.O. Box 681069, Schaumburg, IL 60168-1069, (888) 462-DERM. A group of doctors who treat skin diseases.
http://www.aad.org

American Society for Dermatologic Surgery, 930 N. Meacham Road, Schaumburg, IL 60173, (800) 441-2737. A group of doctors who do surgery on the skin.
http://www.asds-net.org

National Institute of Arthritis and Musculoskeletal and Skin Diseases, 1 AMS Circle, Bethesda, MD 20892-3675, (301) 495-4484. A federal agency that studies skin diseases.
http://www.nih.gov/niams

Sleep Apnea

Sleep apnea (AP-nee-a) is a disorder in which a person temporarily stops breathing while sleeping.

Will He Snooze or Snore?

James loved his grandfather, but he was dreading this year's visit. When James shared his room with Grandpa last year, he did not sleep all week. Sometimes the snoring would stop, but then James had to hop out of bed to make sure his grandfather was breathing. Each time, Grandpa started breathing again after about 10 seconds, but he would choke and gasp for air before starting to snore again. In the morning, he had no memory of the night's noisy events.

When Grandpa arrived, the first thing he told James was that he would be a better roommate this year. His snoring had been caused by sleep apnea, and his doctor had given him a device to wear in his nose at night to make it easier for him to breathe.

What Is Sleep Apnea?

While sleeping, a person with sleep apnea stops breathing briefly, usually for about 10 seconds at a time. This can happen hundreds of times a night. The result is that the body does not get enough oxygen* or a restful night's sleep. People with sleep apnea often are very tired during the day, have trouble concentrating, and may feel anxious and have difficulty falling asleep at night. Sometimes, they wake up in a panic, because they think they are choking, and many wake up with headaches and are depressed and moody.

Obstructive sleep apnea (OSA) is the most common type of sleep apnea. It occurs when something in the throat, such as the tongue or tonsils*, blocks the airway. Central sleep apnea occurs when the brain temporarily "forgets" to tell the body to breathe. Mixed apnea is a combination of OSA and central apnea.

People of all ages have sleep apnea, but it is most common in older people. OSA occurs most often in men over 50, and many people with OSA are overweight. People with sleep apnea often do not know that they have it. Family members, however, are well aware of the problem, because the most common symptom is loud snoring.

Living with Sleep Apnea

In some people, sleep apnea is just an annoying problem; in others, it can lead to heart problems and stroke*. To determine if someone has sleep apnea, doctors monitor the person while he or she sleeps. Sometimes, this is done at sleep clinics, which are special places where researchers measure people's brain waves, heart rate, eye movement, body muscle tone, breathing, snoring, and blood oxygen levels while they sleep.

People with sleep apnea should not drink alcohol or take sleeping pills before bed, and they should try to lose weight if they are too heavy. For many people, sleeping on their sides eliminates, or at least lessens, snoring. Various prescription drugs relieve apnea in some people. Special devices worn in the nose or mouth can keep the airways clear as well. In some cases, surgery to remove tissues that block the airway (such as tonsils and adenoids) can be performed.

Resources

SleepNet provides information and support for people with sleep apnea at its website.
http://www.sleepnet.com

The Apnea Patient's News, Education, and Awareness Network (APNEA Net) provides information and support for people with sleep apnea at its website.
http://www.apneanet.org

Snoring

One of the symptoms of sleep apnea is snoring. But snoring can have other causes, including drinking alcohol, taking sedative medication, chronic nasal congestion, or obstruction caused by enlarged adenoids (AD-e-noidz) and tonsils.

The most common cause of snoring is not known—some people just snore. Snoring is a symptom of sleep apnea only if the snoring is punctuated by extended quiet periods before snoring resumes.

* **tonsils** (TON-silz) are paired clusters of lymphoid tissues in the throat.

* **stroke** is a blocked or ruptured blood vessel within the brain, which deprives some brain cells of oxygen and thereby kills or damages these cells. Also called apoplexy (AP-o-plek-see).

▶ See also
Insomnia
Obesity
Sleep Disorders

Researchers use electroencephalograms (EEGs) and positron emission tomography (PET scans) to study sleep disorders. These PET scans show various stages of sleep and wakefulness. When awake (left), the brain shows active areas in red and yellow, with inactive areas in blue. During normal sleep (center), the brain is less active, and most areas show as blue. During deep sleep and non-REM sleep (right), the brain is active but not as active as during REM sleep (not shown) or wakefulness. © *Hank Morgan, Science Source/Photo Researchers, Inc.*

▼

Sleep Disorders

A sleep disorder is just what its name implies: something abnormal about the way a person is sleeping. It might be that he or she cannot get enough sleep, as is the case in insomnia (in-SOM-nee-a). In hypersomnia (HY-per-SOM-nee-a), the individual sleeps too much. In still other kinds of sleep disorders, events such as night terrors may interfere with sleep.

Why Are Sleep Disorders Important?

When people do not get a normal refreshing sleep, they are not at their best. They may be impatient or careless, or they may show poor judgment in the things they do. They also may be irritable with family and friends. Sleeplessness can cause serious accidents, as when someone "nods off" while driving a car or operating machinery.

An estimated 30 million to 40 million Americans have serious sleep problems that can be damaging to their health. In the case of insomnia alone, estimates of the cost in terms of lost productivity reach many billions of dollars.

In order to understand sleep disorders, it is necessary to understand something about sleep itself and the wide range of normal variations in the way people sleep.

What Is Normal Sleep?

On average, about one-third of a person's life is spent sleeping. However, the amount and timing of sleep vary considerably in different people, based on their age and lifestyle. Newborn infants may sleep up to 20 hours a day. Young and middle-aged adults sleep about 8 hours on average. Elderly people tend to get less sleep at night but may take naps during the day.

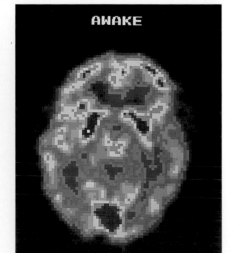

AWAKE

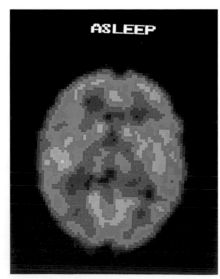

ASLEEP

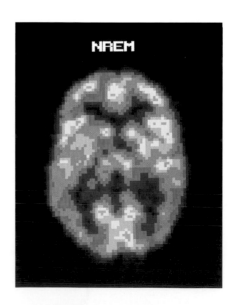

NREM

The timing of sleep often is determined by such factors as work schedules, but it is affected by lifestyle as well. Some individuals seem to be morning people, or "early birds," by nature, whereas others are "night owls," preferring to stay up late.

What Are the Types and the Stages of Sleep?

Scientists at sleep laboratories have discovered that there are two distinct types of sleep. One is called rapid eye movement, or REM, sleep, because the eyes can be seen moving rapidly beneath the closed eyelids. Dreaming takes place during REM sleep, and the brain waves of someone in REM sleep look much like those of someone who is awake when the waves are measured on an electroencephalogram (ee-LEK-tro-en-SEF-a-lo-gram), or EEG.

The other type is non-REM sleep. It consists of four stages in which the brain waves progressively become deeper and slower but then speed up again until the REM stage occurs. This cycle normally is repeated with some variation at approximately 90-minute intervals, with REM sleep usually taking up about 25 percent of the total.

Studies conducted at sleep laboratories have contributed greatly to the diagnosis and treatment of sleep problems. The following are some of the more common sleep disorders.

Insomnia   Insomnia is a general term for trouble sleeping ("somnia" comes from the Latin *somnus,* which means sleep). The disorder is very common, as can be inferred from the fact that sleeping pills are among the most widely used of all medications. People with insomnia may have difficulty falling asleep, or they may wake up too early in the morning. Some wake up frequently during the night and then find it hard to go back to sleep.

Because people need different amounts of sleep, insomnia is not defined by hours of sleep. Insomnia is classified according to how long it lasts. Transient, or short-term, insomnia lasts from one night to a few weeks. Causes may include stress, excitement, or a change in surroundings. Chronic* insomnia, which occurs almost every night for a month or more, is a complex disorder with multiple causes.

Sleep apnea   A person with sleep apnea (AP-nee-a) stops breathing intermittently while asleep, for periods of about 10 seconds or more. The most common and severe type is obstructive sleep apnea. In this disorder, the muscles at the back of the throat relax and sag during sleep, until they obstruct the airway. The pressure to breathe builds up until the sleeper gasps for air. These episodes may occur hundreds of times a night and are accompanied by wakings so brief that they usually are not remembered. People with sleep apnea typically complain of being very tired during the day. Severe sleep apnea can induce high blood pressure and increase the risk of stroke*, heart attack, and even heart failure.

Narcolepsy   Narcolepsy (NAR-ko-lep-see), like sleep apnea, involves excessive daytime sleepiness. In narcolepsy, however, the person cannot resist falling asleep. Sleep attacks crop up at odd and inappropriate times,

* **chronic** (KRON-ik) means continuing for a long period of time.

* **stroke** is a blocked or ruptured blood vessel within the brain, which deprives some brain cells of oxygen and thereby kills or damages these cells. Also called apoplexy (AP-o-plek-see).

such as while eating or talking to someone. Another symptom is cataplexy (KAT-a-plek-see), a sudden attack of muscular weakness that can make the person go limp and fall. Some people with narcolepsy also experience frightening hallucinations* or sleep paralysis*, an inability to move or speak, while falling asleep or waking up. Research has shown that during a sleep attack, the REM stage of sleep intrudes suddenly into the waking state. Narcolepsy is a lifelong condition of unknown cause. Narcoplesy does run in families. Sometimes socially embarrassing or inconvenient, this disorder can also be severely disabling and cause injury.

Hypersomnia   People with hypersomnia may sleep excessively during the day or longer than normal at night. Drowsiness or sleep periods last longer than with narcolepsy. Psychological depression* often is the main cause. A rare type of hypersomnia called Kleine-Levin syndrome* is characterized by periods of overeating as well as oversleeping. It occurs most often in teenage boys.

Jet lag   When an air traveler crosses several time zones, jet lag occurs. The body's internal "clock" then is desynchronized (or out of sync) with local time. Temporarily, people with jet lag may find it difficult to stay awake during the day or be unable to sleep at night.

Nightmares   Almost everyone has nightmares occasionally. These unpleasant, vivid dreams occur during REM sleep, usually in the middle or late hours of the night. Upon awakening, the dreamer often remembers the nightmare clearly and may feel anxious. Nightmares are especially common in young children. In adults, they may be a side effect of certain drugs or of traumatic events, such as accidents.

* **hallucinations** (ha-loo-si-NAY-shunz) are sensory perceptions without a cause in the outside world.

* **paralysis** (pa-RAL-i-sis) is the loss or impairment of the ability to move some part of the body.

* **depression** (de-PRESH-un) is a mental state characterized by feelings of sadness, despair, and discouragement.

* **syndrome** means a group or pattern of symptoms that occur together.

THE POETS ON SLEEP AND SLEEP DISORDERS

William Shakespeare expressed in poetic terms the value and purpose of sleep when he wrote, "Sleep that knits up the ravell'd sleave of care,/The death of each day's life, sore labour's bath,/Balm of hurt minds, great nature's second course,/Chief nourisher in life's feast" (*Macbeth,* Act II, Scene 2).

In modern times, the humorous poet Ogden Nash, who delighted in creating whimsical rhymes, showed familiarity with sleep problems in this verse: "Sleep is perverse as human nature,/Sleep is as perverse as a legislature,/Sleep is as forward as hives or goiters,/And where it is least desired, it loiters" (*The Face Is Familiar. Read This Vibrant Exposé*).

Night terrors and sleepwalking   A night terror is quite different from a nightmare. It occurs in children during deep non-REM sleep, usually an hour or two after going to bed. During an episode, they may sit up in bed shrieking and thrashing about with their eyes wide open. Typically, the next day they remember nothing of the event. Night terrors occur chiefly in preschool children. Although frightening, they generally are harmless and are soon outgrown.

Sleepwalking also occurs during non-REM sleep. It was once believed to be the acting out of dreams, but this is not the case. It takes place most commonly in children. The sleepwalker wanders about aimlessly, appearing dazed and uncoordinated, and remembers nothing of the episode afterward.

How Do Doctors Diagnose and Treat Sleep Disorders?

Most sleep disorders can be treated successfully if diagnosed properly. Anyone who sleeps poorly for more than a month or has daytime sleepiness that interferes with normal activities may wish to consult a doctor or be referred to a specialist in sleep disorders.

At a sleep clinic, patients first are asked questions about their medical history and sleep history. A polysomnogram (pol-ee-SOM-no-gram) is sometimes used to measure brain waves, muscle activity, breathing, and other body functions during sleep.

Many sleep disorders, such as jet lag, short-term insomnia, and most nightmares, do not need treatment. Some others, such as night terrors, are outgrown.

Chronic insomnia often is treated successfully with behavior therapy, which involves various relaxation techniques and reconditioning to change poor sleeping habits. Sleeping pills may be used temporarily, but their long-term use is controversial because of unwanted side effects.

Obstructive sleep apnea often is treated with dental appliances or a device known as CPAP (continuous positive airway pressure) to keep the airway open. Operations sometimes are performed to treat severe obstructive sleep apnea.

Hypersomnia due to depression is often helped by psychotherapy*.

There is no cure for narcolepsy, but medications can help control or ease symptoms.

Guidelines for Prevention

Most sleep disorders can be prevented or minimized by making a few changes in one's lifestyle. The following are some simple guidelines:

- Avoid excessive amounts of caffeine or alcoholic beverages, especially soon before bedtime. The same goes for smoking cigarettes. Avoid frequently disrupted sleep-wake schedules.

- Avoid excessive napping in the afternoon or evening.

- Exercise regularly, but not just before retiring.

Melatonin

Some over-the-counter sleep aids contain melatonin (mel-a-TO-nin). Melatonin is a hormone secreted during darkness by the pineal (PIN-e-al) gland, a small structure located over the brain stem*.

Melatonin appears to be part of the system that regulates our sleep-wake cycles. Some research studies have shown that a small dose of melatonin at night helps make falling asleep easier, and that melatonin may be beneficial to travelers who have jet lag.

Melatonin is available for sale without a prescription, but the U.S. Food and Drug Administration does not regulate its production or sale. Studies still are being conducted to determine whether melatonin is safe for use.

* **brain stem** is the part of the brain that connects to the spinal cord. The brain stem controls the basic functions of life, such as breathing and blood pressure.

* **psychotherapy** (SY-ko-THER-a-pee) is the treatment of mental and behavioral disorders by support and insight to encourage healthy behavior patterns and personality growth.

Did You Know?

- Our eyes move when we dream much as they do when we are awake.

- A person who lived to be 70 would spend about 6 years dreaming.

- In one sleep disorder, apnea, people can stop breathing hundreds of times each night.

- In another, narcolepsy, someone can fall asleep while having a conversation.

- Night terrors are different from nightmares.

- People who sleepwalk are not acting out their dreams.

▶ See also

Depressive Disorders

Insomnia

Jet Lag

Sleep Apnea

**Sudden Infant Death
Syndrome (SIDS)**

KEYWORDS
for searching the Internet
and other reference sources

Skeletal disorders

Spine

Resources

Book

Remmes, Ann, and Roxanne Nelson. *If You Think You Have a Sleep Disorder.* New York: Dell Publishing Co., 1998.

Organizations

The National Heart, Lung, and Blood Institute (NHLBI), part of the U.S. National Institutes of Health (NIH), posts information about insomnia on its website.
http://www.nhlbi.nih.gov/health/public/sleep/insomnia.htm

The National Institute of Neurological Disorders and Stroke (NINDS), part of the U.S. National Institutes of Health (NIH), posts information about sleeping disorders on its website.
http://www.ninds.nih.gov/patients/Disorder/SLEEP/brain-basics-sleep.htm

The National Sleep Foundation posts a fact sheet, *The Nature of Sleep,* on its website.
http://www.sleepfoundation.org/publications/nos.html

Center for Narcolepsy Research (CNR), College of Nursing, The University of Illinois at Chicago, 845 South Damen Avenue, Room 215, Chicago, IL 60612-7350. CNR posts information about narcolepsy on its website.
Telephone 312-996-5176
http://www.uic.edu/depts/cnr

The Nemours Foundation posts a fact sheet, *Coping with Night Terrors,* on its website.
http://kidshealth.org/parent/behavior/nghtter.html

Slipped Disk

Slipped disk is a condition in which a disk in the spinal column becomes displaced from its normal position in the spine and presses on the spinal nerves, causing pain and sometimes muscle weakness.

What Is a Slipped Disk?

The spine is made up of bones called vertebrae (VUR-te-bray) that protect the delicate spinal cord. These vertebrae are separated from each other and cushioned by disks. The disks contain a soft inner layer and a tough outer layer. If the outer layer tears, the soft inner layer can push out and put pressure on the spinal nerves. This can cause severe pain as well as muscular weakness. Slipped disks are also called "herniated," "protruded," and "bulging."

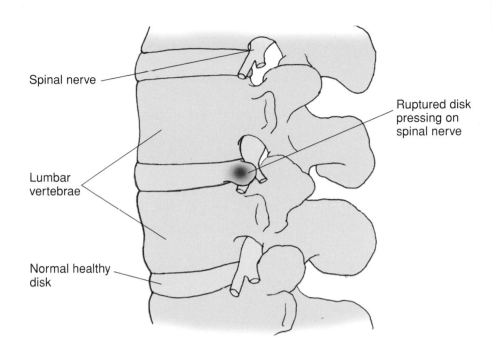

Spinal nerve

Ruptured disk pressing on spinal nerve

Lumbar vertebrae

Normal healthy disk

Healthy disk between vertebrae, compared to slipped disk pressing on spinal nerve.

Most slipped disks occur in the lower back. However, slipped disks can occur in any part of the spine, including the neck.

What Causes Slipped Disks?

In most cases, the condition develops gradually over a number of years. A person may be totally unaware that anything is wrong, until the disk begins to cause pain. There are a small number of cases of slipped disk that occur to people who have made a sudden difficult movement, such as lifting a heavy object or making a sudden awkward movement. Slipped disks can also be the result of normal wear and tear on the disks due to aging.

How Common Is Slipped Disk?

Slipped disk is a fairly common disorder that happens mainly to people between the ages of 30 and 40. However, it can occur in younger people and even in children. After the age of 40, disks become more stable because extra tissue forms around them. Between the ages of 30 to 40, disks tend to lose fluid and become less resistant to pressures put on them. Slipped disk is more common in men than in women. People of either sex, however, who sit for long periods of time are more susceptible to the condition.

How Is Slipped Disk Diagnosed?

A person suffering from severe, sudden back pain should be evaluated by a physician to determine if he or she has a slipped disk, particularly if there is muscular weakness or pain and numbness in the legs or feet. The doctor administers nerve-reflex and muscle-strength tests after taking a personal history of the patient.

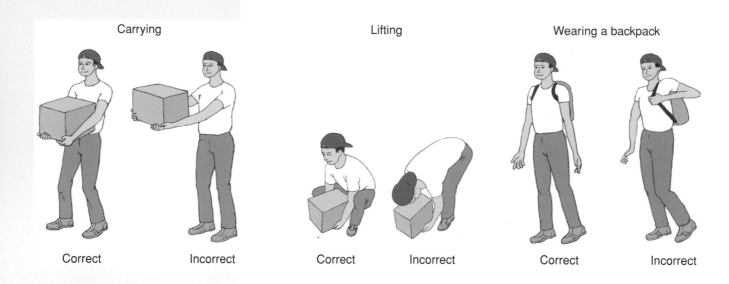

Carrying

Correct   Incorrect

Lifting

Correct   Incorrect

Wearing a backpack

Correct   Incorrect

▲

Correct versus incorrect posture: carrying loads, lifting, wearing backpack

▶ *See also*

Sciatica

KEYWORDS
*for searching the Internet
and other reference sources*

Infectious disease

Viral infection

Among the tests used to locate and confirm a diagnosis, x-rays and other imaging tests may be performed. Another test, an electromyogram (e-LEK-tro-MY-o-gram) can measure the amount of electrical activity in the muscles and help determine how much muscle or nerve damage the patient has.

What Is the Treatment for Slipped Disk?

Total bed rest used to be prescribed for 2 weeks. Doctors now believe that this much bed rest does not help, and patients may be told to stay in bed 2 to 3 days. Medications are given to help relax muscle spasms and to relieve pain. After their initial symptoms have improved, patients are given certain exercises to strengthen the muscles of the back and abdomen and they are told to avoid twisting the spine. Lifting should be done by bending the knees first and keeping the spine upright. Most patients recover within 3 months.

However, if these treatments are not successful, surgery may be necessary. Disk surgery involves removing a part of the disk that has slipped against a nerve. Exercise, weight management, and lifestyle changes are recommended following surgery to avoid a recurrence of the injury.

Smallpox

Smallpox is a highly infectious and often fatal viral disease that leaves permanent pits in the skin. Before smallpox was wiped out, it killed, disfigured, and blinded millions of people.

A Different Kind of War

Beginning in 1966, the World Health Organization declared war against an enemy that throughout history had caused governments to fall and

EDWARD JENNER

E dward Jenner was born in England in 1749. He worked as a country doctor. In Europe, it was believed that milkmaids who developed cowpox (a disease that affects the udders of cows but is harmless to humans) did not get smallpox. To test this belief, in 1796 Jenner began inoculating (i-NOK-yoo-layt-ing) people with cowpox virus. In an experiment that would not be permitted today because it would be considered too dangerous, he later injected these same people with smallpox virus. They remained disease-free. Jenner's experiment with cowpox proved the value of vaccination and led to its widespread use. Modern immunology, that is, the study of how organisms fight infection, began with Jenner.

wiped out entire populations. The allies in this battle were mostly ordinary people in villages and towns, and their main weapon was a vaccine. Ten years later, they achieved one of the finest victories in the history of medicine: the global destruction of smallpox. The last known outbreak of the disease, which killed 2 million people in 1967, was in Somalia in 1977. In 1980, the World Health Assembly declared the world free of smallpox. Today people have nothing to fear from this disease.

What Is Smallpox?

Smallpox is an infection caused by the variola virus. The virus was spread when one person breathed in droplets from the air that an infected person had breathed out, for instance by sneezing or coughing. It could also be spread by simply touching someone with the disease. Once inside the

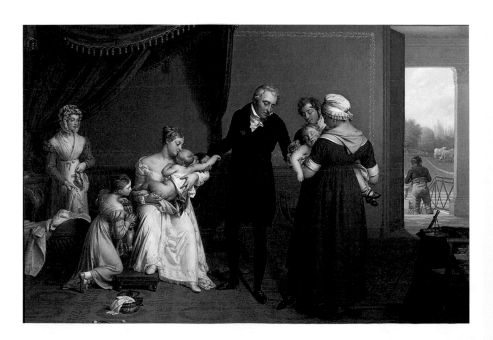

◀

This painting by Constant Desbordes shows a doctor (Dr. Alibert) performing a smallpox vaccination on an infant in the year 1800. The doctor scratched the skin with cowpox, which conferred immunity against smallpox. *Jean-Loup Charmet/Science Photo Library/Photo Researchers, Inc.*

Should the Smallpox Virus Be Destroyed?

As of 1999, the smallpox virus officially remained only in two high-security laboratories in Atlanta and Moscow. These "stocks" of the virus were kept because they have value for scientific research. But some people argue that they should be destroyed because the damage the virus would cause if it were ever released would pose too great a risk. The World Health Organization fixed the date of June 30, 1999, to destroy the remaining stocks of smallpox, but then changed its mind because of the strong debate in the scientific community. Scientists argue that a future smallpox epidemic could occur, and without these stored viruses, newer vaccines and antiviral drugs could not be made. They say that stored vaccines are old and deteriorating. Also, the old vaccine is a live virus that could not be given to people who have impaired immune systems or who have had organ transplants. The virus itself might be needed to develop effective vaccines for these people.

body, the virus multiplies and spreads throughout the bloodstream, invading the various tissues of the body. It destroys the cells of the skin, and these dying cells form blisters. The eyes and internal organs such as the liver and spleen are also affected by the virus.

What Causes Smallpox?

Social factors played a major role in the transmission of smallpox. Because it spread by face-to-face contact with another person, it thrived in the crowded conditions of poverty. Smallpox is highly infectious, but it is not as contagious as measles or the flu. If the virus ran out of humans to infect, it could not spread. However, the lesions that appeared on the skin as the disease progressed were infectious and could contaminate nonliving objects such as clothes or blankets for long periods. Children, the elderly, and people who were sick from other diseases would catch smallpox more easily, but the virus could infect anyone.

What Are the Symptoms of Smallpox?

Smallpox would begin very suddenly, and in the beginning it was like a bad case of the flu. After a few days, the flu-like symptoms went away, and the skin broke out in bumps. At first the bumps were solid, but soon they became filled with liquid, like blisters, and then with pus. Finally, after about 2 weeks, the blisters dried up and formed scabs. When the scabs fell off, they left permanent pits in the skin, most often on the face. Many people who developed this form of smallpox recovered. However, in severe cases, where a high fever and bleeding rash were present, a person might have died in a few days.

How Did Doctors Diagnose Smallpox?

Before smallpox was wiped out, it was easy to tell whether people had the disease simply by their appearance. Sometimes, the initial fever might have been mistaken for the flu. Or the rash might have been confused

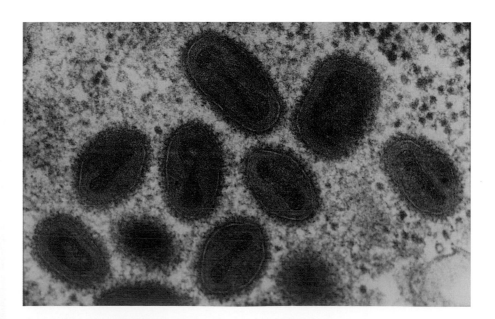

The remaining stock of smallpox virus is kept in a secure vault. © *Hans Gelderblom/Visuals Unlimited*

with chickenpox, which is a much less serious disease. When it was necessary to confirm the diagnosis, fluid taken from the lesions could be examined using special techniques.

How Was Smallpox Treated?

In the past, treatment for smallpox was aimed at making patients comfortable and limiting the spread of the disease. If possible, patients were separated from other people, and the area around them and the things they touched were kept very clean to prevent further infection.

Vaccination Prevents Smallpox

Hundreds of years ago, in Asia, it was observed that people who survived smallpox never got it again. This observation led to a practice later called variolation (var-ee-o-LAY-shun), which involved, for example, rubbing pus from a smallpox lesion into small scratches or cuts in the skin of healthy people in the hope of protecting them. Although these people still developed smallpox, it was often a mild form.

Variolation was unknown in Europe and North America until the 1700s. In 1796, Edward Jenner showed that variolation using cowpox instead of smallpox could protect a person completely from the disease, sparing the person from even a minor case of smallpox. Jenner's vaccine (from the Latin word for "cow") made it possible to control smallpox in many countries. But it was only in 1980 that enough people around the world had been vaccinated to stop the disease forever.

In the past, children were routinely immunized against smallpox before their first birthday. But now that smallpox has been wiped out, vaccination is no longer necessary.

What Are Viruses?

Viruses are organisms that are smaller than cells, so tiny that they can be seen only with a special kind of microscope. To multiply and cause disease, viruses need the help of a living cell. Although viral particles may be present in large numbers, some viruses can remain in the body for a long time, even many years, before people begin to feel sick. The AIDS (acquired immune deficiency syndrome) virus is a good example of this kind of virus. Other viruses, like influenza or smallpox, make people ill very quickly.

Resources

Books

Giblion, James Cross, and David Frampton. *When Plague Strikes: The Black Death, Smallpox, AIDS.* New York: HarperCollins, 1995.

Goodfield, June. *Quest for the Killers.* Boston: Birkhauser, 1985, pp. 191–244.

McNeill, William H. *Plagues and Peoples.* Garden City, NY: Anchor Books, 1989.

Article

Henderson, David A. The Eradication of Smallpox. *Scientific American,* 1976, Vol. 235, pp. 25–33.

Tutorial

"A Dose of the Pox," a self-teaching guide about smallpox and Edward Jenner's vaccine.
http://www-micro.msb.le.ac.uk/Tutorials/Pox/Pox1.html

Organizations

World Health Organization (WHO), Avenue Appia 20, 1211 Geneva 27, Switzerland. The WHO led the campaign to eradicate smallpox. Their Web site provides information about public health around the world.
http://www.who.org

Centers for Disease Control and Prevention (CDC), 1600 Clifton Road, N.E., Atlanta, GA 30333. The United States government authority for information about infectious and other diseases.
http://www.cdc.gov

Smoking *See* Tobacco-Related Diseases

Snake Bites *See* Bites and Stings

Spastic Colon *See* Irritable Bowel Syndrome

Speech Disorders

A speech disorder is a condition that interferes with a person's ability to speak clearly and understandably. It may be caused by developmental delays, hearing problems, accidents, strokes, or defects in any of the organs or muscles involved in producing speech or in any of the areas of the brain that control speech.

KEYWORDS
for searching the Internet
and other reference sources

American Sign Language

Aphasia

Articulation

Augmentative communication devices

Broca's area

Communication disorders

Neurology

Stuttering

Wernicke's area

How Does Speech Develop?

Speech and language develop most intensively during the first three years of life. When babies are born, they can make sounds by pushing air out of the lungs and through the vocal cords in the throat. The air vibrates these vocal cords, located in the larynx (LAR-inks) or voice box, creating sound.

Newborns learn that a cry will bring food, comfort, and companionship, and they begin to recognize certain sounds. As the jaw, lips, tongue, throat and brain develop over the first nine months of life, infants learn how to use the voice to mimic simple controlled sounds, such as "ba ba" or "da da." During this time, they learn to regulate the action of muscles in the face, mouth, neck, chest, and abdomen to produce speech-like sounds. At first, these sounds are filled with nonsense syllables. Eventually, children begin to use words that others can understand. The responses they get encourage them to speak more and more. With practice, words become more understandable.

During the preschool years, children increase their mastery of speech sounds, word and sentence formation, word and sentence understanding, the tone and rhythm of speech, and effective use of language.

What Can Go Wrong?

Speech disorders arise from many different conditions and have a wide range of causes. Two main parts of the brain are involved in producing and understanding speech: Broca's area and Wernicke's area. Broca's area coordinates the muscles of the lips, tongue, jaw, and vocal cords to produce understandable speech. Wernicke's area controls the comprehension, or understanding, of others' speech. Damage to these or other portions of the brain—or to the nerve connections to the organs that make speech (tongue, mouth, chest, and so forth)—can result in disordered speech.

Stroke, trauma, or infection may be the root cause of these disruptions. Severe mental retardation often has a negative impact on speech development. In some cases, anatomy plays a role in speech disorders, for example cleft palate, cleft lip, hearing problems, and damage to the larynx all can interfere with speech.

Speech disorders are fairly common in children. Many children show delays in developing speech, a condition that frequently is outgrown. Often the cause of a child's speech disorder is never known.

When adults develop a speech disorder after years of speaking normally, it usually is easier to locate the cause. For instance, a stroke, head injury, brain tumor, or dementia* may involve damage to the areas of the brain that affect speech or speech understanding. In other cases, an accident, a surgical procedure, or a viral infection can cause damage to the nerves that control the functions of the larynx.

> *__dementia__ (de-MEN-sha) is a general loss of intellectual abilities involving impairment of memory, judgment, and abstract thinking, and often changes in personality.

Articulatory Disorders

Articulatory (ar-TIK-yoo-la-tor-ee) disorders interfere with the process whereby the muscles of the mouth, tongue, jaw, throat, and diaphragm work together to produce clear, understandable sounds. These problems typically begin in childhood and can persist into adulthood. They also may be called fluency disorders.

It is normal for children to have problems with articulation as they are learning to speak. For instance, many children between the ages of 2 and 3 are unable to pronounce the sound "th." Other children in this age group stutter, which means that they repeat sounds occasionally or hesitate between words. Most children outgrow such problems rather quickly. If problems persist, however, they are considered speech disorders.

Lisp   A lisp is a relatively common speech disorder in which a person has trouble pronouncing the sounds of the letters "s" and "z." One of the most well-known lispers is the cat, Sylvester, featured in the Tweety Bird cartoons, whose favorite exclamation is "thuffering thuccotash!"

Lisping can happen for a variety of reasons: an abnormal number or position of teeth; unconscious imitation of other lispers; defects in the structure of the mouth, such as a cleft palate; or hearing loss. Usually lisps can be corrected by working with a speech-language therapist who coaches the person with the lisp to make the sound correctly.

Stuttering Stuttering often begins in early childhood and may persist into adulthood. People who stutter repeat certain speech sounds, or prolong certain sounds, or hesitate before and during speaking. Stuttering often is referred to as a fluency disorder because it disrupts the smooth flow of speech. Over 3 million Americans stutter, and most began stuttering between the ages of 2 and 6.

Stuttering can have social and emotional consequences. People who stutter may be self-conscious about their speech. Some show signs of tension, such as twitching, unusual facial expressions, or eye blinks, when trying to get words out. Experts are not sure what causes stuttering, although some studies show that stuttering has a tendency to run in families, suggesting that it may have a genetic component.

Other cases of stuttering may be neurogenic (noor-o-JEN-ik), meaning that that they are caused by signal problems between the brain and the nerves or muscles that control speech. Stuttering also may result from emotional trauma, stress, or other psychological causes.

Researchers have found that stuttering affects males about four times more often than females. Certain situations, such as speaking before a group

SIGN LANGUAGES

Spoken language is not the only way that people can communicate. Many people who are deaf and/or unable to speak learn to communicate through manual communication or signed language. Currently, there are three signed languages used in the United States.

In the mid-1700s, a French educator working with poor deaf children developed a system for spelling out French words with a manual alphabet, expressing whole concepts with one or two hand signs, and adding emphasis with standardized facial expressions. In 1816, Thomas Gallaudet (1787–1851) brought French Sign Language to the United States. French Sign Language was modified to incorporate English terms, while maintaining French sentence structure, to form what now is American Sign Language (ASL). Gallaudet University in Washington, D.C., is named for Thomas Gallaudet.

Signed Exact English was developed by educators in California who worked with children with hearing loss and deafness. This language takes the same alphabet and hand signs as American Sign Language, but places them into English sentence structure.

Cued Speech, developed in 1966 by the American scientist R. Orin Cornett, uses hand signs to represent sounds, rather than letters or concepts. It is used in conjunction with mouthing of word cues, such as the most prominent vowel in each word.

of people or talking on the telephone, may make stuttering more severe for some, whereas singing or speaking alone often improve fluency.

Most young children outgrow their stuttering, and it is estimated that fewer than 1 percent of American adults stutter. However, children who do not outgrow stuttering by the time they enter elementary school may need speech therapy. Many people have overcome stuttering and gone on to achieve success in careers that require public speaking, acting, and singing.

Brain Disorders

Speech disorders in adults usually are the result of damage to the portions of the brain that control language. Damage may be caused by head injury, brain tumor, or stroke. Adults who have aphasia (a-FAY-zha) not only have trouble speaking, but also have difficulty understanding what others are saying. Dysphasia (dis-FAY-zha) is a condition that causes similar, but less severe, challenges in speaking and understanding. The symptoms of aphasia and dysphasia depend on which area of the brain is affected: Broca's area or Wernicke's area.

Broca's aphasia Broca's aphasia results from damage to the area that coordinates the muscles of the lips, tongue, jaw, and vocal cords that produce understandable speech. People with damage to Broca's area frequently speak in short, meaningful phrases that are produced with great effort, omitting small words such as "is," "and," and "the." People with Broca's aphasia often are aware of their speech difficulties and may become frustrated by their speech problems.

Wernicke's aphasia Wernicke's aphasia results from damage to the area of the brain responsible for understanding speech. These people have trouble understanding others and often are unaware of their own problems. They may speak in long rambling sentences that have no meaning, often adding unnecessary words. They may even create nonsense words.

Global aphasia Global aphasia results from damage to large portions of the language areas of the brain. Individuals with global aphasia have severe communication difficulties and may be extremely limited in their ability to speak or to comprehend language.

How Are Speech Disorders Diagnosed and Treated?

Diagnosis Many adults recognize when they develop a speech difficulty and seek help from doctors and trained speech-language therapists. Parents of children with speech disorders often are the first to call the condition to the attention of health care providers.

Speech-language therapists often make an initial evaluation to help determine what problems exist and the best way to treat them. Because talking and hearing are closely related, children with speech disorders often undergo a hearing evaluation done by an audiologist (aw-dee-OL-o-jist), who is educated in the study of the hearing process and hearing loss. The

Successful Speakers

What do singers Carly Simon and Mel Tillis, television journalist John Stossel, and actors James Earl Jones, Marilyn Monroe, and Bruce Willis have in common? All share the problem of stuttering. Their public successes point to one of the unique features of stuttering: although it is a problem in everyday conversation, often it disappears when someone is singing or delivering memorized lines. Further, people who stutter often can learn strategies for overcoming the problem as they grow older.

James Earl Jones

In his autobiography, actor James Earl Jones describes how he overcame his stuttering problem by reading Shakespeare aloud to himself and then reading to audiences, debating, and acting. Jones has provided the voices for Darth Vader in *Star Wars* and King Mufasa in the animated *Lion King*, and has acted on stage and in numerous films.

John Stossel

As a reporter for the television news magazine *20/20*, John Stossel depends on his voice to make a living. He stuttered as a child and worked hard to hide the condition. Stossel started his career in news as a researcher, but eventually was asked to go on the air. He considered quitting when he found himself stumbling over certain words, but he got help overcoming his stuttering through speech therapy at the Hollins College speech clinic in Roanoke, Virginia. Stossel now is a spokesman for the National Stuttering Association.

audiologist can determine if a person has a hearing loss, the type of loss, and recommend how the person can make the best use of any remaining hearing. When the speech disorder is caused by damage to the nerves or brain, a neurologist may also be involved in the evaluation process.

Treatment People with aphasia often benefit from speech-language therapy, which focuses on helping people make the most of their remaining abilities and learning other methods of communicating. Supplemental methods of communication that assist an individual in speaking are called Augmentative Communication Devices (ACDs). Available ACDs include portable communication computers, personalized language boards, and picture exchange programs. As technology continues to improve and become more portable, communication possibilities for aphasic and dysphasic adults will continue to expand.

Resources

Books

Bobrick, Benson, and Deborah Baker, Eds. *Knotted Tongues: Stuttering in History and the Quest for a Cure.* New York: Kodansha, 1996.

Jezer, Marty. *Stuttering: A Life Bound Up in Words.* New York: Basic Books, 1997.

Organizations

U.S. National Institute on Deafness and Other Communication Disorders, National Institutes of Health, 31 Center Drive, MSC 2320, Bethesda, MD 20892-2320.
Telephone 800-241-1044
http://www.nih.gov/nidcd

American Speech-Language-Hearing Association (ASHA), 10801 Rockville Pike, Rockville, MD 20852.
Telephone 888-321-ASHA
http://www.asha.org

National Aphasia Association, 156 Fifth Avenue, Suite 707, New York, NY 10010.
Telephone 800-922-4622
http://www.aphasia.org

National Stuttering Project, 5100 East LaPalma Avenue, Suite 208, Anaheim Hills, CA 92807.
Telephone 800-364-1677
http://www.nspstutter.org

Stuttering Foundation of America, P.O. Box 11749, 3100 Walnut Grove Road, Number 603, Memphis, TN 38111.
Telephone 800-992-9392
http://www.stuttersfa.org

▶ *See also*

Alzheimer's disease

Brain tumor

Cleft palate

Deafness and Hearing Loss

Infection

Laryngitis

Mental Retardation

Stroke

Trauma

Viral infections

Spina Bifida

Spina bifida (SPY-na BI-fi-da) is a birth defect in which the spinal column does not form properly, leaving a gap or opening in the spine.

KEYWORDS
for searching the Internet and other reference sources

Meningocele

Myelomeningocele

Neural tube defects

Neurology

Orthopedics

Brian Teaches Class

As part of a sixth grade science project, Brian chose to report on a condition called spina bifida. He showed a picture of the ring-shaped bones, or vertebrae, of the spine and demonstrated how the vertebrae protect the spinal cord and anchor muscles. He explained that in people with spina bifida, some of the bony plates that should cover the spine do not close, leaving an unprotected opening at the back of the spine.

No one in Brian's class had ever heard of spina bifida, and they all were surprised to learn that Brian had been born with it. He had a mild form of the condition that was corrected surgically when he was an infant. He ended his presentation by showing the small scar on his lower back.

What Is Spina Bifida?

Spina bifida is a Latin term meaning "split spine" or "open spine." It is the most common of several birth defects called neural tube defects. The neural tube contains the cells that ultimately make the spinal cord and the brain, and it develops during the first three to four weeks of pregnancy (often before a woman even knows that she is pregnant).

Spina bifida results when the sides of the neural tube fail to join together properly, leaving an open area. Often the gap occurs in the lower back at the base of the spine. The spinal cord is part of the central nervous system, which allows a person to move and sense the world around them. Thus, because spina bifida involves the central nervous system, it can cause a range of physical and mental problems.

Prenatal Testing for Spina Bifida

Sometimes parents can find out whether their baby has spina bifida before the baby is born. There are several commonly used tests.

The **maternal-serum alfa-fetoprotein (AFP) test** is performed between the sixteenth and eighteenth weeks of pregnancy. Alfa-fetoprotein is a substance made by the developing fetus. Because the mother and fetus are connected via their circulatory systems, AFP from the fetus gets into the mother's bloodstream. By measuring the amount of AFP in the mother's blood, doctors get an indication of the likelihood that the fetus has certain birth defects. This test does not give a definite answer, and high levels of AFP only suggest that the fetus *might* have spina bifida. If AFP levels are high, the test is repeated. If still high, other tests are needed to confirm that the fetus has spina bifida. Many times, high AFP readings are false alarms and the baby is just fine.

Ultrasound can be used to confirm or rule out spina bifida. An ultrasound works by bouncing sound waves off of internal structures. A

Babies born with spina bifida often have an unprotected opening at the back of the spine.

▼

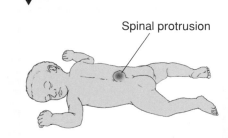

Spinal protrusion

computer converts the returning sound waves into an image of the fetus inside the uterus. Sometimes the defect in the developing spine is visible on the ultrasound image.

Amniocentesis is a procedure performed between the sixteenth and eighteenth week of pregnancy. In this procedure, a needle is passed through the mother's belly into her uterus to collect some of the fluid in which the fetus lives. This fluid, called amniotic fluid, contains cells and chemicals from the fetus. Levels of AFP can be measured to determine whether the fetus has spina bifida.

Is Spina Bifida Always Serious?

Spina bifida is a common birth defect, but it does not always cause serious problems. At birth, the gap may be so slight that it is invisible and harmless. On the other hand, sometimes the spinal cord bulges out through the mal-formed vertebrae and there are serious neurological (nerve) problems.

Spina bifida occulta   Brian was born with spina bifida occulta, the mild-est form of spina bifida. "Occulta" means hidden, and in many cases, the gap in the spine is never detected. Often there is an opening in one or two of the vertebrae but the spinal cord is not affected. A dimple, a birthmark, or a patch of hair may be visible on the skin overlying the site of the gap.

Scientists estimate that about 40 percent of all Americans have this form of spina bifida, but not many ever know they have it. Most people with spina bifida occulta never need treatment. Brian was an exception. He needed surgery because as he grew, the lower end of his spinal cord got caught against his vertebrae, causing him to have problems controlling his bladder. The doctors "unhooked" the spinal cord and closed the gap surgically.

Spina bifida manifesta   Spina bifida manifesta includes two forms of spina bifida that together represent one of the most common disabling birth defects. On average, 1 out of 1,000 babies in the United States is born with either meningocele (me-NING-go-seel) or myelo-meningocele (MY-e-lo-me-NING-go-seel).

Meningocele   Of babies born with spina bifida manifesta, about 4 per-cent have the meningocele form. The meninges (me-NIN-jez) consist of three layers of tough membranes that cover and protect the brain and spinal cord. The brain and spinal cord also are bathed in a fluid called cerebro-spinal fluid (CSF). A meningocele is a CSF-filled sac formed when the meninges balloon through the gap in the vertebrae. It looks like a large blister covered by a thin layer of skin. The sac can range in size from as small as a grape to as large as a grapefruit.

A meningocele is harmless if the sac contains only CSF. However, if nerves are caught in the sac, the affected baby can have problems con-trolling muscles and the bladder. Babies with this form of spina bifida usually have surgery during infancy to put the meninges back inside the vertebrae and to close the gap in the vertebrae.

Myelomeningocele   When most people think of spina bifida, they think of the myelomeningocele form. Approximately 96 percent of babies born with spina bifida manifesta have myelomeningocele, and it is the most serious type of spina bifida. As in meningocele, the meninges bulge out through the gap in the spine, but in myelomeningocele, part of the spinal cord bulges out as well. The sac can be covered with skin or the nerves can actually be exposed.

People with myelomeningocele have a variety of physical and mental problems, the severity of which depends on where the defect in the spine occurs. A gap high up on the spinal column will create more problems than a gap at the lower back. People with this condition usually experience loss of movement and feeling (paralysis) below the abnormal vertebrae. The most severely impaired children cannot walk or control their bowel or bladder. Most babies born with myelomeningocele also have hydrocephalus, which means that they have too much fluid inside and surrounding their brain. If hydrocephalus is not treated, the excess pressure in the skull can cause blindness and permanent brain damage.

Myelomeningocele requires surgery within 24 to 48 hours of birth. Surgeons must close the gap in the vertebrae to protect the spinal cord and prevent infection. They also must treat hydrocephalus, if present. They do this by placing a device called a shunt into the brain to drain excess fluid and relieve pressure on the brain.

What Causes Spina Bifida?

Spina bifida sometimes runs in families, which suggests that genes may play a role in some cases, but 90 to 95 percent of babies with spina bifida are born to families that have never before had a child with the condition. Mothers who have diabetes, a high fever during pregnancy, or who have taken a drug called valproic acid to treat epilepsy seem to have a greater chance of having a baby with spina bifida than mothers without these conditions. There also appears to be a link between a deficiency of folic acid (a B vitamin) in the mother's diet and having a baby with spina bifida. Adding folic acid to the diet significantly reduces the chance that a baby will be born with spina bifida.

Living with Spina Bifida

Most children with spina bifida occulta, and many with meningocele, live normal lives without any impairment. Children born with myelomeningocele, however, often have multiple problems resulting from damage to their spinal cord. Surgery to repair the gap in the vertebrae and to place a shunt in the brain can prevent further damage to the nervous system. However, it cannot reverse the nerve problems that already are present at birth.

The severity of symptoms caused by myelomeningocele varies from child to child. Common problems, however, include the inability to control the bowel and bladder. Catheters*, diapers, and attentive caregivers can help alleviate embarrassment caused by these problems.

Many affected children cannot walk without crutches or leg braces, and many need a wheelchair. In addition, some children have learning problems, particularly with reading and math. For children with these problems, special education classes can help to prepare them for school.

Preventing Spina Bifida: The Role of Folic Acid

Scientists estimate that the incidence of spina bifida can be decreased by as much as 75 percent if all women of child-bearing age consume 0.4 mg of folic acid each day.

Spina bifida has been linked to a deficiency of folic acid during the first weeks of pregnancy. Folic acid is one of the B vitamins and it is essential for proper functioning of the human body. When the body is growing quickly, such as during pregnancy and during fetal development, the body needs more folic acid than usual.

Good sources of folic acid include dark green leafy vegetables (like spinach and broccoli), eggs, and orange juice. In addition, the U.S. Food and Drug Administration requires breads and enriched grains and cereals to have folic acid added to them. Even with folic acid supplements added to common foods, the average American diet does not contain 0.4 mg of folic acid per day. Most multivitamins, however, now contain the recommended dose of folic acid.

* **catheters** (KATH-e-terz) are tubes inserted into parts of the body to allow fluids to flow in and out. Catheters into the bladder through the urethra (the last part of the urinary tract) allow urine to flow into an outside container.

Children with spina bifida often develop sensitivity or an allergy to latex (natural rubber), which is used in such healthcare products as gloves and catheter tubes, probably because they come into contact with latex so often and from such a young age.

Even with the disabilities caused by spina bifida, children with the disease often live well into adulthood. With the help of early and continuing medical, psychological, and educational treatment, children with spina bifida can lead full and productive lives.

Resources

Books

Sandler, Adrian. *Living with Spina Bifida: A Guide for Families and Professionals.* Chapel Hill: University of North Carolina Press, 1997.

Lutkenhoff, Marlene. *Spinabilities: A Young Person's Guide to Spina Bifida.* Bethesda: Woodbine House, 1997.

Organizations

Spina Bifida Association of America, 4590 MacArthur Boulevard, Suite 250, Washington, DC 20007.
Telephone 800-621-3141
http://www.sbaa.org

Association for Spina Bifida and Hydrocephalus, 42 Park Road, Peterborough, PE1 2UQ, England.
Telephone 01733-555988
http://www.asbah.demon.co.uk

March of Dimes Foundation, 1275 Mamaroneck Avenue, White Plains, NY 10605.
Telephone 888-663-4637
http://www.modimes.org/

▶ *See also*
Birth Defects
Hydrocephalus
Incontinence
Paralysis

Stomach Cancer

Stomach cancer, also called gastric cancer, is a disease in which the cells in the stomach divide without control or order and take on an abnormal appearance. These cancerous cells often spread to nearby organs and to other parts of the body.

KEYWORDS
for searching the Internet and other reference sources

Digestive system

Oncology

How Does Stomach Cancer Develop?

The stomach is the sac-like organ located in the upper abdomen, under the ribs, which plays a role in the digestion of food. It connects the esophagus (e-SOF-a-gus), the tube that carries swallowed food, with the small intestine, which absorbs the nutrients needed by the body. When food enters the stomach, the muscles in its wall create a rippling motion that mixes and mashes it. The glands in the lining of the stomach release juices that help to digest the mixture. After a few hours, the food becomes a liquid and moves into the small intestine. This makes it easier for the intestine to absorb the substances that the body needs for energy.

Stomach cancer begins when some of the cells in its lining take on an abnormal appearance and begin to divide without control or order. If left untreated, these cancer cells can grow through the stomach wall, and they can spread to nearby organs, or to nearby lymph nodes. Through the lymphatic system, the cancer cells can spread to distant areas of the body, including the lungs and the ovaries.

Who Gets Stomach Cancer, and Why?

Each year, about 24,000 people in the United States learn that they have cancer of the stomach. Like most other forms of cancer, stomach cancer occurs most frequently in older people, usually aged 55 or older. Fortunately, for reasons that scientists cannot fully explain, the number of people who get this disease has been dropping steadily for the past 60 years.

Stomach cancer is much more common in other countries, especially Japan, Chile, and Iceland. Researchers think the reason may be that people in these countries eat many foods that are preserved by drying, smoking, salting, or pickling. Eating foods preserved in this way may raise someone's risk for developing stomach cancer. People who smoke cigarettes also may be at higher risk of developing stomach cancer.

What Happens When People Have Stomach Cancer?

Symptoms   At first, stomach cancer does not cause any symptoms. And when it does eventually cause symptoms, they often are mistaken for less serious stomach problems, such as indigestion, heartburn, or a virus. Therefore, it is hard to find stomach cancer early, which makes it more difficult to treat. Possible symptoms include:

- indigestion or a burning sensation in the stomach
- discomfort or pain in the abdomen
- nausea and vomiting after meals
- bloating of the stomach after meals
- anemia
- weakness, fatigue, or weight loss
- vomiting blood or passing black, tar-like stools.

Diagnosis   When people report these symptoms to their family doctor, they may be referred to a gastroenterologist (gas-tro-en-ter-OL-o-jist), a doctor who specializes in diagnosing and treating digestive problems. The gastroenterologist may order additional diagnostic tests to figure out what is wrong.

One of the most common procedures is called endoscopy (en-DOS-ko-pee), which involves passing a very thin, lighted tube down the esophagus and into the stomach. This allows doctors to look directly at the inside of the stomach. If an abnormal area is seen, they can remove some tissue through the tube and have it examined under a microscope. This process, called a biopsy (BY-op-see), determines whether or not cancer cells are present.

A person also might have an upper GI series, which is a series of x-rays of the upper gastrointestinal (gas-tro-in-TES-ti-nal) tract, including the esophagus and stomach. These pictures are taken after the person drinks a thick, chalky liquid called barium (BA-ree-um). The barium outlines the stomach on the x-rays, helping doctors locate tumors or other abnormal areas.

The doctor also might want to test for blood in the stool, the solid waste that people produce when they go to the bathroom. This involves placing a small amount of stool on a slide and having it tested in the laboratory. Sometimes, blood in the stool is a sign of stomach cancer or other cancers of the digestive tract.

If cancer is diagnosed, then doctors need to find out whether it has spread to other parts of the body. They often use imaging tests such as CT scans* or ultrasound* to check for this possibility.

*CT scans (CAT scans) are computerized axial tomography (to-MOG-ra-fee), which uses x-rays and computers to view structures inside the body.

*ultrasound is a painless procedure in which sound waves passing through the body create images on a computer screen.

How Is Stomach Cancer Treated?

Because the symptoms associated with stomach cancer seem so minor at first, people rarely report them right away. Therefore, the cancer usually has spread into the stomach wall or even beyond the stomach when it is found. This makes it difficult to cure.

The most common treatment is an operation called gastrectomy (gas-TREK-to-mee), during which surgeons remove part or all of the stomach and some of the surrounding tissue. If all of the stomach needs to be removed, then surgeons connect the esophagus directly to the small intestine. The nearby lymph nodes usually are removed, too.

People with stomach cancer may also be treated with radiation therapy or chemotherapy, either in an attempt to destroy some of the cancer cells or to ease some of their symptoms, such as pain. Radiation therapy focuses high-energy rays on the body to destroy cancer cells and to stop or slow their growth. During chemotherapy, anti-cancer drugs are given by mouth or by injection into a muscle or blood vessel.

Because stomach cancer is so difficult to cure, researchers are looking at new ways to treat this disease. Studies called clinical trials are being conducted to evaluate some of these new treatments in cancer patients. One example is biological therapy, which triggers the body's own immune system to attack and destroy cancer cells.

Living with Stomach Cancer

Because people with stomach cancer often have part or all of the stomach removed, they need time to readjust to eating after the surgery. At first, patients are fed intravenously (in-tra-VEE-nus-lee), through a vein in the hand or arm. Within several days, they usually can start taking in liquids, then soft foods, and then more solid foods. Often they need to follow a special diet until they can adjust to having a smaller stomach or none at all. People with stomach cancer need to work with dietitians and nutritionists to make sure that they are getting the nutrients their bodies need.

Resources

U.S. **National Cancer Institute (NCI)**, Bethesda, MD 20892. NCI posts the fact sheet *What You Need to Know About Stomach Cancer* at its website, along with a glossary, referrals, information about healthy eating for cancer patients, and information about clinical trials. Telephone 800-4-CANCER
http://cancernet.nci.nih.gov/wyntk_pubs/stomach.htm

American Cancer Society (ACS), 1599 Clifton Road N.E., Atlanta, GA 30329-4251. ACS has a *Stomach Cancer Resource Center* at its website, which answers frequently asked questions and posts information about survivorship, prevention, and treatment. Telephone 800-ACS-2345
http://www3.cancer.org/cancerinfo

United Ostomy Association (UOA), 36 Executive Park, Suite 120, Irvine, CA 92612-2405.
Telephone 800-826-0826

▶ *See also*
Cancer
Colorectal Cancer
Pancreatic Cancer
Peptic Ulcer
Tumor

Stomach Ulcer *See* Peptic Ulcer

Strabismus

Strabismus is a condition in which the eyes cross or do not work together normally, which may lead to permanent loss of vision in one eye.

KEYWORDS
for searching the Internet and other reference sources

Amblyopia

Ophthalmology

Optometry

Vision

When people cross their eyes, the world suddenly doubles. Images, like the words on this page, become blurred, and it appears as if there are two of everything. When the eyes function correctly, they work together to focus images and to allow the brain to develop a three-dimensional view of the world. But when the eyes cannot work together, as when people cross their eyes, the brain sees two of everything. The result is double vision.

Fortunately, both eyes work together for most people. But some people have an eye disorder that causes the eyes to fail to line up properly, resulting in blurred or double vision. This condition is called strabismus (stra-BIZ-mus), which comes from a Greek word that means squinting. Often in strabismus, one eye may remain straight and the other eye may turn in, as if the person is crossing one eye.

Why Do People Have Strabismus?

Strabismus usually develops during infancy or early childhood. In most cases, there is no known cause, although sometimes several members of the same family have the disorder. This may mean that in some cases strabismus is inherited, like eye color. Other possible causes include:

- Farsightedness, causing focus difficulties
- Damage to one eye or to the part of the brain that controls the muscles involved in eye movement
- Other disorders that affect the brain, including Down syndrome, cerebral palsy, and hydrocephalus
- Less commonly, vision is blocked by a tumor* or cataract that causes cloudiness in the normally clear lens of the eye

* **tumor** usually refers to an abnormal growth of body tissue that has no physiologic purpose and is not an inflammation. Tumors may or may not be cancerous.

DID ABE LINCOLN HAVE STRABISMUS?

President Abraham Lincoln (1809–1865) is known for many things, from his work as a rail-splitter, to his legendary debates with Stephen A. Douglas, to serving as president of the United States during the Civil War.

Lincoln's physical characteristics caused much discussion. He was unusually tall for his time, standing 6 feet 4 inches. He also was extremely thin for that height and probably weighed about 160 pounds when elected to Congress in 1847.

"He was not a pretty man by any means—nor was he an ugly one," wrote William Herndon. "He was a homely looking man." The assessment goes on and sounds extraordinarily harsh, considering that Herndon was Lincoln's friend, law partner, and biographer.

Historical researchers have speculated that Lincoln had strabismus. In photographs, his eyes appear slightly off center. His right eye was thought to be abnormal, sometimes described by biographers as "wandering." Researchers also believe that Lincoln may have had Marfan syndrome, a rare disorder that causes exceptional height in combination with especially long legs, hands, and feet. Eye trouble is another characteristic of the syndrome. Some of Abraham Lincoln's descendants are known to have had Marfan syndrome, and it is known to be an inherited disorder.

Strabismus affects about 3 to 5 percent of children in the United States. It occurs in boys and girls equally. Fortunately, if it is diagnosed and treated early, there is a good chance of saving or improving vision in the affected eye.

Some adults have strabismus. This may be because they were not treated for it as a child, or because the treatment was not effective. Other adults may develop strabismus when a disorder such as stroke* causes the eyes to cross or not work together normally.

How Do Six Muscles in Each Eye Work as One?

The eyes and the nerves that connect them to the brain work like the two lenses of binoculars. They merge the images seen by each eye into one image. Six muscles are attached to each eye, and they control how the eyeball moves left and right or up and down. To make it possible for the brain to develop a single three-dimensional image, the muscles must work together to focus, just as the two lenses of binoculars must be aligned to focus together.

People with strabismus have trouble with one or more of the muscles in an eye. Instead of working together, one eye is out of step. Sometimes strabismus seems to come and go, depending on how tired the eyes are, and sometimes the eyes remain out of step. There are different forms of strabismus:

- When one eye points inward toward the nose, which makes the person look cross-eyed, the condition is called "esotropia" (es-o-TRO-pe-a).

- When one eye points away from the nose, as if looking to the outside, the condition is called "exotropia" (ek-so-TRO-pe-a) or "walleye."

- When the brain turns off the vision in the turned eye in favor of the vision in the straight eye, the condition is called "strabismic amblyopia" (stra-BIZ-mik am-blee-O-pee-a) or "lazy eye."

Amblyopia does not mean that the eye is lazy. Instead, the brain turns off the image coming from the optic nerve in that eye so the person sees only one clear image of the world instead of having blurred or double vision.

A Little Pirate

Mrs. Apple noticed that the eyes of her baby Chloe often did not work together. She had read in a book how babies sometimes appear cross-eyed or how it seems one eye is looking off in another direction from the other. This can be normal for a very young baby. But when Chloe was about four months old, Mrs. Apple became worried. Chloe's left eye seemed to be looking at her nose when Mrs. Apple moved her face close, and the right eye seemed to be looking straight ahead. Mrs. Apple took the baby to an ophthalmologist* for an eye exam and was told that Chloe likely had strabismus.

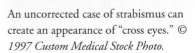

An uncorrected case of strabismus can create an appearance of "cross eyes." © *1997 Custom Medical Stock Photo.*

* **stroke** may occur when a blood vessel bringing oxygen and nutrients to the brain bursts or becomes clogged by a blood clot or other particle. As a result, nerve cells in the affected area and the specific body parts they control do not properly function.

* **ophthalmologist** is a medical doctor who specializes in treating diseases of the eye.

Will Crossed Eyes Become Stuck?

It seems almost everyone has received this warning from a parent or teacher: "If you keep crossing your eyes like that, they could stay that way forever!"

Although the warning may be a way for parents to make children stop silly behavior, it is not medically true. Voluntarily crossing the eyes will not harm them or put them at risk of strabismus.

It is usually a parent who first notices the signs of strabismus when children are infants or preschoolers. The children are too young to complain about double or poor vision. If Mrs. Apple had not taken action because of her worries, the strabismus might have developed into amblyopia, leaving Chloe without vision in the crossed eye. Without treatment, amblyopia may become permanent.

The ophthalmologist recommended that Chloe wear an eye patch over her normal eye. The doctor explained that this could force the weaker eye to develop vision more properly.

How Do Doctors Diagnose Strabismus and Amblyopia?

Diagnosis   Doctors use a variety of methods to diagnose strabismus and amblyopia. Most involve observation of how the child looks at objects, since most children are too young to recognize the letters on a standard eye chart. The doctor will cover one eye and then the other, holding and moving objects, and watching to see if the child squints or tries to cover or close one eye in favor of the other. The doctor also will check the alignment of the eyes by shining a light in both eyes to see if the reflection falls in the same place in the pupils (the black spot in the center of the eye) of both eyes.

Many children do not like to have their eyes covered during these exams. Some are frightened of the equipment that may be held close to their faces. New techniques under development use computers to track eye movements from a distance, sometimes while the child is watching a cartoon.

Treatment   The most common treatment of strabismus involves wearing a patch like Chloe's over the stronger eye. The brain now starts to try to send and receive signals from the weaker eye, and the muscles that control it try to bring the eye back to a normal focus. The same result often is achieved with eye drops that blur the vision in the normal eye to make the other eye work harder. Doctors also may prescribe special eyeglasses for some children with strabismus. Some of these eyeglasses use prisms that change how the image is sent into the eye.

New techniques involve disabling or weakening one or more of the muscles in the eye. This is done to force the other muscles to work harder to bring the affected eye into focus with the normal eye. This can be done surgically by repositioning the eye muscles of one or both eyes. The operations can leave the eyes straight and vision normal, although sometimes the eyes appear straight but people still need eyeglasses to achieve good vision. Sometimes, injections are used to disable one or more eye muscles for a period of time. This may achieve similar results to surgery.

Treatment is most effective when children are young, which is why vision testing and early diagnosis are important. Strabismus and amblyopia do not simply go away, as some people believe. With treatment, children like Chloe can have almost normal vision and no restrictions on activities as they grow up.

Resources

Book

Ophthalmic Disorders Sourcebook, Health Reference Series, Vol. 17. Detroit: Omnigraphics Inc., 1997. Includes reports from government agencies and other groups about various eye disorders.

Organizations

American Academy of Ophthalmology, P.O. Box 67424, San Francisco, CA 94120-7424. The American Academy of Ophthalmology posts a fact sheet at its website about strabismus and amblyopia. Telephone 415-561-8500 http://www.eyenet.org/public/faqs/strabismus_faq.html

American Optometric Association, 243 North Lindbergh Boulevard, St. Louis, MO 63141. The American Optometric Association posts a fact sheet about crossed-eyes and strabismus at its website, which also includes a Teachers' Center and a *Just for Kids!* educational center. http://www.aoanet.org/cvc-crossed-eyes.html

▶ See also
Cataracts
Farsightedness
Marfan Syndrome

Strains and Sprains

Strains and sprains are injuries to the body's soft tissues. Strains are injuries to muscles and/or tendons, which are the cords that connect muscles and bones. Sprains are injuries to ligaments, which are bands of connective tissue that support the joints and connect the bones to each other. Strains and sprains may result from sudden injury or from long-term overuse.

KEYWORDS
for searching the Internet and other reference sources

Orthopedics

Sports medicine

Strains and sprains are injuries to the muscles, tendons, and ligaments.

▼

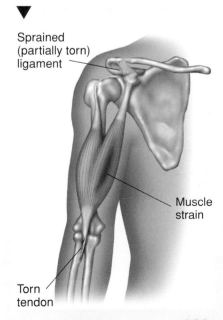

Sprained (partially torn) ligament

Muscle strain

Torn tendon

What Are Strains and Sprains?

Strains and sprains are injuries to the body's soft tissues—its muscles, tendons, and ligaments. They are everyday occurrences for athletes but can happen to anyone as the result of a fall, a twist, or any other sudden blow to the body.

Strains are injuries to muscles or to tendons, which support the bones and connect them to the muscles. Sprains are injuries to ligaments, which are bands of connective tissue that support the joints and connect the bones to each other.

Strains occur most often in the muscles and tendons of the legs and back—hamstring pulls, groin pulls, and sore back muscles are common forms of strain. Sprains most often affect the joints, such as the ankles, knees, and wrists. Both strains and sprains cause pain, swelling, and inflammation*. The injured area also may be discolored if it has been bruised and blood pools underneath the skin.

*__inflammation__ (in-fla-MAY-shun) is the body's reaction to irritation, infection, or injury that often involves swelling, pain, redness, and warmth.

*__edema__ (e-DEE-ma) means swelling in the body's tissues caused by excess fluids.

Bracing with compression bandages or splints can help most sprains heal quickly. © *M. and D. Long/Visuals Unlimited.*

Most people recover from strains and sprains if they see their doctor promptly and follow the doctor's instructions, which often involve a R.I.C.E. protocol: rest, ice, compression, and elevation.

What Are the Different Types of Strains and Sprains?

Doctors usually classify strains and sprains by the degree of damage done to the muscles or ligaments.

First degree A first-degree strain or sprain causes the least amount of damage or stretching of ligaments or muscle fibers. There are no tears in the tissue fibers, pain and swelling are minimal, and range of motion (movement up and down or sideways) usually is not affected to any important degree. There may be some slight disability in using the affected joint, but on the whole, people can resume normal activities after a short recovery period.

Second degree In a second-degree strain or sprain, about 80 percent of the tissue fibers are ruptured. There is more pain, there is edema*, and range of motion is reduced. Unlike first-degree injuries, it may be 2 to 3 weeks before the pain and swelling begin to show real improvement. For athletes who resume their sports activity too soon, there is the possibility that a second-degree injury will turn into a third-degree injury. A third-degree injury takes about 8 to 10 weeks before it begins to show signs of improvement.

Third degree In third-degree injury, there is a 100 percent rupture in all the tissues that surround the joint capsule—-muscles, tendons, and ligaments. A person with a third-degree sprain or strain can no longer use the injured part of the body, and there will be pain and visible bruising. X-rays may show that even though bones have not been broken, there may be chips pulled from the bone called avulsion (a-VUL-shun) fractures. The injury usually will have to be protected for 8 to 10 weeks, and surgery may be necessary to repair damaged joints.

What Is the Treatment for Strains and Sprains?

Doctors who treat strains and sprains use the term "Rice Diets" to describe the steps required for healing:

■ **R: Rest.** How much rest depends on the degree of injury.

■ **I: Ice.** Ice is used to reduce inflammation.

■ **C: Compression.** Bandages and wraps are used to reduce pain and swelling, and to help ruptured small blood vessels heal more quickly.

■ **E: Elevation.** Lifting the injured area above the heart helps keep swelling down and blood from pooling in the area of damage.

■ **D: Drugs.** Doctors may recommend use of aspirin, ibuprofen, or other anti-inflammatory medications during the first few days after the injury.

■ **I: Incision, drainage, and injection.** These procedures sometimes are necessary for third-degree sprains.

■ **E: Exercise.** It is important to learn the proper way to exercise after these injuries.

■ **T: Therapy.** Sometimes physical therapy may be necessary to get the injured part of the body back in use without injuring it again.

■ **S: Surgery.** As with bone fractures, a bad strain or sprain may need surgery to repair damaged tissue.

Can Strains or Sprains Be Prevented?

Many strains and sprains can be avoided. Precautions at home include:

■ Clearing ice away from porches, steps, and sidewalks.

■ Wearing shoes and boots with nonskid soles.

■ Using hand rails on stairways.

■ Using rubber mats in tubs and shower stalls.

■ Using rugs with nonskid backing.

■ Making sure there is adequate lighting for night-time entrances.

■ Keeping a night light or wall light between bedroom and bathroom.

■ Making sure always to keep tools, toys, and other items away from places where people can trip over them.

■ Making sure ladders are steady.

Rules for athletes include starting slowly, stretching frequently, and always remembering to warm up and cool down before and after strenuous exercise.

Resources

U.S. National Institute of Arthritis and Musculoskeletal and Skin Diseases (NIAMS), Building 31, Room 4C05, Bethesda, MD 20892-2350. NIAMS posts information about shoulder problems at its website. Telephone 301-496-8188
http://www.nih.gov/niams/healthinfo/shoulderprobs/shoulderqa.htm

Sports Medicine

Athletes and those who exercise for physical fitness are at risk for strains and sprains. The branch of medicine that specializes in treating these injuries is called "sports medicine."

Doctors who specialize in sports medicine can help athletes improve performance without injuring the body. They also can test athletes for drug use, treat injuries that result from exercise or sports, advise about proper clothing and protective gear, and supervise diet and fluid intake during training and travel to foreign places.

American Academy of Orthopaedic Surgeons (AAOS), 6300 North River Road, Rosemont, IL 60018-4262. AAOS posts *Sprains and Strains* and *Shoulder Pain* patient education fact sheets at its website.
Telephone 800-346-AAOS
http://www.aaos.org

Arthritis Foundation, 1330 West Peachtree Street, Atlanta, GA 30309. The Arthritis Foundation publishes brochures and posts fact sheets about many different kinds of soft tissue injuries at its website.
Telephone 800-283-7800
http://www.arthritis.org

American Physical Therapy Association (APTA), 1111 North Fairfax Street, Alexandria, VA 22314-1488.
Telephone 703-684-2782
http://www.apta.org

▶ *See also*
Broken Bones and Fractures
Carpal Tunnel Syndrome
Repetitive Stress Syndrome
Trauma

Strep Throat

Strep throat, an infection of the throat common in children, is caused by bacteria in the Streptococcus (strep-to-KOK-us) family. Its main symptoms are sore throat and fever. The medical term for strep throat is streptococcal pharyngitis (fa-rin-JY-tis).

KEYWORDS
for searching the Internet and other reference sources

Infectious diseases

Streptococcal pharyngitis

What Are the Symptoms of Strep Throat?

In addition to having a sore throat and fever, people with strep throat feel generally weak and tired. They may also have a runny nose, have a headache, or the lymph nodes* in their neck may become enlarged. In some cases, toxins (poisons) from streptococcal bacteria may lead to a red, sandpapery rash, which is called scarlet fever.

* **lymph nodes** are bean-sized round or oval masses of immune system tissue that filter bodily fluids before they enter the blood-stream, helping to keep out bacteria and other undesirable substances.

How Are Strep Throat Bacteria Transmitted?

Children between the ages of 5 and 15 are most at risk for streptococcal infections, although they can occur in people of any age. If children who have strep throat sneeze or cough in a classroom, playground, or other crowded environment, they can spread the infection to the other people. Moisture droplets from their coughing or sneezing are passed into the air. Other children inhale these germs, and then they too become infected. Within 2 to 4 days they may begin to show symptoms.

Another way the bacteria can be passed along is by hand to hand contact or by touching objects that an infected person has recently handled. That is why doctors tell people to wash their hands often.

How Do *Streptococcus* Bacteria Operate in the Body?

Streptococci (strep-to-KOK-sigh) are round bacteria. They grow like beads on a string. These bacteria are responsible for many different types of diseases. Certain types of *Streptococci* are harmless. They remain in the mouth and throat where they do no damage. If they should enter the bloodstream they usually are killed quickly by the body's natural defense systems.

If the same *Streptococci* reach the heart, however, they may be able to survive there and can later cause heart damage. Bacteria that make it to the urinary system can cause urinary tract infections.

If a streptococcal infection does not go away on its own or respond to treatment, there are a number of possible serious complications. These include:

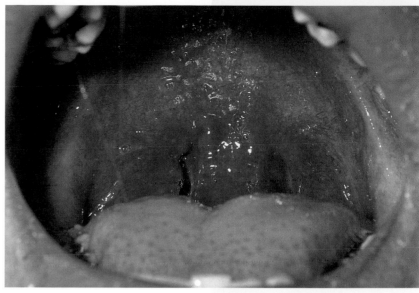

Strep throat causes redness and inflammation. *Dr. P. Marazzi/Science Photo Library, Photo Researchers, Inc.*

- Nephritis (nef-RY-tis), an inflammation of the kidneys

- Rheumatic fever, a condition involving the heart, joints and other parts of the body, which can cause permanent damage to heart valves

- Deeper tissue infections that spread from the original infection

How Is Strep Throat Diagnosed and Treated?

A doctor who suspects strep throat will have to take a throat culture before the diagnosis can be confirmed. This is done by touching a swab to the back of the person's throat to pick up a sample of bacteria. The bacteria can be grown in a laboratory dish overnight and then identified under a microscope. Alternately, "instant" tests exist that can tell almost immediately if strep bacteria were picked up on the swab.

The antibiotic* penicillin (pen-i-SIL-in) is freqently prescribed to treat the infection. If the patient is allergic to penicillin, then another antibiotic is used. Usually the infection will clear up within a week after treatment has begun.

*__antibiotics__ (an-ty-by-OT-iks) are drugs that kill bacteria.

Resources

Organization

The National Institute of Allergy and Infectious Diseases posts information on strep throat on its website.
http://www.niaid.nih.gov/factsheets/strep.htm

▶ See also
Bacterial Infections
Nephritis
Rheumatic Fever
Scarlet Fever

* **hormone** is a chemical that is produced by different glands in the body. A hormone is like the body's ambassador: it is created in one place but is sent through the body to have specific regulatory effects in different places.

Stress-Related Illness

Stress is an intense physical and/or emotional response to a difficult or painful experience. Stressful events can range from taking a test in school to dealing with a loved one's death. Reacting to such events, the body's stress response system can cause a rapid heartbeat, a rise in blood pressure, and other physical changes. Stress-related illnesses are physical or mental problems that sometimes seem to be brought on by or made worse by stress. They can include headaches, stomachaches, sleeplessness, depression, anxiety, and many other conditions.

Stress Is Not All in the Head

Imagine Alicia, the goalie on the traveling soccer team, with the opposing team barreling toward her with the ball in possession. Imagine Eduardo at 7:59 a.m., running for the school bus that leaves at 8:00 a.m. Imagine Maria, whose dog has just been run over by a car. Anyone who has been in situations such as these knows what stress feels like: The pulse quickens, the heart races, breathing becomes heavier, and muscles tense. Some people feel nauseated and start to sweat. Others freeze and feel a sense of dread.

The stress response All these changes in the body happen because stress sets off an alarm in the brain. This alarm triggers the release of hormones*, which trigger the release of oxygen and glucose, which send emergency energy to the brain and muscles. This is called the "fight or flight" response because it prepares the body to fight or run.

The stress hormone response: When the brain perceives stress, the hypothalamus releases corticotropin-releasing factor (CRF) (1), which triggers the release of adrenocorticotropin (ACTH) (2) from the pituitary gland. ACTH (2) travels through the bloodstream and (along with signals from the brain sent through the nervous system) stimulates the adrenal glands to release cortisol and epinephrine into the bloodstream (3). Cortisol and epinephrine (3) help provide energy, oxygen, and stimulation to the heart, the brain, and other muscles and organs (4) to support the body's response to stress.

▶

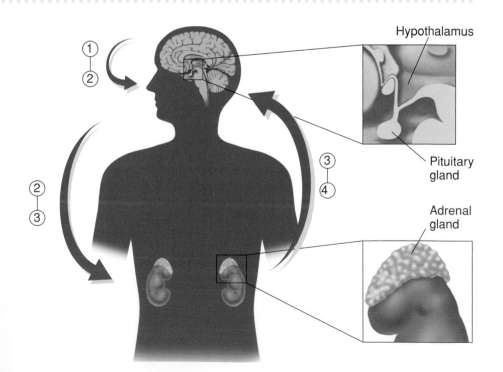

Hypothalamus

Pituitary gland

Adrenal gland

The hypothalamus is a part of the brain that produces hormones. When the stress response begins, the hypothalamus sends a hormone called corticotropin-releasing factor (CRF) to the pituitary gland, which then sends a hormone called adrenocorticotropin (ACTH) through the bloodstream to the adrenal glands. The adrenal glands produce cortisol (in response to ACTH) and epinephrine (in response to signals sent from the brain through the nervous system), which help the body produce emergency energy and support the "fight or flight" response. As long as the brain perceives stress, it continues to produce CRF. The body's stress response ends when the brain relaxes, allowing hormone levels to return to normal. Scientists think the "fight or flight" response developed because it helped primitive humans deal with such threats as attacks by wild animals. In many cases, the stress response is still helpful—it may help Alicia react more quickly to block the ball and Eduardo race to the bus stop in time. And a certain amount of stress helps keep life exciting and challenging. But in other cases, like Maria's grief over her dog, the natural stress response may not be helpful at all.

Chronic stress   Events that trigger the stress response usually do not last for very long. When long-term problems with school or family or illness create chronic* stress, however, they keep the body's stress response system activated over too long a period of time. This can contribute to many psychological disorders. Doctors think it also can lead to physical problems, such as chest pain, headaches, and upset stomach. Researchers suspect that, over time, high stress levels can contribute to more serious illnesses, such as high blood pressure and heart disease. They also suspect that chronic stress may suppress the immune system, the body's natural defense against infection, leaving people more prone to illness, perhaps even to some forms of cancer. Much work must still be done, however, to determine whether those suspected links are real and to unravel the complex relationships between physical and psychological factors in health.

Which Illnesses Are Stress-Related?

It is hard for researchers to establish a definite cause and effect relationship between stress and specific physical symptoms or illnesses. Not only do people's minds and bodies react differently to stress, but there also are other factors at work when someone gets sick. The following conditions are known or believed to be stress-related (as opposed to stress-caused):

- Pain caused by muscular problems, such as tension headaches, back pain, jaw pain, and repetitive stress syndrome. Pain of many kinds seems to be caused or made worse by stress.
- Gastrointestinal (gas-tro-in-TES-ti-nal) problems, such as heartburn, stomach pain, and diarrhea.
- Insomnia, or difficulty sleeping.
- Substance abuse, including smoking, drug addiction, and heavy drinking of alcohol. Substance abuse, in turn, can lead to other illnesses, including heart disease and cancer.

*__chronic__ (KRON-ik) means continuing for a long period of time.

Stress and Neglect

Research using animals suggests that neglect early in life can cause animals to respond more intensely to stress when they grow up. In one study, researchers compared two sets of rat pups: Group A rats were removed from their mothers for 15 minutes a day, while Group B rats were separated for 3 hours.

When the pups were returned to their rat mothers, the mothers tended to respond differently: After 15-minute separations, the rat mothers intensively licked and groomed their returned pups. After 3-hour separations, the rat mothers ignored the pups, at least at first. In subsequent tests, the "neglected" pups in Group B were shown to respond to stress more intensely than the Group A pups. This response appeared to last into adulthood.

Another study reported that infant monkeys whose mothers had difficulty providing them with food had higher levels of corticotropin-releasing factor (CRF), one of the key hormones in the stress response. Because the monkey mothers were distressed about finding food, they behaved inconsistently toward their offspring, sometimes neglecting them. These young monkeys were more anxious than usual when confronted with separation or new environments; in other words, their stress response was more intense. "Stressing out" these animals as babies seemed to shape the way their brains and nervous systems responded to stress when they grew up.

Support Groups and Stress Reduction

When people are diagnosed with illnesses such as cancer or AIDS, they usually take powerful drugs that can reverse or slow down the biological processes of the disease. Studies suggest that patients also benefit by joining support groups. Social relationships are believed to increase feelings of well-being and to reduce stress.

In the 1970s, a psychiatrist in California led support groups for women with advanced breast cancer. Group members expressed their emotions and concerns during regular meetings. A decade later, the same psychiatrist went back and reviewed the women's records. He found that the women who participated in the support groups survived twice as long as similar patients who did not.

In a later study, another California psychiatrist concluded that group therapy was helpful to people diagnosed with a serious form of skin cancer. Those who participated in the support group were found to have greater numbers of active tumor-killing cells than patients who did not.

A researcher at the University of Miami completed a similar study with men who tested positive for HIV, the virus that causes AIDS. Men who were trained in stress-management showed a slower rate of decline in the immune system cells that the virus attacks, compared to those who did not. More work remains to be done, but these and other studies suggest that support groups can have an important effect on the body's ability to fight off disease.

- Asthma attacks in people who already have the condition or who are susceptible to it.

- Post-traumatic stress disorder, a mental disorder in which people repeatedly relive a terrifying experience in dreams and memories long after the event has passed; and acute stress disorder, in which they have similar symptoms immediately after the event.

- Other mental disorders, including eating disorders, anxiety, depression, and possibly schizophrenia.

- Cardiovascular (car-dee-o-VAS-kyu-lar) problems, such as irregular heartbeat, hardening of the arteries, and heart attack. Stress makes the heart beat more quickly and increases blood pressure temporarily. Although long-term effects have not been proven, many scientists suspect that they exist.

The Mind-Body Connection

Why do scientists believe that stress plays a role in causing illness? Although they still are unraveling the complex relationship between physical and psychological health, many studies suggest links between stress, illness, and the immune system's ability to fight off illness. Some examples:

- Studies have found that people who recently lost a husband, wife, or other loved one—which causes intense stress—are more likely to die themselves, from a wide variety of causes.

- Workers who reported high levels of stress were estimated to incur nearly 50 percent more in health care expenditures.

- Researchers reported that two groups of people under stress—medical students taking exams and people caring for Alzheimer's disease patients—showed decreases in their immune system activity.

Learning to Deal with Stress

Stress is inevitable, but people can learn how to cope with it. Doctors sometimes suggest the following strategies for managing stress:

- Exercising takes the mind off stressful thoughts, and causes the release of chemicals called endorphins (en-DOR-fins) in the brain that provide feelings of calmness and well-being.

- Making time for hobbies and enjoyable activities outside school and work can decrease stress levels.

- Relaxation techniques such as deep breathing, visualizing pleasant images, meditation, and yoga can lower the heart rate and blood pressure while reducing muscle tension.

- Scaling back on activities and responsibilities and managing one's time effectively can head off stress-causing situations.

- Participating in support groups or sessions with professionally trained counselors or psychologists can help provide an outlet for emotional stresses.

Using drugs, alcohol, and smoking to cope with stress can make stress-related problems and illnesses worse.

Resources

U.S. National Institute of Mental Health, National Institutes of Health, 6001 Executive Boulevard, Room 8184, MSC 9663, Bethesda, MD 20892-9663.
Telephone 301-443-4513
http://www.nimh.nih.gov

American Psychological Association (APA), 750 First Street N.E., Washington, D.C. 20002-4242. The APA's on-line Help Center features useful information about the stress-illness connection.
Telephone 202-336-5500
http://helping.apa.org

KidsHealth.org from the Nemours Foundation posts fact sheets that spotlight stress in children and in teenagers.
http://www.kidshealth.org/teen/bodymind/stress.html

American Institute of Stress, 124 Park Avenue, Yonkers, NY 10703.
Telephone 914-963-1200
http://www.stress.org

National Mental Health Association, 1021 Prince Street, Alexandria, VA 22314.
Telephone 800-969-6642
http://www.nmha.org

Stroke

A stroke is the sudden destruction of brain cells when blood flow to the brain is disrupted, usually by a blockage in a blood vessel. It can cause weakness, speech problems, paralysis, and death, although most people survive.

Carmen Visits Her Grandparents

While eating lunch with her grandfather on a sunny afternoon, fourteen-year-old Carmen was in the midst of describing her summer camp plans when suddenly one side of her grandfather's face went slack. He tried to speak, but he was slurring his words. Without warning, he clutched the picnic table, and the drinking glass he held smashed to the ground.

Relaxation Meditation

Many people find that relaxation meditation is a good way to relieve some of the stresses of everyday life. People who meditate regularly recommend the following:

- Finding a quiet room or place away from disturbances.

- Sitting in a comfortable position with the spine straight.

- Repeating a special word or phrase throughout the session.

- Keeping eyes closed or eyes focused on an object.

- Clearing the mind of distracting thoughts, repeating the chosen phrase, and concentrating on the chosen point of focus.

▶ *See also*
Alcoholism
Anxiety Disorders
Asthma
Cancer
Depressive Disorders
Eating Disorders
Heart Disease
Hypertension
Insomnia
Irritable Bowel Syndrome
Post-Traumatic Stress Disorder
Repetitive Stress Syndrome
Substance Abuse
Temporomandibular Joint Syndrome
Trauma

KEYWORDS
for searching the Internet
and other reference sources

Circulatory system

Ischemia

Stenosis

Thrombosis

Tissue plasminogen activator (t-PA)

"Grandma!" Carmen called. As her grandmother rushed to dial for emergency aid, Carmen held her grandfather's trembling hand.

In a few minutes, the ambulance arrived to carry him to the hospital, where the doctors quickly ordered a brain scan. The brain scan showed that Carmen's grandfather had undergone an ischemic (is-KEE-mik) stroke. The doctors gave him t-PA, a powerful drug that dissolved a blood clot that was blocking the flow of blood to the brain. In a few days, he was ready to return home. Over several months, with the help of physical, occupational, and speech therapies, Carmen's grandfather was able to make a full recovery.

What Is a Stroke?

A stroke occurs when the blood supply to part of the brain is suddenly interrupted, or when a blood vessel in the brain bursts, spilling blood into the spaces surrounding neurons (nerve cells). Like other cells, brain cells die when they no longer receive oxygen and nutrients from the bloodstream, or when they are damaged by sudden bleeding into or around the brain.

There are two major types of strokes: ischemic strokes involve a reduced blood flow to the brain. Hemorrhagic (hem-o-RAJ-ik) strokes involve bleeding in the brain. Ischemia (is-KEY-me-a) is the term used to describe the loss of oxygen and nutrients when there is inadequate blood flow. If ischemia is left untreated, it can lead to infarction (in-FARK-shun), or cell death and tissue death in the surrounding area.

Ischemic Strokes

Ischemic strokes occur when a blood vessel to the brain becomes blocked, suddenly decreasing or stopping blood flow and ultimately causing an infarction. Ischemic strokes account for approximately 80 percent of all strokes. A blood clot (also called a thrombus) is the most common cause of vessel blockage and brain infarction.

A blockage in an artery that supplies blood to the brain can cause an ischemic stroke.

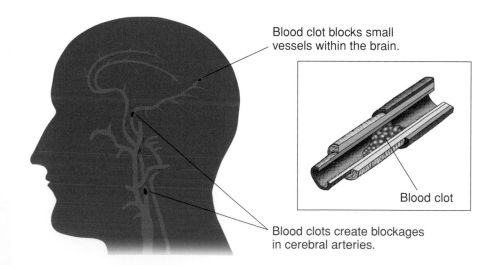

Blood clot blocks small vessels within the brain.

Blood clot

Blood clots create blockages in cerebral arteries.

Blood clots   Blood clotting is necessary in the body to stop bleeding and to allow repair of damaged areas, but when blood clots develop in the wrong place within an artery, they can cause injury by stopping the normal flow of blood. Problems with clots develop more frequently as people age.

An embolus is a clot that has formed in a blood vessel somewhere in the body, often in the heart. It can break away from the wall of the vessel where it was formed, travel through the circulatory system, and become wedged in the brain, causing an embolic stroke. Ischemic strokes also can be caused by the formation of a blood clot in one of the cerebral arteries (arteries supplying blood to the brain). If the clot grows large enough it will block blood flow.

Stenosis   Stenosis, or a narrowing of the arteries, also can cause ischemia. Stenosis can occur in large arteries or small arteries, and is called blood vessel disease or small vessel disease. The most common blood vessel disease that causes stenosis is atherosclerosis. Deposits of plaque (a mixture of cholesterol and other fatty substances) build up along the inner walls of larger and medium sized arteries causing thickening, hardening, and loss of elasticity of the artery walls.

Transient ischemic attacks (TIAs)   Some people get a warning that they may be headed for a future stroke. A transient ischemic attack (TIA) is a very small stroke caused by a temporarily blocked blood vessel. Unlike a full stroke, a TIA leaves no permanent damage. Symptoms are similar to those of a full stroke, but they usually last 24 hours or less. It is impossible to know whether the symptoms are caused by a stroke or by a TIA, so any symptoms should receive immediate medical attention. Having a TIA increases the risk of having a full stroke in the future, and medical attention can sometimes prevent or lessen the severity of the stroke.

Hemorrhagic Strokes

Hemorrhagic strokes are caused by burst blood vessels. In a healthy brain, the neurons do not come into direct contact with blood. Oxygen and nutrients move across a membrane from the blood vessel to the brain cells. Neuroglial (noo-ro-GLEE-al) cells help control which fluids and nutrients reach the neurons of the brain. When an artery in the brain bursts, blood spills out into the surrounding tissue, overriding the control of neuroglial cells and disrupting the delicate chemical balance of the brain.

Hemorrhagic strokes may occur in several ways. Aneurysms, or weak spots on artery walls, can stretch or "balloon" until eventually they break and spill blood into surrounding brain cells. Hemorrhages also can happen when plaque-encrusted arteries lose their elasticity and become brittle and thin enough to crack. Hypertension (high blood pressure) increases the risk that a brittle artery wall will give way and release blood into surrounding brain tissue.

A person who has an arteriovenous (ar-ter-ee-o-VEN-us) malformation (a tangle of defective blood vessels and capillaries within the brain that can rupture) also can be at increased risk for hemorrhagic stroke.

The U.S. and the World

- Stroke is the third leading cause of death in the United States, killing more than 150,000 people each year.

- According to the U.S. Centers for Disease Control and Prevention (CDC), the overall stroke death rate in the U.S. has been declining since 1950.

- The American Heart Association reports that, on average, someone in the U.S. has a stroke every 53 seconds. About 600,000 strokes occur each year, including 100,000 strokes in people who have had at least one previous stroke.

- About 4.4 million people in the U.S. have experienced a stroke and survived.

- Stroke occurs about 20 percent more often in men than in women. But if a woman has a stroke, her chance of dying is about 20 percent higher than a man's chance.

- The World Health Organization (WHO) estimates that strokes killed approximately 5.1 million people worldwide in 1998.

- WHO reports that strokes are increasing worldwide and estimates that stroke and related heart disease could rival infectious disease as the leading cause of death in the developing world by 2020. Reasons cited for the increase include the rise of cigarette smoking as well as changes in diet and lifestyle.

Strokes can affect many different parts of the brain. ▶

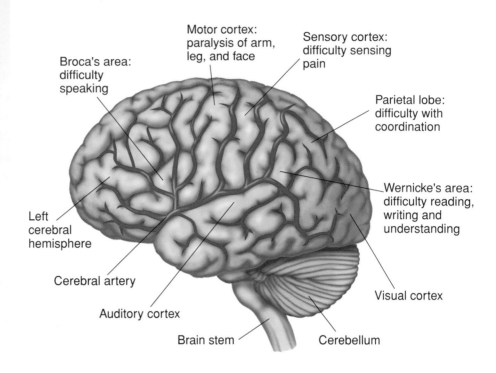

Broca's area: difficulty speaking

Motor cortex: paralysis of arm, leg, and face

Sensory cortex: difficulty sensing pain

Parietal lobe: difficulty with coordination

Left cerebral hemisphere

Cerebral artery

Auditory cortex

Brain stem

Wernicke's area: difficulty reading, writing and understanding

Visual cortex

Cerebellum

Although hemorrhagic strokes are less common than ischemic strokes, they have a much higher fatality rate, because more brain tissue can be damaged more quickly.

How Do People Know They Are Having a Stroke?

Symptoms of stroke, such as those experienced by Carmen's grandfather, appear suddenly. They may include:

- Numbness or weakness of the face, arm, or leg, particularly on one side.
- Confusion, trouble talking, and trouble understanding speech.
- Difficulty seeing in one or both eyes.
- Dizziness, difficulty walking, loss of balance, or loss of coordination.
- Severe headache with no known cause.

Strokes are medical emergencies and require immediate medical attention.

How Is Stroke Diagnosed?

Doctors have diagnostic techniques and imaging tools to help diagnose strokes quickly and accurately. When a person with signs and symptoms of stroke arrives at the hospital, the first diagnostic step is a physical examination and a medical history. Often, an electrocardiogram and a CT scan* will be done to check for signs of heart disease, evidence of prior TIAs, and heart rhythm disturbances. The patient may be asked to

* **CT scans** (CAT scans) are computerized axial tomography (to-MOG-ra-fee), which uses x-rays and computers to view structures inside the body.

814

answer questions and to perform several physical and mental tests to evaluate the possibility or severity of brain damage.

Imaging tests also help health care professionals to evaluate stroke. The CT scan may rule out a hemorrhage or may show evidence of early infarction. If the stroke is caused by a hemorrhage, a CT scan can reveal any bleeding into the brain. MRI scans* may be taken to detect subtler changes in brain tissue or areas of dead tissue soon after a stroke.

*** MRI,** which is short for magnetic resonance imaging, produces computerized images of internal body tissues based on the magnetic properties of atoms within the body.

How Is Stroke Treated?

Stroke treatment often involves medication, surgery, and rehabilitation. Acute stroke therapy uses medication to stop a stroke while it is happening by quickly dissolving the blood clot that is causing the stroke or by stopping the bleeding of a hemorrhagic stroke.

Medication and surgery Physicians have a number of different medications that can be used to treat stroke:

- Antithrombotics work to counteract the chemicals in the body that cause blood to clot.

- Antiplatelet drugs prevent clotting by decreasing the activity of cells that contribute to the clotting properties of blood. They can reduce the risk of ischemic stroke.

- Anticoagulants reduce the stroke risk by thinning the blood and reducing its clotting properties.

- Thrombolytic agents are used to treat an ongoing stroke. These drugs stop the stroke by dissolving the blood clot that is blocking the blood vessel supplying the brain. Tissue plasminogen activator (t-PA) can be effective if given intravenously within 3 hours of the onset of stroke symptoms when a CT scan confirms that a person has suffered an ischemic stroke.

Surgery may be used to prevent stroke, to treat acute stroke, or to repair vascular malformations in and around the brain.

Rehabilitation Post-stroke rehabilitation helps people overcome the disabilities that result from stroke damage. For some people, like Carmen's grandfather, acute stroke treatment and post-stroke therapy led to a full recovery. For others, recovery is only partial.

Although strokes occur in the brain, they may affect the entire body and all activities of daily living. Some of the disabilities that may result from a stroke include paralysis, or partial paralysis, of many different parts of the body, difficulties with memory and concentration, speech problems, and emotional distress as people cope with their changed circumstances. Rehabilitation may involve several different forms of therapy:

- Physical therapy helps people to regain movement, balance, and coordination and to reestablish skills such as sitting, walking, and moving from one activity to another.

Physical therapy helps people who have had strokes regain movement, balance, and muscular coordination. © *Will and Deni McIntyre/Photo Researchers, Inc.*

▶

- Occupational therapy helps people who have had strokes readapt to everyday life by relearning practical skills needed at home, such as dressing, eating, bathing, reading, and writing.

- Speech therapy addresses the speech and language problems that arise when a stroke causes brain damage in the language parts of the brain. Speech therapy helps people who have no deficits in cognition or thinking but have problems understanding written words, or problems forming speech. One common problem for people who have suffered stroke is aphasia (a-FAY-zha), a condition in which comprehension or expression of words is impaired. Speech therapists help stroke patients by working to improve language skills, develop alternative ways of communicating, and develop coping skills to deal with the frustration of not being able to communicate easily.

- Psychotherapy often is useful following a stroke, because depression, anxiety, frustration, and anger are common post-stroke symptoms.

Preventing Stroke

* **risk factors** are any factors that make it likelier a person will get a certain disease.

The most important risk factors* for stroke are hypertension (high blood pressure), heart disease, diabetes, and smoking. Others things that increase the risk of having a stroke include heavy alcohol consumption, high cholesterol levels, and genetic or congenital conditions, such as vascular (blood vessel) abnormalities.

Hypertension People with hypertension or high blood pressure have a risk for stroke that is four to six times greater than those without hypertension. One third of adults in the United States have high blood pressure. Antihypertensive drugs and attention to diet can decrease a person's risk for stroke.

Heart disease   After hypertension, the second most powerful risk factor for stroke is heart disease, particularly the condition known as atrial fibrillation*. This condition is more prevalent in older people. Other forms of heart disease that can increase the chances of having stroke include malformations of heart muscle and some heart valve diseases. Cardiac surgery to correct heart malformation or the effects of heart disease also can cause stroke. Strokes occurring during surgery often are the result of dislodged plaques.

Diabetes   People with diabetes have three times the risk of stroke as those without diabetes. The relative risk is highest in the fifth and sixth decades of life and decreases after that. People with diabetes who control their blood sugar level well, who avoid smoking, and who avoid or control hypertension, are less likely to have strokes.

Cigarette smoking   Smokers have a 40 to 60 percent greater chance of having a stroke than nonsmokers. Smoking increases a person's chance for ischemic stroke, independent of all other risk factors.

Blood cholesterol levels   High cholesterol levels can contribute to the risk of stroke. Too much cholesterol in the blood is associated with plaque developing in the walls of arteries (atherosclerosis), leading to stenosis of blood vessels. By lowering cholesterol through diet and exercise, a person can lower the risk for atherosclerosis and stroke. Doctors may prescribe cholesterol-lowering medication for people with high cholesterol levels.

Lifestyle changes   Many strokes can be prevented with changes in lifestyle. These changes include:

- Stopping smoking.
- Avoiding binge drinking and overconsumption of alcohol.
- Avoiding illicit drugs: cocaine and crack cocaine can cause stroke, and marijuana may damage blood vessels, which can cause stroke.

Medical measures   To prevent stroke, doctors may prescribe medications to lower blood pressure and cholesterol levels. In some cases, particularly if a person has atrial fibrillation, doctors may prescribe regular doses of aspirin, coumadin, or other medications that prevent blood clotting. If carotid (ka-ROT-id) arteries (arteries supplying the brain) are partially blocked by plaque, surgery can clear them and prevent strokes in many cases.

* **atrial fibrillation** (AY-tree-al fib-ri-LAY-shun) is the arrhythmic or irregular beating of the left upper chamber of the heart. This leads to an irregular flow of blood and to the formation of blood clots that can leave the heart and travel to the brain, causing a stroke.

Ike

Dwight D. Eisenhower (1890–1969) was a U.S. Army general and the thirty-fourth president of the United States. "Ike," as he was known, had a meteoric rise as a military commander during World War II. In 1953, he was elected to his first term in the White House. Despite having a stroke and a heart attack, he was elected to a second term. Eisenhower completed his presidency in 1961, when John F. Kennedy was sworn in as thirty-fifth president.

Strokes can happen to people of either sex no matter what their age or racial background. Transient ischemic attacks (TIAs) multiply a person's risk of having a full stroke and should receive immediate medical attention.

Resources

U.S. National Institute of Neurological Disorders and Stroke (NINDS), Building 31, Room 8A16, 31 Center Drive, MSC 2540, Bethesda, MD 20892-2540. The NINDS website posts many useful fact sheets about stroke, with information on stroke prevention, treatment, research, and clinical trials.
Telephone 800-352-9424
http://www.ninds.nih.gov/patients/Disorder/STROKE/strokehp.htm

National Stroke Association, 96 Inverness Drive East, Suite 1, Englewood, CO 80112-5112.
Telephone 800-787-6537
http://www.stroke.org

American Heart Association, 7272 Greenville Avenue, Dallas, TX 75231.
http://www.amhrt.org

World Health Organization (WHO), Avenue Appia 20, 1211 Geneva 27, Switzerland. WHO's website posts information about stroke and other non-communicable diseases worldwide.
http://www.who.org/home/map_ht.html

▶ *See also*
Aneurysm
Diabetes
Dysrhythmia
Heart Disease
Hypertension
Paralysis
Speech Disorders
Substance Abuse
Thrombosis

Substance Abuse

KEYWORDS
for searching the Internet and other reference sources

Addiction

Drug abuse

Narcotics

Tobacco

Substance abuse is the misuse of alcohol, tobacco, illegal drugs, prescription drugs, and other substances (such as paint thinners or aerosol gasses) that change how the mind and body work. It is possible to abuse some substances without becoming physically, emotionally, or psychologically dependent on them, but continued use does tend to make people dependent. Dependency on some substances happens very quickly and is difficult to reverse.

What Is Substance Abuse?

Substance abuse is a serious problem in the United States. People who abuse substances can get sick, ruin their relationships with other people, destroy their lives and the lives of family members, and even die. Substance abuse contributes to accidents, crime, violence within the family, and lost productivity at work.

Substance abuse is the use of any substance for an unintended purpose or in an excessive amount. All substances, whether legal or illegal, have an impact on health when used in the wrong way. Different substances have different effects on the body. Substances that are commonly abused in the United States include:

- alcohol
- amphetamines
- anabolic steroids
- cocaine
- depressants
- hallucinogens
- inhalants
- marijuana
- narcotics
- prescription medications
- nonprescription (over-the-counter) medications
- tobacco

Dependency and addiction   People can abuse some substances without being physically, emotionally, or psychologically dependent on them, although continued use often leads to dependency. With continued use, the tolerance for a substance tends to grow, so that to get the same effect a person must use more and more of the substance. Some substances are very quickly addictive.

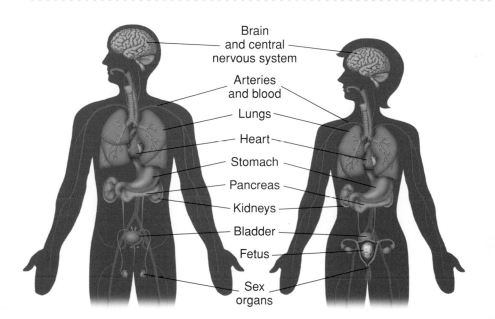

Brain
and central
nervous system

Arteries
and blood

Lungs

Heart

Stomach

Pancreas

Kidneys

Bladder

Fetus

Sex
organs

Substance abuse and addiction affect many different parts of the body.

Addiction is a special type of dependence in which people have a compulsive need to use the substance no matter what the consequences are. People who are psychologically addicted want to keep using the substance to feel satisfied. People who are physically addicted feel sick and have physical withdrawal symptoms if they stop using the substance. The risk and type of dependence varies by substance. Substance abuse occurs among people of all ages, from children to the elderly, including those with good educations and professional jobs.

Alcohol

Although moderate drinking (up to two drinks a day for men and one drink a day for women and older people) is not normally considered harmful, millions of people in the United States abuse alcohol or are alcoholics (people who are physically dependent on alcohol). A 1996 national survey found that 11 million Americans are heavy drinkers, and that 32 million people engage in binge drinking (more than five drinks on one occasion). This includes 1.9 million people with alcoholism and 4.4 million binge drinkers between the ages of 12 and 20.

Alcohol depresses the central nervous system. It interferes with messages to and from the brain, and alters the way that drinkers feel, see, hear, and move. People who drink too much may lose muscle coordination, may become abusive to friends, may exhibit poor judgment, may drive while drunk and cause accidents, may anger easily and get into fights, may take foolish risks, may vomit violently, or may get arrested because of their behavior while under the influence of alcohol.

People with alcoholism are at risk for serious, even life-threatening diseases and problems. It increases the risk for certain cancers, and causes liver damage, immune system problems, and brain damage. Pregnant women who drink may permanently harm the development of their unborn children. Alcohol also increases the risk of death from car, on-the-job, and other accidents, and is a factor in many murders and suicides. Every year about 100,000 deaths are wholly or partially attributed to drinking alcohol. Alcoholism tends to run in families, and is a problem throughout the world.

Amphetamines

Amphetamines are man-made stimulants that speed up the central nervous system, creating a sense of euphoria, and increased energy. Amphetamines can be taken orally, injected, smoked, or sniffed. They may be legally prescribed to treat attention deficit hyperactivity disorder (ADHD), to suppress appetite, and to combat fatigue or narcolepsy (a disorder that causes uncontrolled falling asleep). Amphetamines include benzedrine, dexedrine, and methedrine. Street names for amphetamines include black beauties, crystal, hearts, ice, speed, and meth.

People who abuse amphetamines need more and more of the drug to achieve the same effect or high. When they become dependent, amphetamine users may be jittery, lose weight, feel depressed, anxious, restless, hostile, and lack energy. An overdose may cause a very fast heartbeat (tachycardia), high blood pressure, seizures, fever, delirium, paranoia*, psychosis*, coma, and cardiovascular collapse.

Anabolic Steroids

Anabolic steroids are synthetic compounds that are closely related to testosterone, the male sex hormone. Taken orally or injected, they may promote the growth of skeletal muscle and lean body mass, increase physical endurance, and cause serious side effects.

Steroids are used medically as hormone replacement therapy. Athletes, especially weight lifters and body builders, sometimes use steroids illegally to enhance their performance and to create extremely bulky muscles. A 1997 study by the National Institute on Drug Abuse estimated that up to 1.5 percent of all eighth, tenth, and twelfth graders in the United States had tried anabolic steroids. Men, however, are many times more likely to use steroids than women.

Some of the short-term side effects of steroids often are reversible, including aggressive behavior, jaundice (a liver problem causing yellow skin, tissues, and body fluid), fluid retention, high blood pressure, severe acne, and trembling. Other side effects include:

- In males: shrinking testicles, infertility, reduced sperm count, baldness, development of breasts.

- In females: growth of hair on the face and body, a deepened voice, changes in the menstrual cycle, enlargement of the genitalia.

- In teenagers: acceleration of puberty and shortening of adult height because the skeleton matures too fast.

The effects of long-term, high-dose use of steroids are not completely known. They may cause increases in cholesterol, heart disease, liver tumors, cancer, and cataracts.

Cocaine

Cocaine, a white powder extracted from the leaves of the South American coca plant, is a stimulant that creates a rush of euphoria, increased physical energy, and sleeplessness. Cocaine can be snorted or sniffed, injected, or smoked. Street names include coke, dust, blow, and crack. Crack is a less expensive form of cocaine that has been processed for smoking. Crack produces a very intense, but short-lived high. Crack is the most addictive form of cocaine.

Cocaine is a dangerous drug. It constricts the blood vessels, dilates pupils, and increases temperature, heart rate, and blood pressure. It can make users restless, irritable, and anxious. First time users occasionally have died suddenly. People who use a lot of cocaine, or who have been using it for a long time, may become paranoid and violent, may damage the soft tissue in their noses to the point where part of the nose collapses, may lose their

...the World

- About 15 million people "incur a significant risk to their health" by abusing drugs, the World Health Organization said in 1996. Between 100,000 and 200,000 deaths per year are linked with injecting drugs, mostly from contracting AIDS and hepatitis from shared needles.

- Drug use is stabilizing in many industrial nations. But the use of drugs that are injected is rising in developing nations of Africa and Asia, leading to increases in hepatitis, HIV infections, and AIDS.

- Among the most commonly used drugs worldwide is marijuana. A 1997 estimate was that 141 million people, or 2 percent of the world's population, had used marijuana.

* **paranoia** (pair-a-NOY-a) refers to behavior that is based on delusions of persecution or grandeur. People with persecution delusions falsely believe that other people are out to harm them. People with delusions of grandeur falsely believe that they have great importance or ability.

* **psychosis** (sy-KO-sis) is a serious mental illness that leads to thoughts and behaviors that are out of touch with reality.

Athletic Competitions

The International Olympic Committee and most other organizations sponsoring national and international athletic competitions have banned more than 20 different anabolic steroids. The ban is enforced through sometimes-controversial drug testing. In 1983, 19 athletes were disqualified from the Olympics for use of banned steroids.

Cocaine disrupts body processes by blocking the neurons' (nerve cells) normal handling of neurotransmitters that carry messages from the brain to other parts of the body. ▶

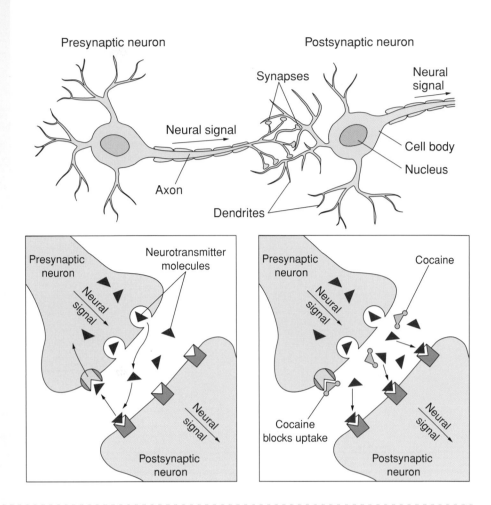

sex drive, and may die of respiratory arrest, seizure, stroke, or heart attack. Children born to mothers addicted to cocaine also are addicted. They are jittery, respond poorly to people, and must go through withdrawal.

Cocaine, especially when smoked as crack, is very addictive. People who develop a tolerance to the drug need to use more to get the same high as the first time they used it, which may lead to participation in criminal activities. Withdrawal from cocaine addiction leaves the person feeling depressed, tired, sleepy, and sometimes suicidal, as well as having a strong craving for cocaine.

Depressants

Depressants slow down the nervous system, relieving anxiety, irritability, and tension. Depressants include barbiturates, methaqualone, and tranquilizers. They may be prescribed legally as a sedative, an anesthetic, to control anxiety, or to control seizures. Street names include barbs, roofies, and tranks. When depressants are combined with alcohol, the slowing effects on the nervous system are more powerful than when alcohol or depressants are used alone. Abuse of depressants causes users to become uninhibited, in a way similar to being drunk, which may be followed by sleepiness. An overdose may cause respiratory distress, coma, and death. Most depressants are physically and psychologically addictive.

Hallucinogens

Hallucinogens, also called psychedelic drugs, cause hallucinations*, delusions*, altered perceptions, and unpredictable behavior. LSD (lysergic acid diethylamide), usually called "acid," is one of the strongest hallucinogens. Taken orally, the effects of LSD are unpredictable, depending on the amount taken, the user's personality, mood, expectations, and the surroundings in which the drug is taken. LSD usually changes the user's sense of time and self, and can produce strange feelings ("hearing" colors or "seeing" sounds). Some users have scary thoughts and feelings about losing control, insanity, death, and despair. Physically, LSD causes dilated pupils; increases in body temperature, heart rate, and blood pressure; loss of appetite; sweating; dry mouth;

THE OPIUM TRADE

Ancient Chinese medical texts indicated that opium, imported to the west from China by Arab traders in the eighth century, was used originally for medicinal purposes. When tobacco was introduced to China from the Philippines, the mixing of tobacco with opium became popular. British colonial traders recognized the strong demand for opium. Despite an eighteenth century edict by the Chinese government banning the sale of opium and the operation of opium houses, the British continued its sale on the black market. During the late eighteenth century, opium was at times the largest single commodity in trade.

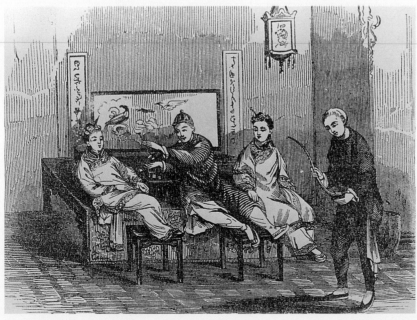

In 1882, *Gaillard's Medical Journal* published this illustration of an opium den. *National Library of Medicine, Science Photo Library/Photo Researchers, Inc.*

Medicinal Marijuana

Marijuana is an illegal drug. In some states, however, legislation has been passed that allows doctors to prescribe marijuana for certain purposes. Research indicates that marijuana may help in the treatment of glaucoma, and may relieve the nausea and wasting away that people with AIDS and cancer sometimes experience as a side effect of other treatments. But research also shows that marijuana smoke contains more tar than cigarette smoke and may contain high levels of other cancer-causing agents. Further research is needed and public policies regarding marijuana are likely to remain controversial.

* **hallucinations** are false perceptions. People hear voices, see visions, or otherwise sense things that are not really there.

* **delusions** are false beliefs that a person clings to, despite their lack of basis in reality.

Acupuncture

Acupuncture is a component of Chinese traditional medicine that has been practiced for at least 2,500 years. The treatment consists of inserting small needles into designated points in the body.

Acupuncture is sometimes used to reduce the physical symptoms of withdrawal from addictive substances and to relieve the depression, anxiety, and insomnia that often accompany treatment. Acupuncture is not a replacement for medical care, counseling, and self-help programs but may add to their effectiveness.

sleeplessness; and tremors. Users may experience flashbacks (recurrences) within a few days to more than a year after using LSD.

Other widely used hallucinogens are DMT (dimethyltryptamine), psilocybin (the main ingredient in "magic" mushrooms), MDMA ("ecstasy"), and mescaline. The effects of psilocybin and mescaline are similar to LSD. MDMA makes people feel less inhibited and distorts judgment.

Hallucinogens are not physically addictive, but people using them are at risk for accidents, violence, panic attacks, and other consequences of impaired judgment. All of these substances are illegal to use, make, or sell.

Inhalants

Inhalants are chemical vapors that can be breathed to produce mind-altering effects. Users inhale the vapors through their noses or mouths. The vapors then enter the lungs. There are three types of inhalants: solvents (such as paint thinners, gasoline, glues, felt-tip marker fluid), gases (such as butane lighters, whipping cream aerosols, spray paints, deodorant sprays, and nitrous oxide or "laughing gas"), and nitrites.

The physical effects of inhalants depend on the chemical being inhaled. Many cause serious, often irreversible health problems, and sometimes cause death. Users can lose consciousness. Other serious, but potentially reversible, effects include liver damage, kidney damage, and depletion of blood oxygen. Irreversible effects of inhalers include hearing loss, loss of muscle control and limb spasms, damage to the central nervous system and brain, damage to the bone marrow, lung damage, and heart failure.

Marijuana

Marijuana is a tobacco-like substance made from the hemp plant *Cannabis sativa*. Also called pot, weed, Mary Jane, and many other names, marijuana is usually smoked as a cigarette (called a joint or a nail). Some users mix marijuana into foods or brew it as tea.

Some marijuana users feel relaxed, experience mild euphoria, and become more sociable. Their perception is distorted, causing problems with memory, learning, thinking, and problem solving. Physically, marijuana causes loss of coordination and makes the heart beat faster. Occasionally other drugs are mixed with or sprinkled on marijuana, causing hallucinations, paranoia, and delirium.

Long-term use of marijuana affects the brain, lungs, and heart. Learning and memory can be impaired, and people who smoke marijuana are at risk for the same health problems as people who smoke tobacco: coughing, chronic bronchitis, respiratory infections, and lung damage.

Marijuana is psychologically rather than physically addictive. Medical use of marijuana to treat glaucoma and increase the appetite in people with cancer and AIDS is controversial and continues to be studied.

Narcotics

Narcotics are drugs that dull the senses. They are used medically to relieve pain. Narcotics can produce a sense of euphoria (a "high") followed by sleepiness, and a feeling of being in a fog. At least 20 opiates, a type of narcotic, are available in the United States. These include morphine, heroin, meperidine, and codeine. Many opiates have legitimate medical uses, but heroin, the most commonly abused opiate, does not.

Heroin is made from the seed of the Asian poppy plant. It is usually a brown or white powder that users inject, smoke, or sniff. Long-term use of heroin can lead to miscarriages, collapsed veins, infections of the heart lining and valves, abscesses, liver disease, pneumonia, and fatal overdoses. Infectious diseases such as AIDS and hepatitis can be spread from person to person by sharing needles used to inject heroin. Withdrawal from heroin causes pain, nausea, sweating, and a great deal of physical and mental discomfort. Withdrawal symptoms are most commonly treated with maintenance doses of methadone, but withdrawal from methadone must later be accomplished.

Tobacco

Nicotine, the active ingredient in tobacco, is one of the most widely used addictive drugs in the United States. Nicotine both stimulates and sedates the central nervous system. Tobacco is usually smoked, but it can also be snuffed (placed between the lip and gum or under the tongue), or chewed. Smoking cigars and pipes also is harmful.

Tobacco contains thousands of chemicals, including carbon monoxide and tar. Many of these play a role in disease. The more people smoke, the greater their risk of disease. Smoking accounts for about 30 percent of all cancer deaths, 20 percent of heart disease deaths, and more than 80 percent of chronic obstructive lung disease cases. People who smoke tend to get more colds and respiratory tract infections than other people. Pregnant women who smoke have a greater risk of having a miscarriage or stillborn child. Babies of smokers usually weigh less, have more respiratory infections, are at higher risk of ear infections and asthma, and have less effective lungs than other babies. Being around people who smoke (called passive smoking) also is harmful. Passive smoking increases the risk that nonsmokers will have the same health problems as smokers.

Smokers feel physical symptoms of withdrawal when they stop smoking. A patch that delivers nicotine through the skin, when combined with counseling, behavior modification, and self-help groups, often can be effective in helping people quit smoking.

Prescription and Over-the-Counter Drugs

People can abuse legal medicines by taking more than prescribed, using them for nonmedical reasons, or using them to treat unrelated illnesses. The most commonly abused prescription and over-the-counter medicines are stimulants, pain relievers, depressants (such as sleeping pills), cough and cold medicines, and laxatives.

Abusing these substances can cause physical and psychological dependence. Some prescription medications contain alcohol and narcotics—such as codeine—that are physically addicting. Combining alcohol with prescription and over-the-counter drugs, or mixing drugs, can change the effectiveness of the drugs and cause harmful side effects.

How Is Substance Abuse Diagnosed and Treated?

Diagnosis   Substance abuse often is difficult to diagnose and treat. Doctors can screen for substance abuse through a medical history, a physical exam, and sometimes blood or urine testing, but doctors and family members often have a hard time convincing substance abusers that they need help. In many cases, substance abusers are more afraid of losing the drug and of withdrawal symptoms than of the health and safety consequences of continued use.

Treatment   Treatment for substance abuse consists of helping people stop using the substance, treating withdrawal symptoms, and preventing people from returning to substance abuse afterwards. Outpatient psychotherapy* and self-help groups can be effective. People with severe problems may require residential treatment programs. Treatment often is provided by doctors and organizations that specialize in substance abuse programs. Successful programs:

* **psychotherapy** is treatment of mental disorders and behavioral problems through support, suggestion, persuasion, reeducation, reassurance, and insight.

- Evaluate people for psychiatric or medical disorders.
- Teach them about the effects of the drug and their addiction.
- Offer mutual support and self-help groups.
- Provide individual and group psychotherapy.
- Offer a replacement for the substance being given up.
- Emphasize behavior changes that promote not using the substance.
- Offer rehabilitation and life skills training.

Even people who are successfully treated must guard against starting to use the abused substance again. People with serious medical or psychiatric symptoms, people who overdose on drugs, and people who have toxic reactions to drugs require immediate medical treatment.

Resources

U.S. National Institute on Drug Abuse (NIDA), National Institutes of Health, 6000 Executive Boulevard, Bethesda, MD 20892-7003. NIDA's website posts fact sheets about anabolic steroids, heroin, inhalant abuse, marijuana, methamphetamine, and many other topics. It also provides hyperlinks to more than 50 other organizations that provide information about substance abuse and its treatment. http://www.nida.nih.gov

U.S. National Clearinghouse for Alcohol and Drug Information. This service of the Substance Abuse and Mental Health Services Administration (SAMHSA) focuses on prevention. Its website has a *Kids Area* in English and Spanish.
Telephone 800-487-4890
http://www.health.org/kidsarea.htm

U.S. National Institute on Alcohol Abuse and Alcoholism (NIAAA), National Institutes of Health, 6000 Executive Boulevard, Bethesda, MD 20892-7003. NIAAA's website posts fact sheets in English and in Spanish about alcoholism, alcoholism and pregnancy, and treatment. http://www.niaaa.nih.gov

Alcoholics Anonymous (AA) World Services, 475 Riverside Drive, 11th floor, New York, NY 10115. This self-help organization provides referrals to local support groups and has information about the AA program.
Telephone 212-870-3400
http://www.alcoholics-anonymous.org

▶ See also
AIDS and HIV
Alcoholism
Cirrhosis of the Liver
Eating Disorders
Glaucoma
Growth Disorders
Hepatitis
Mental Disorders
Pregnancy, Complications of
Prematurity
Seizures
Tobacco-Related Diseases

Sudden Infant Death Syndrome

Sudden Infant Death Syndrome (also known as SIDS) refers to the sudden death of an apparently healthy infant under 1 year of age whose death cannot be explained even after a complete investigation.

KEYWORDS
for searching the Internet and other reference sources

Obstetrics

Pediatrics

Prenatal Care

Taking Care

Mrs. Wyatt is doing all the things her doctor told her to do with her new baby. She puts him to sleep for naps and at night on his back instead of on his stomach. She makes sure the crib has a mattress that is firm, and that there are no blankets, pillows, or toys around the baby. She refrains from bundling her baby in thick clothing before putting the baby to bed.

The doctor recommended these things because they reduce the risk of Sudden Infant Death Syndrome (SIDS), a mysterious disorder that is a leading cause of death for children between the age of 1 month and 1 year.

SIDS kills more than 3,000 babies a year in America, usually while they are asleep in cribs. But since mothers like Mrs. Wyatt started to put their babies to sleep on their backs, and to adopt other preventive strategies, the number of SIDS deaths has dropped more than 40 percent.

No one knows for sure why these babies die. Most of the babies appear to be healthy until their deaths.

Parents often feel guilt mixed with their grief over the death. They think perhaps there was something they could have done. But SIDS is no one's fault.

What Is SIDS?

Researchers have not discovered a cause for Sudden Infant Death Syndrome in the more than 30 years they have been studying it. In fact, it is easier to say what SIDS is not than what it is. SIDS does not result from suffocation, choking, vomiting, or a fatal reaction to a vaccination*. A baby does not catch it like a cold.

* **vaccination** (vak-si-NAY-shun) is taking into the body a killed or weakened germ, or a protein made from such a microbe, in order to prevent, lessen, or treat a disease.

* **autopsy** (AW-top-see) is the examination of a body after a person has died, to determine the cause of death.

* **immune system** is the system that protects the body from diseases. It includes elements such as the thymus, spleen, lymph nodes, bone marrow, and antibodies (AN-te-bod-eez).

The Back to Sleep Campaign

For decades, parents thought it was best to put babies to sleep on their stomachs. They thought that if babies were on their backs, they would choke on their vomit if they threw up.

Doctors today say that should not be a concern. In fact, a national Back to Sleep Campaign was launched in 1994 by the U.S. National Institute of Child Health and Human Development (NICHD) and other organizations to inform parents that they should put healthy babies to sleep on their backs, because doing this appears to reduce the risk of SIDS.

It was in 1992 that the American Academy of Pediatrics first recommended that babies sleep on their backs. Between 1992 and 1997, the number of children sleeping on their stomachs dropped from 70 percent to 21 percent, and the death rate from SIDS dropped by 42 percent.

The only time doctors say that a baby has died of SIDS is if no other cause of death is found after there has been an autopsy*, an investigation of the place where the baby died, and a review of the baby's medical history.

Recent research suggests that infants who die of SIDS might have a problem in an area of the brain that controls two functions while they are asleep: breathing and waking up. This problem area in the brain, however, might not be enough on its own to cause SIDS. Other things may have to happen to reduce the amount of oxygen a baby gets, or to disrupt the baby's breathing and heart rate.

For example, babies might not get enough oxygen when they breathe air that is trapped in soft beds or in folds of blankets near their mouths. This is not the same as suffocation, which usually involves completely blocking a person's ability to take in air. In SIDS, the babies may be getting air but not enough oxygen, because they are breathing in their own exhaled breath.

Respiratory infections such as a cold or other ailment also can make breathing difficult for a baby.

Usually, babies would wake up and cry if they were not breathing well. But it may be that some babies cannot process the signals in the brain when they are not breathing properly.

These examples could help explain why babies who sleep on their stomachs or have infections are at higher risk of SIDS. It also might explain why SIDS is more likely to occur in the winter, when the risk of infection is higher and babies might be sleeping with more bedclothes or blankets.

Researchers are investigating other possible physical problems that could contribute to the risk of SIDS. One possible factor is an immune system* disorder that creates too many white blood cells and proteins, which disrupt the brain's control over breathing and heart rate.

Like many disorders, SIDS might have a combination of factors that cause it, including some that have not been discovered.

Who Is at Risk for SIDS?

Although research is beginning to suggest causes for SIDS, there is still no way to predict who will die of the disorder. The vast majority of babies who are laid to sleep on their stomachs, have infections, or sleep with blankets do not die from SIDS. Others who sleep on their backs in ideal conditions still die of the disorder.

There are no warning signs of SIDS before a baby dies. Doctors only diagnose it after ruling out other possible causes of death.

Certain things *are* known. SIDS can happen any time within the first year, but it occurs most often between the first and fourth month after birth. Seldom does it occur within the first 2 weeks following birth or after 6 months.

What Are the Risk Factors for SIDS?

A baby is more likely to die of SIDS if the baby has:

■ A mother who smoked during pregnancy

- A mother less than 20 years old
- A mother who did not receive proper medical care before her baby was born
- A birth before the full 9 months of a normal pregnancy
- A lower than normal birth weight
- Family members who smoked around the baby.

However, babies who are breast-fed have a lower risk of SIDS than babies who are fed with a bottle. One possible reason might be because breast-feeding helps reduce the risk of the types of infections that may contribute to breathing problems.

Resources

Books

Horchler, Joani Nelson, and Robin Rice Morris. *The SIDS Survival Guide: Information and Comfort for Grieving Family and Friends and Professionals Who Seek to Help Them.* Revised and updated edition. Hyattsville, MD: SIDS Educational Services, 1997.

Guntheroth, Warren G. *Crib Death: The Sudden Infant Death Syndrome.* Third edition. Armonk, NY: Futura Publishing Company, Inc., 1993.

Organizations

The National Institute of Child Health and Human Development (NICHD), part of the U.S. National Institutes of Health (NIH), posts information about SIDS on its website, which also includes information on the Back to Sleep Campaign.
Telephone 800-505-2742
http://156.40.88.3/publications/pubs/sidsfact.htm
http://www.nichd.nih.gov/sids/sids.htm

Sudden Infant Death Syndrome Network, P.O. Box 520, Ledyard, CT 06339. This organization is dedicated to providing information on SIDS, and support for families who lose a baby. It features information in more than a dozen languages.
http://sids-network.org

National SIDS Resource Center, 2070 Chain Bridge Road, Suite 450, Vienna, VA 22182.
Telephone 703-821-8955
http://www.circsol.com/SIDS

SIDS Alliance, 1314 Bedford Avenue, Suite 210, Baltimore, MD 21208. SIDS Alliance is a national network of SIDS support groups.
Telephone 800-221-7437 or 410-653-8226
http://www.sidsalliance.org

The Back to Sleep campaign also informed health professionals and the general public about other ways to lower the risk of SIDS. These include:

- Having the mother avoid smoking during pregnancy
- Making sure the mother gets medical care during pregnancy
- Having family members avoid smoking around the baby after it is born
- Making sure the baby gets ongoing medical care after it is born
- Having the mother breast-feed the baby
- Providing the baby with a firm mattress
- Keeping pillows, blankets, and toys in the crib from crowding the baby
- Not dressing a baby in too many clothes when the baby is sleeping.

Not all babies should sleep on their backs. A few have problems with their airways or keeping food down. Doctors may recommend in these rare cases that the babies be placed on their stomachs on a firm mattress without soft pillows, blankets, or plush toys.

Some parents have misunderstood the intent of the Back to Sleep Campaign. They never put their children on their stomachs, even when they are awake. Doctors say it is important for children's physical and mental development to spend some time on their stomachs while they are awake, so long as an adult is watching.

▶ *See also*
Cold
Prematurity
Tobacco-Related Diseases

Syphilis

Syphilis (SIF-i-lis) is a sexually transmitted disease that is easily cured, but if left untreated can cause blindness, deafness, paralysis, and insanity many years after a person becomes infected.

KEYWORDS

for searching the Internet and other reference sources

Sexually transmitted diseases

The Story of the Great Pox

It was 1494, not long after Christopher Columbus had returned from his first voyage to the New World. Spanish soldiers, including some of Columbus's men, were fighting the French in Italy. When the war ended and the soldiers returned home, they seemed to carry with them a terrible new illness. The Great Pox, as it was called, raged across Europe and Asia. It caused joint pain, genital sores, rashes, and wounds that gnawed away at the face, disfiguring people before it killed them after years of suffering.

The Great Pox was syphilis, scientists think, but in a more severe and contagious form than we know it today. One of the great debates of medical history is whether the men who sailed with Columbus brought syphilis back from the Americas or whether it had long been present in the Old World, perhaps confused with leprosy, and suddenly became more virulent*. The question is still unsettled.

What Is Syphilis?

Syphilis is caused by the spirochete (SPY-ro-keet) *Treponema pallidum* (trep-o-NEE-ma PAL-i-dum), a corkscrew-shaped type of bacteria that spreads throughout the body and can infect almost any organ. It usually is transmitted by contact with syphilitic lesions, or sores, during sexual activity, although in rare cases it can spread by nonsexual touching of a sore.

Today, syphilis is still a serious disease, but the antibiotic* penicillin (pen-i-SIL-in) can cure it easily and prevent its spread. In the United States in 1995, health officials detected 1,500 cases of syphilis in newborns and 68,000 cases of syphilis in adults. By 1997, recently acquired infections were at the lowest levels ever reported in the United States. Health officials are especially eager to prevent syphilis because people who have syphilitic sores are more likely to become infected with HIV, the virus that causes AIDS.

Getting Sick in Stages

The symptoms of syphilis appear in stages. The first stage, called primary syphilis, usually occurs about three weeks after infection when a sore called a chancre (SHANG-ker) appears on the body, usually in the genital area*. People often ignore the sore because it does not hurt and goes away on its own in a few weeks. Sometimes they do not notice it at all.

The secondary, or disseminated stage, usually starts about six weeks after infection. People feel achy, tired, and feverish. They usually have a rash that may be prominent on the palms of the hand and soles of the

** **virulent** comes from the Latin word for poisonous, and describes a microbe that is especially adept at overcoming the body's immune system defenses.*

** **antibiotics** (an-ty-by-OT-iks) are drugs that kill bacteria.*

** The **genital area** is the area around the external sex organs.*

The spirochete *Treponema pallidum* is seen under the electron microscope.
© *Chris Bjornberg/Photo Researchers, Inc.*

▼

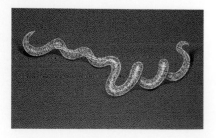

feet. They often lose patches of hair, giving their head a moth-eaten appearance. This bout of illness also goes away on its own. People may think they had influenza or measles, and that they are all better.

Syphilis then enters a latent, or hidden, phase. For a year or two, people may develop an occasional sore, but after that they seem healthy. In most people, the bacteria either are gone or remain inactive forever. But about one-third of infected people go on to develop late or tertiary* syphilis anywhere from 3 to 40 years after they were first infected.

Tertiary syphilis can cause problems in almost any organ. Wounds called gummas may form in the skin, bones, lungs, liver, or other internal organs and can eat away tissue in the nose or mouth, much as leprosy does. Cardiovascular syphilis (kar-dee-o-VAS-ku-lar syphilis) damages the heart or blood vessels. Neurosyphilis (NYOOR-o-sif-i-lis), which affects the nervous system, can cause headache, dizziness, and convulsions. With the most severe form of neurosyphilis, called general paresis (pa-REE-sis), people lose their memory, their reasoning ability, and their sanity. They may become blind, deaf, or paralyzed before dying.

Untreated, syphilis causes the death of 10 to 20 percent of those it infects. If a pregnant woman has untreated primary or secondary syphilis, her baby may be stillborn (dead at birth) or born already infected with syphilis (congenital syphilis). An infected baby may appear healthy at first or may have symptoms that include a rash and bloody mucus* in the nose. Later the baby may have abnormalities of the bones and teeth, mental retardation, blindness, or deafness.

As recently as the early 1930s, 60,000 children a year were born with syphilis in the United States, and as many as 20 percent of the people in American mental institutions suffered from its effects. Because of the impact it used to have on society, syphilis has been likened to AIDS, the terrible epidemic of our own age.

How Is Syphilis Diagnosed?

Syphilis can affect so many organs and resemble so many other diseases that doctors used to call it "the great impostor." Today, when doctors suspect syphilis from the symptoms, they use a microscope to look for the spirochete in fluid taken from a sore, or they can check for syphilis with blood tests.

If the syphilis spirochete is present, doctors may want to check whether the bacteria have entered the central nervous system. This requires a spinal tap, a procedure in which a needle is inserted next to the spinal cord to remove some spinal fluid for testing. Doctors usually will recommend testing for other sexually transmitted diseases including HIV, too. They also will recommend that anyone who had sex with the infected person be tested for syphilis and other sexually transmitted diseases.

How Is Syphilis Treated?

The antibiotic penicillin, developed in the 1940s, revolutionized syphilis treatment. A single injection was enough to cure primary or secondary

*tertiary (TER-she-air-ee) means the third stage.

*mucus (MYOO-kus) is a kind of body slime. It is thick and slippery, and it lines the inside of many parts of the body. The linings that make mucus are called mucous membranes.

THE TUSKEGEE SYPHILIS STUDY

They were poor black men, sharecroppers, mainly, who were trying to scratch out a living in Macon County, Alabama, during the Great Depression of the 1930s. Doctors from the United States government promised them free medical care if they would take part in a study of "bad blood," the local term for a number of illnesses, including anemia, diabetes, and syphilis.

Of those who agreed, 399 had syphilis. They got free medical examinations, burial insurance, and some free meals, but for 40 years (from 1932 to 1972) federal doctors knowingly let their syphilis go untreated without ever telling them that they were being denied treatment. Even after penicillin, a quick and easy cure for syphilis, was developed in the 1940s, researchers did not treat the men, but simply observed as some of the men went on to sicken and die. The doctors' goal was to understand more about syphilis by seeing how it behaves when left untreated.

The Tuskegee syphilis study ended in 1972 when newspaper stories made it public and brought a wave of revulsion from the public. In 1974 new rules were developed to protect the rights of people taking part in federally sponsored experiments. In 1997 President Bill Clinton apologized on behalf of the nation to the survivors of the most notorious medical experiment in United States history.

Issues raised by the study are still with us today. For instance, even today African Americans are less likely to get needed medical treatments, from AIDS drugs to organ transplants, than other Americans. The reasons are complicated but many researchers think racism is a factor as it was in the Tuskegee study.

syphilis and to prevent congenital syphilis. Today, more than 50 years after the discovery of penicillin, that is still true. In latent, tertiary, and congenital syphilis, multiple doses of penicillin can eliminate the bacteria, but some internal organs may already be permanently damaged. Although penicillin is still the best medicine for syphilis, other antibiotics sometimes are used in special cases.

How Can Syphilis Be Prevented?

Syphilis can be prevented by refraining from sexual activity with an infected person. Using condoms can prevent transmission, but only if the condom covers all sores.

Once people have been effectively treated for syphilis, they no longer can transmit the disease. If untreated, syphilis stops being contagious when lesions stop appearing, usually a year or two after the person became infected.

PAUL EHRLICH AND SAHACHIRO HATA

For centuries doctors attacked syphilis with dangerous compounds like mercury that could rot the bones. Some even infected patients with malaria in order to raise a fever and "sweat out" the disease. But early in the twentieth century, a German doctor named Paul Ehrlich (1854–1915) had a better idea.

Dr. Ehrlich, who studied the immune system, thought he could create chemical compounds that would act as "magic bullets." By this he meant that they would target the microbes that caused specific diseases without harming the rest of the body, much as the antibodies of the immune system do. Working with a Japanese colleague, Sahachiro Hata (1872–1938), Dr. Ehrlich tested hundreds of compounds against syphilis. In 1890, their six hundred and sixth experiment worked. They had found a cure for syphilis, an arsenic compound called Salcarsan or 606.

Treatment was still quite risky, since arsenic can be a poison. But the drug marked the beginning of the modern age of medicines that have saved countless lives. One of those modern medicines, the antibiotic penicillin, later proved to be closer to a magic bullet for syphilis, often curing the dreaded disease with a single shot.

Resources

Organizations

The Centers for Disease Control and Prevention's Division of STD Prevention posts information, including a fact sheet and background on the Tuskegee syphilis study, on its website.
http://www.cdc.gov/nchstp/dstd

The Centers for Disease Control and Prevention National Sexually Transmitted Diseases Hotline has counselors on hand to answer questions. Telephone 800-227-8922

▶ *See also*
Sexually Transmitted Diseases

Systemic Lupus Erythematosus *See* **Lupus**

T

Tapeworm

Tapeworms are long, flat, intestinal worms found in humans and many other animals.

Tapeworms, also called cestodes (SES-todes), infect humans worldwide, although they are rare in the United States. The most common species in humans are *Taenia saginata*, the beef tapeworm, and *Taenia solium*, the pork tapeworm. As adults, these worms stay in the intestines and usually do little harm. But if people become infected with the cysts (immature stage) of the pork tapeworm, they can develop a condition called cysticercosis (sis-ti-ser-KO-sis), which can damage the brain. This is a major health problem in many tropical countries.

What Is the Life Cycle of the Beef Tapeworm?

The adult beef tapeworm is usually a whopping 15 to 30 feet long (4.5 to 9 meters) and lives in the small intestine. An infected person usually has only one or two worms. The tapeworms use their head, called the scolex, to attach themselves to the intestinal wall. They have 1,000 to 2,000 body segments, called proglottids, each containing 80,000 to 100,000 eggs.

The eggs can survive for months or years in the environment. When cattle or other herbivores (plant-eaters) eat egg-contaminated vegetation, the eggs hatch and burrow through their intestinal wall. The larvae* burrow into muscles and form fluid-filled cysts, which are protective capsules. If humans eat raw or undercooked beef containing cysts, the cysts develop over a 2-month period into adult tapeworms. Adult beef tapeworms can live for more than 30 years.

What Is the Life Cycle of the Pork Tapeworm?

The adult pork tapeworm is about half as long as the beef tapeworm, usually 8 to 11 feet (2.5 to 3.5 meters) long. It also has a scolex for attaching to the intestinal wall and a body of about 1,000 proglottids. Each proglottid contains about 50,000 eggs.

The life cycle is similar to the beef tapeworm's except that the worms infect pigs instead of cows. When humans eat raw or undercooked pork

KEYWORDS
for searching the Internet
and other reference sources

Cestodes

Infestation

Neurocysticercosis

*** larvae** are worms at an intermediate stage of the life cycle between eggs and adulthood.

The head of the beef tapeworm *Taenia saginata,* which is where the worm attaches to the intestine. © *1995 Science Photo Library/Custom Medical Stock Photo.*

▼

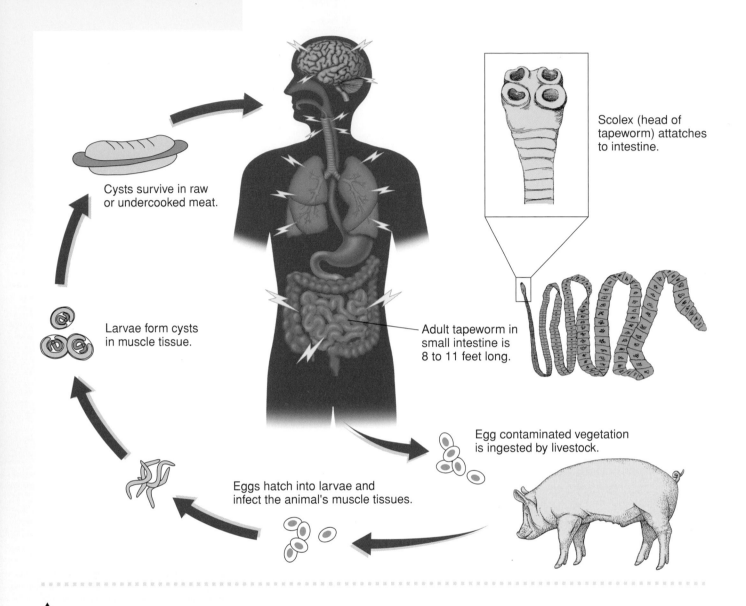

Scolex (head of tapeworm) attaches to intestine.

Cysts survive in raw or undercooked meat.

Larvae form cysts in muscle tissue.

Adult tapeworm in small intestine is 8 to 11 feet long.

Egg contaminated vegetation is ingested by livestock.

Eggs hatch into larvae and infect the animal's muscle tissues.

▲

Life cycle of the pork tapeworm.

containing cysts, the cysts develop into adult tapeworms in humans. Adult pork tapeworms can live up to 25 years.

Cysticercosis   Pork tapeworms also can cause a more serious infection, called cysticercosis. This happens if people eat or drink something contaminated with human waste containing pork tapeworm eggs. The eggs hatch into cysts in the intestines, and the cysts travel through the blood to the rest of the body, especially the muscles and brain.

What Are the Signs and Symptoms of Tapeworm Infection?

Beef tapeworm infections produce only mild symptoms that may include diarrhea, abdominal pain, and weight loss. Pork tapeworm infections generally produce no symptoms. Cysticercosis, however, can cause muscle pain, weakness, and fever. If the central nervous system is involved, it can also cause epilepsy* or inflammation of the brain and the membranes around it (meningoencephalitis).

*** epilepsy** is a disorder in which a person repeatedly has seizures, sudden attacks in which the person may jerk, grow rigid, or lose consciousness briefly.

How Do Doctors Diagnose and Treat Tapeworm Infection?

Eggs and proglottids can be seen in stool samples by microscopic examination. But to tell which tapeworm—beef or pork—is involved, a scolex would have to be removed and examined. This is seldom done, as doctors usually can prescribe the same medication for both types of infection. Stools are checked at 3 and 6 months after treatment to ensure that the infection is gone.

Cysticercosis is diagnosed by examining the muscles or brain with a CT scan* that can show the cysts. Blood tests for antibodies, which are substances the body makes to fight the infection, can confirm the diagnosis. Cysticercosis is also treated with medication but, in rare instances, cysts may be removed surgically.

Prevention   Tapeworm infection may be prevented by thoroughly cooking meat until juices run clear and the centers are no longer pink. This ensures that any tapeworm cysts in the meat are destroyed.

*CT scans or CAT scans are the short form for computerized axial tomography, which uses x-rays and computers to view structures inside the body.

Resource

The U.S. National Center for Infectious Diseases has a fact sheet about cysticercosis at its website.
http://www.cdc.gov/nciod/focus/vol6no4/dpd.htm

▶ *See also*
Encephalitis
Parasitic Diseases
Worms

Tay-Sachs Disease

Tay-Sachs disease is a rare inherited disorder that results in slow destruction of the central nervous system (brain and spinal cord).

KEYWORDS
for searching the Internet and other reference sources

Hexosaminidase A (Hex-A)

Neurology

What Is Tay-Sachs Disease?

Tay-Sachs disease is a rare metabolic disorder with severe neurologic (nervous system) symptoms. "Metabolic" refers to the body's chemical processes that produce protein and other substances, and break down nutrients to release energy. Tay-Sachs disease is a metabolic disorder because it is caused by the absence of the enzyme (a type of protein) hexosaminidase A (Hex-A). Hex-A is necessary for breaking down fatty substances called lipids. Without Hex-A, these lipids build up in, and eventually destroy, the nerve cells in the brain. Ultimately, the nervous system stops functioning properly.

How Does Tay-Sachs Disease Affect the Body?

Classical Tay-Sachs   The most common form of Tay-Sachs disease (classical Tay-Sachs) affects children and usually is fatal. It is caused by a complete lack of Hex-A. Destruction of nerve cells begins before birth,

* **seizures** are sudden attacks of disease, often referring to some type of violent spasms.

but an affected baby does not begin to lose nerve function until he or she is about six months old. By age two, the child may have seizures* and begins to lose skills such as crawling, sitting, turning over, and reaching for things. Eventually, the child will be blind, paralyzed, and mentally retarded. Children with this form of Tay-Sachs disease do not live past age five.

A variation of this scenario is when children develop symptoms between the ages of two and five rather than as an infant. The same symptoms emerge, but the disease progresses more slowly. Children with this form usually die by age 15.

Late onset Tay-Sachs (LOTS) Late onset Tay-Sachs disease (LOTS) is less common than the infantile form. It affects teenagers and adults in their twenties and thirties by causing a gradual loss of nerve function. People with LOTS have low levels of Hex-A rather than a complete lack of it. As LOTS develops, people affected by it may grow clumsy, uncoordinated, and moody. They may experience muscle weakness, twitching, slurred speech, and intellectual impairment. The symptoms vary in type and severity from person to person. Because this form develops so gradually, life expectancy of affected people seems to be similar to that of unaffected people.

How Do People Get Tay-Sachs Disease?

Tay-Sachs disease is caused by a mutation (abnormal change) in the gene that codes for Hex-A, and it is a recessive trait. This means that people will have the disease if they have two copies of the defective gene, but they will not have the disease if they have at least one unaffected copy. People with one normal copy and one defective copy are called carriers, because they can pass the disease on to their children.

Just about anyone can be a carrier of the gene for Tay-Sachs disease. In the general population, about 1 in 250 people carries the gene.

People inherit Tay-Sachs disease when they inherit a defective gene from both parents, resulting in two defective genes that make the body unable to produce Hex-A correctly. People who have only one defective gene are called carriers. Carriers do not have the disease, because they have inherited one healthy gene to code for Hex-A, but they may pass the defective gene on to their children. If both parents are carriers, each child born to them has a 1 in 4 liklihood of having the disease. ▶

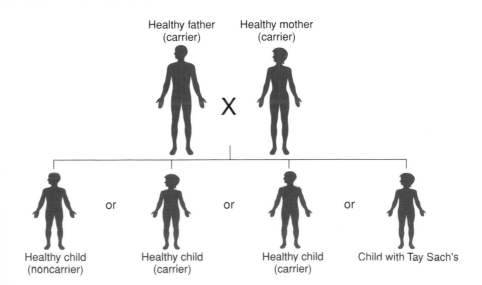

Healthy father (carrier) X Healthy mother (carrier)

Healthy child (noncarrier) or Healthy child (carrier) or Healthy child (carrier) or Child with Tay Sach's

WHAT'S IN A NAME?

Tay-Sachs disease was named for two scientists working on opposite sides of the Atlantic Ocean.

Warren Tay (1843–1927) was a British eye doctor. In 1881, he described a patient with a cherry red spot on the retina of eye (the structure inside the eye that receives light). This spot is characteristic of the classical form of the disease.

An American neurologist (nerve and brain specialist) named Bernard Sachs (1858–1944) described the changes in cells caused by the disease. He also recognized that it was an inherited condition that ran in families and that most babies with the disease were of eastern European Jewish descent.

However, some populations of people include more carriers than others. For example, 1 in 27 people of eastern European Jewish (Ashkenazi) descent in the United States is a carrier. People of French-Canadian ancestry from one part of Quebec and the Cajun population in Louisiana also have a higher than usual risk of carrying the Tay-Sachs gene.

Is There a Cure for Tay-Sachs Disease?

Although researchers are actively looking for a way to prevent or treat Tay-Sachs disease, currently no treatment or cure exists. However, tests have been developed that allow people to find out if they carry the defective gene. Blood tests can determine the level of Hex-A in people's blood (carriers have about half as much as noncarriers) and DNA tests may find evidence of mutations in the Hex-A gene. Testing is particularly useful for people who have had relatives with Tay-Sachs disease and for people in high-risk populations. Finding out about risk before having a baby can prevent the anguish of watching a child develop and then die from Tay-Sachs disease.

Prenatal tests also exist for women who already are pregnant. The amniotic fluid (the fluid in which the fetus develops) or the chorionic villus (structures inside the mother's uterus) both contain fluid from the developing baby that can be sampled and tested for the presence of Hex-A. If Hex-A is present, that means that the fetus does not have Tay-Sachs disease.

Resources

National Tay-Sachs and Allied Diseases Association, Inc., 2001 Beacon Street, Suite 204, Brookline, MA 02146.
Telephone 800-906-8723
http://www.ntsad.org/

Late Onset Tay-Sachs Foundation, 1303 Paper Mill Road, Erdenheim, PA 19038.
Telephone 800-672-2022

March of Dimes Foundation, 1275 Mamaroneck Avenue, White Plains, NY 10605.
Telephone 888-663-4637
http://www.modimes.org/

TB *See* Tuberculosis

▶ *See also*
Genetic Diseases
Metabolic Diseases

Temporomandibular Joint Syndrome (TMJ)

Temporomandibular (tem-po-ro-man-DIB-yoo-lar) joint syndrome refers to symptoms caused by problems with the joint that joins the jawbone to the skull.

KEYWORDS
for searching the Internet and other reference sources

Bruxism

Malocclusion

Whiplash injuries

What Is TMJ?

Technically, TMJ stands for temporomandibular joint, or jaw joint, one of which is located on each side of the head. These joints are where the lower jaw, or mandible (MAN-di-bul), meets the temporal (TEM-po-ral) bone, which is one of a pair of bones that form the lower part of the

Side view of a temporomandibular joint.

▶

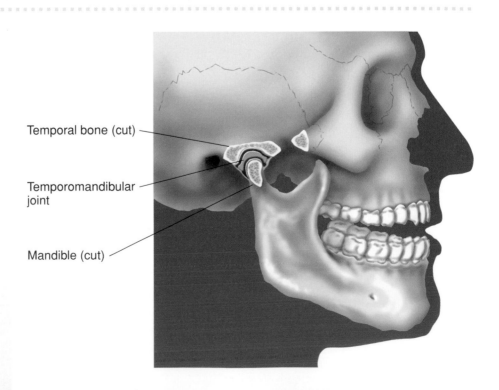

Temporal bone (cut)

Temporomandibular joint

Mandible (cut)

skull. Each temporomandibular joint acts as both a hinge and a gliding joint; they allow the jaw to open and to slide from side to side.

TMJ also refers to temporomandibular joint syndrome (or disorder), in which the joints do not function properly. This may cause pain, difficulty opening and closing the mouth easily, or problems with chewing and swallowing, as well as other symptoms.

What Are the Causes of TMJ?

TMJ can be caused by dislocated temporomandibular joints or by inherited problems with the joints. In a condition called bruxism (BRUK-sizum), some people grind their teeth during sleep or times of stress, which can lead to TMJ. Malocclusion (mal-o-KLOO-zhun), when teeth do not fit together properly; whiplash injuries* from car accidents; being hit on the head or jaw; and arthritis* are other causes of TMJ.

What Are the Symptoms of TMJ?

Since the TMJ joint is located near many important nerves going between the brain and many parts of the body, the symptoms can be felt in parts of the body that do not seem related to the TMJ joint. Millions of Americans report some of the following symptoms:

- Frequent headaches
- Pain in the face, sinuses, ears, eyes, teeth, neck, and back
- Clicking sounds in the jaw
- Difficulty in opening or closing the mouth
- Trouble chewing or swallowing

*whiplash injuries describe general injuries to the spine and spinal cord at the junction of the fourth and fifth vertebrae (VER-te-bray) in the neck occurring as a result of rapid acceleration or deceleration of the body.

*arthritis (ar-THRY-tis) refers to any of several disorders characterized by inflammation (in-fla-MAY-shun) of the joints.

How Is TMJ Diagnosed and Treated?

Doctors or dentists will ask the patient to describe the symptoms and will then examine the patient. Sometimes, x-rays and MRIs* are used to examine the joints to diagnose TMJ.

Hot compresses and over-the-counter pain medications may help relieve TMJ. Stress management and mouth guards worn at night can help eliminate teeth grinding and its effects.

*MRI, which is short for magnetic resonance imaging, produces computerized images of internal body tissues based on the magnetic properties of atoms within the body.

Resources

The National Institute of Dental and Craniofacial Research (NIDCR), part of the U.S. National Institutes of Health (NIH), posts information about TMJ on its website.
http://www.nidr.nih.gov/news/pubs/tmd/main.htm

TMJ Association, Ltd., P.O. Box 26770, Milwaukee, WI 53226-0770. The TMJ Association provides information and support for people who have TMJ.
Telephone 414-259-3223
http://www.tmj.org

▶ *See also*
Arthritis
Headache

Jaw Joints and Allied Musculo-Skeletal Disorders Foundation, Inc. (JJAMD), Forsyth Dental Research Center, 140 Fenway, Boston, MA 02115-3799. This organization, founded in 1982, provides information and support for people with TMJ.
Telephone 617-266-2550

Tendinitis *See* Repetitive Stress Syndrome

Tennis Elbow *See* Repetitive Stress Syndrome

Testicular Cancer

Testicular (tes-TIK-yoo-lar) cancer occurs when cells in the testicle (TES-ti-kul), one of the two male sex glands located in the scrotum* below the penis, divide without control or order, forming a tumor*. Over time, these cancer cells can spread to other parts of the body.

A Skater's Story

In February of 1997, while on tour with his professional ice skating show, former Olympic champion Scott Hamilton started experiencing sharp, shooting pains in his abdomen* and lower back. Assuming that he had pulled a muscle, he continued along with the tour. Several weeks later, though, the pain became unbearable, and Hamilton underwent testing at a nearby hospital. Doctors found a grapefruit-sized tumor in his abdomen, which they soon discovered had originated in his testicle. At that point, the skater left the tour and returned home to be treated for cancer*.

For the next 3 to 4 months, Hamilton underwent chemotherapy* in the hope that it would shrink his tumor. Fortunately it worked, and over time the tumor became considerably smaller. That made it much easier for doctors to remove. However, the course of treatment was difficult and weakened Hamilton physically. It took time for him to get back to the level of stamina and flexibility that figure skating requires. Showing the same drive that propelled him to an Olympic gold medal in 1984, Hamilton worked hard and was able to return to the ice within the year.

What Is Testicular Cancer?

The testicles, also called the testes or male gonads, are the male sex glands located below the penis in a pouch of skin called the scrotum. The testicles are the body's main source of male hormones*, which control the

KEYWORDS
for searching the Internet and other reference sources

Chemotherapy

Neoplasm

Testicular self-examination

* **scrotum** (SKRO-tum) is the pouch on a male body that contains the testicles.

* **tumor** (TOO-mor) usually refers to an abnormal growth of body tissue that has no known cause or physiologic purpose and is not an inflammation.

* **abdomen** (AB-do-men), commonly called the belly, is the portion of the body between the chest or thorax (THOR-aks) and the pelvis.

* **cancer** is any tumorous (TOO-mor-us) condition, the natural (untreated) course of which is often fatal.

* **chemotherapy** (kee-mo-THER-a-pee) is the treatment of cancer with powerful drugs that kill cancer cells.

development of the reproductive organs and male sex characteristics such as body and facial hair, low voice, and muscular arms. They also produce and store sperm, the tiny, tadpole-like cells that fertilize the female egg.

Testicular cancer usually begins when cells begin to divide without control or order, forming a tumor. Cells can break away from the tumor and enter the blood or the lymph, an almost colorless fluid produced by tissues all over the body. The fluid passes through lymph (LIMF) nodes*, the bean-shaped organs that filter the lymph, fight infection, and produce certain kinds of blood cells. When testicular cancer spreads, cancer cells usually are found in the nearby lymph nodes, the liver*, or the lungs.

The Importance of Early Detection

Like most types of cancer, testicular cancer can be treated most easily when it is found early. That is why doctors encourage all teenage boys and men to perform monthly testicular self-examination (TSE), which involves rolling each testicle between the fingers and thumb. The testicles are smooth, oval-shaped, and rather firm, and men who examine themselves regularly become familiar with the way their testicles feel. If any change occurs, it should be reported to a doctor. For most men, it takes time to get comfortable with doing TSE, but it is the best way to find a lump early. This usually is the first sign of testicular cancer.

Other possible symptoms of testicular cancer include:

- Any enlargement of a testicle
- A feeling of heaviness in the scrotum
- A dull persistent ache in the lower abdomen or the groin
- A sudden collection of fluid in the scrotum
- Pain or discomfort in a testicle or in the scrotum.

It is important for all men to be aware of these symptoms, because doctors cannot predict who will get testicular cancer and who will not. They have not been able to identify what causes it. They do know that boys who are born with undescended testicles (located in the lower abdomen, rather than in the scrotum) have a higher risk of developing testicular cancer later in life. However, it usually develops for no apparent reason.

How Is Testicular Cancer Diagnosed?

Doctors begin by examining the scrotum and testes carefully and ordering urine and blood tests. These tests can help determine whether an infection or some other disorder might be causing the symptoms. Also, if a tumor is present, certain substances in the blood may be found at higher levels. These substances are called tumor markers, because they often are found in abnormal amounts in patients with some types of cancer. The doctor may also order tests that create images of the inside of the body, such as a CT scan* or an ultrasound*.

After all of these tests, the doctor can be reasonably certain about the diagnosis. However, the only sure way to determine whether cancer is

* **hormones** are chemicals that are produced by different glands in the body. Hormones are like the body's ambassadors: they are created in one place but are sent through the body to have specific regulatory effects in different places.

* **lymph nodes** are round masses of tissue that contain immune cells that filter out harmful microorganisms.

* **liver** is a large organ located in the upper abdomen that has many functions, including storage and filtration of blood, secretion of bile, and participation in various metabolic (met-a-BOLL-ik) processes.

* **CT scan** or CAT scan are the shortened names for computerized axial tomography (to-MOG-ra-fee), which uses x-rays and computers to view structures inside the body.

* **ultrasound** is a painless procedure in which sound waves passing through the body create images on a computer screen.

843

* **metastases** (me-TAS-ta-seez) are new tumors formed when cancer cells from a tumor spread to other parts of the body.

present is to examine a sample of tissue under a microscope. In an operation, surgeons remove the affected testicle.

Once cancer is diagnosed, doctors need to figure out whether it has spread to other parts of the body and formed metastases*. They may perform other tests to look for cancer elsewhere. Because the cancer frequently spreads through the lymph nodes in the abdomen, these may be removed and then checked for cancer cells.

How Is Testicular Cancer Treated?

The removal of the testicle, which is necessary to diagnose the cancer, is also the first step in treating it. In addition, tumors that have spread to other parts of the body may be removed partly or entirely by surgery. In most cases, surgery will be followed by radiation therapy, which focuses high-energy rays on the remaining tumor to kill cancer cells and stop their growth.

In some cases, chemotherapy may be used either before or after surgery. During chemotherapy, anticancer drugs are given by mouth or by injection into a muscle or vein.

Life after Testicular Cancer

Fortunately, this disease responds well to treatment, even when it has spread from the testicle to other parts of the body. Men who have had testicular cancer need to see their doctors for regular follow-up appointments to make sure that the cancer has not recurred.

A man with one healthy testicle can still have sex and father children. Radiation therapy and chemotherapy may cause a temporary drop in sperm production, but it usually returns to normal within a few months. Patients who are concerned about how they look can also have an artificial testicle, called a testicular prosthesis*, placed in the scrotum. It looks and feels just like a normal testicle.

* **prosthesis** (pros-THEE-sis) is an artificial substitute for a missing body part. It can be used for appearance only or to replace the function of the missing part (as with a prosthetic leg).

Resources

The National Cancer Institute (NCI), part of the U.S. National Institutes of Health (NIH), posts information about testicular cancer on its website. From the Publication Index, follow the links Types of Cancer, "What You Need To Know About Cancer" Series, and Testis. Telephone 800-422-6237

http://rex.nci.nih.gov/NCI_PUB_INDEX/PUB_INDEX_DOC.html

The American Cancer Society's website features a section devoted to testicular cancer. Telephone 800-227-2345

http://www.cancer.org

▶ See also

Cancer

Prostate Cancer

Tetanus

Tetanus (TET-a-nus) is one of the oldest diseases known to afflict human beings. It is a disease that attacks the central nervous system, causing lockjaw and other symptoms. Tetanus is caused by infection of a wound by the bacterium Clostridium tetani.

KEYWORDS
for searching the Internet
and other reference sources

Bacterial infection

Vaccination

What Is Tetanus?

The bacteria *Clostridium tetani* are present in soil and in animal feces. The bacteria can produce spores, which are a special form of the bacteria that is resistant to heat and disinfectants. When spores enter the skin through a wound, they can germinate into the more active form of *Clostridium tetani.* The bacteria can then produce a substance that is very toxic (poisonous) to human beings. This toxin causes the symptoms of tetanus.

Tetanus is a rare disease in the United States (about 100 cases a year) because children are routinely vaccinated against it. But the disease is more common in places that do not have rigorous immunization policies. In the United States people who get tetanus tend to be older; many of them have not been adequately immunized. Without treatment, tetanus can be fatal.

How Do People Get Tetanus?

People get tetanus through an infected open wound. If a person steps on a rusty nail, for example, he or she could become ill from the spores of the tetanus bacteria. The bacteria produce a substance that is toxic to the central nervous system. Because the spores cannot germinate and the

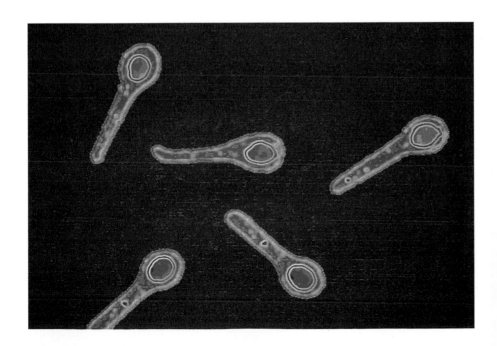

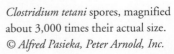

Clostridium tetani spores, magnified about 3,000 times their actual size.
© *Alfred Pasieka, Peter Arnold, Inc.*

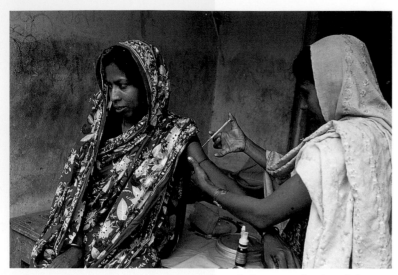

▲

A government health worker gives a
tetanus injection to a pregnant woman at
a rural clinic in Bangladesh. © *Shehzad
Noorani/Still Pictures/Peter Arnold, Inc.*

bacteria cannot live when there is a high
level of oxygen, wounds that do not have a
good blood supply or are not exposed to air
are more likely to lead to tetanus.

Once the bacteria have entered the body,
it may take from 3 to 50 days (with an average of 5 to 10 days) for symptoms to appear.

What Are the Symptoms of Tetanus?

Stiffness of the jaw (lockjaw) is the most common symptom of tetanus. A person with
tetanus has difficulty opening his or her
mouth. Other muscles become stiff (back,
abdomen, face). If the muscles of the face stiffen, a person with tetanus
looks as if he or she has a fixed smile that does not change.

The patient may also have a fever, perspire heavily, have a rapid
pulse, feel restless, and have muscle spasms. Noise and light may cause
seizures in a person with tetanus. Infants with tetanus are unable to
nurse because they lose their ability to suck.

How Is Tetanus Diagnosed and Treated?

There are no reliable tests for tetanus. The doctor makes a diagnosis
from the symptoms a person has and from a recent history of open
wounds. It is, unfortunately, easier for a doctor to diagnose tetanus in its
later rather than its earlier stages. Some of the symptoms of tetanus
could indicate a different disease.

When the doctor does determine that tetanus is present, the patient
should be given an injection of tetanus antitoxin. The antitoxin contains

THE DISCOVERY OF TETANUS

The German physician Arthur Nicolaier discovered the tetanus
bacillus in 1884. He was not able, however, to obtain a pure
culture of the tetanus, which would have allowed him to study it
more closely. Instead, he confirmed that the bacteria generated the
tetanus toxin by injecting garden soil containing the bacteria into animals and observing the resultant symptoms of tetanus. Five years later,
the Japanese bacteriologist Shibasaburo Kitasato cultivated the tetanus
bacterium in pure culture and a year later developed an effective tetanus
antitoxin. After World War I, English scientists developed an improved
antitoxin that was put to use after World War II when the establishment
of active immunization for all children became a standard practice.

antibodies that attach to and neutralize the tetanus toxin. The person is also immunized for tetanus. After being treated with antitoxin, the infected areas are cleansed thoroughly. Then antibiotics are given to the patient to destroy bacteria in the wound. Other drugs are given to control the symptoms that are present. In some cases, a mechanical ventilator (breathing machine) is needed to help regulate the person's breathing. The patient is kept in a dark and quiet environment, since light and noise stimulate symptoms of the disease.

Can Tetanus Be Prevented?

Tetanus can be prevented by vaccination. In combination with vaccines against diphtheria (a bacterial infection that causes sore throat and fever) and pertussis (whooping cough), a tetanus vaccination is given routinely to children in the United States. The vaccine will protect a person for 10 years, after which a booster shot is recommended. When a person has a serious wound to the skin and has not been immunized for over 10 years, tetanus antitoxin injections are administered as a precaution.

Resources

Henderson, Alan D. "Neonatal Tetanus." *Health Letter on the CDC,* December 28, 1998, p. 10.

The U.S. Centers for Disease Control and Prevention (CDC), 1600 Clifton Road, N.E., Atlanta, GA 30333. The United States government authority for information about infectious and other diseases, the CDC posts information about tetanus at its website. http://cdc.gov/nip/vaccine/nip-dtp.htm

Weinberg, Winkler. *No Germs Allowed.* New Brunswick, NJ: Rutgers University Press, 1996.

Thrombosis

Thrombosis is the formation of a blood clot, called a thrombus, that blocks part or all of a blood vessel, such as a vein.

KEYWORDS
*for searching the Internet
and other reference sources*

Cardiovascular system

Circulatory system

Within moments after a finger is cut, platelets in the blood begin to gather at the injury. Platelets are tiny disc-shaped cells in the blood, much smaller than even a red blood cell. The platelets react with calcium and with other substances in the body's tissues to form a semi-solid, stringy protein. The cut covers with a scab and eventually heals. For injuries like cuts, clots are good things. But when clots form inside blood vessels, the condition is called thrombosis, and it can be life threatening.

* **phlebitis** (fle-BY-tis) refers to inflammation of a vein.

* **tumor** refers to an abnormal growth of body tissue. Tumors may or may not be cancerous.

* **pulmonary** refers to the lungs.
* **embolism** is a blockage in a blood vessel caused by a blood clot, air bubble, fatty tissue, or other substance that traveled through the bloodstream from another part of the body.

How Does Thrombosis Happen?

Phlebitis   Thrombosis usually begins as an inflammation of the vein known as phlebitis*. Phlebitis develops when blood flows slowly or pools in veins. This usually occurs in the legs and causes injury to the walls of the vein. Just as platelets gather to form clots on cut fingers, they also may start to form clots along the injured walls of veins. People with phlebitis may experience pain and tenderness along the vein, skin discoloration, swelling and edema, a rapid pulse, and mild fever. If untreated, many people with phlebitis develop thrombosis in the inflamed vein.

Causes   There are many possible causes. Inactivity, such as sitting for long periods of time or resting in bed, is a major cause. Surgery, tumors*, and injuries to the leg also may cause thrombosis. Certain infections and cancers may alter the clotting substances in the blood and cause thrombosis.

Women are especially at risk, because the female hormone estrogen is linked to thrombosis. Pregnant women have very high levels of estrogen. Estrogen is also found in birth control pills and in the hormone replacement medications that some women use after menopause, although thromboses due to these medications are not very common.

What Are the Signs and Symptoms of Thrombosis?

The major symptoms of thrombosis are pain in the affected area and swelling, which can occur suddenly. If the thrombosis involves a leg vein, the leg also might appear red and feel warm to the touch. Veins close to the skin surface may look larger than normal and reddish-blue in color.

The biggest danger is when a clot forms in the large veins that are deep within the legs. If the blood clot grows, it may break off. The clot may then travel toward and then through the heart and block the pulmonary* artery, which is a major blood vessel, causing a pulmonary embolism*. This serious complication of thrombosis may cause death if not treated rapidly and effectively.

How Do Doctors Diagnose and Treat Thrombosis?

Doctors use several tests to determine if patients have thrombosis. They may inject a dye into the veins and then use an x-ray to look for clots. They may use an ultrasound machine, which uses sound waves to create an internal view of veins similar to an x-ray. Or they may test blood pressure above and below the suspected location of the clot to measure differences.

Thrombosis can be treated with medications that prevent the blood from clotting as easily. This can stop the clot from growing larger and lower the risk that the clot will break free and cause an embolism. Clot-dissolving drugs also may be injected into the vein. A procedure called balloon angioplasty widens the vein around the clot by inserting and inflating a small balloon that pushes out the narrow walls of the vein. Another surgery involves inserting a small, mesh tube within the vein to keep it open.

For people at high risk for developing thrombosis, doctors sometimes recommend preventive measures such as the use of drugs that interfere with blood clotting and special compression stockings that help keep blood from pooling in the deep veins of the legs.

Resource

The Venous Educational Institute of North America posts information and graphics about clots and surgical procedures at its website. http://www.venous-info.com/

▶ *See also*
Clotting
Embolism
Phlebitis
Stroke

Thrush

Thrush is an infection that causes raised white patches in the mouth and throat that can look like cottage cheese. It is caused by the Candida albicans *fungus that also causes diaper rash and vaginal yeast infections.*

What Is Thrush?

Candida albicans is a single-celled fungus that is a natural inhabitant of the mouth. Usually, the body maintains a natural balance of microbes* in the mouth. But if that natural balance has been disturbed, *Candida* and other fungi may begin to grow in the warm moist environment of the mouth and throat. Other names for thrush are oral candidiasis (kan-di-DY-a-sis) and oral moniliasis (mon-i-LY-a-sis).

Thrush and the immune system   Thrush is common in newborns. In older children, and adults, it may be a sign of an immune system disorder. People whose immune systems have been damaged by the AIDS virus, for example, may develop thrush. People who are treated with antibiotics for bacterial infections and people who use steroid inhalers for asthma may also develop thrush.

Neonatal thrush   Infants may get thrush during childbirth, if their mothers have vaginal yeast infections, or they may get thrush from bottles or nipples or family members with contaminated hands. Thrush looks like white patches of cottage cheese on the tongue, palate (roof of the mouth), inner cheeks, or throat. If the white patches of thrush are scraped, however, the sores will bleed, and infants may refuse to suck because of pain in the mouth. *Candida* also causes diaper rash, but those sores are reddish rather than white.

How Is Thrush Diagnosed and Treated?

Thrush usually goes away by itself. Because thrush may be a sign of an immune system disorder, however, it is important to check with a doctor

KEYWORDS
for searching the Internet and other reference sources

Candidiasis

Infection

Moniliasis

Mycotic stomatitis

*****microbes** are small organisms that usually can be seen only under a microscope. They include bacteria, protozoa, and fungi.

Candida albicans coats the tongue of this infant, who has thrush. Infants with thrush may refuse to suck because of pain in the mouth, or they may spread the infection to their fingernails if they suck their thumbs. *Dr. P. Marazzi/Science Photo Library, Photo Researchers, Inc.*

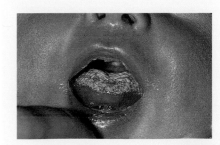

or dentist, who may identify the yeast under a microscope, check for possible causes, and suggest ways to prevent its recurrence.

Thrush usually is treated by prescription medication, taken orally or applied directly to the sores, and by careful hygiene, which includes frequent hand washing, frequent diaper changes, and use of mouth washes.

▶ *See also*
  AIDS and HIV
  Asthma
  Fungal Infections
  Immunodeficiency
  Yeast Infection, Vaginal

Resource

The U.S. Centers for Disease Control and Prevention (CDC) posts *ABCs of Safe and Healthy Child Care* at its website, which includes a fact sheet about thrush.
http://www.cdc.gov/ncidod/hip/abc/facts43.htm

Thyroid Disease

Thyroid disease is an impairment in the normal functioning of the thyroid, an important gland located at the base of the neck. A major function of the thyroid is to regulate metabolism, the biochemical processes in the body. Thyroid disease may speed up or slow down metabolism, producing a wide range of physical and mental symptoms.

KEYWORDS
for searching the Internet and other reference sources

Endocrine system

Goiter

Graves' disease

Hashimoto's thyroiditis

Metabolism

Thyroid-stimulating hormone (TSH)

Thyrotoxicosis

Thyroxine

* **hormones** are chemicals that are produced by different glands in the body. A hormone is like the body's ambassador: it is created in one place but is sent through the body to have specific regulatory effects in different places.

* **metabolism** is the total of all the chemical activities in cells that release energy from nutrients or use energy to make other substances, such as proteins.

What Is the Thyroid?

The thyroid is an H-shaped gland that has two main parts, or lobes, that lie on either side of the trachea (TRAY-key-a) or windpipe. The lobes are connected by a narrow segment called the isthmus. The principal hormone* produced by the thyroid is thyroxine. Production of this hormone is in turn controlled by another hormone, called thyroid-stimulating hormone (TSH), secreted by the pituitary gland located at the base of the brain. Thyroxine is released into the bloodstream and controls the rate of metabolism*. In children, thyroid hormones are essential for normal growth and development.

What Is Thyroid Disease?

Disorders of the thyroid can cause overproduction of thyroid hormones (hyperthyroidism), or underproduction of thyroid hormones (hypothyroidism). Sometimes the thyroid becomes enlarged, a condition known as goiter.

Hyperthyroidism: a revving engine   The most common type of hyperthyroidism, or thyrotoxicosis (thy-ro-tox-i-KO-sis), is called Graves' disease. It is an autoimmune disorder, a disturbance of the immune system. Antibodies stimulate the thyroid to produce excessive quantities of hormone, thereby raising the rate of metabolism. Graves' disease can occur at any age, but the highest incidence of this disorder is in women between 20 and 40 years of age.

Symptoms of Graves' disease include an increased heart rate, nervousness and irritability, tremor, loss of weight, enlarged thyroid gland (goiter), abnormalities of the menstrual periods, sweating and heat intolerance, restless overactivity, and sleeplessness. Sometimes there is also exophthalmos (eks-off-THAL-mus), a condition in which the eyeballs protrude (bulge outward).

Less commonly, hyperthyroidism results from a form of thyroiditis (thyroid-EYE-tus) inflammation of the thyroid caused by a viral infection or by thyroid nodules (lumps or growths) that may produce excess hormones.

Hypothyroidism: a slowing down Whereas hyperthyroidism abnormally raises the metabolic rate, hypothyroidism slows it down too much. Many of the symptoms of hypothyroidism are thus the reverse of those seen in hyperthyroidism. The most common cause of hypothyroidism is Hashimoto's thyroiditis, which occurs most often in young and middle-aged women.

Hashimoto's thyroiditis, like Graves' disease, is an autoimmune disorder. The immune system damages the thyroid rather than stimulating it, resulting in an underproduction of hormone. Symptoms of Hashimoto's thyroiditis include a slow heart rate, tiredness, muscular weakness, weight gain, abnormal menstrual periods, intolerance of cold, dry skin, hair loss, hoarseness, enlarged thyroid (goiter), and mental dullness. In more severe cases, there may be myxedema (mik-se-DEE-ma), a thickening and puffiness of the skin most noticeable in the face.

Less often, hypothyroidism is caused by surgical removal of part or all of the thyroid gland to treat other thyroid conditions, or by insufficient iodine in the diet, which is now a rare occurrence in developed countries.

When hypothyroidism occurs in infancy and is not treated cretinism (KREET-in-izm) results. A child with cretinism has stunted growth and mental deficiency. Older children who become hypothyroid show slowing of growth and delayed sexual maturation.

Goiter Goiter is not itself a disease. The term simply refers to enlargement of the thyroid, sometimes visible as a swelling in the front of the neck. Enlargement of the thyroid can be a sign of hyperthyroidism or hypothyroidism. It even can occur when thyroid function is normal.

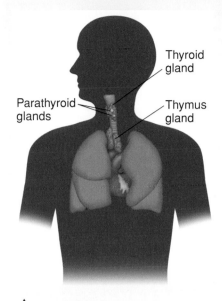

▲
Anatomy of the thyroid glands, parathyroids, and thymus.

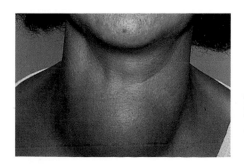
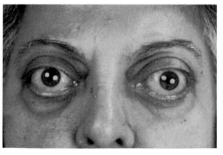

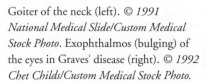
◀
Goiter of the neck (left). © *1991 National Medical Slide/Custom Medical Stock Photo.* Exophthalmos (bulging) of the eyes in Graves' disease (right). © *1992 Chet Childs/Custom Medical Stock Photo.*

IODIZED SALT

Goiter and other thyroid disorders sometimes are the result of too little iodine in the diet. In ancient Greece, iodine-rich seaweed was eaten in response to enlarged thyroid glands. In 1811, the French chemist Courtois identified iodine, which began being used internally in the treatment of thyroid disorders in 1821.

In 1922, the Swiss Goiter Commission introduced the first program of adding iodine to salt as a preventive measure against goiter in Switzerland. Also in 1922, Michigan physician David Murray Cowie expressed interest in eliminating goiter by means of iodized salt. Cowie worked with the Michigan State Medical Society to have iodized salt placed on Michigan grocery shelves and, eventually, in stores across the United States. In areas with such programs, iodine deficiency is rarely seen.

*inflammation (in-fla-MAY-shun) is the body's reaction to irritation, infection, or injury that often involves swelling, pain, redness, and warmth.

A goiter can be seen in hyperthyroidism of Graves' disease, in which the thyroid enlarges due to stimulation of the gland by the malfunctioning immune system. In hypothyroidism, it enlarges as part of the body's attempt to produce enough hormone to compensate for damage done to it by the disease, or because of inflammation* caused by the disease, or both.

Goiter also can occur in parts of the world where there is inadequate iodine in the diet. Found in seafood and most table salt preparations, iodine is an element essential for the formation of thyroid hormones in the body.

Nodules   Distinct swellings or lumps within the thyroid are called nodules. They are most common in women and their incidence increases with age. The large majority of thyroid nodules are benign, but some may be cancerous. They therefore require prompt medical evaluation.

Sometimes the thyroid temporarily enlarges slightly during puberty or pregnancy, without impairing its function or causing any other symptoms.

How Are Thyroid Diseases Diagnosed and Treated?

Diagnosis   To diagnose a suspected thyroid disorder, the doctor will take a medical history and perform a physical examination. Blood samples usually are taken to measure the levels of thyroid hormones and TSH, the pituitary hormone that stimulates the thyroid. The thyroid also may be checked using various scanning techniques. If a thyroid tumor is suspected, a sample of thyroid tissue may be removed for examination.

Treatment   Most thyroid diseases are highly treatable. Hyperthyroidism may be treated with a single dose of radioactive iodine, which destroys overactive thyroid cells. Alternatively, antithyroid medications may be prescribed to suppress formation of thyroid hormones. Surgical removal of most of the thyroid is another treatment. Hypothyroidism is treated with hormone replacement medication, which usually must be continued for life.

A goiter of uncertain cause may disappear on its own, or it may be small and not need treatment. Goiters caused by thyroid disease usually shrink with treatment. Occasionally, surgery is needed for removing a very large goiter. Thyroid disease is not contagious. It often runs in families, and there is no way a person can prevent it. People who live in parts of the world where seafood is scarce and table salt is not iodized, however, need to make sure they take in sufficient amounts of iodine to avoid hypothyroidism and goiter.

Resources

Books

Wood, Lawrence C., M.D., David S. Cooper, M.D., and E. Chester Ridgway, M.D. *Your Thyroid: A Home Reference*, third edition. New York: Ballantine Books, 1996.

Rubenfeld, Sheldon, M.D. *Could It Be My Thyroid.* Houston: Thyroid Society for Education and Research, 1996.

Organizations

American Thyroid Association, Montefiore Medical Center, 111 East 210 Street, Bronx, NY 10467. The American Thyroid Association works with the Thyroid Foundation of America to publish patient education brochures and to provide referrals to patient support organizations. http://www.thyroid.org

National Graves' Disease Foundation, 2 Tsitsi Court, P.O. Box 1969, Brevard, NC 28712.
Telephone 828-877-5251
http://www.ngdf.org/index.htm

Columbia-Presbyterian Medical Center in New York has an online Thyroid Center with information about hyperthyroidism and hypothyroidism.
http://cpmcnet.columbia.edu/dept/thyroid/

Tics *See* Tourette Syndrome

Tinnitus

Tinnitus (ti-NY-tus) is the sense of ringing, whistling, or similar noise in the ear even when there is no external sound.

George and Barbara Bush

When George Bush was President of the United States (1989–1993), he and his wife, Barbara, both were diagnosed with Graves' disease, a type of hyperthyroidism (overactive thyroid).

Because only 1 or 2 of every 100 women, and even fewer men, get Graves' disease, the likelihood of any husband and wife having the disorder at the same time is extremely rare. Since one person cannot catch Graves' disease from another, this was an amazing medical coincidence.

▶ *See also*
Dietary Deficiencies
Growth Disorders
Immunodeficiency
Mental Retardation
Metabolic Diseases

KEYWORDS
for searching the Internet and other reference sources

Auditory disorders

What Is Tinnitus?

Tinnitus is a mysterious disorder that affects as many as 50 million Americans. The sound that people with tinnitus hear is often described as a ringing, but it also can resemble whistles, sizzles, clicks, roars, or other sounds too complex to describe easily. Some people experience the noise only at certain times or notice it only when it is quiet, such as at bedtime. Others, however, live with a constant unpleasant sound.

The noise can be high-pitched like a baby's whine or low like a rumbling train. It might sound like a continuous tone or cycle in a rhythm, often in time with the heartbeat.

What Causes Tinnitus?

Tinnitus is usually a symptom of other problems, such as too much earwax or an ear or nasal infection. Other causes include cardiovascular disease, tumors, jaw misalignment, anemia, and neck and head injuries. Certain medicines, such as aspirin and some antibiotics, as well as carbon monoxide and alcohol, can also cause tinnitus. Long-term exposure to loud sounds like a jet plane or loud music can lead to tinnitus.

What Can a Doctor Do?

The first thing a doctor will do is look for the cause. If it is something that can be corrected, such as removing earwax or treating an infection, the tinnitus usually will go away.

Some people must find ways to live with tinnitus. Hearing aids are a common way to help, if the cause is related to hearing loss. Sometimes the person uses a device like a hearing aid that covers the tinnitus with another sound that is less noticeable or less disturbing.

▶ See also
Ear Infection
Vertigo

Tobacco-Related Diseases

Tobacco-related diseases, including lung disease, heart disease, stroke*, and cancer*, are illnesses caused by tobacco use, the leading preventable cause of death in the United States.

KEYWORDS
*for searching the Internet
and other reference sources*

Addiction

Cigarettes

Nicotine

* **stroke** is a blocked or ruptured blood vessel within the brain, which deprives some brain cells of oxygen and thereby kills or damages these cells..

* **cancer** is any tumorous (TOO-mor-us) condition, the natural (untreated) course of which is fatal.

What Is Tobacco-Related Disease?

Where there is smoke, there is disease. Tobacco use is the leading cause of preventable death in the United States. It leads to more than 430,000 deaths each year, or one in every five deaths. Hundreds of studies have found that cigarette smoking can cause lung disease, heart disease, and stroke. Smoking also can cause cancer of the lung, mouth, larynx*, esophagus*, and bladder*. In addition, it plays a role in cancer of the cervix*, pancreas*, and kidney*. Smokeless tobacco and cigars can have deadly results, too, including cancer of the mouth, larynx, and esophagus.

The harmful effects of smoking do not end with the smoker. Women who smoke during pregnancy are more likely to have babies with a low birth weight, a leading cause of death among babies. Nonsmokers are affected by secondhand smoke, also known as environmental tobacco smoke, which is smoke from other people's cigarettes. Each year, second-hand smoke kills about 3,000 nonsmokers in the United States by lung cancer. It also causes up to 300,000 children to get infections of the lower airways and lungs. In addition, there is some evidence that second-hand smoke may increase nonsmokers' risk of getting heart disease.

Who Uses Tobacco, and Why?

Tobacco eventually leads to death or disability for half of all regular users. Nevertheless, about 47 million adults in the United States smoke cigarettes. Four out of five adults who ever smoked began by age 18. This means that students who stay smoke-free through high school probably will never light up. Young people who start smoking are more likely to get low grades in school than nonsmokers. These students often have low self-esteem, and they may turn to smoking because they think it will make them more attractive or popular. Because such teenagers lack self-confidence, they may have trouble saying no to tobacco.

Who smokes cigarettes in the United States? According to federal figures, people of all ages and ethnic groups smoke. But some patterns are evident. During the 1990s, the highest rates of smoking were among white high school students, and adults of Native American and Native Alaskan ancestry. In those groups, almost 40 percent smoked. African-American men were somewhat more likely to smoke than white men. Least likely to smoke were Asian-American women (about 6 percent). Among high school students, African-Amercan students' rate of smoking nearly doubled in the 1990s, alarming health officials. But even so, they were far less likely to smoke than white or Hispanic students.

* **larynx** (LAR-inks) a structure in the throat, composed of muscle and cartilage (CAR-ti-lij) and lined with a mucous membrane (MU-kus MEM-brayn), that guards the entrance to the windpipe and contains the vocal cords.

* **esophagus** (e-SOF-a-gus) is the tube connecting the stomach and the throat.

* **bladder** (BLAD-er) is the sac that stores urine produced by the kidneys prior to discharge from the body.

* **cervix** (SER-viks) is the lower, narrow end of the uterus (YOO-ter-us), the organ in females for containing and nourishing the young during development in the period before birth.

* **pancreas** (PAN-kree-us) is a large gland located behind the stomach that secretes various hormones and enzymes necessary for digestion and metabolism (me-TAB-o-liz-um), notably insulin.

* **kidney** is one of the pair of organs that filter blood and get rid of waste products and excess water as urine.

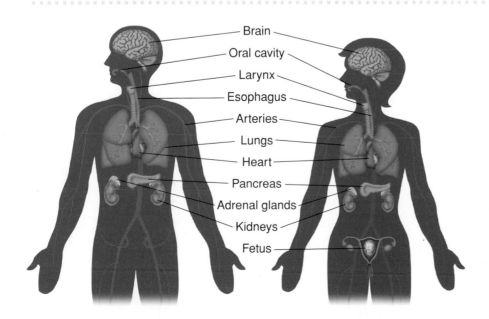

Parts of the body affected by tobacco in males and females.

*   **addiction** (a-DIK-shun) is a strong physical or psychological dependence on a physical substance.

How Do Smokers Become Hooked?

Tobacco contains a chemical known as nicotine (NIK-o-teen). Smokers can become addicted to this substance, which means they can become dependent on it physically and suffer unpleasant symptoms when it is taken away. For some people, the addiction* to nicotine is as strong as that to heroin or cocaine. In fact, when nicotine is breathed in cigarette smoke, it reaches the brain even faster than drugs that enter the body through a vein.

What About Smokeless Tobacco and Cigars?

Some people use smokeless tobacco, chewing tobacco, or snuff, because they think it is safer than cigarettes. However, tobacco is tobacco, and it can cause problems in any form. Smokeless tobacco can cause bleeding gums, tooth loss, and sores of the mouth that never heal. Eventually, it can lead to cancer. In addition, young people who use smokeless tobacco are more likely to start using cigarettes, too. Other people prefer cigars because of their glamorous image. However, cigar smokers, like cigarette smokers, have higher death rates from heart disease than nonsmokers. They are also more likely to get cancer of the mouth, larynx, and esophagus.

*   **inflammation** (in-fla-MAY-shun) is the body's reaction to irritation, infection, or injury that often involves swelling, pain, redness, and warmth.

*   **mucus** (MU-kus) is a kind of body slime. It is thick and slippery, and it lines the inside of many parts of the body.

*   **chronic** (KRON-ik) means continuing for a long period of time.

What Health Problems Does Tobacco Cause?

The following are just some of the diseases that are caused by or linked to tobacco:

Chronic bronchitis   Bronchitis (brong-KY-tis) refers to inflammation* of the bronchial (BRONG-kee-al) tubes, the airways that connect the windpipe to the lungs. This leads to a cough that brings up lots of thick, sticky mucus*. About 14 million Americans have chronic* bronchitis, and smoking is by far the most common cause.

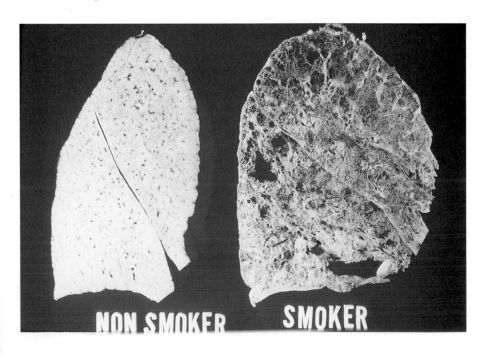

Healthy lung of a nonsmoker compared with damaged lung of a smoker.
© *O. Auerbach, Visuals Unlimited.*

Emphysema   Emphysema (em-fe-ZEE-ma) is a chronic lung disease in which the air sacs of the lungs are overly large. This condition makes the lungs work less efficiently and leads to shortness of breath. About 2 million Americans have emphysema, and most of these cases are caused by smoking.

Heart disease   A heart attack occurs when the blood supply to part of the heart muscle is decreased or stopped. This happens when one of the large blood vessels that bring blood to the heart is blocked, usually by a buildup of fatty deposits inside the vessel. More than 470,000 Americans die each year from a heart attack. Smokers are twice as likely as nonsmokers to have a heart attack, and two to four times as likely to die suddenly of heart problems.

Stroke   A stroke occurs when a blood vessel to the brain is blocked or bursts, which can damage the brain. This is the leading cause of serious, long-term disability in the United States. Strokes also kill almost 160,000 people a year. Smoking raises the risk of having a stroke.

Lung cancer   Lung cancer kills more people than any other kind of cancer. Each year, more than 170,000 new cases of lung cancer occur in the United States, and about 160,000 people die from it. Smoking is the direct cause of almost 90 percent of all lung cancer cases.

Other cancers   Cigarette smoke contains more than 4,000 different chemicals, and more than 40 of these have been shown to cause cancer in humans and animals. Smokers are more likely to get several kinds of cancer, including that of the mouth, larynx, esophagus, bladder, cervix, pancreas, and kidney.

How Can These Problems Be Prevented?

By far the best way to prevent tobacco-related diseases is never to start smoking. There is still good news for people who already are smokers, though. Those who quit, no matter how old they are, live longer than those who keep smoking. Quitting is hard. It usually takes people two or more tries to succeed. However, studies have shown that each time a person tries to quit, he or she learns more about what works and what does not. Eventually, all people can succeed if they really want to stop smoking. Half of all people who have ever smoked have quit.

Some people see a health care provider or join a program to help them stop smoking. Three methods seem to work.

Using the nicotine patch or gum   Research shows that almost all smokers can benefit from temporarily wearing a small patch or chewing gum that contains nicotine. The nicotine passes through the skin and reduces the craving for this substance. Using the prescription patch or gum doubles the odds of success. A prescription nicotine nose spray is also approved for use in the United States.

Butting Out

These tips may help smokers who want to quit give up the habit:

Set definite goals.

- Pick a quit date, and tell friends and family members of these plans. Write down all the reasons for quitting. Ask other people for their understanding.

- Ask friends and family members who are smokers to consider quitting at the same time.

- Change the surroundings.

- Get rid of cigarettes and ashtrays at home and in the car.

- Stay away from the smell of tobacco smoke.

- Think about past attempts to quit. Try to figure out what worked and what did not.

- Stop smoking *completely* on the quit date. Do not just cut back on smoking. People who try to smoke fewer cigarettes usually wind up smoking the same amount again soon.

- Keep a list of slips and near-slips. Look for patterns. Try to figure out what caused the slips and how to avoid them in the future.

- Be ready for short-term symptoms. Quitting smoking can lead to a dry mouth, cough, scratchy throat, and feelings of edginess.

- Get professional help, if needed. A doctor, dentist, therapist, or school nurse may be a good source of advice and support.

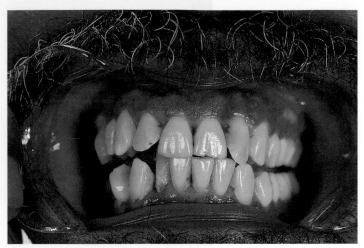

▲

Teeth and gums of a smoker stained from tobacco. No one will want to kiss someone like this. © *1997 Custom Medical Stock Photo.*

Getting support and encouragement   Personal counseling or a quit-smoking program can help someone learn how to live life as a nonsmoker. Studies have shown that the more counseling people have, the greater their chances of success. Look for a quit-smoking program that offers at least four to seven sessions over a period of at least 2 weeks. Friends and family members can also give support. In addition, self-help books and telephone hotlines may be helpful.

Learning to handle the urge to smoke   People benefit from becoming aware of the things that make them want to smoke. For example, many people like to smoke when they are around other smokers or are feeling sad or frustrated. It is a good idea to avoid these situations as much as possible when trying to quit. To reduce stress, do physical things that are fun and healthy, such as going for a walk or bike ride. Keep the mind busy, too, to help control thoughts of smoking.

Resources

Book

Izenberg, Neil, M.D., with Robert P. Libbon. *How to Raise Non-Smoking Kids.* New York: Byron Preiss Multimedia Company, 1997.

Organizations

American Cancer Society (ACS), 1599 Clifton Road N.E., Atlanta, GA 30329-4251. ACS is a nonprofit group that sponsors the Great American Smokeout to help people quit smoking.
Telephone 800-227-2345
http://www.cancer.org/gasp/index.html
http://www.cancer.org/smokeout

American Heart Association (AHA), National Center, 7272 Greenville Avenue, Dallas, TX 75231. AHA is a nonprofit group that provides information on tobacco and heart disease. From the homepage, follow the links Family Health, Risk Factors for Heart Disease and Stroke That Can Be Changed, and Smoking.
Telephone 800-242-8721
http://www.americanheart.org

American Lung Association (ALA), 1740 Broadway, New York, NY 10019. ALA is a nonprofit group that provides information on tobacco and lung disease.
Telephone 800-586-4872
http://www.lungusa.org

Teen Smoking

- Each day, about 3,000 teenagers start smoking regularly.

- However, most young people, 87 percent to be exact, do not smoke.

- More than four in five teenagers say that they would rather date a nonsmoker.

- About two-thirds of teenagers say that seeing someone smoke turns them off.

- Some problems, such as coughing, shortness of breath, nausea, and dizziness, begin with a person's first cigarette.

- Problems such as coughing and wheezing have been found in young people who smoke as little as one cigarette a week.

- About two in five young people who smoke say they have tried to quit but failed.

Office of the U.S. Surgeon General, 200 Independence Avenue S.W., Washington, DC 20201. A government office that has issued several reports on the dangers of smoking.
Telephone 202-690-7694
http://www.surgeongeneral.gov

SGR4KIDS. A site for young people about the dangers of smoking from the U.S. Surgeon General.
http://www.cdc.gov/nccdphp/osh/sgr4kids/sgrmenu.htm

Office on Smoking and Health, National Center for Chronic Disease Prevention and Health Promotion, U.S. Centers for Disease Control and Prevention (CDC), 4770 Buford Highway N.E., Mail Stop K-50, Atlanta, GA 30341. A government agency that provides facts and statistics on tobacco-related diseases.
Telephone 800-232-1311
http://www.cdc.gov/tobacco

U.S. Food and Drug Administration (FDA), 5600 Fishers Lane, Rockville, MD 20857. A government agency with a program to reduce tobacco use by children and teenagers.
Telephone 888-332-4543 or 888-463-6332
http://www.fda.gov/opacom/campaigns/tobacco.html

QuitNet. A site that helps smokers kick their habit and provides up-to-date news about tobacco.
http://www.quitnet.org

National Center for Tobacco-Free Kids, 1707 L Street N.W., Suite 800, Washington, DC 20036. A group that aims to protect children from tobacco use and secondhand smoke.
Telephone 800-284-5437
http://www.tobaccofreekids.org

Stop Teenage Addiction to Tobacco (STAT), Northeastern University, 360 Huntington Avenue, 241 Cushing Hall, Boston, MA 02115. STAT is a group that aims to stop smoking by teenagers and children.
Telephone 617-373-7828
http://www.stat.org

Action on Smoking and Health (ASH), 2013 H Street N.W., Washington, DC 20006. ASH fights smoking and supports the rights of nonsmokers.
Telephone 202-659-4310
http://www.ash.org

Smoke-Free Kids and Soccer. A site that urges girls not to smoke and to stay physically fit through soccer.
http://www.smokefree.gov

Americans for Nonsmokers' Rights (ANR), 2530 San Pablo Avenue, Suite J, Berkeley, CA 94702. A group that fights smoking and supports the rights of nonsmokers.
Telephone 510-841-3032
http://www.no-smoke.org

Passive Smoke

Choosing not to smoke usually is enough to prevent lung cancer—but not always. Studies have shown that smoke from the cigarettes of others contains carcinogens (car-SIN-o-jenz), cancer-causing chemicals that can affect people who are around smoke often. The secondhand smoke from cigarettes contains more tars and other chemicals than does the smoke inhaled by the smoker. Most cigarettes are filtered and remove at least some of the harmful chemicals. To protect yourself and others:

- Avoid places where people are smoking whenever possible.

- Encourage smokers to quit for their health and yours.

- Prevent children from regularly being exposed to smoke.

- Encourage restaurants, stores, and other social settings to provide no-smoking areas.

▶ See also
Asthma
Birth Defects
Bronchitis
Cancer
Emphysema
Environmental Diseases
Halitosis (Bad Breath)
Heart Disease
Hypertension
Kidney Cancer
Lung Cancer
Mouth Cancer
Pancreatic Cancer
Pregnancy, Complications of
Substance Abuse
Sudden Infant Death Syndrome (SIDS)
Uterine/Cervical Cancer

Tonsillitis

KEYWORDS
for searching the Internet
and other reference sources

Inflammation

Otolaryngology

Palatine tonsils

Respiratory system

Tonsillitis is an infection of the tonsils, which are lumps of tissue located at the back of the mouth near the opening of the throat.

Until recent decades, the removal of tonsils was very common in child-hood. Many adults today recall the unlimited ice cream they were given to soothe throat pain after surgery. Today, it is uncommon to remove the tonsils unless they become infected repeatedly or are large enough to obstruct breathing.

What Is Tonsillitis?

The tonsils are collections of lymphatic tissue* involved in helping the body to prevent and fight infection. Sometimes, however, the tonsils themselves become infected with viruses or bacteria. The tonsils swell and sometimes become coated with whitish spots or pus. This commonly happens with pharyngitis*, influenza, or other respiratory* infections.

The first symptom of tonsillitis is usually a sore throat. Fever and chills may follow, and the lymph nodes (glands) under the jaw and in the neck may become swollen and sore. Tiredness and loss of appetite are common. Swallowing may become difficult. Sometimes there is also a middle ear infection, because the eustachian (yoo-STAY-ke-an) tube, which con-nects the throat and middle ear, becomes blocked.

* **lymphatic tissue** is tissue where white blood cells fight invading germs.

* **pharyngitis** (far-in-JY-tis) is a sore throat.

* **respiratory** (RES-pi-ra-tor-ee) refers to the breathing passages and lungs.

Who Gets Tonsillitis?

Tonsillitis can happen to anyone, but it is more common in children. A doctor will try to determine whether a virus or a bacterium is causing the tonsillitis. A cotton swab is touched to the tonsillar area and used to test for the presence of streptococci bacteria, which cause strep throat and can be killed with antibiotics. If, however, a virus is causing the ton-sillitis, then antibiotics will not work. The body's own defenses must fight the virus.

A non-aspirin pain reliever can lessen soreness in the throat. Soft food, soups, milkshakes, and ice pops also help. Getting adequate rest is important, as is drinking enough liquid. Most people start to feel better within five days after the sore throat starts. It might take longer if the tonsillitis is the result of a viral infection.

Can Tonsillitis Be Prevented?

The best way to avoid a bout of tonsillitis is to avoid close contact with people who have respiratory infections. This is especially important for people who have had tonsillitis before. It is important not to share cups or utensils with people who have sore throats or who are coughing and sneezing. It is always important to wash the hands frequently to help prevent the spread of this and other infections.

Tonsils

▲
Anatomy of the tonsils.

Will the Doctor Cut Out the Problem?

Recurrent bouts of tonsillitis may cause a doctor to recommend tonsillectomy (ton-si-LEK-to-mee), which means surgery to remove the tonsils. Often, the surgeon removes the adenoids (also lymphatic tissue near the tonsils) at the same time. Surgery may be considered when a child has had many infections. This surgery was common for many years, although today it is done less frequently. In some cases, the tonsils are removed to help people with sleep apnea, which is a disorder that causes breathing to stop for brief periods during sleep.

> ▶ See also
> **Ear infections**
> **Sleep Apnea**
> **Strep Throat**

Tooth Decay *See* Cavities

Tourette Syndrome

Gilles de la Tourette (ZHEEL de la too-RETT) syndrome is a neurological disorder that causes a person to make sudden movements or sounds, which are called tics. Many scientists think Tourette syndrome is caused by a chemical imbalance in the brain.

KEYWORDS
*for searching the Internet
and other reference sources*

Attention Deficit Hyperactivity Disorder

Neurological Disorders

Tics

Daniel's Story

When Daniel yelped out loud like a dog, and his classmates erupted with laughter, Ms. Jones sent him to the school office. The teacher knew Daniel was being treated for hyperactivity, but recently he had been blinking his eyes, twitching his nose, and shuffling his feet. Ms. Jones decided she could no longer tolerate his interruptions. She also was concerned about Daniel. Was he just showing off, or could he have a more serious condition? She had read about a condition called Tourette syndrome that involved strange movements and sounds. Was that Daniel's problem?

What Is Tourette Syndrome?

Gilles de la Tourette syndrome is named for the French physician Georges G.A.B. Gilles de la Tourette (1857–1904) who first described the disorder in 1885. It is sometimes referred to as Tourette syndrome and abbreviated TS. The symptoms are tics: abrupt, rapid, and repeated movements or vocal sounds. Researchers have identified more than 80 tics, including grunts, barks, babbling, eye movements, head or neck motions, throat clearing, grimaces, shrugging, sniffing, leg and mouth motions, and motions of the torso.

Tics are categorized as either simple or complex. Simple motor tics include twitching of an eye or a jerking movement of the arm. Simple vocal tics include grunts, barks, or other noises. Complex tics involve several coordinated muscle movements, including twirling or doing

LITERARY GIANT: SAMUEL JOHNSON

Samuel Johnson (1709–1784) is a towering figure in English literature. He wrote essays, poetry and, in 1755, the monumental *Dictionary of the English Language*. Dr. Johnson's friends recognized that he was a brilliant writer. They also thought he was quite eccentric.

Johnson was always in motion, rocking or swerving. He twitched and grunted and blew out his breath like a whale. His friends noticed he had obsessive-compulsive behaviors. For example, when he walked outside he maneuvered so that he never walked on cracks in the paving stones, and he touched every post he passed. If he missed a post, he would go back to touch it. He also would scrape his fingernails and joints with a knife until they were raw.

When Samuel Johnson died in 1784, a physician examined his brain, looking for evidence of disease. He found none. Based on the observations and letters of his friends, most modern scholars believe Dr. Johnson had Tourette syndrome.

deep knee bends when walking. Complex vocal tics include stuttering, babbling, uttering profanities, or echoing sounds. Among the more common tics in Tourette syndrome:

- Echolalia (eh-koh-LAY-lee-uh): echoing other people's words.

- Palilalia (pal-ee-LAY-lee-uh): repeating one's own last words, sounds, or sentences.

- Coprolalia (ko-pro-LAY-ee-uh): "babbling about feces" and refers to people with TS who use explicit and obscene language or sounds.

- Echopraxia (eh-koh-PRAK-see-uh): imitating other people's movements.

- Copropraxia (ko-pro-PRAK-see-uh): making obscene and socially unacceptable gestures.

People with more severe tics may mutilate themselves by biting their lips or banging their heads. Others may exhibit obsessive-compulsive behavior such as excessive hand washing. In addition to tics, a person with Tourette syndrome may show signs of hyperactivity, poor coordination, or attention deficit hyperactivity disorder (ADHD).

People with TS can sometimes control their tics for minutes but, like a suppressed sneeze, the tic returns sooner or later. Tics get worse when a person is tired or anxious; they get better when a person is focused and concentrating on something. Severe tics can be more pronounced around family and close friends and better in the presence of strangers. Tics are less pronounced in the morning, worse at night, and, generally, not evident when a person is sleeping.

The disorder usually begins in childhood. Symptoms appear around age 7, and 90 percent of cases develop before age 10. Boys are four times more likely to develop TS than girls. About 1 person in 2,000 has Tourette syndrome.

At least 25 percent of all children display a simple tic. However, these tics go away within a year and are not a sign of TS. A person with Tourette syndrome may have tics for a lifetime, though the frequency and type of tic may change. About 35 percent of people with TS experience an easing of symptoms in adolescence; most others find that, even if they do not disappear, tics become less frequent and less severe in adulthood. The reverse can also be true: Some people with mild symptoms develop severe tics in their twenties or early thirties.

People with Tourette syndrome may suffer social embarrassment or emotional stress because of their tics. The disorder does not affect their intelligence or ability to lead a full life.

HOME RUN HITTER: JIM EISENREICH

Jim Eisenreich was different from other children. His body was constantly in motion, but not in the same way as other active children. His head twitched from side to side, and his shoulders jerked and shrugged. He often grunted, suddenly, for no apparent reason. His classmates laughed at his odd behavior. Doctors said Eisenreich was hyperactive and nervous and would outgrow the behavior. He did not.

Because he was embarrassed by his behavior, Eisenreich kept to himself and concentrated on something he excelled at: baseball. He was a terrific baseball player and, in 1982, he won a spot on the Minnesota Twins.

Baseball in the big leagues was competitive and stressful. Much to his embarrassment, Eisenreich began to experience tics on the field in front of thousands of fans. His neck and shoulders twitched. His face twitched. One day, deeply embarrassed, Eisenreich walked off the field.

Eisenreich retired from baseball for four years. During those years, he sought medical help and discovered the reason for the tics: He had Tourette syndrome. Medication helped ease the tics, and counseling helped Eisenreich accept himself.

Eisenreich returned to baseball and became a star hitter and outfielder for the Philadelphia Phillies. In the second game of the 1993 World Series, he smacked a three-run home run that helped Philadelphia beat the Toronto Blue Jays. Eisenreich had returned to baseball with a new outlook on life and on a condition known as TS.

What Causes Tourette Syndrome?

In the Middle Ages, people who displayed movement and vocal tics were thought to be possessed by demons. Gilles de la Tourette, the French physician who studied the disorder in the 1800s, thought TS had a physiological basis, which means that its cause was physical, not mental. Modern scientists think Gilles de la Tourette was right.

Scientists believe TS is caused by an abnormality in the brain's neurotransmitters, which are chemicals that carry signals from one nerve cell to another. One of the affected neurotransmitters is dopamine, a chemical that controls movement. Research indicates that some forms of TS are inherited, which means they are passed down from parent to child.

How Do Doctors Treat Tourette Syndrome?

An accurate and prompt diagnosis is important to a person with Tourette syndrome, especially if the symptoms surface during childhood. People with TS often are misunderstood or ridiculed, and children may be punished for behavior that is out of their control.

Most people with Tourette syndrome do not need medication. For those with severe tics, medication can reduce the frequency and severity of their symptoms so they can function at school, at work, and in social settings.

Resources

Books

Fowler, Rick. *The Unwelcome Companion: An Insider's View of Tourette Syndrome.* Cashiers, NC: Silver Run Publications, 1996. A review of symptoms, causes, and treatments.

Rubio, Gwyn Hyman. *Icy Sparks.* New York: Viking, 1998. A novel about a 10-year-old girl who tries to conceal her tics and the unhappiness they cause her.

Organizations

U.S. National Institute of Neurological Disorders and Stroke (NINDS), Bethesda, MD 20892. NINDS is a division of the National Institutes of Health. It posts a fact sheet about Tourette syndrome at its website. http://www.ninds.gov/patients/Disorder/tourette/tourette.htm

Tourette Syndrome Association, Inc., 42-40 Bell Boulevard, Suite 205, Bayside, NY 11361. A national organization providing medical information and support.
Telephone 800-237-0717
http://tsa.mgh.harvard.edu

▶ See also
Attention Deficit Hyperactivity Disorder
Obsessive-Compulsive Disorder

Toxemia of Pregnancy *See* Pregnancy, Complications of

Toxic Shock Syndrome

Toxic shock syndrome (TSS) is an uncommon but sometimes life-threatening form of bacterial poisoning usually associated with **Staphylococcus** *or* **Streptococcus** *bacteria.*

KEYWORDS
for searching the Internet
and other reference sources

Blood poisoning

Septicemia

What Is Going On?

Between October 1979 and May 1980, doctors all over the United States began reporting a new illness to the Centers for Disease Control and Prevention (CDC) in Atlanta, Georgia. Fifty-five women between the ages of 13 and 52 had shown up with symptoms of serious infections. The cooperation of doctors, health officials, epidemiologists, and laboratory scientists in the months that followed revealed a surprising coincidence—all the women were menstruating and used tampons*. This discovery led to recommendations that reduced the risk for the illness.

What Is Toxic Shock?

Bacteria are microscopic one-celled organisms found all over the earth. Many bacteria play a beneficial role in producing antibiotics and nutrients such as vitamins for use by humans, plants, and animals. Bacteria are also essential ingredients in foods such as yogurt and sauerkraut. But bacteria can also cause disease. *Staphylococcus aureus* (staf-i-lo-KOK-us AW-ree-us) is a bacterium that normally lives harmlessly on the skin and in the nose, armpit, groin, or vagina*, but which can cause disease under certain circumstances.

For reasons that no one understands, certain forms of bacteria sometimes produce, or secrete, poisonous substances called toxins. People whose bodies are not equipped to fight these toxins may develop a severe reaction to them called toxic shock syndrome. In human beings, the toxin does not poison the cells directly. Instead, it stimulates the immune cells—the body's defenders against disease—to secrete huge amounts of cytokines (SI-to-kines), which are proteins that act on other cells. The action of these cytokines produces the symptoms of TSS.

A second kind of TSS, caused by *Streptococcus* (strep-to-KOK-us) bacteria and called STSS, was officially recognized in 1987. This illness behaves similarly to TSS and is treated in the same way, but it is much rarer and is related to injured skin and wounds, not to tampon use.

How Does a Person Get Toxic Shock?

Anyone—men, women, and children—can get TSS. TSS is not contagious like the cold or flu, but a person who has the bacteria on his or her hands can infect areas of broken skin or wounds anywhere on the body. Half of TSS cases involve women who use tampons during menstruation* or who have had injuries to the vagina from other causes, and half are related to infections arising from burns, insect bites, chickenpox blisters, or wounds resulting from surgery.

* **tampon** is a plug of cotton or other material placed in the vagina during menstruation to absorb menstrual blood and other fluids.

* **vagina** In girls and women, the vagina is the canal that leads from the uterus—the womb (the organ where a baby develops)—to the outside of the body.

* **menstruation** (men-stroo-AY-shun) refers to the monthly flow, or discharge, of the blood-enriched lining of the uterus that occurs in women who are old enough to bear children. Most girls have their first period between the age of 9 and 16. Menstruation ceases during pregnancy and after menopause.

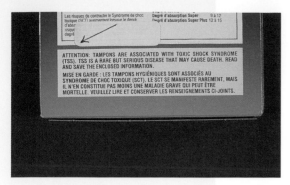

▲

The outer packaging of a tampon box shows a warning about Toxic Shock Syndrome. © *Leonard Lessin, Peter Arnold, Inc.*

Introducing *Staphylococcus aureus*

The staphylococci were among the first human disease-causing organisms to be discovered. They grow in various shapes, including irregular bulky clusters from which they get their name (the Greek word *staphulé* means "grapelike"). Staphylococci are the most common causes of infections that people get in hospitals. In fact, they are at the root of about 2 million hospital infections each year. There are various kinds of staphylococci. Some are particularly dangerous to people whose systems are already weak from other diseases. *Staphylococcus aureus,* the bacterium that causes TSS, is a major public health worry because it is very destructive and the infections it causes can be hard to treat.

Signs and Symptoms

TSS begins with vomiting, a high fever, diarrhea, and muscle aches. A sunburn-like rash develops over the body during the first two days of illness. Curiously, the place on the body where the bacteria are multiplying and producing toxin may appear perfectly normal. The early signs and symptoms of TSS go away within a few days. As the rash heals, the skin on the torso, face, hands, and feet begins to peel. Later symptoms may include low blood pressure and heart and kidney failure.

Most people with TSS recover in 7 to 10 days, but 3 percent of people who get TSS die from it. People are more likely to die from TSS that is unrelated to menstruation.

Diagnosis

The early symptoms of TSS may resemble those of severe allergic drug reactions or other illnesses. Lacking any other explanation, a doctor will suspect TSS in certain patients, such as women who use vaginal methods of birth control (for example, a diaphragm) or anyone who has recently had an operation. A blood test can confirm the diagnosis.

How Is TSS Treated?

Hospitalization is usually recommended for TSS. Doctors treat TSS with antibiotics and anti-inflammatory drugs. The place on the body where the toxin is being produced is disinfected. During the worst part of the illness, a person is given fluids to maintain normal blood pressure, a breathing machine (ventilator) may be required, and if the kidneys fail, waste products may have to be removed from the blood in a procedure called dialysis (di-AL-a-sis).

Can TSS Be Prevented?

There is no sure way to prevent TSS, but women can take precautions against it. Menstruating women should avoid using superabsorbant tampons, change tampons frequently, and never leave a tampon inserted overnight. They also should wash their hands before and after inserting tampons. Girls and women who have had TSS should check with their doctor before using tampons again.

Resources

Books

Dusenberry, David B. *Life at Small Scale: The Behavior of Microbes.* New York: W. H. Freeman, 1996.

Snedden, Robert, and Steve Parker. *Yuck! A Big Book of Little Horrors.* New York: Simon and Schuster, 1996.

Organization

Centers for Disease Control and Prevention (CDC), 1600 Clifton Road, N.E., Atlanta GA 30333. The United States government authority for information about infectious and other diseases.
http://www.cdc.gov

Tutorials

"Introduction to the Bacteria." An engaging, easy-to-read primer on bacteria, with very good links.
http://www.ucmp.berkeley.edu/bacteria/bacteria.html

"Toxic Shock Syndrome." A guide to toxic shock syndrome for parents and children from the experts at the Nemours Foundation.
http://www.kidshealth.org/parent/common/toxic_shock.html

Toxocariasis

Toxocariasis (TOK-so-ka-RY-a-sis) is an infection in people caused by parasitic roundworms found in the intestines of cats and dogs. It most commonly affects young children who come in contact with contaminated dirt.

Many cats and dogs, especially kittens and puppies, have intestinal worms called *Toxocara canis* (in dogs) or *Toxocara cati* (in cats). Eggs from *Toxocara* pass with the stools from infected cats and dogs and then contaminate the soil.

When children play in contaminated areas, the eggs can stick to their hands or toys and then be swallowed. When the eggs enter the digestive system, they hatch. The larvae* burrow through the intestinal wall and move to the liver, lung, and sometimes to other sites, including the central nervous system, eye, kidney, and heart. The larvae may stay alive for many months and cause damage to tissues or organs. Because the larvae are cat or dog parasites, they do not complete their life cycle in humans.

What Happens When People Have Toxocariasis?

Symptoms   Most people with toxocariasis have no symptoms. If symptoms occur, they may include fever, cough or wheezing, and seizures. Other symptoms may include abdominal pain, enlarged liver or spleen, loss of appetite, rash, and enlarged lymph nodes*. Toxocariasis can also affect the eyes and cause decreased vision, swelling around the eyes, and a cross-eyed appearance.

Naming Bacteria

Bacteria, like all other organisms, are named by a pair of Latin words that identify them in the same way that a person's name identifies him or her. For organisms, the family name is called the genus, and the first name, or given name, is called the species. So, for example, some members of the genus *Staphylococcus* are named *Staphylococcus aureus, Staphylococcus epidermidis,* and *Staphylococcus saprophyticus* to distinguish them from one another. Like members of a family, they are all related, but each acts in a different way.

▶ *See also*
Bacterial Infections
Shock

KEYWORDS
for searching the Internet and other reference sources

Infestation

Parasites

Roundworms

Toxocara canis

Toxocara catis

*larvae** are worms at an intermediate stage of the life cycle between eggs and adulthood.

*lymph nodes** are round masses of tissue that contain immune cells whose job it is to filter out harmful microorganisms; lymph nodes can become enlarged during infection.

Diagnosis and Treatment Toxocariasis is diagnosed through a blood test. For most cases, no treatment is necessary. Certain medications that are effective against toxocariasis may be used to eliminate the infection.

How Can Toxocariasis Be Prevented?

As with other infections, good hygiene and frequent handwashing are essential. Important safety measures include:

- Keeping children from playing in areas contaminated by cats and dogs.

- Teaching children not to put their hands and toys in their mouths after playing with cats and dogs.

- Teaching children to wash their hands thoroughly after playing outside, after playing with pets, and before eating.

- Keeping pets away from sandboxes, which should be covered when not in use.

Pets should be checked for parasites periodically by veterinarians and treated if they are found to be infected.

Resource

The U.S. Centers for Disease Control and Prevention (CDC), 100 Clifton Road N.E., Atlanta, GA 30333. CDC's Division of Parasitic Diseases posts a fact sheet about toxocariasis at its website. Telephone 404-639-3534
http://www.cdc.gov/ncidod/dpd/toxocar.htm

► *See also*
Parasitic Diseases
Worms
Zoonoses

Toxoplasmosis

Toxoplasmosis (tok-so-plaz-MO-sis) is an infection caused by the **Toxoplasma gondii** *parasite that animals can transmit to people.*

KEYWORDS
for searching the Internet and other reference sources

Infection

Parasites

Pregnancy

Toxoplasma gondii

* **parasites** are creatures that live in and feed on the bodies of other organisms. The animal or plant harboring the parasite is called its host.

Toxoplasmosis is a disease caused by the microscopic parasite* *Toxoplasma gondii*, which infects the cells of warm-blooded animals, especially cats. People get toxoplasmosis primarily by eating infected meat that has been undercooked. It is estimated that 14 percent of pork and 10 percent of lamb meat contain this parasite. The parasite can be killed by thorough cooking.

People also can get toxoplasmosis by touching infected cat stool. This may happen when cleaning cat litter boxes, when gardening, or when petting a cat. Pregnant women can pass the disease to their unborn babies. In rare cases, blood transfusions, organ transplants, and laboratory accidents also can cause toxoplasmosis.

Toxoplasmosis is a life-long infection, although usually it is latent (inactive). Most people with toxoplasmosis do not get sick. The disease can be life threatening, however, for people with weakened immune systems* and for babies born with the disease, who can have severe organ damage, especially to the eyes and brain. Toxoplasmosis also may cause miscarriage or stillbirth (the baby is born dead).

*__immune system__ is the body's defense system, fighting off attacks by viruses, bacteria, fungi, and other foreign substances that can cause illness or hurt the body.

What Are the Symptoms of Toxoplasmosis?

Most people with toxoplasmosis, including pregnant women, have no symptoms. When symptoms do appear, they usually appear within 10 days of exposure, and they vary with age and the response of the immune system. Children with toxoplasmosis fall into three groups:

- **Babies born with toxoplasmosis:** Congenital infection occurs when babies get toxoplasmosis before birth from their mothers. Most of these babies (85 percent) appear normal at birth but later have learning disabilities, movement disorders, mental retardation, and loss of vision.

- **Healthy children who become infected:** These children may have no symptoms, or they may have swollen glands, fever, general tiredness, and weakness.

- **Children with immune disorders such as AIDS or cancer:** These children may have severe infections, which attack the central nervous system, brain, lungs, and heart. Symptoms may include fever, seizures, headache, psychosis (severe mental disturbance), and problems in vision, speech, movement, or thinking.

For most people who get toxoplasmosis after birth, symptoms may include:

- fever
- night sweats
- weight loss
- general tiredness
- sore throat
- muscle pain
- swollen glands
- calcium deposits in the brain.

How Is Toxoplasmosis Diagnosed and Treated?

Toxoplasmosis is diagnosed through blood tests, laboratory tests of fluid surrounding the brain and spinal cord, and x-rays of the head. It can be diagnosed in pregnant women and in their unborn babies. Toxoplasmosis can be treated with prescription medication, but women who are pregnant must be careful about taking medication because of the harm that may be done to the developing baby.

How Is Toxoplasmosis Prevented?

Toxoplasmosis can be prevented by careful attention to hygiene and sanitation. Preventive steps include:

- Thoroughly cooking meats.
- Washing hands, utensils, and food preparation surfaces after handling meats.
- Washing fruits and vegetables before eating them.
- Keeping flies and cockroaches away from food.
- Washing hands after petting cats, changing litter boxes, working in the garden, or cleaning sandboxes.
- Keeping outdoor sandboxes covered when not in use so that they will not be used as litter boxes by cats.

▶ *See also*

AIDS and HIV

Cancer

Parasitic Diseases

Pregnancy, Complications of

Zoonoses

Resource

U.S. Centers for Disease Control and Prevention (CDC), 100 Clifton Road N.E., Atlanta, GA 30333. CDC's Division of Parasitic Diseases (DPD) posts a fact sheet about toxoplasmosis at its website. Telephone 404-639-3534
http://www.cdc.gov/ncidod/dpd/toxoplas.htm

Transient Ischemic Attack *See* Stroke

Trauma

Trauma occurs when a person experiences a sudden or violent injury. Safety and prevention of injury should be foremost in people's minds. It is easier to prevent than to treat trauma.

KEYWORDS
for searching the Internet
and other reference sources

Accidents

Burns

Emergency medicine

Injuries

Prevention

Safety

Shock

Violence

Seat Belts Saved Marcus

Marcus was 16 years old and in a car with four other teenagers. The driver was going too fast, missed a curve, and smashed into a tree. The compact car flipped over, tossing the teens who were not wearing seat belts out of the car. Paramedics found Marcus conscious and still belted in the back seat with only a broken arm and leg. The four other passengers died. "Without them," Marcus said of seat belts, "I'd be dead."

What Is Trauma?

Trauma may be physical or psychological. Physical trauma is an injury or wound caused by external force or violence: motor vehicle accidents, falls, burns, drowning, elecric shock, stabbings, gunshots, and other physical assaults. Physical trauma may cause permanent disability, and it is the leading cause of death for people under age 40 in the United States. Even surgery is a trauma—it is planned and controlled, but the body reacts in many of the same ways.

The majority of deaths occur in the first several hours after trauma. Trauma also may cause psychological shock that produces confusion, disoriented feelings and behaviors, and long-term after effects.

Trauma Emergencies

Traumatic injuries may include broken bones, severe sprains, head injuries, burns, and internal or external bleeding. They may occur at any time, and they are medical emergencies that require immediate treatment.

Burns   Burns are tissue damage that results from scalds, fires, flammable liquids, gases, chemicals, heat, electricity, sunlight, or radiation. There are approximately 2 million burn injuries each year in the United States. Burn injuries may cause swelling, blistering, dehydration, infection, and destruction of skin and other body organs. Treatment of burns may require antibiotics, transfusions, and surgery.

Traumatic brain injury (TBI)   Traumatic brain injury is the form of trauma most likely to result in permanent disability or death, with gun injuries as the leading cause, followed by motor vehicle accidents, and falls. In the United States, estimates of the number of people affected by traumatic brain injuries each year include:

- 1 million people treated in hospital emergency rooms
- 230,000 people survive
- 80,000 people discharged with TBI-related injuries
- 50,000 people die.

Traumatic brain injuries affect many different parts of the body, and they may impair vision, memory, mood, concentration, strength, coordination, and balance. TBIs sometimes cause epilepsy and coma. They affect males about twice as often as females, with people between the ages of 15 and 24 at highest risk.

Shock   Shock may occur if the body's circulatory system shuts down as a result of trauma. Shock may result from internal or external bleeding, dehydration, vomiting, other loss of body fluids, burns, drug overdoses, severe allergic reactions, bacteria in the bloodstream (septic shock), and severe emotional upset. The symptoms of shock include cold and sweaty skin, weak and rapid pulse, dilated pupils, and irregular breathing. Doctors who treat trauma patients often begin transfusions of salt solutions to maintain fluid levels and blood pressure and prevent shock even before they treat other traumatic injuries.

Preventing Trauma

In the United States, trauma kills more people under age 40 than any other disease or medical condition. It is one of the most preventable cause of death. Preventive measures include:

- Motor vehicle seatbelts, restraints, and airbags
- Child safety seats for cars
- Bicycle helmets
- Home smoke detectors
- Firearm safety procedures
- Enforcement of vehicle, firearm, and workplace safety laws.

The Trauma May Last

Survivors of traumatic events, or other situations that involve intense fear and loss of control, are at risk for psychological problems in addition to their physical ones. Emotional support and counseling immediately after the trauma are important as people adjust to the sudden (and often irreversible) changes the trauma causes in their lives. If left untreated, they may develop post-traumatic stress disorder, which can interfere with activities of daily living long after physical wounds have healed. Signs and symptoms of ongoing psychological trauma include:

- Dreams, flashbacks, or intrusive thoughts during which people re-experience the traumatic event
- Avoiding places and people that remind them of the traumatic event
- Insomnia or difficulty concentrating
- Anxiety or depression
- Physical problems that did not exist before the trauma.

Preventing traumatic injury requires individual, group, and government attention to public health and safety.

Resources

U.S. National Institute of General Medical Sciences (NIGMS), 45 Center Drive, MSC 6200, Bethesda, MD 20892-6200. The NIGMS website posts facts and figures about trauma, burn, shock, and injury in the United States, with referrals to other resources. http://www.nih.gov/nigms/news/facts/traumaburnresources.html

U.S. Centers for Disease Control and Prevention (CDC), 1600 Clifton Road N.E., Atlanta, GA 30333. The CDC website posts fact sheets about firearm injuries and fatalities, sexual assault (rape), traumatic brain injury, and other health topics.
http://www.cdc.gov/health/diseases.htm

American Trauma Society, 8903 Presidential Parkway, Suite 512, Upper Marlboro, MD 20772-2656. The American Trauma Society website features a *Caution* board game for children and a *Troo the Traumaroo* injury prevention program for children.
Telephone 800-556-7890
http://www.amtrauma.org

▶ See also
Broken Bones and Fractures
Burns
Concussion
Hemorrhage
Post-Traumatic Stress Disorder
Seizures
Shock
Strains and Sprains

Trichinosis

Trichinosis (trik-i-NO-sis) is an infection of the muscles by parasitic roundworms found in infected meat.

KEYWORD
for searching the Internet and other reference sources

Nematodes

One winter day in 1995, a hunter in Idaho shot a cougar and decided to use it to make jerky, a kind of dried meat. After soaking it in saltwater, he smoked the meat. And he liked the results enough to give his cougar jerky to 14 other people.

About 10 days later, the hunter came down with fever, muscle aches, fatigue, and swelling of the face. His doctor suspected trichinosis, an infection caused by eating raw or undercooked meat that contains the larvae* of roundworms. Eventually, health officials confirmed trichinosis in the hunter and in nine others who had eaten his jerky. In fact, they found larvae still living in cougar meat the hunter had frozen.

*****larvae** are worms at an intermediate stage of the life cycle between egg and adult.

What Kinds of Worms Cause Trichinosis?

Trichinosis, which is also known as trichinellosis (trik-i-nel-LO-sis), is caused by five species of roundworms called *Trichinella*. The most common species is *Trichinella spiralis*, which is found worldwide in many warm-blooded animals that eat meat. The most common carriers are pigs and wild game, including bears, boar, walrus, and cougar. In the United States, domesticated pigs rarely become infected, thanks to laws against feeding uncooked garbage to pigs. As a result, only 13 cases of trichinosis were reported in the United States in 1997.

How Does Trichinosis Spread?

Once *Trichinella* larvae get into muscle, they enclose themselves in protective capsules called cysts. When a person or animal eats meat containing these cysts, acid and enzymes in the stomach release the larvae from their capsules.

Cysts in muscle tissue containing *Trichinella* larvae. © *Ed Reschke, Peter Arnold, Inc.*

▶

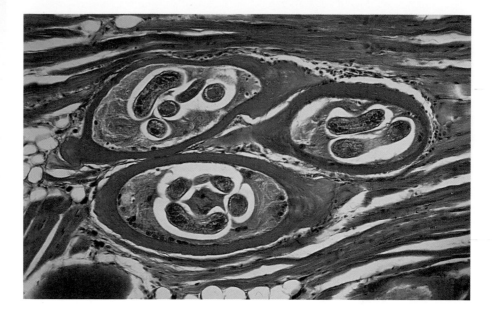

The larvae invade the mucous lining of the intestine. After about two days they mature into adult worms and mate. Females are about 3.5 mm long (less than 2/10 of an inch), and males are about 1.5 mm long. After about a week, the female worms release larvae that enter the bloodstream and lymphatic system, which distribute them to the muscles. There they form cysts, which takes four to five weeks. Larvae in cysts remain viable* for months to years.

What Are the Symptoms of Trichinosis?

The incubation* period may be from two to seven days. At first, there may be no symptoms or only mild ones, with fever, diarrhea, abdominal pain, and vomiting. The initial stage lasts from one to six weeks. It overlaps with the second stage, the muscle invasion stage, which begins at the end of the first week and continues for about six weeks. Symptoms include fever, muscle aches, swelling of the face, especially around the eyes, conjunctivitis (inflammation of eye membranes), and rash. If the larvae infect the heart, lungs, or central nervous system, this can be life-threatening. In the third stage, the larvae form cysts. Symptoms are muscle aches and weakness, which may last for several months before fading away.

How Is Trichinosis Diagnosed and Treated?

Diagnosis   During the first stage, the symptoms are common ones and no diagnostic test is available. During the second and third stages, a biopsy (tissue sample) of the muscle may show larvae or cysts. Within two weeks of infection, blood tests generally become positive. These tests look for antibodies, which are substances the immune system produces to fight the worm.

Treatment   The doctor may prescribe anti-parasite and anti-inflammatory medications to help get rid of the worms in the intestine and to ease the symptoms caused by the cysts.

*viable means an organism can survive, grow, develop, and function.

*incubation (in-ku-BAY-shun) means the period of time between infection and first symptoms.

How Is Trichinosis Prevented?

Smoking, pickling, and preserving meats are not enough to prevent trichinosis. The only way to prevent trichinosis is to make sure that all meat is completely cooked before it is eaten. Meat must be cooked until it is gray inside, not pink, which means heating it to a temperature of at least 150 degrees Fahrenheit (150°F). Freezing meat at 16 degrees Fahrenheit (16°F) for two or three days may also be effective, but researchers believe that much lower temperatures may be required for meat from Arctic animals.

Resources

The U.S. National Institute of Allergy and Infectious Diseases (NIAID) has a fact sheet about trichinosis and other roundworm infections at its website.
http://www.niaid.nih.gov/factsheets/roundwor.htm

The U.S. Centers for Disease Control (CDC) publish a *Morbidity and Mortality Weekly Report (MMWR)* about disease outbreaks, injuries, and other public health topics. The Idaho story was reported in *MMWR*, volume 45, issue 205, 1996, as "Outbreak of trichinellosis associated with eating cougar jerky—Idaho, 1995."
http://www.cdc.gov (CDC)
http://www2.cdc.gov/mmwr/mmwr_wk.html (MMWR)

▶ See also
Ascariasis
Parasitic Diseases

Tuberculosis

Tuberculosis (too-ber-ku-LO-sis) is a bacterial infection that spreads through the air and usually affects the lungs. Worldwide, it kills more people than any other infectious disease.

KEYWORDS
for searching the Internet and other reference sources

Consumption

Infection

Lung diseases

Mycobacterium tuberculosis

TB or Not TB

Hippocrates, a Greek physician who today is called "the father of medicine," accurately described tuberculosis (TB) about 2,400 years ago when he coined the term "phthis," which means to melt and to waste away. In later years, tuberculosis was called consumption, because people with TB tended to waste away as if they were being slowly consumed.

What Is Tuberculosis?

Tuberculosis is a potentially serious infection caused by *Mycobacterium tuberculosis* bacteria that are spread mainly through the air from one person to another. TB usually infects the lungs, but can also cause symptoms that affect the whole body.

immune system is the body's defense system, fighting off attacks by viruses, bacteria, fungi, and other foreign substances that can cause illness or hurt the body.

lymph node a round mass of tissue that contains immune cells that filter out harmful microorganisms; lymph nodes can become enlarged during infection.

peritoneum is the membrane that lines the abdominal cavity.

The U.S. and the World

In the United States, tuberculosis is a serious disease but is not a leading cause of death or illness. In 1996, for instance, it caused about 21,000 new cases of illness and about 1,200 deaths. It is estimated that 10–15 million people in the U.S. have primary (in other words, nonactive) TB infection. Of these about 1 in 10 will eventually become ill with the disease.

In the U.S., TB is most common among people with HIV, people in homeless shelters and prisons, other poor people who live in big cities and elderly people. Rates are higher for men than for women and far higher for people of African ancestry than for people of European ancestry. This may be because a higher proportion of African Americans are poor. Another factor may be that, over the centuries, TB was largely a European disease and Europeans who survived it may have evolved resistance to it.

In the U.S., tuberculosis was on the decline until the mid-1980s, when it began to make a comeback. A main reason was the rise of HIV, the AIDS virus, which weakens the immune system. HIV-infected people are more likely to get new TB infections and to have old, inactive infections become

Not everyone who is infected with tuberculosis bacteria (called primary infection) gets sick or infects other people. About 10 million people in the United States are infected with tuberculosis, but only one out of every 10 of these people will develop active TB (called secondary infection).

People with primary TB infection are protected from developing active TB by their body's immune system*, but they still carry the bacteria in their bodies. As long as the infection is inactive, they cannot spread TB. They can, however, develop active (secondary) TB years later if their immune systems are weakened by other diseases such as AIDS, diabetes, or by alcohol or drug abuse. Most people with active TB who are treated can be cured. If left untreated, however, TB is fatal 40 to 60 percent of the time.

How Does Tuberculosis Spread?

When people with active tuberculosis of the lungs or throat cough or sneeze, they spread bacteria through the air. Other people who breathe the same air may become infected with the bacteria, which can lodge in the lungs and begin to grow. From there, the bacteria can move through the blood and settle in almost any other part of the body, including the urinary tract, brain, lymph nodes*, bones, joints, peritoneum*, and heart.

People with active tuberculosis are most likely to give it to those they spend a lot of time with over a long period, such as family members, close friends, and coworkers. Even with close contact, however, only one third of people who are exposed to TB infection become infected. People who have primary tuberculosis cannot spread it to others. TB in parts of the body other than the lungs and throat usually is not contagious.

Who Gets Tuberculosis?

Tuberculosis can strike anyone, but some people are more likely to get it than others:

- Babies and young children who have weak immune systems.
- People with medical problems such as HIV (the virus that causes AIDS) infection, alcohol or drug abuse, poor nutrition, diabetes, certain types of cancer, or severe kidney diseases that weaken their immune systems.
- People who take certain medications, such as corticosteroid drugs that weaken their immune systems.
- People who have had organ transplants and take drugs to suppress their immune systems.
- People who do not get good medical care due to poverty or homelessness.

What Are the Symptoms of Tuberculosis?

Primary tuberculosis does not cause any symptoms. The symptoms of secondary (active) tuberculosis depend on where in the body the tuberculosis bacteria are growing. Tuberculosis of the lungs may cause a cough

TUBERCULOSIS TIMELINE

Archeologists have found evidence of tuberculosis in skeletons from Peru that are 1,300 years old and in Egyptian skeletons dating back 3,400 years. But TB apparently did not emerge as a major killer until the 1600s in Europe.

By the 1800s, the Industrial Revolution had created ideal conditions for TB to spread—overworked, underfed people crowded together in tenements and factories with poor ventilation. TB became the leading killer in many European and U.S. cities. It even took on an aura of romance, as it sapped the life from many literary figures, both real (the poet John Keats) and fictional (the heroine of the opera "La Boheme").

It was unclear whether TB was inherited or infectious until the 1880s, when the German physician Robert Koch (1843–1910) identified the TB bacterium. Treatment consisted of rest, rich food, and fresh air, often provided in special TB hospitals called sanitoriums that were built in mountain areas.

Streptomycin, an antibiotic that kills TB bacteria, was introduced in the 1940s. Isoniazid, another effective antibiotic, came into use in the 1950s. Both are still used today, along with other drugs. As drug-resistant strains of TB continue to emerge, research toward better treatment continues as well.

that does not go away, pain in the chest, and coughing up blood or sputum*. Other common symptoms include feeling tired all the time, weight loss, lack of appetite, fever, chills, and sweating at night. However, some people with active TB feel well and only cough occasionally.

Tuberculosis bacteria typically infect the lungs, but they can settle in almost any part of the human body:

- Urinary tract. Symptoms may include repeated urinary tract infections, repeated fevers, or pus or blood in the urine for which there is no other explanation.
- Brain. Tuberculosis bacteria can infect the membranes surrounding the brain and spinal cord (the meninges), especially in babies and young children. Symptoms of tuberculosis meningitis may include headaches, seizures, or abnormal behavior.
- Lymph nodes. Tuberculosis bacteria can infect the small organs commonly known as lymph nodes. Symptoms may include inflammation and swelling of the nodes anywhere in the body, including in the neck.
- Bones and joints. Tuberculosis bacteria can infect the skeleton, especially in the elderly. Symptoms may include fever, pain, and stiff, swollen joints. The lower spine and weight-bearing joints are most often affected.

active and cause illness. Health officials responded to the upsurge with better TB control programs, and rates of TB went down again. By the late 1990s, the number of new U.S. illesses was the lowest ever and was dropping each year.

- Worldwide, TB causes more deaths than any other infectious disease. In 1997, it was estimated to cause about 8 million new cases of illness and about 2 million deaths, on top of 16 million existing cases of illness. It is estimated that one-third of the world's people have primary (inactive) TB infection. That means 2 billion infected people.

- Worldwide, most tuberculosis cases occur in Asia. About 4.5 million of the 8 million new cases each year occur in India, China, Bangladesh, Pakistan, Indonesia, and the Philippines. But the rates —the number of cases that occur for each 100,000 people—tend to be highest in some African countries. That's because HIV is particularly common there and HIV-infected people are more like to get sick with TB. Many cases of tuberculosis also occur in the Mideast and South America. In the developing world, TB is most common among young men and women of reproductive age.

- Worldwide as well, the spread of tuberculosis has been fueled by the rise of HIV, but it has not been brought under control. The World Health Organization has been trying to get countries to use the kind of control measures that worked in the U.S. in the 1990s. But the control measures are expensive and difficult to do on the large scale that is needed, and the countries that need them most are not as wealthy as the U.S.

* **sputum** mucus and other matter coughed out from the lungs, bronchi, and trachea.

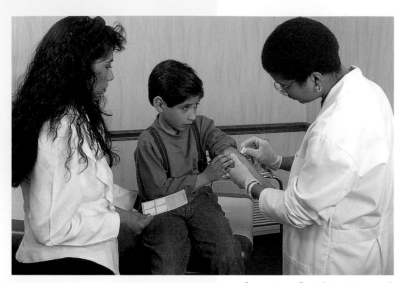

A lab technician performs a TB test on a young boy while his mother watches.
Blair Seitz/Photo Researchers, Inc.

■ The measures advocated by the World Health Organization are called DOTS, for "directly obseved treatment—short term." Under this system, health workers watch patients take their medicines each day for six months to a year, either at a clinic or on visits to the patient's home. This ensures that the patients complete their treatment, rather than stopping whenever they feel better. That cuts down on the spread of the illness and on the emergence of drug-resistant strains.

■ Peritoneum. Tuberculosis bacteria can infect the inner lining of the abdomen. Symptoms may include a fever and buildup of fluid inside the abdomen. This often goes along with a buildup of fluid around the lungs.

■ Heart. Tuberculosis bacteria can infect the sac enclosing the heart. Although this is extremely rare, the death rate is high when it does occur. Symptoms may include shortness of breath, chest pain, and fever.

How Is Tuberculosis Diagnosed?

A skin test is used to diagnose primary tuberculosis. For this test, a small amount of testing fluid is injected with a fine needle just beneath the skin on the lower part of the arm. Two to three days later, a healthcare professional checks the arm. If a bump of a certain size is present, the test is positive, and a diagnosis of primary tuberculosis is made. Doctors may order more tests, such as a chest x-ray and a test of sputum that is coughed up, to see if secondary (active) tuberculosis is present.

The U.S. Centers for Disease Control and Prevention recommends that certain people at risk for getting tuberculosis get the skin test. These include:

■ People who have spent a lot of time with other people who are infected with TB.

■ People who think they may have caught the disease for other reasons.

■ People who have HIV infection or other medical problems that put them at high risk for getting tuberculosis.

■ People who inject street drugs.

■ People who come to the United States from countries where tuberculosis is more common (most countries in Latin America and the Caribbean, Africa, and all of Asia except for Japan).

■ People who live in the United States in environments where tuberculosis is common (homeless shelters, migrant farm camps, prisons, and some nursing homes).

How Is Tuberculosis Treated?

Primary tuberculosis   People with primary tuberculosis who are in high-risk groups for developing active TB may be given medication to help ward off the illness. This is called preventive therapy. People under age 35 with primary tuberculosis who are not in high-risk groups also may benefit from preventive therapy. The goal is to kill the bacteria that are not doing any harm now, but that could cause active TB in the future. The medication usually given for this purpose is called isoniazid (INH). To kill these bacteria, however, INH must be taken every day for 6 to 12 months.

Secondary (active) tuberculosis Secondary (active) tuberculosis can often be cured with medication. People with secondary TB usually take several different drugs, because this does a better job of killing all the bacteria and preventing the formation of resistant bacteria that cannot be killed by drugs.

Although they usually feel better after a few weeks of treatment, people with active TB must continue to take their medication correctly for the full length of the treatment or they can become sick again. Since people with tuberculosis of the lungs or throat can spread the infection to others, they need to stay home from school or work until they are no longer infectious to others; this usually takes a couple of weeks.

People with tuberculosis who are sick enough to go to the hospital may be put in a special room with an air vent system that keeps the bacteria from spreading. Doctors, nurses, and others who work in such rooms must wear special facemasks to protect themselves from breathing the bacteria.

How Can the Spread of Infection Be Stopped?

People who have tuberculosis can keep from spreading the infection by taking all their medication exactly as prescribed, visiting their doctors regularly, staying away from people until they are no longer infectious to others, covering their mouths with a tissue when they cough, sneeze, or laugh, and airing out the room often.

Tuberculosis bacteria can only be spread through the air. Other people cannot be infected by shaking hands, sitting on toilet seats, or sharing dishes or personal items with people who have tuberculosis.

Is There a Vaccine for Tuberculosis?

Bacillus Calmette-Guerin (BCG) is a vaccine that can help protect people against tuberculosis infection. It does not always work and may cause a positive reaction to the tuberculosis skin test, making it harder to tell if people become infected despite the vaccine. BCG is not widely used in the United States, but it often is given to babies and young children in countries where tuberculosis is common.

Resources

U.S. National Center for HIV, STD and TB Prevention, 1600 Clifton Road N.E., Atlanta, GA 30333. This government agency, part of the U.S. Centers for Disease Control and Prevention, is a good source of tuberculosis information.
Telephone 888-CDC-FACT
http://www.cdc.gov/nchstp/tb/faqs/qa.htm

U.S. National Institute of Allergy and Infectious Diseases (NIAID), Office of Communications and Public Liaison, Building 31, Room 7A-50, 31 Center Drive, MSC 2520, Bethesda, MD

Germs That Resist Arrest

Multi-drug resistant (MDR) tuberculosis, caused by bacteria that cannot be killed by regular tuberculosis drugs, is very dangerous. Even with treatment, 40 to 60 percent of people with MDR tuberculosis die. People with MDR tuberculosis must take special medications that do not work as well as the usual tuberculosis drugs and that have more side effects.

People with tuberculosis who do not take their medication correctly, or who do not finish it all, can get MDR tuberculosis, and they can spread the infection to others. MDR tuberculosis is common in some parts of the world, including Southeast Asia, Latin America, Haiti, and the Philippines.

The red spot on the arm indicates a positive skin test for TB. *Ken Greer/Visuals Unlimited*

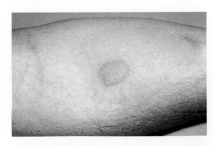

20892-2520. NIAID also posts information about tuberculosis at its website.
Telephone 301-496-5717
http://www.niaid.nih.gov

American Lung Association. 1740 Broadway, New York, NY 10019. This group has information about tuberculosis on its website.
Telephone 800 LUNG-USA
http://www.lungusa.org

World Health Organization (WHO), Avenue Appia 20, 1211 Geneva 27, Switzerland. WHO posts information about tuberculosis and other vaccine preventable diseases at its website.

▶ *See also*
AIDS and HIV
Bacterial Infections
Pneumonia

Tumor

A tumor (TOO-mor) is an abnormal growth of new tissue that can occur in any of the body's organs. Many people automatically associate tumors with the disease called cancer*, but that is not always the case.

KEYWORDS
for searching the Internet and other reference sources

Cancer

Neoplasm

* **cancer** is any tumorous (TOO-mor-us) condition, the natural (untreated) course of which is fatal.

What Is a Tumor?

The human body is made up of many types of cells that are constantly dividing to produce new, younger cells that can "take over" for aging or damaged cells. Through this process, the body heals its injuries and keeps tissues healthy. Sometimes, this process gets out of control, and new cells continue to be produced even when they are not needed, forming a clump of extra tissue, a tumor.

There are two types of tumors:

- malignant (ma-LIG-nant), or cancerous, tumors are made up of abnormally shaped cells that grow quickly, invade nearby healthy tissues, and often make their way into the bloodstream. When these cells travel to other parts of the body, they form additional tumors.

- Benign (be-NINE) tumors are not cancer. They grow slowly and are self-contained; that is, they do not invade and destroy the tissue around them, nor do they spread to other parts of the body. Their cells are usually normally shaped.

Who Gets Tumors?

People of all ages can develop tumors, but generally they are more common as people grow older. Researchers believe that malignant tumors result from a combination of causes, the most important being genetic and environmental. People may inherit a tendency to develop certain kinds of tumors from their parents. Also, repeated exposure to harmful substances such as cigarette smoke, pollutants, and too much sunlight can damage cells and trigger the process of tumor formation.

When a tumor first starts to develop, it is so small that it does not cause symptoms. As it grows, it usually causes symptoms that vary according to its location. For instance, a tumor in the lung may cause a feeling of irritation or a nagging cough. People with brain tumors may experience headaches, dizziness, blurry vision, or lack of coordination. A person with a tumor in the colon* may notice that going to the bathroom is painful or produces blood.

How Are Tumors Diagnosed and Treated?

A doctor can usually diagnose a tumor with one of many tests that create images of the inside of the body, such as x-rays, ultrasound*, CT scans*, or MRI*. The next step is to figure out whether the tumor is benign or malignant through a process called biopsy (BY-op-see). Surgeons remove part or all of the tumor and examine a sample under the microscope. The appearance of the cells will indicate whether a tumor is cancerous or not.

Even though a benign tumor is not harmful, it may have to be removed if it causes pain, pressure, or other symptoms. In many cases of a malignancy, the tumor and any affected surrounding tissue will be removed. Sometimes, radiation therapy (directed high-energy x-rays) or chemotherapy (cancer-fighting drugs) may be used to shrink the tumor.

Resource

The National Cancer Institute, part of the U.S. National Institutes of Health (NIH), has a fact sheet, *What You Need to Know about Cancer*, and a book, *When Someone in Your Family Has Cancer*, available by phone or on its website at the pages given below. For the latter, from the Publication Index, follow the link Living with Cancer/Supporting People with Cancer.
Telephone 800-422-6237
http://cancernet.nci.nih.gov/wyntk_pubs/cancer.htm
http://rex.nci.nih.gov/NCI_PUB_INDEX/PUB_INDEX_DOC.html

* **colon** is part of the large intestine where waste is formed and moved to the rectum, which stores it until it passes out of the body.

* **ultrasound** is a painless procedure in which sound waves passing through the body create images on a computer screen.

* **CT scans** or CAT scans are the shortened names for computerized axial tomography (to-MOG-ra-fee), which uses computers to view structures inside the body.

* **MRI,** which is short for magnetic resonance imaging, produces computerized images of internal body tissues based on the magnetic properties of atoms within the body.

▶ *See also*
Cancer
Tobacco-Related Diseases

Turner Syndrome

Turner Syndrome (also called Turner's Syndrome) is a genetic disorder caused by a missing or partially missing X chromosome. It affects only females and typically causes a variety of physical abnormalities. Girls and women with Turner Syndrome usually are short, and their ovaries and breasts fail to develop normally.

KEYWORDS
for searching the Internet and other reference sources

Gonads

Phenotypes

What Is Turner Syndrome?

Turner Syndrome is a genetic disorder that occurs when one of a girl's X chromosomes is partially or completely missing. Almost every cell in a person's body (except for eggs and sperm cells) has 23 pairs of chromosomes. One pair, the sex chromosomes, makes a person male or female: Boys have an X and a Y chromosome (XY), whereas girls have two X chromosomes (XX). The chromosomes contain all of the information the body needs to function and to develop properly. If part of a chromosome is missing, as in Turner Syndrome, the important information on that chromosome also is missing.

How a girl's body is affected physically by Turner Syndrome depends on how much of the chromosome is missing. Some girls have a mild form of the syndrome that is not detected until they are teenagers or adults. If untreated, nearly all girls with Turner Syndrome will grow slowly and reach a short adult height, and their breasts will not enlarge and they will not have menstrual periods as would be expected in most adolescent girls. Some may have additional problems, including:

- abnormalities in appearance
- hearing loss
- obesity
- heart disorders
- kidney disorders
- thyroid disorders

Most of the physical conditions are treatable, and with good consistent medical care, a person with Turner Syndrome can have a fully productive life and normal life span. Most people with Turner Syndrome have normal intelligence, but some may have specific learning problems, especially with math.

What Causes Turner Syndrome?

About 1 in 2,000 female babies is born with Turner Syndrome, and doctors do not know why. Researchers have tried to find a link between Turner Syndrome and environment, race, geography and socioeconomic status, but these factors have not been proved to play a role.

Living with Turner Syndrome: Carol's Life

Because of physical abnormalities and feeling "different," life might not be easy for a girl with Turner Syndrome. Carol was born with swollen hands and feet, extra skin at the back of her neck (a webbed neck), oddly shaped ears, and arms that tilted outward from the elbows. Based on her appearance, her doctor suspected that she had Turner Syndrome. A test in which Carol's chromosomes were studied confirmed that she was missing one of her X chromosomes.

Carol was teased about her appearance in elementary school, but she was most miserable during her teenage years. She was always the shortest person in her class. When other girls started developing breasts and getting their period, Carol still looked and felt like a little girl. After Carol's doctor prescribed the hormone estrogen to promote sexual development, she finally got her period.

How Do Doctors Treat Turner Syndrome?

Many of the problems associated with Turner Syndrome, such as the failure of the ovaries to develop normally, cannot be prevented, but there are a number of things that can be done to improve an affected person's quality of life:

- Plastic surgery for the neck, face, or ears can improve appearance and self-esteem, if necessary.
- Growth rate and adult height may be increased by treatment with injections of growth hormone.
- Taking the female hormone estrogen promotes sexual development in girls with Turner Syndrome.
- Support groups can help girls with Turner Syndrome develop into confident, successful, and productive adults.
- In some cases, women with Turner Syndrome may be able to become pregnant if a fertilized donor egg is inserted into their uterus.

Resources

Book

Reiser, P. A., and L. E. Underwood. *Turner Syndrome: A Guide for Families*. Wayzata, MN: Turner Syndrome Society, 1992.

Organization

Turner Syndrome Society of America, 1313 Southeast 5th Street, Suite 327, Minneapolis, MN 55415. Telephone 800-365-9944 http://www.turner-syndrome-us.org

▶ See also
Genetic Diseases
Growth Disorders
Menstrual Disorders

Typhoid Fever

Typhoid fever is a bacterial infection that is common in many parts of the world. It is spread by contaminated water and food and primarily affects the digestive system.

KEYWORDS
for searching the Internet and other reference sources

Foodborne diseases

Salmonella typhi

Waterborne diseases

The U.S. and the World

About 16 million cases of typhoid fever occur each year worldwide, and more than 600,000 people die from it.

The disease is common in many underdeveloped nations of the world, especially parts of Asia and in South America with unsanitary water and food preparation. The situation is made more difficult because the disease is showing resistance to some of the traditional antibiotics used to treat those who are infected.

About 400 cases a year are reported in the United States, but about 70 percent of them involve people who had traveled overseas.

In 1998–1999, 13 people in Florida contracted typhoid fever when they drank shakes made with a frozen tropical fruit containing *Salmonelli typhi*.

Typhoid fever is suspected in the deaths of such famous people as Alexander the Great, Wilbur Wright of the Wright Brothers, and poet Gerard Manley Hopkins.

What Is Typhoid?

In many developing countries, typhoid fever is a major problem. It is estimated to cause 16 million illnesses and more than half a million deaths each year worldwide. It is especially common in parts of Asia, Africa, and South America where pure water is not readily available and sewage treatment is limited. In many countries, children are the most likely to get typhoid.

Typhoid used to be a serious problem in the United States as well. Early in the twentieth century, before clean water supplies and sewage systems to dispose of human waste were widely available, it caused about 35,000 illnesses each year. Technological advancements in sewage and water treatment have made typhoid fever rare in industrialized countries. Only about 400 cases are reported each year in the United States. Most of them are acquired while traveling abroad.

What Causes Typhoid Fever?

Typhoid fever is caused by a bacterium called *Salmonella typhi*. It is related to the salmonella bacteria that cause food poisoning, but they are not exactly the same.

Salmonella typhi bacteria are present in the solid wastes (stool) of infected people, including some "healthy carriers" who have no symptoms of illness. The bacteria can spread if human waste gets into water that is used for drinking, irrigating crops, or washing food. Typhoid also occasionally is transmitted through an infected person who is working in food preparation. Once swallowed, the bacteria move from the digestive tract into the bloodstream and then to the liver, spleen, gall bladder, and lymph nodes.

TYPHOID MARY

Some people, called carriers, can be infected with *Salmonella typhi* but not develop typhoid fever. If they prepare food for others, however, they may contaminate the food they handle and pass the bacteria on to other people who eat it and then may get sick.

The most famous typhoid carrier was Mary Mallon, also known as Typhoid Mary, who worked as a cook in homes in New York and New Jersey in the early 1900s. Fifty-one cases of typhoid fever resulting in three deaths were traced to her. Mallon never was sick herself, however, and she never accepted that she had infected anyone else.

Against her will, the authorities confined Mallon to a hospital on North Brother Island in New York's East River. Three years later, in 1910, they released her on condition that she never work as a cook again. But in 1915, typhoid struck a maternity hospital in Manhattan, and it turned out that Mallon had cooked there. She spent the rest of her life, 23 years, as a captive on North Brother Island.

What Happens When People Have Typhoid Fever?

Symptoms The symptoms of typhoid fever come on gradually. At first, people may get a headache, stomachache, and constipation*. They develop a fever and lose their appetite. In some cases, they may get rose spots, a rash mostly on the chest and abdomen. As symptoms worsen, the fever may rise as high as 103 to 104 degrees Fahrenheit. People often develop bloody diarrhea, become dehydrated (lose fluids faster than they are replaced), and start acting confused or disoriented. In severe cases, people may go into a coma, a state of deep unconsciousness, and die.

Diagnosis and Treatment A blood or urine test usually can detect the presence of the bacterium that causes typhoid fever. Antibiotic drugs that fight the bacterial infection can make the illness shorter and milder and prevent complications. Fluids may be given as well to counter the effects of diarrhea. Severe infections can lead to a perforation (hole) in the intestine that requires surgery to repair.

How Is Typhoid Fever Prevented?

Clean water supplies and effective waste disposal systems are the best ways of preventing typhoid, but these are lacking in many countries. A vaccine is available that is about 70 percent effective for several years.

Travelers to countries where typhoid fever is common should drink only boiled or bottled water. They should eat only food that has been properly cooked or fruit that they peel themselves and that has not been washed with tap water. The U.S. Centers for Disease Control and Prevention sums up advice for travelers this way: "Boil it, cook it, peel it, or forget it."

*** constipation** is the sluggish movement of the bowels, usually resulting in infrequent, hard stools.

Resources

U.S. Centers for Disease Control and Prevention (CDC), 1600 Clifton Road N.E., Atlanta, GA 30333. CDC posts a fact sheet about typhoid fever at its website.
http://www.cdc.gov/ncidod/dbmd/diseaseinfo/typhoidfever_g.htm

World Health Organization (WHO), Avenue Appia 20, 1211 Geneva 27, Switzerland. WHO's website posts fact sheets about typhoid fever and other vaccine preventable diseases at its website.
http://www.who.org/home/map_ht.html

▶ *See also*
Bacterial Infections
Fever
Gastroenteritis
Salmonellosis

KEYWORDS
for searching the Internet and other reference sources

Endemic typhus

Lice

Murine typhus

Scrub typhus

Rickettsial diseases

Typhus

Typhus (TI-fus) is a group of infections caused by bacteria called rickettsiae that are spread by parasites such as lice that live on people or on other warm-blooded animals such as rats and mice.

TYPHUS EPIDEMICS

It is likely that typhus existed in ancient history, although the first clear historical description of typhus comes from the eleventh century, when an outbreak took place in a monastery in Sicily. Typhus reached epidemic proportions in 1489, during a siege in Granada. Typhus then spread throughout Europe.

Typhus also was present in the Americas, although there is some controversy as to whether Spanish explorers brought the disease in the sixteenth century, or whether the disease already was present in Aztec and other pre-Columbian societies.

In the early nineteenth century, typhus increased dramatically in Europe. In the twentieth century, typhus spread through Europe, North Africa, and the Pacific Islands, killing thousands of prisoners in German concentration camps.

War, Famine, and Typhus

Throughout history, war and famine have brought outbreaks of typhus, a group of infections spread by parasites that live on people or animals such as rats and mice. During World War II, typhus spread through Europe, North Africa, and the Pacific Islands, and it killed thousands of prisoners in German concentration camps. Epidemic typhus still can be a serious threat in parts of the world where a breakdown in society or a natural calamity such as an earthquake leads to unhealthy living conditions.

What Is Typhus?

Typhus is a group of infections caused by rickettsiae, a group of unusual bacteria. Rickettsiae are like other bacteria in that they can be killed by antibiotics. They are also like viruses, however, in that they must invade living cells in order to grow. There are three main types of typhus: epidemic, murine, and scrub.

- **Epidemic typhus**, caused by *Rickettsia prowazekii*, is a severe form of the disease spread by human body lice. In the United States, this type of typhus also occasionally is spread by lice and fleas on flying squirrels. Sometimes the symptoms of people with typhus become active again years after the original attack; this is called Brill-Zinsser disease. Brill-Zinsser disease is milder than epidemic typhus.

- **Murine typhus**, caused by *Rickettsia typhi*, is a milder form of the disease and is spread by fleas on rats, mice, and other rodents.

- **Scrub typhus**, caused by *Rickettsia tsutsugamushi*, is a form of the disease found in the Asian-Pacific area bounded by Japan, Australia, and the Indian subcontinent. It is spread by mites on rats, field mice, and other rodents.

Who Gets Typhus?

Both epidemic and murine typhus are found around the world. However, epidemic typhus is most common in situations where poor hygiene and crowded living conditions exist. Epidemic typhus is rare in the United States. Murine typhus is most common in rat-infested areas. It is the only type of typhus that occurs regularly in the United States, but fewer than 100 cases a year are reported, mainly in Texas and California.

What Happens When People Have Typhus?

Symptoms   The symptoms of typhus include fever, headache, chills, and general aches that are followed by a rash. The rash spreads to most of the body but usually does not affect the face, palms of the hands, or soles of the feet. In murine typhus, the symptoms are similar but milder. In epidemic and scrub typhus, the fever may rise as high as 104 to 105 degrees Fahrenheit and stay high for about two weeks. The headache is intense.

In severe cases of typhus, blood pressure may drop dangerously. Severe illness also may lead to confusion, seizures, coma, or even death. This accounts for the disease's name, which comes from the Greek word "typhos," meaning smoke, a cloud, or a stupor arising from a fever.

Diagnosis and Treatment   Blood tests are used to show if people are infected with typhus rickettsiae. People with typhus who are treated with antibiotics generally recover. If treatment is begun early, they usually get better quickly. If treatment is delayed, however, the improvement usually is slower, and the fever lasts longer. If left untreated, typhus can damage organs, lead to coma, and even to death.

Prevention   Prevention of typhus is based on avoiding the unsanitary conditions in which it spreads. It is always wise to steer clear of animals such as rats and mice that may carry disease. Travelers to areas where typhus is common should be especially cautious. To prevent the spread of typhus, body lice must be destroyed by removing them from people with the disease and by boiling or steaming their clothes.

Resource

U.S. Centers for Disease Control and Prevention (CDC), 1600 Clifton Road N.E., Atlanta, GA 30333. The website for this government agency has information about typhus and other rickettsial infections. Telephone 800-311-3435
http://www.cdc.gov

▶ *See also*
Bacterial Infections
Lice
Rocky Mountain Spotted Fever

U–V

Ulcer *See* Bedsores (Pressure Sores), Canker Sores, (Aphthous Ulcers); Peptic Ulcer

---

Ulcerative Colitis *See* Inflammatory Bowel Disease

Urethritis, Nonspecific

Nonspecific urethritis (NSU) is an inflammation* or infection of the urethra (yoo-REE-thra) in which the cause is not defined. The urethra is the tube through which urine passes from the bladder to the outside of the body.

KEYWORDS
for searching the Internet
and other reference sources

Inflammation

Sexually transmitted diseases

Urinary tract

What Is Nonspecific Urethritis?

Nonspecific urethritis (yoo-re-THRY-tis) is a common urinary tract infection. It is also called nongonococcal (non-gon-o-KOK-al) urethritis. "Nongonococcal" means that the urethritis is not caused by gonococcus, the bacterium (bak-TEE-ree-um) that causes gonorrhea (gon-o-REE-a), a sexually transmitted disease (STD). However, nonspecific or nongonococcal urethritis also is considered to be an STD. It may be caused by *Chlamydia* (kla-MID-ee-a), yeast*, herpesvirus*, intestinal bacteria*, or any of a number of other microorganisms. Although classified as an STD, nonspecific urethritis is not always caused by sexual activity. For example, it can be caused by an infection from intestinal bacteria that enters the urethra from skin around the anus*, or it may result from insertion of an object into the urethra. NSU is more common in females than in males, but it occurs in people of both sexes and of all ages.

What Are the Symptoms of NSU?

A common symptom of NSU is a tingling or burning sensation while urinating. Sometimes, there is also a slight, usually clear discharge. This discharge may be present only in the morning, before urination.

Signs and symptoms of NSU usually appear 2 to 3 weeks after infection. Sometimes, symptoms are very mild or absent, especially in females.

** **inflammation** (in-fla-MAY-shun) is the body's reaction to irritation, infection, or injury that often involves swelling, pain, redness, and warmth.*

** **yeast** is a general term describing single-celled fungi that reproduce by budding.*

** **herpesvirus** (HER-peez-VY-rus) is a virus of the family Herpesviridae (HER-peez-VY-ri-dee), which includes the viruses that cause chickenpox, shingles, genital herpes, and cold sores.*

** **bacteria** (bak-TEER-ee-a) are single-celled microorganisms, which typically reproduce by cell division. Some, but not all, types of bacteria can cause disease in humans.*

** **anus** (AY-nus) is the opening at the end of the digestive system, through which waste is discharged.*

How Is NSU Diagnosed and Treated?

The diagnosis of NSU is made by taking urine and discharge samples and conducting laboratory tests to identify the infecting organism. In many instances, however, the cause cannot be determined.

NSU is treated with antibiotics*. It is extremely important to finish the prescribed amount of these medications. Otherwise, the infecting organisms may not all be killed, and the disease can come back.

Usually, treatment of NSU lasts 2 to 3 weeks. During this time, sexual activity must be avoided to keep from spreading the infection. Relapses are common, and follow-up visits may be needed to confirm a cure.

What Are the Possible Complications from NSU?

Sometimes, treatment of NSU is unsuccessful, especially if the cause is not found. Possible complications may include chronic* urethritis and cystitis (sis-TY-tis), a bladder infection. The infection sometimes may reach the kidneys*.

How Can NSU Be Prevented?

General measures that can decrease the likelihood of NSU include frequent bathing. Especially good hygiene is needed in the genital area. Bubble baths should be avoided, because they can irritate the urethra.

With regard to sexual transmission, as for any STD, not having sex is the only sure means of prevention. The risk of getting NSU is lowered by limiting the number of one's sexual partners. Condoms can decrease the rate of transmitting the infection.

NSU and other urinary tract infections are not contagious* in people who are not sexually active.

Resources

The Nemours Foundation has information concerning NSU and other urinary tract infections at its website.
http://kidshealth.org/teen/bodymind/body/infection/uti.html
http://kidshealth.org/parent/common/urinary.html

The Wardenburg Health Center has information on NSU at its website.
http://www.colorado.edu/wardenburg/healthbrochure/std/nsu.html

The Health Library has information on NSU at its website.
http://thriveonline.aol.com/health/Library/illsymp/illness542.html

Urinary Tract Infection

Urinary tract infections are infections that occur in any part of the urinary tract. The urinary tract is composed of the kidneys*, bladder*, *and urethra*. The main cause of these infections is bacteria*. Sometimes, the infection is carried through the bloodstream to other areas of the body.*

What Is Urinary Tract Infection?

When an infection causes inflammation* in the urethra, it is called urethritis (yoo-re-THRY-tis). Infections that inflame the bladder are called cystitis (sis-TY-tis). Infections that inflame the kidneys are called pyelonephritis (py-e-lo-ne-FRY-tis).

The primary cause of urinary tract infections is bacteria. Sometimes, the formation of stones or tumors* in the kidneys can cause a blockage in the urinary tract, which puts people at risk of developing a urinary tract infection. Sometimes, other diseases result in urinary tract infection. Urinary tract infection occurs about 10 times more often in women than in men, although infants of both sexes contract the disease at about the same rate.

Urethritis . Urethritis usually is not the result of a urinary tract infection but arises from a sexually transmitted disease such as a chlamydial (kla-MID-ee-al) infection. The main symptom of urethritis is a burning sensation during urination. The condition can be diagnosed with a urine test. Urethritis that is not treated can cause blockage and scarring in the urethra.

Cystitis When the bladder becomes inflamed from bacteria, a person with cystitis will have a burning sensation during urination. The condition also causes a person to feel the need to pass urine often. Low back pain, mild fever, a tired feeling, and blood in the urine sometimes also are present in cystitis, particularly if the kidneys also are involved.

Pyelonephritis A urinary tract infection that spreads to the kidneys can be quite serious. The infection needs to be treated properly to avoid any permanent damage to the kidneys. Some symptoms that may be present in kidney infection are back pain, pain in the lower abdomen*, fever, chills, nausea, and vomiting.

How Are Urinary Tract Infections Treated?

First a diagnosis is made, which might be done by procedures that include examining the urine and sending a sample to the laboratory to identify the bacteria. In some cases, doctors use x-ray, ultrasound*, and other methods to diagnose urinary tract disease. Antibiotics* may be prescribed to fight the bacterial infection.

How Can Urinary Tract Infections Be Prevented?

Practicing good hygiene can help prevent urinary tract infections. It is important to keep the genital, urinary, and anal areas of the body clean. Wiping the rectum separately from the urinary tract opening is important to avoid spreading fecal matter to the urethra, which can cause

* **kidneys** (KID-nees) are the pair of organs that filter blood and get rid of waste products and excess water as urine.

* **bladder** (BLAD-er) is the sac that stores urine produced by the kidneys prior to discharge from the body.

* **urethra** (yoo-REE-thra) is the tube through which urine is discharged from the bladder to outside of the body.

* **bacteria** (bak-TEER-ee-a) are single-celled microorganisms, which typically reproduce by cell division. Some, but not all, types of bacteria can cause disease in humans.

* **inflammation** (in-fla-MAY-shun) is the body's reaction to irritation, infection, or injury that often involves swelling, pain, redness, and warmth.

* **tumors** (TOO-morz) usually refer to abnormal growths of body tissues that have no physiologic purpose and are not inflammations. Tumors may or may not be cancerous.

* **abdomen** (AB-do-men), commonly called the belly, is the portion of the body between the chest or thorax (THOR-aks) and the pelvis.

* **ultrasound** is a painless procedure in which sound waves passing through the body create images on a computer screen.

* **antibiotics** (an-ty-by-OT-iks) are drugs that kill bacteria.

infection, particularly in females. Urinary tract infections also can be spread through sexual activity; avoiding risky sexual practices will reduce the chances of contracting a urinary tract infection.

Resources

Organization

National Institute of Diabetes and Digestive and Kidney Diseases (NIDDK). Office of Communications and Public Liaison, NIDDK, NIH, 31 Center Drive, MSC 2560, Bethesda, MD 20892-2560. This organization, part of the National Institutes of Health (NIH), posts fact sheets on urinary tract infections on its website.
http://www.niddk.nih.gov/health/urolog/pubs/utiadult/utiadult.htm
http://www.niddk.nih.gov/health/urolog/pubs/utichild/utichild.htm

▶ *See also*
Bacterial Infections
Chlamydial Infections
Infection
Kidney Disease
Kidney Stones
Nephritis
Sexually Transmitted Diseases
Urethritis, Nonspecific

KEYWORDS
for searching the Internet
and other reference sources

Human papillomavirus

Pap test

* **uterus** (YOO-te-rus) is the organ in females for containing and nourishing the young during development in the period before birth. Also called the womb.

* **cervix** (SER-viks) is the lower, narrow end of the uterus.

* **tumors** (TOO-morz) are new growths of tissue in which the multiplication of cells is uncontrolled.

* **cancer** is any tumorous (TOO-mor-us) condition, the natural (untreated) course of which is often fatal.

Uterine and Cervical Cancer

Uterine (YOO-te-rin) and cervical (SER-vi-kal) cancers are two cancers that occur in the reproductive tract of women.

What Are Uterine and Cervical Cancer?

The uterus* is the hollow, pear-shaped organ in which a baby develops when a woman is pregnant. The cervix* is the lower part of the uterus, which extends into the vagina (va-JY-na), the canal that connects to the outside of the body. Uterine and cervical cancers occur when cells in a woman's uterus or cervix undergo abnormal changes and start dividing without control or order, forming tumors*.

How are uterine and cervical cancer similar? Both types of cancer* begin in the uterus, but in different parts. Uterine cancer usually begins in the cells of the endometrium (en-do-MEE-tree-um), the thin layer of tissue that lines the inside of the main part of the uterus. That is why it is sometimes called endometrial (en-do-MEE-tree-al) cancer. Cervical cancer originates in the thin, flat cells on the surface of the cervix, the lower necklike portion of the uterus.

Both kinds of cancer are more common in women aged 50 and older, but they can occur at any age. Also, both types usually develop gradually, with some of the cells first undergoing precancerous changes. These cells are not yet cancerous, but they have undergone some abnormal changes that indicate that they could turn into cancer.

If they are not caught early, both types of cancer can grow through the wall of the uterus or cervix and spread to nearby organs. The cancer cells also can enter nearby lymph nodes* and be carried to other parts of the body.

How do uterine and cervical cancer differ? Uterine and cervical cancer differ in many important ways: how frequently they occur, what causes them, and how likely they are to be detected early.

Uterine cancer is more common, affecting about 35,000 women each year. Cervical cancer affects about 15,000 women each year.

Doctors have been able to identify an important risk factor* for cervical cancer. Cervical cancer usually is caused by infection with a certain type of virus* called the human papillomavirus (pap-i-LO-ma-VY-rus), or HPV. This virus is transmitted during sex. Women who started having sex at an early age (usually in their teens), have had many sex partners, or have sex without using a condom increase their risk for HPV, and for developing cervical cancer. These behaviors also increase the risk of developing HIV, or human immunodeficiency (im-yoo-no-de-FISH-en-see) virus, which has also been identified as a cause of cervical cancer. Poor nutrition and smoking also may contribute to the development of cervical cancer.

Though the causes of uterine cancer are not fully known, cancer of the uterus occurs more frequently in those women who have an imbalance of reproductive hormones*, particularly estrogen (ES-tro-jen). Researchers still are trying to unravel the connection between estrogen and uterine cancer.

Perhaps the most important difference between the two types of cancer is that cervical cancer is much more likely to be caught early. About 50 years ago, a scientist named George Papanicolaou developed a simple method of examining tissue cells shed by an organ in the body. Doctors use this method, now called the Pap test or Pap smear, to examine cells scraped from the surface of the cervix under a microscope. They can tell whether the cells have undergone any of the abnormal changes that could develop into cancer, or whether cancer already is present in its earliest stage. When found early, cervical cancer is highly curable. Therefore, doctors recommend that women start having yearly Pap tests as soon as they start having sex or they reach age 18, whichever comes first. The Pap test is such a powerful tool because cervical cancer does not cause symptoms right away. As cervical cancer progresses, it usually causes abnormal bleeding from the vagina.

Uterine cancer also usually is curable if it is found early, but unfortunately there are no reliable routine tests for this disease (although a Pap test sometimes can detect early forms). Typically, it is found only after a woman experiences symptoms, such as unusual bleeding or other discharge from the vagina, pain or pressure, or weight loss.

How Is Cervical Cancer Diagnosed and Treated?

If doctors suspect that cancer is present based on Pap test results, they may wish to do further tests. One test is called colposcopy (kol-POS-ko-pee), which involves applying a vinegar-like solution to the cervix and then using a very thin lighted instrument to examine it closely. Doctors also

*   **lymph nodes** are round masses of tissue that contain immune cells that filter out harmful microorganisms.

*   **risk factor** is something that is associated with the appearance of a disease.

*   **virus** (VY-rus) is a tiny infectious agent that lacks an independent metabolism (me-TAB-o-lizm) and can only reproduce within the cells it infects.

*   **hormones** are chemicals that are produced by different glands in the body. Hormones are like the body's ambassadors: they are created in one place but are sent through the body to have specific regulatory effects in different places.

893

* **lesion** (LEE-zhun) is any sore, irregularity, or damaged tissue caused by illness or a wound.

* **chemotherapy** (kee-mo-THER-a-pee) is the treatment of cancer with powerful drugs that kill cancer cells.

* **fallopian tubes** (fa-LO-pee-an tubes) are two long slender tubes in females that connect the ovaries and the uterus. Typically, a fallopian tube is where conception takes place.

* **ovaries** (O-va-reez) are the organs in females that contain and release eggs (ova).

* **menstrual** (MEN-stroo-al) refers to menstruation (men-stroo-AY-shun), the discharging through the vagina of blood and tissue from the uterus that recurs each month in women of reproductive age.

may decide to remove a small amount of tissue from the cervix and have it examined under a microscope, a procedure called biopsy (BY-op-see).

Treatment depends on how abnormal the cells look. Some lesions* that have a close-to-normal appearance do not require treatment, but they do need to be checked regularly. Other growths, or tumors, that appear likely to develop into cancer may need to be removed. This often is done by using a special instrument to freeze them off, a procedure called cryosurgery (KRY-o-sur-jer-ee), to burn them off by cauterization (kaw-ter-i-ZAY-shun), or to direct high-energy laser beams at them. These procedures can destroy the abnormal areas without affecting nearby healthy tissue.

These procedures also may be used to remove tumors that definitely are cancerous but have remained on the surface of the cervix. If they have grown into the wall, surgeons either need to remove the tumor and the surrounding tissue, or they need to remove the entire uterus and cervix, an operation called a hysterectomy (his-ter-EK-to-mee). Surgery is the most common treatment for cervical cancer, but it also may be used together with radiation therapy and chemotherapy*. These treatments can help prevent the cancer from spreading, or they help destroy cancer cells that already have traveled to other parts of the body. Radiation therapy uses high-energy rays to damage cancer cells and stop them from growing. Chemotherapy involves giving powerful anticancer drugs either by injection into a vein or by mouth.

How Is Uterine Cancer Diagnosed and Treated?

If doctors suspect uterine cancer, based on a woman's symptoms and a physical examination, a biopsy is necessary to confirm the diagnosis. As with cervical cancer, the most common treatments are surgery, radiation therapy, and chemotherapy. Surgery involves removing the uterus and nearby reproductive organs such as the fallopian tubes* and ovaries*. Lymph nodes near the tumor also may be removed during surgery to see if they contain cancer.

After the treatment is finished, most women can lead normal lives. If their uterus was removed, however, they can no longer bear children. This often is not an issue for women in their fifties and sixties, but younger women in their twenties, thirties, and forties may find it hard to adjust to this reality.

How Can Cervical and Uterine Cancer Be Prevented?

Because cervical cancer is so closely connected with the sexually transmitted virus called HPV, not having sexual intercourse is an effective way to prevent HPV infection. Those who do have sex should always use a condom. Smoking should be avoided, and it is essential that women see their doctors yearly for an examination and a Pap test.

The causes of uterine cancer are less clearly defined, and so it is difficult to say how it might be prevented. Women who have irregular menstrual* periods, which may mean that they have a hormonal imbalance, should be evaluated by a doctor. Hormonal treatment may reduce the risk of uterine cancer. As with other forms of cancer, eating a healthful diet high in fruits and vegetables and low in animal fat, as well as

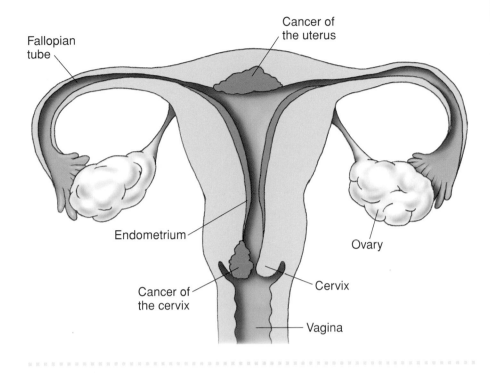

Cancer of
the uterus

Fallopian
tube

Endometrium

Ovary

Cancer of
the cervix

Cervix

Vagina

Anatomy of the female reproduction system showing cervical and uterine cancers.

maintaining a proper body weight, seems to play some role in lowering the risk of developing it.

Resources

Book

Runowicz, Carolyn D., M.D., Jeanne A. Petrek, M.D., and Ted S. Gansler, M.D. *Women and Cancer: A Thorough and Compassionate Resource for Patients and Their Families.* New York: Villard Books, 1999.

Organizations

The National Cancer Institute (NCI), part of the U.S. National Institutes of Health (NIH), publishes *What You Need to Know about Cancer of the Cervix* and *What You Need to Know about Cancer of the Uterus,* which are available by phone or at its website.
Telephone 800-422-6237
http://cancernet.nci.nih.gov/wyntk_pubs/index.html

The American Cancer Society (ACS) posts information on cervical and uterine cancer on its website.
Telephone 800-227-2345
http://www.cancer.org

The National Cervical Cancer Coalition (NCCC) posts information about cervical cancer on its website.
http://www.nccc-online.org

Ovarian Cancer

Cancer of the ovaries, the organs in women that produce eggs, is the most dangerous of the cancers that can form in the female reproductive system. Although it is generally treatable if caught early, it is not usually caught early. Unlike uterine cancer, it usually causes no symptoms until it is advanced. And unlike cervical cancer, which can be found with the Pap test, there is no screening test reliable enough to be recommended for all women.

Women at high risk, however, can be screened with a blood test and a sonogram, which uses sound waves to "see" inside the body. Such women include those with close relatives who have had ovarian cancer, those who have mutations in the breast cancer genes BRCA-1 and BRCA-2, and those who have had breast cancer.

When symptoms do occur, they can include swelling of the abdomen, gas, bloating, stomach and leg pain, and a feeling of pressure in the pelvis, as though the woman needs to go to the bathroom.

Diagnosis begins with various imaging procedures, but requires a biopsy, a surgical sampling of tissue, since noncancerous tumors also can occur in the ovaries. As treatment, the ovaries are removed and chemotherapy is usually given.

Can ovarian cancer be prevented? If a woman needs to have her uterus removed for another reason (through an operation called a hysterectomy) and she is past childbearing age, removing the ovaries as well is sometimes advised. Taking birth control pills over a period of years appears to decrease ovarian cancer risk, as does having children before age 30 and breastfeeding.

 See also
Cancer
Genital Warts
Tobacco-Related Diseases

Varicose Veins

Varicose veins are veins that become stretched, enlarged, or twisted. They can often be seen on the legs, just below the surface of the skin, and they may give legs a lumpy appearance.

KEYWORDS
for searching the Internet
and other reference sources

Circulatory system

Vascular system

What Are Veins and Arteries?

The body has two systems for carrying blood to and from all its cells, tissues, and organs. Arteries carry blood from the heart to the organs, and veins return blood back to the heart. Although veins and arteries are similar in structure, veins usually carry blood with less oxygen than arteries do, and vein walls are thinner and weaker than arterial walls. When veins become injured or empty, they sometimes dilate* or collapse and become varicose*.

Where Do People Get Varicose Veins?

Varicose veins develop on the inside areas of the leg or on the back of the calf. The veins look bluish in color and may become swollen, which gives the leg a lumpy appearance. About 15 percent of adults in the United States develop varicose veins. Women sometimes develop varicose veins during pregnancy and develop them more often than men do. There is a tendency for varicose veins to run in families.

* **dilate** (DY-late) means to become enlarged or stretched beyond the usual boundaries.

* **varix, varices, varicose** are the Latin words that describe veins, arteries, or lymph vessels that have become stretched or enlarged.

A healthy vein compared with a varicose vein.

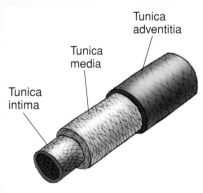

Tunica
adventitia

Tunica
media

Tunica
intima

Vein

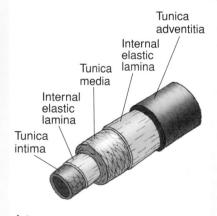

Tunica
adventitia

Internal
elastic
lamina

Tunica
media

Internal
elastic
lamina

Tunica
intima

Artery

What Is the Treatment for Varicose Veins?

Many people with varicose veins have no symptoms, but some people feel pain in their legs, especially when they stand for long periods of time.

Mild cases In mild cases, doctors usually suggest that people with varicose veins exercise to improve circulation and that they wear support hose or stockings around the swollen veins to help relieve pain. People with varicose veins are usually told to sit with their feet up as often as possible and to avoid standing for prolonged periods of time.

Severe cases When people have more severe cases of varicose veins, doctors sometimes inject a solution into the vein to block it. The body then reroutes the blocked vein's blood supply to nearby veins that are healthier. Sometimes doctors "strip" varicose veins, which means they remove them surgically. This process takes about 30 minutes and is often quite successful.

Resource

The U.S. National Institutes of Health (NIH) has a search engine at its website that locates information about varicose veins at the U.S. National Heart, Lung, and Blood Institute (NHLBI) and elsewhere. http://www.nih.gov

Vertigo

Vertigo (VER-ti-go) is dizziness in which people feel that they or their surroundings are moving, often causing loss of balance.

KEYWORD
for searching the Internet and other reference sources

Otology

What Is Vertigo?

Vertigo is different from other forms of dizziness because it is caused by disturbances in the structures that control the sense of balance. These structures include the vestibule and semicircular canals in the ear, the vestibular (ves-TIB-u-lar) nuclei in the brain stem, and the eyes. There are many different kinds of vertigo.

Benign paroxysmal vertigo of childhood Benign* paroxysmal (par-ok-SIZ-mal) vertigo is a condition that sometimes affects toddlers, who may suddenly lose their balance, roll their eyes, and become pale, dizzy, or nauseated for a few minutes. They usually recover quickly and often outgrow this form of vertigo.

> *** benign** (be-NINE) means a condition is not cancerous or serious and will probably improve, go away, or not get worse.

Positional vertigo Positional vertigo may occur following changes in head position, especially when lying on one ear or when tipping back the head to look up. The symptoms tend to appear in clusters that last for several days. The vertigo begins several seconds after head movement and usually stops in under a minute. Some of the causes of positional vertigo are trauma to the ear, an ear infection, ear surgery, or degeneration because of aging inner ear organs that are involved in balance. Surgery can sometimes correct positional vertigo.

Ménière's disease This is sometimes called Ménière's syndrome* or recurrent aural vertigo. It is caused by damage to the balance organs in the ears, although doctors often do not know the cause of the damage. In addition to vertigo, symptoms often include tinnitus (ti-NY-tis), which is a ringing, buzzing, or roaring in the ears. It may also cause gradual deafness in the affected ear. Ménière's disease can be controlled but not cured with medication.

> *** syndrome** means a group or pattern of symptoms and/or signs that occur together.

Labyrinthitis Labyrinthitis (lab-i-rin-THY-tis) is an inflammation of the labyrinth in the inner ear, possibly as a result of viral infection in the upper respiratory tract. The labyrinth is a group of canals in the inner ear that is important for balance. Symptoms of labyrinthitis are sudden onset of severe vertigo lasting for several days, hearing loss, and tinnitus in the affected ear. During the recovery period, which may last several weeks, rapid head movement causes temporary vertigo.

Vestibular neuronitis Vestibular neuronitis (noo-ro-NY-tis) is sometimes called epidemic vertigo and is thought to be the result of a virus that causes inflammation of the vestibular nerve cells. Vestibular neuronitis

How the world looks to a young boy with vertigo. It feels like he's spinning and the world around him is spinning, too. © 1993 J.S. Reid/Custom Medical Stock Photo.

▶ *See also*

Deafness

Ear Infections

Motion Sickness

Tinnitus

usually causes a single attack of severe vertigo with nausea and vomiting that lasts for a few days. There is no hearing loss or tinnitus, and doctors will often prescribe medication to help with the dizziness and nausea.

Traumatic vertigo Traumatic vertigo is one of the most common types of vertigo. It usually follows a head injury. The symptoms generally start to improve within several days but may last for weeks. Deafness often accompanies the vertigo on the side of the head that received the trauma. In some cases, surgery may be required to correct damage to the ear structures.

Acoustic neuromas Acoustic neuromas are benign tumors that form in the vestibular nerve, affecting nerve signals for balance and hearing from the ear to the brain. Symptoms are hearing loss, tinnitus, dizziness, and unsteadiness. Surgery to remove the tumor improves the vertigo.

How Do Doctors Treat Vertigo?

Doctors often prescribe medication to reduce the dizziness, nausea, and sense of motion of vertigo. Other treatments will vary according to the cause of the vertigo.

Resources

The U.S. National Institute on Deafness and Other Communication Disorders (NIDCD) posts information about hearing and balance at its website, which includes a special section called *Kids and Teachers*. http://www.nih.gov/nidcd

Vestibular Disorders Association, P.O. Box 4467, Portland, OR 97208-4467. The Vestibular Disorders Association posts information at its website about vertigo, labyrinthitis, neuronitis, Ménière's disease, and other inner-ear balance disorders. It also offers a video and brochure called *Dealing with Dizziness*. http://www.vestibular.org

Viral Infections

Viral infections occur when viruses enter cells in the body and begin reproducing, often causing illness. Viruses are tiny germs that can reproduce only by invading a living cell.

How Are Viruses Different from Bacteria?

Viruses are far smaller than bacteria. They are so small that they could not be seen until the electron microscope was invented in the 1940s. Unlike most bacteria, viruses are not complete cells that can function on their own. They cannot convert carbohydrates to energy, the way that bacteria and other living cells do. Viruses depend on other organisms for energy. And viruses cannot reproduce unless they get inside a living cell. Most viruses consist only of tiny particles of nucleic acid (the material that makes up genes) surrounded by a coat of protein. Some have an outer envelope as well.

Thousands of viruses There are thousands of viruses, and in humans they cause a wide range of diseases. For instance, rhinoviruses cause colds, influenza viruses cause flu, adenoviruses cause various respiratory problems, and rotaviruses cause gastroenteritis. Polioviruses can make their way to the spinal cord and cause paralysis, while coxsackieviruses (sometimes written as Coxsackie viruses) and echoviruses sometimes infect the heart or the membranes surrounding the spinal cord or lungs. Herpesviruses cause cold sores, chickenpox, and genital herpes, a sexually transmitted disease. Other viruses cause a variety of conditions from measles and mumps to AIDS.

The body's defense system Most viruses do not cause serious diseases and are killed by the body's immune system—its network of natural defenses. In many cases, people never even know they have been infected. But unlike bacteria, which can be killed by antibiotics, most viruses are not affected by existing medicines. Fortunately, scientists have been able to make vaccines, which help the body develop natural defenses to prevent many viral infections.

How Do Viruses Infect the Body?

Viruses can enter the human body through any of its openings, but most often they use the nose and mouth. Once inside, the virus attaches itself to the outside of the kind of cell it attacks, called a host cell. For example, a rhinovirus attacks cells in the nose, while an enterovirus binds to cells in the stomach and intestines. Then the virus works its way through the host cell's outer membrane.

After entering the cell, the virus begins making identical viruses from the host cell's protein. These new viruses may make their way back out through the host cell's membrane, sometimes destroying the cell, and then attacking new host cells. This process continues until the body develops enough antibodies* and other defenses to defeat the viral invaders.

Not all viruses attack only one part of the body, causing what is called a localized infection. Some viruses spread through the bloodstream or the nerves, attacking cells throughout the body. For instance, HIV, the human immunodeficiency virus that causes AIDS, attacks certain cells of the immune system that are located throughout the body.

Are Viruses Alive?

It would seem to be a simple matter to tell if something is alive. But biologists disagree on whether viruses are a form of life.

Viruses lack certain features that other forms of life have. They cannot convert carbohydrates, proteins, or fats into energy, a process called metabolism. They cannot reproduce on their own, but must enter a living cell and use the host cell's energy. On the other hand, like all life forms, viruses do have genes made of nucleic acid that contain the information they need to reproduce.

Biologists have an elaborate way of classifying every form of life. Each is grouped into a kingdom (such as the Animal Kingdom) and smaller sub-categories called the phylum, class, genus, and species.

Bacteria and fungi each have a kingdom of their own, but viruses are left out of this system. Many biologists think that, unlike the forms of life grouped into kingdoms, viruses did not evolve (develop) as a group. Instead, viruses may have developed individually from the kind of cells they now infect—animal cells, plant cells, or bacteria.

* **antibodies** are proteins made by the body's immune system to target a specific kind of germ or other foreign substance.

How Long Do Viral Infections Last?

In most types of viral infection, the immune system clears the virus from the body within days to a few weeks. But some viruses cause persistent or latent* infections, which can last for years. In these cases, a person may get infected and seem to recover or may not be aware of being infected at all. Then years later, the illness will occur again, or symptoms will start for the first time. Viruses that can cause latent infections include herpesviruses, Hepatitis B and C viruses, and HIV.

How Do Viruses Cause Illness?

Viruses can cause illness by destroying or interfering with the functioning of large numbers of important cells. Sometimes, as mentioned earlier, the cell is destroyed when the newly created viruses leave it. Sometimes the virus keeps the cell from producing the energy it needs to live, or the virus upsets the cell's chemical balance in some other way. Sometimes the virus seems to trigger a mysterious process called "programmed cell death" or apoptosis (ap-op-TO-sis) that kills the cell.

Some persistent or latent viral infections seem to transform cells into a cancerous state that makes them grow out of control. It has been estimated that 10 to 20 percent of cancers are caused by viral infections. The most common are liver cancer caused by persistent infection with Hepatitis B or Hepatitis C virus, and cancer of the cervix (the bottom of a woman's uterus or womb), linked to certain strains of the human papillomavirus.

Sometimes a viral illness is caused not by the virus itself, but by the body's reaction to it. The immune system may kill cells in order to get rid of the virus that is inside them. This can cause serious illness if the cells being

** **latent** infections are dormant or hidden illnesses that do not show the signs and symptoms of active diseases.*

There are thousands of kinds of viruses. Most consist only of tiny particles of genetic material surrounded by a coat of protein and sometimes an outer envelope. Specific viruses attach themselves to the outsides of specific host cells, and then work their way inside through the host's outer membranes. Once inside their host cells, the viruses reproduce. The new viruses can destroy their host cells and then move on to attack new host cells. ▶

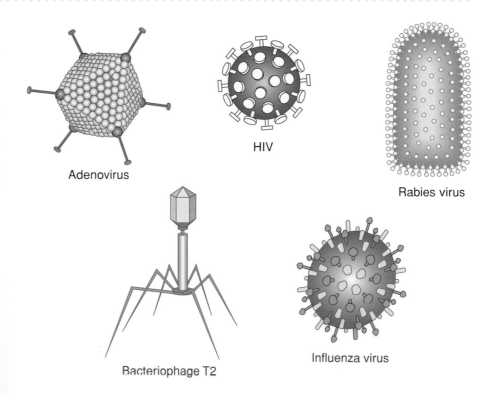

Adenovirus

HIV

Rabies virus

Bacteriophage T2

Influenza virus

killed are very important to the body's functioning, like those in the lungs or central nervous system, or if the cells cannot reproduce quickly enough to replace the ones being destroyed.

How Are Viral Infections Diagnosed and Treated?

Symptoms   Symptoms vary widely, depending on the virus and the organs involved. Many viruses, like many bacteria, cause fever, and either respiratory symptoms (coughing and sneezing) or intestinal symptoms (nausea, vomiting, diarrhea). Viral illnesses often cause high fevers in young children, even when the illnesses are not dangerous.

Diagnosis   Some viral infections, such as influenza, the common cold, and chickenpox, are easily recognized by their symptoms and no lab tests are needed. For many others, such as viral hepatitis, AIDS, and mononucleosis, a blood sample is analyzed for the presence of specific antibodies to the virus. If present, these antibodies help confirm the diagnosis. In some cases, a virus may be grown in the laboratory, using a technique called tissue culture, or identified by its nucleic acid, using a technique called polymerase chain reaction (PCR). Tests like PCR or tissue culture are used when antibody tests are not precise enough or when the actual amount of a virus in the body must be determined.

Treatment   Viruses cannot be treated with the antibiotics that kill bacteria. Fortunately, a few drugs, such as ribavirin and acyclovir, can control the spread of viral invaders without destroying host cells. Intense research to find better treatments for AIDS has led to development of many drugs that help fight the virus. Unfortunately, none of these drugs has been able to treat viral infections as effectively as antibiotics treat bacterial infections.

How Are Viral Infections Prevented?

Hygiene and sanitation   The first step in preventing the spread of viral infections is simply to practice good hygiene. This means washing the hands often, and eating only food that has been prepared properly. It also means building and maintaining facilities for getting rid of sewage safely and for providing clean drinking water.

Vaccination   Another important preventive measure is immunizing people against viruses. This involves giving people vaccines that stimulate the immune system to make antibodies, proteins that target a specific germ. Vaccines to prevent Hepatitis B, polio, mumps, measles, rubella (German measles), and chickenpox are usually given to babies and young children in the United States. Vaccines also can prevent influenza and Hepatitis A.

Vaccines are useful only against certain kinds of viruses. For example, the polioviruses that cause poliomyelitis (polio), a great crippler of children in the past, are few in number and relatively stable. So it was possible in the 1950s to make a vaccine that protects children from getting

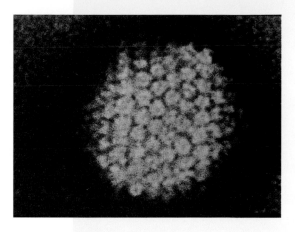

▲

An individual adenovirus viewed under an electron microscope. Viruses are so small that they could not be seen until the electron microscope was invented in the 1940s. This one was photographed at 800,000 times its original size. © *Hans Gelderblom/Visuals Unlimited.*

What Is a 24-Hour Virus?

When people have a mild illness—perhaps fever and an upset stomach, perhaps nausea and diarrhea—they often say they have a "24-hour virus" or a "stomach virus." Many viruses can cause these kinds of symptoms, but there are many other possible causes as well, including bacterial infection or bacterial food poisoning. People usually recover from these brief or mild illnesses before doctors can do the tests that determine the causes. So a "stomach virus" may or may not be a virus at all.

KEYWORDS
*for searching the Internet
and other reference sources*

Depigmentation

Dermatology

Melanocytes

Photochemotherapy

Psoralens

* **pigment** (PIG-ment) is a sub-stance that imparts color to another substance.

polio (although the illness still occurs in the developing world where fewer children are vaccinated). On the other hand, influenza viruses change in minor ways every few years and in a major way about every ten years, so a flu vaccine is useful for only a year or two.

One reason a vaccine for the common cold has never been developed is that there are at least a hundred different rhinoviruses that cause colds, and so far it has not been possible to make a vaccine that works against all of them. A similar problem with HIV, which has many different and fast-changing strains (variations), is one of several reasons why progress toward an AIDS vaccine has been slow.

Vitamin Deficiencies *See* Dietary Deficiencies

Vitiligo

Vitiligo is a condition that causes white patches of skin due to a loss of pigment in the cells and tissues of the body.

What Is Vitiligo?

Melanocytes (MEL-a-no-sites) are special skin cells that make the pigment* that colors the skin, hair, eyes, and body linings. If these cells die or cannot make pigment, the affected skin gets lighter or completely white, causing vitiligo (vit-i-LY-go). The hair in affected areas also may turn white, and people with dark skin may notice a loss of color inside their mouths. No one knows for sure what makes melanocytes die or stop working in vitiligo.

Who Gets Vitiligo?

Vitiligo affects people of all races and both sexes equally. It affects one or two out of every 100 people. About half of all people who have vitiligo begin to lose pigment before they are 20 years old.

Vitiligo is common in people with certain immune system diseases and in children with parents who have the condition. However, most people with vitiligo have no immune system disease, and most children will not get vitiligo even if a parent has it. In fact, most people with vitiligo are in good general health and do not have a family history of the condition.

Vitiligo is more obvious in people with dark skin. Light-skinned people may notice the contrast between patches of vitiligo and areas of suntanned skin in the summer. The amount of pigment that is lost varies from person to person. The first white patches often occur on the hands, feet, arms, face, or lips. Other common areas for patches to appear are the armpits, the groin (the area where the inner thighs join the trunk), and around the navel (belly button) and genitals.

There is no way to know if vitiligo will spread to other parts of the body, but it usually does spread over time. For some people, this spread occurs rapidly, but for other people, it takes place over many years. Both sides of the body usually are affected in a similar way. There may be a few patches or there may be many.

How Is Vitiligo Diagnosed and Treated?

Diagnosis   To diagnose vitiligo, the doctor may ask about such things as a person's symptoms, whether or not the person has an immune system disorder, and whether or not vitiligo runs in the person's family. The doctor also may suggest various tests to rule out other medical problems that can cause light skin patches.

Treatment   Vitiligo does not always need treatment. For some people with light skin, simply avoiding a suntan on areas of normal skin is enough to make the patches of vitiligo almost unnoticeable. Other people use makeup, skin dyes, or self-tanning products to cover up the vitiligo. Self-tanning products are creams that give the skin a tan color, but not a true tan. The color tends to wear off after a few days. None of these things changes the condition, but they can make the vitiligo less noticeable. In children, vitiligo usually is just covered up.

In adults, if covering up the vitiligo is not enough, a medical treatment may be tried, although results often cannot be seen for 6 to 18 months. The choice of treatment depends on the person's wishes, how many white patches the person has, and how widespread the patches are. Not every treatment works for every person. There are several choices:

- Corticosteroid (kor-ti-ko-STEER-oid) creams can be applied to the skin and sometimes can return color to small areas of vitiligo.

- PUVA, which stands for psoralen (SOR-a-len) and ultraviolet A therapy. Ultraviolet A is the part of sunlight that can cause the skin to tan, and psoralens are substances that react with ultraviolet light to darken the skin. This medication is taken by mouth or applied to the skin, and then the light patches of skin are exposed to ultraviolet A light from a special lamp.

- Skin grafting is an operation that involves moving skin from normal areas to white patches. It is useful only for a small number of people with vitiligo.

- Depigmentation therapy involves using medication to fade the normal skin to match the whitened areas of vitiligo.

Living with Vitiligo

The white patches of vitiligo have no natural protection from the sun and are very easily sunburned. People with vitiligo should be careful to avoid exposure to midday sun, to cover up with clothing and a hat, and to use a sunscreen with a high SPF (sun protection factor) rating.

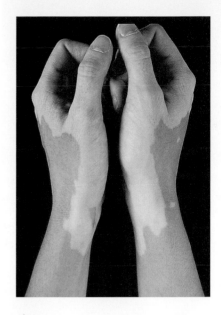

▲

This young woman has vitiligo on her wrists, hands, and thumbs. She does not use makeup to cover it. *1997 Custom Medical Stock Photo.*

► See also
Albinism
Immunodeficiency
Skin Conditions

Resources

American Academy of Dermatology, 930 North Meacham Road, Schaumburg, IL 60173. The American Academy of Dermatology publishes a pamphlet called *Vitiligo* and posts a fact sheet about it at its website.
Telephone 888-462-DERM
http://www.aad.org/aadpamphrework/Vitiligo.html

The U.S. National Institute of Arthritis and Musculoskeletal and Skin Diseases posts a fact sheet called *Questions and Answers About Vitiligo* at its website. To order a pamphlet, contact the NIAMS Information Clearinghouse, 1 AMS Circle, Bethesda, MD 20892-3675.
Telephone 301-495-4484
http://www.nih.gov/niams/healthinfo/vitiligo.htm

National Vitiligo Foundation, Inc., P.O. Box 6337, Tyler, TX 75703. This is a national group for people with vitiligo.
Telephone 903-531-0074
http://nvfi.org

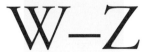

W–Z

Wall Eyes *See* Strabismus

Warts

Warts are small, hard bumps on the skin or inner linings of the body that are caused by the human papillomavirus (HPV).

KEYWORDS
for searching the Internet and other reference sources

Human papillomavirus (HPV)

Verrucae

What Are Warts?

Despite all the stories, warts are not caused by touching a frog. Warts are small, hard bumps on the skin or inner linings of the body that are caused by a virus—too small to be seen with the naked eye—called human papillomavirus (pap-i-LO-ma-VY-rus), or HPV. Warts can affect any part of the body, but most often they appear on the fingers, hands, arms, and feet. Warts also may occur in the genital area.

About one in four people have had a wart at some time. Children get warts more often than adults do. The virus that causes warts is passed from person to person. However, the chance of catching hand and foot warts is small. Warts grow more readily if the skin has been injured. This explains why people who bite their nails get warts so often. In addition, some people just seem to be more likely to get warts, just as some people catch colds more easily than others do.

What Do Warts Look Like?

The way a wart looks depends on where it is growing. Most warts are skin-colored, raised, and rough to the touch. However, some are dark, flat, or smooth. Warts usually are painless, except for plantar warts that grow on the bottoms of the feet. Plantar warts may have black dots in the center. When the pressure of walking causes plantar warts to flatten, they can be painful, feeling like a small rock in the shoe.

How Are Warts Treated?

In children, warts often go away without any treatment, sometimes after a few months and sometimes after a few years. In adults, however, warts usually do not go away without treatment. Methods of treatment include:

- Dissolving warts with non-prescription lotions available over the counter at drugstores
- Dissolving warts with stronger lotions prescribed by doctors

See also
Genital warts
Skin Conditions
Viral Infections

*laser surgery uses a very narrow and intense beam of light that can destroy body tissue.

■ Removing warts by laser* surgery

■ Freezing warts with liquid nitrogen or other cold liquid

■ Burning warts with an electric needle

It is important to check with a doctor before using non-prescription lotions to remove warts. Many treatments for warts can remove healthy skin along with the wart itself, and treatments may cause scarring or infection, particularly for people who have diabetes or other conditions that affect the circulatory system. Doctors usually can identify warts by looking at them, and can make sure that the growth being treated really is a wart and not a different skin condition or skin cancer.

Resources

American Academy of Dermatology, 930 North Meachum Road, Schaumburg, IL 60173. The AAD posts a fact sheet about warts, in both English and Spanish, at its website.
Telephone 888-462-DERM
http://www.aad.org/aadpamphrework/warts.htm

KidsHealth.org, sponsored by the Nemours Foundation, posts a fact sheet about warts, with pictures, at its website.
http://www.KidsHealth.org

American Podiatric Medical Association, 9312 Old Georgetown Road, Bethesda, MD 20814-1698. The APMA posts a fact sheet about plantar warts at its website.
Telephone 800-FOOTCARE
http://www.apma.org/topics/Warts.htm

Whooping Cough (Pertussis)

Whooping cough, also known as pertussis, is an infection of the respiratory system caused by Bordetella pertussis *bacteria.*

What Is Whooping Cough?

Whooping cough is an infection of the respiratory system that occurs most frequently in young children. It is caused by two related bacteria: *Bordetella pertussis* (bor-de-TEL-a per-TUS-is) and *Bordetella parapertussis* (bor-de-TEL-a par-a-per-TUS-is).

What Happens When Children Get Whooping Cough?

Symptoms Whooping cough can last for as long as seven weeks. During the first or second week, children feel tired and feverish, and they develop a short, dry cough that gets worse at night.

KEYWORDS
for searching the Internet
and other reference sources

Catarrh

Infection

Pertussis

Respiratory system

During the next few weeks, the children experience coughing spasms that last for several minutes, during which they take in loud, sudden breaths that sound like a "whoop." They also may cough up mucus*, which can cause choking and vomiting. In some cases, whooping cough may lead to ear infections and pneumonia. The coughing spells are very tiring, and they interfere with sleep.

During the last few weeks, when children begin to recover, their coughing becomes less frequent and their vomiting stops.

Diagnosis When parents or doctors hear the characteristic "whooping" sound, they often will suspect that whooping cough is the cause. The doctor sometimes will take a swab of mucus from the nose or throat to examine under the microscope for evidence of *Bordetella pertussis* or *Bordetella parapertussis* bacteria.

Treatment Usually, treatment involves trying to make the child as comfortable as possible until the infection runs its course. The doctor may prescribe medication to make it easier to sleep and will usually recommend frequent light meals and snacks to replace the nutrients lost due to vomiting. Sometimes the doctor will suction the child's lungs to remove mucus and make it easier to breathe. The doctor may prescribe antibiotics to treat ear infections and pneumonia, and to prevent the disease from spreading to other members of the child's family, but the antibiotics usually cannot shorten the duration of the coughing. Whooping cough can be very dangerous for infants and young children, and the doctor may recommend that a child with whooping cough be hospitalized.

How Is Whooping Cough Prevented?

In the United States, infants and children receive pertussis vaccinations as part of their normal childhood shots. Children are required to be immunized against whooping cough, as well as against several other diseases, before they enter school.

Vaccination with earlier ("whole cell") forms of pertussis vaccine sometimes caused side effects* in infants, with reactions that included fever, irritability, and (in rare instances) seizures. Researchers have developed a new "acellular" pertussis vaccine, which causes fewer side effects and still protects against whooping cough.

Pertussis vaccination during childhood does not give lifetime immunity, and adults should check with their doctors about receiving booster shots.

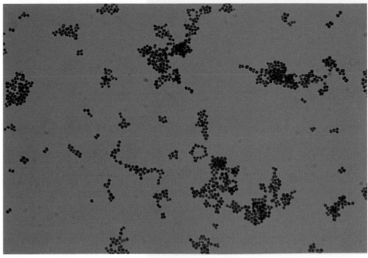

▲

Bordetella pertussis bacteria seen under a microscope. © *George J. Wilder/Visuals Unlimited.*

* **mucus** (MU-kus) is a kind of body slime. It is thick and slippery, and it lines the inside of many parts of the body.

* **side effects** are unwanted symptoms that may be caused by vaccines or medications.

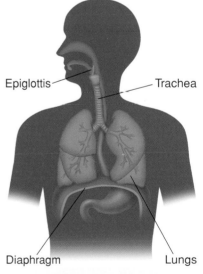

Epiglottis — Trachea

Diaphragm — Lungs

▲

Whooping cough can cause fever and quick short coughs due to spasms of the glottis as the air leaves the lungs.

▶ See also

Bacterial Infections

Worms

KEYWORDS
for searching the Internet
and other reference sources

Cestodes

Infestation

Nematodes

Parasites

Trematodes

* **infestation** occurs when parasites
are living on or in the body tissues
of a human or other host.

* **parasites** are creatures that live
in and feed on the bodies of other
organisms.

▶ See also
Ascariasis
Hookworm
Parasitic Diseases
Pinworm (Enterobiasis)
Schistosomiasis
Tapeworm
Toxocariasis
Trichinosis

*Worms are invertebrate (in-VER-te-bret) animals, which means
they lack spinal columns (backbones). Worms can cause certain
types of parasitic infestation* in humans.*

Diseases and conditions caused by worms are as varied as the types of
worms that cause them. Worms that act as parasites* come in thousands
of different species, including roundworms, tapeworms, flatworms, flukes,
and leeches. The worms may be microscopic, or they may be as long as
9 meters (almost 30 feet).

Some worms cause painful and deforming conditions, while others
are barely noticed by the host. Some worm infestations clear up after a
short time, while others cause long-term problems that affect many different body organs and may even cause death. Common garden earth-
worms do not cause human illness.

Frequent hand-washing, good hygiene, good sanitary conditions,
and clean water can help prevent worm infections. Prompt diagnosis
and treatment by a doctor can help clear up worm infestations.

Resources

The World Health Organization's Division of Control of Tropical
Diseases posts many fact sheets about worm infections at its website.
http://www.who.int/ctd/html/intest.html

The U.S. National Institute of Allergy and Infectious Diseases posts a
fact sheet about parasitic roundworm diseases at its website.
http://www.niaid.nih.gov/factsheets/roundwor.htm

KEYWORDS
for searching the Internet
and other reference sources

Candida albicans

Candidiasis

Fungal infections

Vulvovaginal Candidiasis

* **fungus** (FUN-gus) is any organism
belonging to the kingdom Fungi
(FUN-ji), which includes mushrooms, yeasts, and molds.

* **yeast** is a general term
describing single-celled fungi that
reproduce by budding.

Yeast Infection, Vaginal

*The vaginal yeast infection candidiasis (kan-di-DY-a-sis) is caused
by an overabundance of a certain kind of fungus* in the genital
area. Its symptoms include an itching or burning sensation in the
genital area and, very typically, a white discharge from the vagina.
Almost all cases of candidiasis affect women, although men also can
show related signs of the infection.*

What Is Candidiasis?

The fungus that causes vaginal yeast* infection is usually *Candida albicans* (KAN-di-da AL-bi-kanz). It is naturally present in many parts of

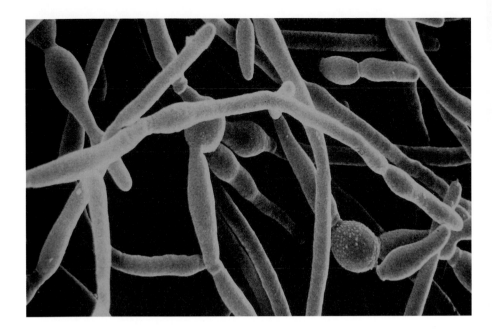

The *Candida albicans* fungus, photographed at 18,000x actual size. © *David M. Phillips, Visuals Unlimited.*

◀

the body and grows in the vagina (va-JY-na), the gastrointestinal* tract, and the mouth. It is usually kept under control by a balance with various bacteria* that also are normally found in these naturally moist areas. Candidiasis will occur when this balance is disrupted and too many of the fungus cells are present in the vaginal area. (When *Candida* infection involves the mouth, it is called thrush. When it involves babies' diaper area, it is called candidal diaper rash.)

Candida fungus cells can multiply too much when the use of antibiotics* destroy too many of the bacteria that usually keep them in check. Other situations that may cause the fungus to grow out of control are the use of birth control pills, pregnancy, and the use of drugs that suppress the immune system*. When a woman has a disease like AIDS or diabetes that can cause weakening of the immune system, she will also be more likely to develop a vaginal yeast infection.

It is estimated that 75 percent of women have a yeast infection at least once in their life. Half of them will have the infection more than once.

What Are the Symptoms of Candidiasis?

The most notable symptom of vaginal yeast infection is a white discharge from the vagina. The discharge has the appearance of cottage cheese. The area around the vagina also may itch or feel irritated. In yeast infections in men, the head of the penis becomes inflamed or shows a rash.

How Is Candidiasis Diagnosed and Treated?

Vaginal yeast infection is easily diagnosed by examining a sample of the white vaginal discharge. Treatment is with antifungal drugs* that are applied to the affected area or taken by mouth in the form of a pill.

While some creams for vaginal yeast infections are available without a prescription, it is advisable to see a doctor the first time a vaginal yeast infection is noticed. It is important to have any infection diagnosed

* **gastrointestinal** (GAS-tro-in-TES-ti-nal) means having to do with the stomach and intestines.

* **bacteria** (bak-TEER-ee-a) are single-celled microorganisms, which typically reproduce by cell division. Some, but not all, types of bacteria can cause disease in humans. Many types can live in the body without causing harm.

* **antibiotics** (AN-ty-by-OT-iks) are drugs that kill bacteria.

* **immune system** is the body system that fights disease.

* **antifungal drugs** (an-ty-FUNG-al drugs) are medications that kill fungi.

Antibiotics and Yogurt

Antibiotics prescribed to treat bacterial infections also kill beneficial bacteria. When the beneficial bacteria found normally in the vagina and other mucous membranes are killed, yeast cells can grow unchecked.

Eating active-culture yogurt daily while taking an antibiotic may help replenish the supply of beneficial bacteria.

properly before treatment is started. Health professionals recommend that anyone with a vaginal yeast infection should also have her partner examined for infection.

How Can Candidiasis Be Prevented?

These steps can help prevent a vaginal yeast infection:

- Wearing cotton underwear
- Avoiding tight-fitting underwear made of synthetic fiber, like nylon
- Avoiding the daily use of panty hose
- Using white, nonperfumed toilet paper
- Keeping the genital area clean
- Using a towel (not a blow dryer) to dry the genital area
- Removing a wet bathing suit as soon as possible after swimming
- Avoiding douches and feminine hygiene sprays
- Using sanitary pads or tampons that are free of perfume

Resource

Organization

The U.S. Centers for Disease Control and Prevention (CDC), 1600 Clifton Road N.E., Atlanta, GA 30333. The U.S. government authority for information about infectious and other diseases, the CDC posts information about vaginal yeast infections at its website and sponsors a National Sexually Transmitted Diseases Hotline. Telephone 800-227-8922

http://www.cdc.gov/ncidod/dbmd/diseaseinfo/candidiasis_gen_g.htm

▶ *See also*
Fungal Infections
Infection
Sexually Transmitted Diseases
Thrush

Yellow Fever

Yellow fever is an infectious disease caused by a virus* and transmitted to humans by mosquitoes. It was given its name because of the jaundice* and high fever that accompany severe infections.

KEYWORDS
for searching the Internet and other reference sources

Aedes aegypti

Epidemic

Mosquito

Vaccination

What Is Yellow Fever?

Once causing epidemics* in many parts of the world, including the United States, yellow fever now is confined almost entirely to tropical parts of Africa and South America. There it occurs in two forms, urban and sylvan.

Urban yellow fever is spread from person to person in densely populated areas by the bite of the *Aedes aegypti* (a-EE-deez ee-JIP-she) mosquito. Sylvan (forest) yellow fever occurs among humans and monkeys in sparsely populated jungles and rain forests, where it is spread by various mosquitoes other than *A. aegypti*. One person cannot catch yellow fever directly from another.

Eradication of the mosquito carrying the yellow fever virus from many heavily populated areas long ago has reduced the incidence of yellow fever greatly worldwide. Nonetheless, epidemics still break out occasionally in some African cities today. The disease is endemic* in forests and local populations of many tropical countries.

What Are the Symptoms of Yellow Fever?

The yellow fever virus attacks the central nervous system* and other organs, especially the liver, kidneys, and heart. Fever, headache, and bone pains develop suddenly 3 to 6 days after infection, and they often are accompanied by nosebleeds and stomach distress. Most cases are mild, and the individual recovers in 2 or 3 days.

In severe cases, there is a brief period when symptoms subside. The fever then returns, and the heart rate is unusually slow. The skin turns yellow,

* **virus** (VY-rus) is a tiny infectious agent that lacks an independent metabolism (me-TAB-o-lizm) and can only reproduce within the cells it infects.

* **jaundice** (JAWN-dis) is a yellowing of the skin arising from the deposition of bile pigments; it occurs as a symptom of many liver and bile duct disorders.

* **epidemics** (ep-i-DEM-iks) are outbreaks of diseases, in which the number of cases suddenly becomes far greater than usual.

* **endemic** (en-DEM-ik) describes a disease that is present in a population or geographic area at all times.

* **central nervous system** refers to the brain and the spinal cord, which coordinate the activity of the entire nervous system.

THE ROCKEFELLER COMMISSION

Yellow fever is endemic mostly in the Americas, especially in South American coastal regions. Just prior to the opening of the Panama Canal in 1914, Asian countries feared that yellow fever would be spread from America to the Eastern Hemisphere by means of newly established shipping routes.

In response to protest from countries like Japan, American medical experts testified before a commission that the most effective means of dealing with yellow fever would be through its worldwide eradication. Such an idea seemed feasible, as earlier programs of regional control had been successful.

The Rockefeller Yellow Fever Commission developed a plan to destroy centers where mosquitoes that carry yellow fever were most concentrated. Seemingly successful programs were carried out through the 1920s; however, by the 1930s, it increasingly became evident that eradication of yellow fever was not possible, and that immunization was necessary.

In 1928 the first yellow fever vaccine was prepared by the English physician Edward Hindle. Two more vaccines were developed by the bacteriologist (bak-teer-ee-OL-o-jist) Max Theiler in 1937, for which he was awarded the Nobel Prize for medicine.

The U.S. and the World

- Yellow fever exists in Africa, South America, and some Caribbean islands that are close to the earth's equator. There are an estimated 200,000 cases of yellow fever cases a year and more than 30,000 deaths worldwide. Some researchers suspect the disease is more widespread, because not all cases are reported.

- Europe and North America experienced yellow fever outbreaks before 1900, until it was confirmed the disease was transmitted by mosquito bites. Mosquito control and immunization helped eliminate the problem in developed nations.

- The last recorded outbreak in the United States occurred in New Orleans and other Southern ports. But epidemics continue to strike nations in Africa, where almost 500 million people are at risk of yellow fever.

THE PANAMA CANAL

Yellow fever probably originated in Africa. The disease spread to western Europe and to the American colonies in the 1700s, and during the 1800s severe epidemics regularly broke out in the United States in port cities as far north as New York. It was also rampant in Latin America, taking many lives.

In the early 1900s, the American physician Walter Reed and his coworkers proved that yellow fever is transmitted by mosquitoes. William Gorgas, a U.S. Army physician, then instituted mosquito control measures that virtually eliminated the disease in Havana, Cuba. The successful completion of the Panama Canal in 1914 was due largely to the application of these measures in the canal area.

In 1937, Max Theiler, a South African physician, developed an effective vaccine for yellow fever.

* **delirious** (dee-LEER-ee-us) refers to an acute mental syndrome characterized by confusion, disordered thinking, and hallucinations (ha-loo-si-NAY-shunz).

* **coma** (KO-ma) in an unconscious state, like a very deep sleep. A person in a coma cannot be woken up, and cannot move, see, speak, or hear.

* **immunity** (i-MYOO-ni-tee) is the condition of being protected against an infectious disease.

* **antibodies** (AN-ti-bod-eez) are proteins produced by the immune system to fight specific infections.

* **vaccine** (vak-SEEN) is a preparation of killed or weakened germs, or of proteins made from such microbes, administered in order to prevent, lessen the severity of, or treat a disease.

and bleeding in the stomach causes so-called black vomit. These patients may recover, or they may become delirious* and go into a coma* leading to death.

The mortality rate in yellow fever is estimated to be about 10 percent on the average, but it is higher in severe illness. Patients who recover have a lifelong immunity*.

How Is Yellow Fever Diagnosed and Treated?

Severe cases of yellow fever can be diagnosed readily from the symptoms and can be confirmed with blood tests, which can detect the yellow fever virus and antibodies*.

There is no cure for yellow fever. Treatment consists mostly of complete bed rest and replacement of body fluids.

Immunization is effective. Just one injection of yellow fever vaccine* gives protection for 10 years or more. Vaccination (vak-si-NAY-shun) is essential in countries where the disease is prevalent, and for people planning to travel in those countries. From the public health standpoint, the key to prevention is mosquito control.

Resources

Book

Wills, Christopher. *Yellow Fever, Black Goddess: The Coevolution of People and Plagues*. Pacific Palisades, CA: Perseus Press, 1997.

Organizations

The U.S. Centers for Disease Control and Prevention (CDC), 1600 Clifton Road, N.E., Atlanta, GA 30333. The U.S. government

authority for information about infectious and other diseases, the CDC posts information about yellow fever at its website.
http://www.cdc.gov/ncidod/dvbid/yellowf.htm

The World Health Organization (WHO), Avenue Appia 20, 1211 Geneva 27, Switzerland. This group's website posts a fact sheet about yellow fever.
http://www.who.int/emc/diseases/yellow_fever/index.html

Travel Health Online is a helpful website for travelers that posts information about yellow fever.
http://www.tripprep.com/index.html

▶ *See also*
Bites and Stings
Fever
Infection
Jaundice
Viral Infections

Yersinia *See* Plague

Zoonoses

Zoonoses (zo-o-NO-seez) are diseases that people can catch from animals. Well-known examples include rabies and plague.

KEYWORDS
for searching the Internet and other reference sources

Infection

Infestation

Parasites

Many organisms cause disease only in people. Others affect only certain animals. Zoonotic organisms are those that can spread from animals to humans. There are more than 175 kinds of organisms that can cause zoonoses. They include viruses, bacteria, fungi, and such parasites as mites and worms. Infection can take place by touching an infected animal, by eating undercooked meat, through insect or animal bites, or through contact with infected feces or urine.

Which Animals Cause Zoonoses?

Most zoonoses are caught from animals closely connected to people's lives, such as household pets or farm animals, but wild animals can also spread disease to humans.

Household pets Rabies is a rare but fatal viral disease that can be caught from dogs, usually from a bite. Also rare but less serious is a disease called toxocariasis (tok-so-ka-RY-a-sis), a worm infestation of dogs and cats. Ticks, mites, and fleas from dogs are also common problems.

Cat scratch disease sometimes develops after the scratch or bite of a cat. It may cause swollen glands and fever and occurs mostly in children. Toxoplasmosis (tok-so-plaz-MO-sis), caused by a protozoan (a type of single-celled organism), is picked up by contact with cat feces. It can cause serious medical problems in pregnant women and in people with weakened immune systems. Ringworm is a skin disease caused by a fungus that can be caught from cats.

Parrot owners sometimes get psittacosis (sit-a-KO-sis) by inhaling dust from dried droppings. This pneumonia-like illness, also called

Success In the Germ World

For a disease-causing germ, adaptability bring success. The same is true in animals. The raccoon, for example, is considered successful because it can thrive in areas of human habitation as well as in the wild. The panda, by contrast, can live only in certain remote bamboo forests or in a zoo with controlled conditions, and it is a very rare and endangered species.

In much the same way, germs are more successful—that is, they have a better chance of living and reproducing—if they can infect many different species of animals rather than just one. The zoonoses, therefore, are really success stories in the world of germs.

Echinococcosis

Echinococcosis (ek-KINE-o-kok-o-sis), also called hydatid (hy-DAD-id) disease, is an infection by the larvae of *Echinococcus* tapeworms. Tapeworm eggs or larvae can infect field mice, sheep, and other plant-eating animals. Foxes and coyotes, or household dogs and cats, may pick up the tapeworm eggs or larvae by eating infected animals. And people may pick up the tapeworm eggs or larvae by eating food contaminated with animal droppings (greens or fruits) or by contact with infected farm animals or pets.

Echinococcosis eggs are similar to the *Taenia* eggs that cause other tapeworm infections, and the cyst-like tumors formed by the larvae can infect the liver, the lungs, the brain, and other organs. People may be infected for many years without any symptoms, but if left untreated Echinococcosis infection can be fatal.

This infection is most common in sheep-raising areas, including Australia, New Zealand, South America, and parts of the Mediterranean. It also occurs in Canada, Alaska and other northern states, Russia, China and central Asia, and Japan, especially among hunters, trappers, and veterinarians.

"parrot fever," is caused by the bacterium *Chlamydia psittaci* (kla-MID-e-a si-TA-kee).

Farm animals   Diseases that humans get from such farm animals as cattle, sheep, hogs, and poultry usually come from eating meat. For example, eating undercooked or contaminated meat can cause food poisoning and typhoid fever from Salmonella bacteria. Trichinosis (trik-i-NO-sis) is usually contracted by eating undercooked pork. Some forms of encephalitis can be caught from horses (equine encephalitis) or from the bites of infected mosquitoes.

Wild animals   Many of the diseases that may be transmitted to humans from pets and farm animals are also found in wild animals. Rabies, for example, also occurs in raccoons, foxes, skunks, and bats. Other zoonoses are transmitted only by wild animals. These include:

- Lyme disease, which causes flulike symptoms and joint pain, is a bacterial infection caused by the bites of ticks that feed on the blood of mice carrying the bacteria.

- Hantavirus, which is passed to humans through infected rodent urine or droppings, causes severe respiratory disease.

Some of the most severe viral infections in humans are known or believed to be connected in some way to infections in monkeys and chimpanzees. These include yellow fever, Ebola, and AIDS. The best-known zoonosis historically is probably the bubonic plague, a devastating bacterial infection transmitted from rodents to humans by flea bites.

How Are Zoonoses Treated and Prevented?

Diagnosis and treatment depend upon the specific illness, and doctors should always be consulted following an animal bite. Children should be taught not to approach or pet wild animals or stray dogs, and proper veterinary care is important for household pets.

Good personal hygiene can go a long way toward preventing zoonoses. It is important to wash the hands after using the bathroom and both before and after handling food. Meat should be cooked thoroughly until juices run clear and the inside is no longer pink. Utensils and plates should be washed frequently to avoid recontaminating cooked meat.

Resources

Book

Cockrum, E. Lendell. *Rabies, Lyme Disease, Hanta Virus: And Other Animal-Borne Human Diseases in the United States and Canada.* Tucson: Fisher Books, 1997.

Organizations

The World Health Organization posts fact sheets about many different zoonotic diseases at its website. http://www.who.int/emc/diseases/zoo/index.html#publications

The U.S. Food and Drug Administration's Center for Food Safety and Applied Nutrition posts a *Bad Bug Book* at its website with information about foodborne bacteria, parasites, viruses, and toxins. http://vm.cfsan.fda.gov/~mow/intro.html

U.S. Centers for Disease Control and Prevention (CDC). CDC posts a fact sheet about alveolar hydatid disease (echinococcus) at its website. http://www.cdc.gov/ncidod/dpd/ahd.htm

▶ See also

AIDS and HIV

Animal Bites

Cat Scratch Disease

Chlamydial Infections

Ebola

Encephalitis

Food Poisoning

Hantavirus

Lyme Disease

Plague

Rabies

Ringworm

Rocky Mountain Spotted Fever

Salmonellosis

Trichinosis

Toxocariasis

Toxoplasmosis

Typhus

Yellow Fever

Bibliography

Alberts, Bruce. *Essential Cell Biology: An Introduction to the Molecular Biology of the Cell.* New York: Garland, 1998.

Alberts, Bruce. *Molecular Biology of the Cell.* 3d ed. New York: Garland, 1994.

Anderson, Kenneth N. *Mosby's Medical, Nursing, and Allied Health Dictionary.* 5th ed. St. Louis: Mosby, 1998.

Beers, Mark H. *Merck Manual of Diagnosis and Therapy.* 17th ed. Whitehouse Station, NJ: Merck, 1999.

Behrman, Richard E., ed. *Nelson Textbook of Pediatrics.* 15th ed. Philadelphia: Saunders, 1996.

Bennett, J. Claude, ed. *Cecil Textbook of Medicine.* 20th ed. Philadelphia: Saunders, 1996.

Berkow, Robert, ed. *Merck Manual of Medical Information.* Home ed. Whitehouse Station, NJ: Merck, 1997.

Beutler, Ernest, ed. *Williams Hematology.* 5th ed. New York: McGraw-Hill, 1995.

Bone, Roger C., ed. *Pulmonary and Critical Care Medicine.* St. Louis: Mosby, 1998.

Braunwald, Eugene, ed. *Heart Disease: A Textbook of Cardiovascular Medicine.* 5th ed. Philadelphia: Saunders, 1997.

Braverman, Lewis E., ed. *Werner and Ingbar's The Thyroid: A Fundamental and Clinical Text.* 7th ed. Philadelphia: Lippincott-Raven, 1996.

Brenner, Barry M., ed. *Brenner and Rector's The Kidney.* 5th ed. Philadelphia: Saunders, 1996.

Calkins, Evan, ed. *Practice of Geriatrics.* 2d ed. Philadelphia: Saunders, 1992.

Cassel, Gary H. *The Eye Book: A Complete Guide to Eye Disorders and Health.* Baltimore: Johns Hopkins University Press, 1998.

Cook, G. C., ed. *Manson's Tropical Diseases.* 20th ed. London: Saunders, 1996.

DeVita, Vincent T., ed. *Cancer: Principles and Practice of Oncology.* 5th ed. Philadelphia: Lippincott-Raven, 1997.

Diagnostic and Statistical Manual of Mental Disorders: DSM-IV. 4th ed. Washington, DC: American Psychiatric Association, 1994.

Dorland's Illustrated Medical Dictionary. 28th ed. Philadelphia: Saunders, 1994.

Ellenhorn, Matthew J. *Ellenhorn's Medical Toxicology: Diagnosis and Treatment of Human Poisoning.* 2d ed. Baltimore: Williams and Wilkins, 1997.

Fauci, Anthony S., ed. *Harrison's Principles of Internal Medicine.* 14th ed. New York: McGraw-Hill, 1998.

Glanze, Walter D., ed. *Signet Mosby Medical Encyclopedia.* Rev. ed. St. Louis: Mosby, 1996.

Goldman, L. *Cecil Textbook of Medicine.* 21st ed. Philadelphia: Saunders, 1999.

Goroll, Allan H., ed. *Primary Care Medicine: Office Evaluation and Management of the Adult Patient.* 3d ed. Philadelphia: Lippincott-Raven, 1995.

Habif, Thomas P. *Clinical Dermatology: A Color Guide to Diagnosis and Therapy.* 3d ed. St. Louis: Mosby, 1996.

Kaplan, Harold I., ed. *Comprehensive Textbook of Psychiatry.* 6th ed. Baltimore: Williams and Wilkins, 1995.

Koopman, William J. *Arthritis and Allied Conditions: A Textbook of Rheumatology.* 13th ed. Baltimore: Williams and Wilkins, 1997.

Larson, David E., ed. *Mayo Clinic Family Health Book.* 2d ed. New York: Morrow, 1996.

Lee, G. Richard, ed. *Wintrobe's Clinical Hematology.* 10th ed. Baltimore: Williams and Wilkins, 1999.

Mandell, Gerald L., ed. *Mandell, Douglas, and Bennett's Principles and Practice of Infectious Diseases.* 5th ed. Philadelphia: Churchill Livingstone, 1999.

Markel, Howard. *The Portable Pediatrician.* Philadelphia: Hanley and Belfus, Inc., 1992.

Masci, Joseph R. *Outpatient Management of HIV Infection.* 2d ed. St. Louis: Mosby, 1996.

Merigan, Thomas C., ed. *Textbook of AIDS Medicine.* 2d ed. Baltimore: Williams and Wilkins, 1999.

Middleton, Elliott, Jr., ed. *Allergy: Principles and Practice.* 5th ed. St. Louis: Mosby, 1998.

Pfenninger, John L., ed. *Procedures for Primary Care Physicians.* St. Louis: Mosby, 1994.

Pizzo, Philip A., ed. *Principles and Practice of Pediatric Oncology.* 3d ed. Philadelphia: Lippincott-Raven, 1997.

Rakel, Robert E., ed. *Conn's Current Therapy.* 51st ed. Philadelphia: Saunders, 1999.

Roberts, James R., ed. *Clinical Procedures in Emergency Medicine.* 3d ed. Philadelphia: Saunders, 1998.

Rockwood, Charles A., Jr., ed. *Rockwood and Green's Fractures in Adults.* 4th ed. Philadelphia: Lippincott-Raven, 1996.

Bibliiography

Rosen, Peter, ed. *Emergency Medicine: Concepts and Clinical Practice.* 4th ed. St. Louis: Mosby, 1998.

Rowland, Lewis P., ed. *Merritt's Textbook of Neurology.* 9th ed. Baltimore: Williams and Wilkins, 1995.

Ryan, Kenneth J., ed. *Kistner's Gynecology: Principles and Practice.* 6th ed. St. Louis: Mosby, 1995.

Sabiston, David C., Jr., ed. *Textbook of Surgery.* 15th ed. Philadelphia: Saunders, 1997.

Sande, Merle A. *Medical Management of AIDS.* 6th ed. Philadelphia: Saunders, 1999.

Scott, James R. *Danforth's Obstetrics and Gynecology.* 8th ed. Philadelphia: Lippincott-Raven, 1999.

Taylor, Robert B. *Family Medicine: Principles and Practice.* 5th ed. New York: Springer-Verlag, 1998.

Tierney, Lawrence M., ed. *Current Medical Diagnosis and Treatment.* 37th ed. Stamford, CT: Appleton and Lange, 1998.

Walsh, Patrick C., ed. *Campbell's Urology.* 7th ed. Philadelphia: Saunders, 1998.

Wilson, Jean D., ed. *Williams' Textbook of Endocrinology.* 9th ed. Philadelphia: Saunders, 1998.

Yamada, Tadataka. *Textbook of Gastroenterology.* 2d ed. Philadelphia: Lippincott-Raven, 1995.

Index

Page numbers referring to illustrations are in *italic* type.
See page bottom to find the volume in which any page reference appears.

Index

Index

Amputation saws, *374*

Amygdala, 74

Amyloid, 50, 617

Amyloidosis, 617

Amyotrophic Lateral Sclerosis (ALS),
    59-61

Amyotrophic Lateral Sclerosis
    Association, 61

Anabolic steroids, 821

Anabolism, 581

Anal sex, 28

Anaphylaxis, 46
    latex allergy, 45
    peanut allergy, 47
    shock, 132, 759

Anatomy, *819*
    arteries, *422*
    bones, 158, *397*
    brain, *233,* 563, *814*
    colon, *295*
    digestive organs, *271*
    DNA (deoxyribonucleic acid)
    double helix, *378*
    ears, *255, 256, 312, 590*
    eyes, *184, 236, 350, 388*
    gallbladder, *371*
    heart, *308, 416, 426*
    kidneys, *504*
    liver, *371, 495*
    lungs, *534*
    male reproductive system, *701*
    neurons, *268*
    ovum, *692*
    palate, *212*
    pancreas, *643*
    skin, *771*
    sperm, *692*
    spinal cord, *646*
    temporomandibular joint, *840*
    uterus, *334, 566, 895*
    veins, *423*
    wrist, *182*

Andersen, Hans Christian, 306

Androgenetic alopecia, 406

Androgens, 19, 406

Anemia, 62-69
    Crohn's disease, 483
    hemorrhoids, 440

hookworm infections, 456

iron deficiencies, 290

leukemia, 526

pregnancy, 691, 695

sickle-cell anemia, 760-764

ulcerative colitis, 482

Anesthesia/Anesthetic, 78, 187

Aneurysms, 69-71, 813
    aortic aneurysms, 758
    hemorrhages, 438-439
    Marfan syndrome, 557

Angina. *See* Heart, disease

Angina pectoris, 420, 429

Angiodema, 454

Angiography, 422

Angioplasty, 423

Animals, 913-914
    bites, 71-73
    dander causing asthma, 95, 96
    rabies, 709-712

Anopheles mosquito, 551, *552,* 555

Anorexia nervosa
    amenorrhea, 569
    fasting hypoglycemia, 467
    hirsutism, 408
    See also Eating disorders

Anorexia Nervosa and Related Eating
    Disorders (ANRED), 319

Anovulation, 568

Antacids, 429

Anterior tibial arteries, *422*

Anterior tibial veins, *423*

Anthelmintic medications, 88

Antibiotics
    bacterial infections, 117-118, 119
    bedsores, 121
    campylobacteriosis, 169
    chlamydial infections, 199
    cholera, 202
    colds, 217
    colitis, 223
    cyclosporiasis, 246
    cystic fibrosis, 252
    diarrhea, 283, 284
    diphtheria, 293
    diverticulitis, 295
    Down Syndrome, 299
    ear infections, 314

endocarditis, 332, 333

gangrene, 375

gonorrhea, 391, 392-393

immunodeficiency, 473

inflammatory bowel disease, 483

laryngitis, 514

Legionnaires' disease, 522

Lyme disease, 544-545

meningitis, 564

osteomyelitis, 634

pelvic inflammatory disease
    (PID), 656

peptic ulcers, 659

peritonitis, 661

plague, 670

pneumonia, 678

rheumatic fever, 724

Rocky Mountain spotted fever
    (RMSF), 728

scabies, 734

shock, 759

sickle-cell anemia, 761, 763

strep throat, 807

syphilis, 830

tetanus, 847

trachoma, 140

urethritis, nonspecific (NSU),
    890

urinary tract infections, 891

whooping cough, 907

yogurt, 910

See also Medications

Antibodies, 43-44, 45
    B cell lymphocytes, 471
    body defenses, 475
    lupus, 539
    mumps, 603
    proteins, 581
    rheumatic fever, 722
    rheumatoid arthritis, 82
    sperm, 478
    stress-related illness, 810
    thyrotoxicosis, 850
    trichinosis, 874
    vaccines, 488

Anticoagulants, 815

Antidepressants, 267, 268, 269

Antifungal medications, 100

Index

congenital rubella, 385-386

environmental diseases, 338

fetal alcohol syndrome, 352-353

Birth marks, 772

See also Skin

Bites, 131-135

Bites from animals, 71-73

Black bile, 215

Black Death (plague), 668, 669

Blackheads, 19, *20*

"Blackouts," 37

Black lung disease, 338, 672, 673

See also Pneumoconiosis

Blackwater fever, 554

Black widow spiders, 132-133

Bladder cancer, 135-138

Bladder infections

Urethritis, nonspecific (NSU), 890

urinary tract infections, 891

Blame, 11

Blastomycosis, 368

Blasts (immature white blood cells), 525

Bleeding, 438-440

cervical polyps, 685

dengue fever, 261

ectopic pregnancy, 655

hemophilia, 435

hemorrhagic fever, 411

hemorrhagic strokes, 813-814

menstrual disorders, 569

pregnancy, 696

scurvy, 746-747

See also Blood clotting

Bleuler, Paul Eugene, 740

Blindness, 138-143, 388-390

See also Eyes; Vision

Blindness, color, 228-229

Blisters, 754

Blood, 62

alcohol levels, 40, 41

circulation, 490, 664

clotting of blood, 214

flow to brain, 347-348

glucose, 271, 276

hemolytic jaundice, 495

lipids, 419

loss of, 64

production of, 62-64

Blood clotting, 214

embolisms, 323

hemophilia, 434-438

ischemic strokes, 812-813

liver function, 208

phlebitis, 664

stress-related illness, 809

thrombosis, 847-849

Blood flukes, 736-738

Bloodletting, 153

Blood pressure, 463-464

heart disease, 418

shock, 758-760

tests for phlebitis, 664

typhus, 887

Blood tests

galactosemia, 585

hantavirus, 411

hemorrhages, 439

hepatitis, 446

hypoglycemia, 468

infertility, 479

kidney disease, 503

lactose intolerance, 512

lead poisoning, 519

leukemia, 526

Lyme disease, 544

malaria, 553

menstrual disorders, 570

mononucleosis, 589

muscular dystrophy, 608

osteoporosis, 637

pancreatitis, 644

parasitic infections, 650

pelvic inflammatory disease (PID), 655-656

peptic ulcers, 659

phenylketonuria (PKU), 582

pneumonia, 677

rickets, 726

Rocky Mountain spotted fever (RMSF), 728

schistosomiasis, 737

substance abuse, 826

syphilis, 831

tapeworm, 837

thyroid disease, 852

toxic shock syndrome (TSS), 866

toxocariasis, 868

toxoplasmosis, 869

trichinosis, 874

typhoid fever, 885

typhus, 887

Blood transfusions, 64

blackwater fever, 554

cytomegalovirus, 253

hemophilia, 436, 437

and HIV, 27

shock, 759

sickle-cell anemia, 764

Blood vessels, 69, 278

See also Arteries; Circulatory system; Veins

BMI (Body mass index), 627

Bodily humors, 215

Body fat, 623, 626-627

Body lice, 530

Body mass index, 419, 626, 627

Body systems, 1

Body temperature, 355-359

Body temperature charts, 479

Boils, 15

See also Abscesses

Bone marrow, 63

anemia, 65-66, 68

aspiration, 526

immunodeficiency, 472

lymphatic system, 471

lymphoma, 547

porphyria, 686

transplantation, 253, 526

Bones

anatomy, 158, *397*

broken, 156-160

calcium deficiencies, 290

cysts, 248

of the feet, 164

fragments as embolisms, 324

growth rates, 397

ossicles, *255,* 256

osteomyelitis, 633-635

osteoporosis, 635-639

rickets, 724-726

scans for, 137, 500, 634

spurs, 81

Cerebrospinal fluid (CSF), 459, 794
Cerebrum, *2*
Cerumen, 256
Cervical region of the spine, *646*
Cervix, *566, 895*
    cancer, 173, 753, 892-895
    infertility, 479
    miscarriages, 694
    pelvic inflammatory disease
    (PID), 654
    polyps, 685
    premature birth, 696
Cesarean section, 693, 694
Chad, 201
Chagas' disease, 192-194, 649
Chancres, 650, 830
Charcot, Jean-Martin, 61, 600, 653
Chelates, 519
Chemical exposure
    bladder cancer, 135
    brain tumors, 146
    cancer, 173
    cirrhosis of the liver, 210
    environmental diseases, 339
    leukemia, 526
    See also Environmental factors in
    disease
Chemicals in the brain, 264
Chemistry, word origin, 4
Chemotherapy, 153-154
    brain tumors, 149
    cancer, 175
    cervical cancer, 894
    colorectal cancer, 231
    hair loss, 406
    kidney cancer, 500
    leukemia, 526
    lung cancer, 535
    lymphoma, 548, 549
    mouth cancer, 593
    pancreatic cancer, 642
    skin cancer, 769
    stomach cancer, 798
    testicular cancer, 842, 844
    tumors, 881
Cher, 306
Chernobyl power plant, 713
Chest x-ray, 92

Chewing gum, 857
Chewing tobacco, 592, 856
Chicken meat, 169
Chickenpox, 194-197
    Epstein-Barr virus, 588
    herpes, 451
    pneumonia, 676
    shingles, 756, 757
    smallpox, 787
Chiggers, 131
Chilblains, 222
Childhood asthma, 91
Children and Adults with Attention
    Deficit Disorders, 107
Children's PKU Network, 663
Children With Diabetes, 280
Chile, 797
Chimpanzees, 31
China
    beriberi, 287
    hantavirus, 411
    Japanese encephalitis, 330
    opium, 823
    schistosomiasis, 736
    tuberculosis, 877
Chlamydial infections, 141, 197-200
    gonorrhea, 391
    infertility, 478
    pelvic inflammatory disease
    (PID), 654, 655, 656
    pneumonia, 198, 676
    psittaci, 198, 914
    sexually transmitted diseases
    (STDs), 752
    trachomatis, 140, 198
    urethritis, nonspecific (NSU),
    889
    urinary tract infections, 891
    See also Sexually transmitted dis-
    eases (STDs)
Chlamydia trachomatis, 140, 141
Chloroguanide, 554
Chloroquine, 553, 554
Chocolate cysts, 247
Cholera, 200-203, 282
Cholestrol
    gallstones, 372
    heart disease, 420, 425

    obesity, 624
    strokes, 817
Chorea. *See* Huntington's Disease
Chorionic villus sampling, 381, 579
Chromosomes, 36, 110
    birth defects, 127
    chromosome 21, 296, 297-298
    cystic fibrosis, 250
    definition of, 378
    Down syndrome, 128, 296, 297-
    298
    genetic diseases, 377, 378-380
    hemophilia, 438
    Turner syndrome, 881
    See also X chromosomes
Chrondrodystrophy, 397
Chronic Addison's disease, 23
Chronic back pain, 744
Chronic bronchitis, 161-162, 856
Chronic carbon monoxide poisoning,
    179
Chronic Chagas' disease, 192-194
Chronic cirrhosis of the liver, 207
Chronic colitis, 223
Chronic depression, 264
Chronic diarrhea, 283
Chronic diseases, 11
    growth rates, 397
    HIV (Human immunodeficiency
    virus), 26
Chronic fatigue syndrome, 204-207,
    361
Chronic gout, 393
Chronic hepatitis, 445, 446-447
Chronic illnesses, 6
Chronic inflammatory bowel disease,
    481-485
Chronic insomnia, 491, 779, 781
Chronic kidney disease, 502-503
Chronic Legionnaires' disease, 521
Chronic leukemia, 526
Chronic nephritis, 614
Chronic obstruction bronchitis, 325
Chronic obstructive lung disease, 325
Chronic obstructive pulmonary disease,
    325, 676
Chronic osteomyelitis, 634
Chronic pancreatitis, 644

Index

kwashiorkor, 507-509
obesity, 625, 628
pancreatitis, 644
phenylketonuria (PKU), 582
scurvy, 746-747
See also Nutrition
Di George syndrome, 471, 472
Digestive system, *2, 797*
anatomy, *271*
ascariasis, 87
colorectal cancer, 229-230
inflammatory bowel disease, *482*
lactose intolerance, 511-512
pancreas, 270-271
pounds of waste, 1
See also under individual organs
Digital arteries, *422*
Digital rectal exam, 230
Digital thermometers, 357
Digital veins, *423*
Dilantin, 447
Diphtheria, 291-294
Discoid lupus erythematosus (DLE), 537, 538
Disease, definition of, 5
Disinfecting wounds, 477
Disseminated gonococcal infections, 392
Dissociative identity disorder, 594-598
Diuretic drugs
causing osteoporosis, 637
eating disorders, 317
hypertension, 465
nephrosis, 617
Diverticulitis/Diverticulosis, 294-296
diarrhea, 283
peritonitis, 660
Diving Bell and the Butterfly, The (Bauby), 648
Dizziness. *See* vertigo
Djibouti, 201
DMT (dimethyltryptamine), 824
DNA (deoxyribonucleic acid), 3, 380
anatomy of double helix, *378*
bacterial gene detection, 392
cancer, 171
definition of, 378
and HIV, 31

lymphoma, 547
skin cancer, 767
testing, 437
Dogs
bites, 71, 72
for the deaf, 259
rabies, 710-711
seeing eye, 141
Dole, Bob, 702
Dombey and Son (Dickens), 6
Dominant genetic traits, 127, 378, 379
See also Genes
Dominican Republic, 736
Dopamine, 652
Dorsett, Sybil, 595
Dostoyevsky, Fyodor, 342
Down, John Langdon Haydon, 297
Down syndrome, 7, 128, 296-300
dwarfism, 301
genetic disorders, 380
mental retardation, 577
strabismus, 800
Drafts, 217
Drug abuse/addiction, 439-440, 578, 818-827
See also Substance abuse
Drug-induced lupus, 538
Drug resistant bacteria, 118-119
Drugs, 8
hepatitis, 443
names of, 10
See also Medications
Drugs, illegal. *See* Substance abuse
Drunk driving, 40
Drunkard's Progress: From the First Glass to the Grave (Currier), *39*
Dry beriberi, 287
Dry gangrene, 373, 374
Duchenne, Guillaume Benjamin Amand, 607
Duchenne muscular dystrophy, 605, 606, 607, 608
Duke, Patty, 142
Duodenum, *371, 643,* 644
Du Pré, Jacqueline, 598
Dust mites, 46, 96
Dwarfism, 300-303, 399
Dykstra, Lenny, 593

Dysentery, 56-57, 282, 284
See also Diarrhea
Dysfunctional uterine bleeding, 569
Dyslexia, 303-307
Dysmenorrhea, 569, 571
Dyspepsia, 427-429
Dysphasia, 791
Dysplasia, 397
Dysrhythmia, 307-310, 419
Dystrophin, 605, 606

E

E. coli (Escherichia coli), 116, 282
Eardrum, *255, 256*
conductive hearing loss, 257
ear infections, 312
Ears
anatomy, *255, 256, 312, 590*
deafness, 255-260
infections, 311-315
plugs, 258
positional vertigo, 897
tinnitus, 853-854
tonsillitis infections, 860
vertigo, 897
wax, 256
Eastern equine encephalitis, 330
Eating disorders, 315-319, 573
Ebola fever, 319-321
Echocardiogram, 421, 427, 557
Echolalia, 110, 862
Echopraxia, 862
Echoviruses, 899
Eclampsia, 463, 751
Ecosystem, 1
Ecstacy drug (MDMA), 824
Ectoparasites, 649
Ectopic pregnancy, 655, 656, 693-694
Eczema, 772
Edema, 209
glomerulonephritis, 614
heart disease, 421
kwashiorkor, 508
nephrosis, 615, 617
pregnancy, 692
Edison, Thomas, 306
Education

Index

(RMSF), 728-729
salmonellosis, 731
scarlet fever, 734-738
spina bifida, 795
strep throat, 806
typhoid fever, 885
typhus, 887
viral infections, 901
Fiberoptic instruments, 484
Fibrillin, 556
Fibrin, 291, 434
Fibrinogen, 209, 289, 434
Fibrocystic breast disorder, 359-360
Fibroids
dysmenorrhea, 570
infertility, 479
menstrual disorders, 569
See also Menstrual cycle, disorders in
Fibromyalgia, 80, 84, 360-361
Fibrosis, 673
Fibrositis, 360
Fighter pilots (World War II), 347
"Fight or flight" pattern, 808-809
Filariasis, 131, 321, 649
Fillings for teeth, 187
Filovirus, 320
Finasteride, 407
Finland, 411
Fire ants, 131-132
First degree burns, 165
See also Burns
Flashbacks, 688, 872
Flat feet, 362-363
Fleas, 669-671, 886
Fleisher, Leon, 717
Flesh-eating bacteria, 118
Florida, 84, 553, 884
Floyer, John, 91, 326
Flu, 485-489
compared to colds, 217
Lyme disease, 543
See also Influenza
Fluid in the ear, 314
Fluoride, 188
Folate, 289
Folic acid, 65, 289
anemia, 68

myelomeningocele, 795
sickle-cell anemia, 764
Folk medicine, 518
Follicles, hair, 405, *771*
and acne, 19, 20
definition of, 15
Follicle-stimulating hormone, 567
Folliculitis, 15
Følling, Asbjørn, 583, 661-62
Fonda, Jane, 317
Food poisoning, 117, 143-145, 363-365
campylobacteriosis, 169-170
cans of food, lead poisoning, 517
diarrhea, 281-282
salmonellosis, 731-732
Foods
allergies to, 46
causing migraine headaches, 415
food groups, 628
hives, 453
Foot problems, 163-165, 362-363
Forgetfulness, 50, 52, 55, 58-59
Fox, Michael J., 651
Fractures, 156-160
Fragile X syndrome, 110
See also X chromosomes
France, 411, 489, 669
Frankenstein (Shelley), 263
Franklin, Benjamin, 217, 394, 628
Franks, Wilbur R., 347
Freckles, 768
Free radicals, 54
Freezing temperatures, 218-222
French Sign Language, 790
Freud, Sigmund, 414
Frontal sinuses, *765*
Frostbite, 218, 219-220, 365, 375
Fructose intolerance, 585
Fulguration, 137
Fulminant hepatitis, 442
Fungal infections, 366-369, 476
abscesses, 15
athlete's foot, 99-101
fungi definition, 366
meningitis, 562, 563
osteomyelitis, 634
ringworm, 727

thrush, 849-850
yeast infections, vaginal, 908-910
Fungal pneumonia, 677
Furuncles, 17

G

Gaillard's Medical Journal, 823
Gajdusek, Daniel Carleton, 507
Galactose, 511
Galactosemia, 584-585
Galen, 153
migraine headaches, 412
Parkinson's disease, 653
rabies, 710
Gall, 496
Gallaudet, Thomas, 790
Gallaudet University, 790
Gallbladder, *2,* 371-373
biliary system, 644
heartburn, 428
obesity, 624
Gallstones, 371-373
obstructive jaundice, 495
pancreatitis, 644
sickle-cell anemia, 763
Gama, Vasco da, 746
Gamma knife radiosurgery, *149*
Ganglion cysts, 248
Gangrene, 373-375, 716
Garagiola, Joe, 593
Garrod, Archibald, 580
Gases, substance abuse, 824
Gas gangrene, 374
Gasoline, lead poisoning from, 517
Gastrectomy, 798
Gastric cancer, 796
Gastroenteritis, 282, 375-376
Gastroenterologist, 797
Gastroesophageal reflux disease (GERD), 428
Gastrointestinal conditions, 809
Gehrig, Lou, 59, 61
Gender, 36
General anesthesia, 78
Generalized anxiety disorder, 74-75
Generalized seizures, 342-343, 749
Generalized tonic-clonic seizures, 749

General paresis, 831
Generic drugs, 10
Genes, *2, 3*
    albinism, 34
    alcoholism, 38
    Alzheimer's disease, 51
    arthritis, 81
    autism, 109, 110
    bacterial infections, 118
    birth defects, 127
    breast cancer, 152
    cancer, 171
    cleft palate, 212
    color blindness, 228
    Creutzfeldt-Jakob Disease, 240
    cystic fibrosis, 249, 252
    definition of, 378
    depressive disorders, 264
    diabetes, 273
    dietary deficiencies, 285
    dwarfism, 301
    dyslexia, 304
    genetic diseases, 377-383
    hemophilia, 434-438, 438
    Huntington's disease, 456-458
    immunodeficiency, 469
    inflammatory bowel disease, 482
    lung cancer, 533
    lymphoma, 547
    Marfan syndrome, 556-558
    metabolic disease, 580
    multiple sclerosis, 599-600
    muscular dystrophy, 604-609
    neurofibromatosis, 618
    obesity, 625
    osteoporosis, 636
    porphyria, 685
    Reye's syndrome, 721
    sensorineural hearing loss, 258
    sickle-cell anemia, 66, 760-762
    skin cancer, 767-768
    Tay-Sachs disease, 838-839
    See also Chromosomes; Heredity
Gene therapy, 252, 381, 472
    hemophilia, 438
    lung cancer, 536
    lymphoma, 549
Genetic disorders, 377-383

Down syndrome, 297-298
    genetic childhood rickets, 725
    genetic skeletal dysplasia, 399
    growth rates, 398
    radiation, 713
Genetic testing
    Marfan syndrome, 558
    mental retardation, 579
    muscular dystrophy, 608
    neurofibromatosis, 620
    Tay-Sachs disease, 839
Genital herpes, 450, 752
Genital warts, 383-384, 752
Genome, 378
Genuphobia, 666
George, Otis A., 158
George III, King of England, 584, 686
Georgia, 553
German measles, 128, 384-386
    cleft palate, 212
    growth rates, 397
    hives, 453
    mental retardation, 577-578
Germinoma, 146
Gestational age, 397
Gestational diabetes, 693
Getting to Dry (Maizels, Rosenbaum and Keating), 123
Ghana, 201
Giardia lamblia protozoan, 386, *387, 649*
Giardiasis, 282, 283, 386-387
Gigantism, 399
    See also Growth rate, disorders
Gilles de la Tourette, Georges G. A. B., 861, 864
Gilles de la Tourette syndrome. *See* Tourette syndrome
Ginger root, 591-592
Gingivitis, 401, 746
    See also Gum disease
Ginkgo biloba, 54
GI series. *See* Barium x-rays
Glands, 247, 249
Glare blindness, 286
Glasses, 99
    See also Eyeglasses
Glass Menagerie (Williams), 672

Glaucoma, 388-390, 824
    blindness, 139, 140
    headaches, 413
Glaucoma Research Foundation, 390
Gleason, Jackie, 628
Glioblastoma, 147
Glioma, 146
Global aphasia, 791
Global warming and malaria, 553
Globulin, 443, 444
Glomeruli, 503, 616
Glomerulonephritis, 503, 614, 617
Glomerulus, 613
Glover, Danny, 306
Glucagon, 644
Glucose, 5
    catabolism, 581
    diabetes, 270
    digestive process, 271
    intake by cells, *272*
    lactose intolerance, 511
    metabolism in Alzheimer's disease, 50
Glucose-6-phosphatase deficiency (G6PD), 585
Glycogen, 208, 581, 585
Gogh, Vincent van, 263
Goiter, 289, 851-852, 853
    See also Thyroid gland
Gold, Tracy, 315
Goldberg, Whoopi, 306
Gonadotropin-releasing hormone, 567
Gonococcal arthritis, 392
Gonorrhea, 390-393
    infertility, 478
    pelvic inflammatory disease (PID), 654, 656
    sexually transmitted diseases (STDs), 752
    urethritis, nonspecific (NSU), 889
Goodwill Games, 1998, 645
Gordon, F., 255
Gorgas, William, 912
Gout, 393-394
    arthritis, 80, 84
    obesity, 625
Graham, Billy, 652

Index

sexually transmitted diseases (STDs), 754

tuberculosis, 876

viral infections, 899

See also AIDS (Acquired immune deficiency syndrome)

Hodgkin, Thomas, 547

Hodgkin's disease, 547

shingles, 756

systemic fungal infections, 367

See also Cancer; Lymphoma

Hoffman, Dustin, 112

Holter ECG monitor, 310, 421

Homelessness, 219, 876

Homeostasis, 5

Honduras, 201

Honeybees, 133

Hong Kong, 201, 669

Hooker Chemicals and Plastics Corporation, 337

Hookworm, 454-456, 650

Hopkins, Gerald Manley, 884

Hormones, 19, 243

Addison's disease, 23

cancer treatment, 175

corticotropin-releasing hormone, 243, 809

Cushing's syndrome, 242

dwarfism, 301

endometriosis, 334

growth disorders, 398-400

growth rate, 395-396

hair loss, 406

hypothyroidism, 853

infertility, 478

iodine, 289

melatonin, 781

menstrual disorders, 565, 569, 570

menstruation, 567

obesity, 625

pancreas, 271

post-traumatic stress disorder, 688

proteins, 581

sleep patterns, 491

stress-related illness, 808-809

testicular cancer, 842

therapy with, 500, 702

thyroid disease, 850

urinary incontinence, 474

uterine cancer, 893, 894

Hospital detoxification unit, 42

How and Why We Age (Hayflick), 55

HPS (Hantavirus pulmonary syndrome), 410-411

HPV (Human papillomavirus), 383-384

HTLV-1 (human T-cell lymphotropic virus), 547, 548

Human bites, 72

Human brain, *2*

See also Brain

Human Growth Foundation, 303

Human spongiform encephalopathy, 239

Humidity and the heat index, 432

Humoral immunity, 471

Hungary, 411

Hunter's syndrome, 381

Huntington, George, 457

Huntington's disease, 127, 456-458

genetic disorders, 381

mental disorders, 573

Huntington's Disease Society of America, 458

Hydrocephalus, 302, 458-460

myelomeningocele, 795

strabismus, 800

Hydrocephalus Association, 460

Hydrogen bonds, *378*

Hydrogen breath test, 512

Hydrophobia, 666

Hyperactivity, 102, 103-104

See also Attention deficit hyperactivity disorder (ADHD)

Hyperbaric oxygen chamber, 126, 180, 375

Hypercalcemia, 290

Hyperglycemia, 277, 467

Hyperlipid disorders, 420

Hyperpigmentation, 772

Hyperpituitarism, 399

Hyperplasia, 704

Hypersomnia, 778, 780

Hypertension, 418, 460-465

brain hemorrhages, 439

hemorrhagic strokes, 813

nephrosis, 616

nosebleeds, 621

strokes, 816

See also High blood pressure

Hyperthermia, 355

Hyperthyroidism, 850-851

constipation, 238

secondary osteoporosis, 636

See also Thyroid gland

Hypnosis, 597

Hypochondria, 466

Hypoglycemia, 276-277, 467-468

Hypopigmentation, 772

Hypopituitarism, 398-399

Hypoplastic anemia, 64-65

Hypothalamus, 355, 396

cortisol, 243

stress-related illness, *808,* 809

Hypothermia, 218, 219, 220-222

See also Cold-related injuries

Hypothyroidism, 289-290, 400, 578, 851

See also Thyroid gland

Hypovolemic shock, 758

Hysterectomy, 334, 571, 894

Hysteroscopy, 570

I

Iatrogenic Creutzfeldt-Jakob Disease, 240

Ibuprofen

Alzheimer's disease, 54

causing nephritis, 614

causing peptic ulcers, 658

fever, 358

lupus, 540

mononucleosis, 589

Osgood-Schlatter disease, 633

phlebitis, 664

See also Medications; Over-the-counter medications

Iceland, 797

Ichthyophobia, 666

Idiopathic conditions, 124

epilepsy, 341

osteoporosis, 636

Index

Paint and lead poisoning, 517
Pakistan, 682, 877
Palate, cleft, 211-214
Palilalia, 862
Palmer, Arnold, 702
Palpitations, 308
Palsy. *See* Bell's palsy; Cerebral palsy;
   Parkinson's disease
Panama Canal, 911
Pancreas, 641
   anatomy, *643*
   cystic fibrosis, 249, 251
   diabetes, 270-280
   fasting hypoglycemia, 467
   gallstones, 373
Pancreatectomy, 642
Pancreatic cancer, 641-643
Pancreatitis, 603, 643-645
Pandemics, 487
Panic attacks, 75, 665
Papanicolaou, George, 893
Papillomavirus (HPV)
   cervical cancer, 893
   sexually transmitted diseases
   (STDs), 753
   warts, 905-906
Pap test, 384, 894
Papua, New Guinea, 506
Papule, 774
Paracelsus, 457
Paralysis, 645-648
   acute intermittent porphyria, 686
   multiple sclerosis, 600
   myelomeningocele, 795
   poliomyelitis, 680
   sleep disorders, 780
Paralysis agitans, 653
Paranoia
   porphyria, 586
   schizophrenia, 740
   substance abuse, 821
Paraplegia, 645, *646*
Parasites, 529, 732-734
Parasitic infections, 476, 648-650
   amebiasis, 56
   ascariasis, 86
   babesiosis, 115
   Chagas' disease, 192-194

cirrhosis of the liver, 208
cryptosporidiosis, 245
cyclosporiasis, 245
cysts, 247
diarrhea, 282
elephantiasis, 321
giardiasis, 386-387
hookworm, 454-456
malaria, 551-555
pinworm, 666-668
schistosomiasis, 736-738
toxocariasis, 867-868
toxoplasmosis, 868-870
trichinosis, 873-875
worms, 908
Paré, Ambroise, 394
Parents of Galactosemic Children, 587
Parietal lobe, 814
Parkinson, James, 652, 653
Parkinson's disease, 474, 651-653
Parrot fever, 198, 199, 914
Partial seizures, 750
Pasteur, Louis, 712
Pauling, Linus, 289
PCP (Pneumocystic carinii pneumonia), 677, 678
Peak flow meter, 92-93
Peanuts, allergic reaction to, 47, 49
Peck, Kathy, 255
Pediatric Crohn's and Colitis
   Association, 485
Pediculicides, 531
Pediculosis, 529
Pellagra, 287-288
Pelvic inflammatory disease (PID), 199,
   390, 654
   dysmenorrhea, 570
   infertility, 479
   peritonitis, 660
   sexually transmitted diseases
   (STDs), 753
Pelvic peritonitis, 655
Penetrance, 380
Penicillin
   allergies, 46
   gonorrhea, 392-393
   hives, 453
   scarlet fever, 735

strep throat, 807
syphilis, 830, 832-833
   See also Antibiotics; Medications
Pentosuria, 580
Peptic ulcers, 428, 657-660
Percutaneous umbilical blood sampling,
   381
Periodontal disease, 401-404
Periodontitis, 401-402
   See also Gum disease
Peripheral nervous system, 598-599
   See also Brain; Central nervous
   system
Peripheral vision, 389
Peritoneum, 878
Peritonitis, 77, 660-661
Peritonsillar abscesses, 16
Perlman, Itzhak, 683
Permethrin, 733
Pernicious anemia, 65
Persian Gulf War, 338
Personality changes
   Alzheimer's disease, 49-50
   cirrhosis of the liver, 209
Pertussis, 906-907
   See also Whooping cough
Pervasive development disorde, 109
Pesticides, 336
Pet dander, 44
Petit mal seizures, 343, 749
Pets, 913-914
PET scans, 51, *264, 344*
   Alzheimer's, 51
   epilepsy, 344
   mental disorders, *572*
   schizophrenia, 739
   seizures, 750
   sleep disorders, 778
"P" gene, 35
Pharmacy, word origin, 4
Pharyngitis, 198, 860
   See also Strep throat
Phenylalanine, 249, 582, 661
Phenylketonuria (PKU), 582-583, 661-
   663
   diet, 129
   genetic disorders, 377, 381
Phenylpyruvic acid, 583

Index

Index

"Punch drunk," 235
Punnet squares, 382
Pupaphobia, 666
Pupil of the eye, 389
Purging, eating disorders, 317
Pus
    in abscesses, 15, 17
    gangrene, 375
Pustules, 774
PUVA (Psoralen and ultraviolet A therapy), 903
Pyelonephritis, 503, 891
Pyrexia, 358
Pyrimethamine, 554
Pyrogens, 356

Q

Q fever, 356, 728
Quadriplegia, 645, *646*
    See also Paralysis
Quarantine, 199, 711
Quinine, 554
QuitNet, 858

R

Rabies, 71-72, 709-712
    encephalitis, 330
    virus, *900*
    wild animals, 914
    zoonoses, 913-914
Radial artery, *422*
Radiation, 173
    enterocolitis, 223
    exposure conditions, 712-714
    leukemia, 526
Radiation therapy
    bladder cancer, 137
    brain tumors, 149
    cancer, *174*, 175
    cervical cancer, 894
    colorectal cancer, 231
    leukemia, 526
    lung cancer, 535
    lymphoma, 548
    mouth cancer, 593
    pancreatic cancer, 642
    prostate cancer, 702
    skin cancer, 769

stomach cancer, 798
    testicular cancer, 844
    tumors, 881
Radical prostatectomy, 702
Radioactive iodine, 852
Radiographs, 8
Radiotherapy, 8
Radon, 712
Rain Man (film), 112
Rales, 677
Ramsay Hunt syndrome, 757
Rapid eye movement sleep, 779
    See also Sleeping
Rapoport, Judith L., 632
Rashes. *See* Skin, disorders
Rat-bite fever, 357
Rates of growth, 395
Rats
    Lassa fever, 515
    murine typhus, 886, 887
    See also Rodents
Rattlesnakes, 134
Raynaud's disease, 715-716
Reactions, allergic. *See* Allergies
Reactive hypoglycemia, 467
Reading ability, 304-306
Reading specialists, 306
Reagan, Ronald, 53
Receptors and anxiety disorders, 74
Recessive genetic traits, 127, 378
    albinism, 35
    autosomal disorders, 379
    See also Genes
Recklinghausen, Friedrich von, 618
Rectal cancer, 171
Rectal exam, 230
Rectum, 223, 230
Red blood cells, 62, 552
    See also Blood
Redbugs, 131
Red color, 228
Reduction, 159
Reduviid bugs, *193*
Reed, Walter, 912
Refraction, 611
Refractive surgery, 612
Regional enteritis. *See* Inflammatory
    bowel disease

Regulations for environmental diseases, 339
    See also Environmental factors in disease
Rehabilitation for strokes, 815
Relapsing fever, 357
Relapsing-remitting multiple sclerosis, 599
Relationships and autism, 110
Relaxation techniques, 75, 689, 810
R.E.M. (musical group), 70
Remission and epilepsy, 344
REM sleep, 779
Renaissance, the, 341
Renal artery, *422, 504*
Renal pelvis, 500
Renin, 462
Reno, Janet, 347, 652
Repetitive stress syndrome, 716-720, 809
    See also Carpal tunnel syndrome
Reports of Medical Cases, 613
Repressed memories, 58
Reproductive cells, 378
Reproductive system, 752
    See also Female reproductive system; Male reproductive system
"Rescue missions," 42
Research
    into anemia, 68
    colorectal cancer, 231-232
    cure for cancer, 175-176
    diabetes, 277
    lung cancer, 536
    multiple sclerosis, 601
    rheumatic fever, 724
    skin cancer, 769-770
Research to Prevent Blindness, Inc., 139, 143
RESOLVE, The National Infertility Association, 481
Respiratory syncytial virus, 676
Respiratory system, *2*
    birth defects, 128
    influenza, 486
    See also Lungs
Reston virus, 320
Retina, 98-99, *388*

Salpêtrière Hospital, 600
Salpingitis, 654
Salt, 462, 464, 638
El Salvador, 201
Sanatariums, 341
Sanitation, 10, 57
    See also Environmental factors in
      disease; Water supply
Sarcopetes scabiei, 733
Saudi Arabia, 761
Scabicides, 733
Scabies, 649, 732-734
Scalp reduction surgery, 408
Scarlet fever, 357, 722, 734-738
Schistosoma blood flukes, 649
Schistosomiasis, 649, 736-738
Schizophrenia, 738-741
    autism, 111
    mental disorders, 574
    multiple personality disorder, 596
    See also Mental disorders;
      Multiple personality disorder
Schlatter, Carl, 633
Schools, 105-106, 112, 755
Schwarzkopf, Norman, 702
Sciatica, 741-743, 744
Sclera, 235
Scleroderma, 226, 715
Scleroderma Foundation, 227
Sclerosis, systemic. *See* Scleroderma
Scolex, 835
Scoliosis, 743-745
    Marfan syndrome, 557
    muscular dystrophy, 606
    neurofibromatosis, 619
Scopolamine, 591, 592
Scorpions, 133
Scrapie, 240
Screening tests
    cancer, 176
    colorectal cancer, 231
    Down Syndrome, 299
    See also Tests
Scrotum, 478, 842
Scrub typhus, 886-887
Scuba diving, 125-126
Scurvy, 288, 746-747
Seasickness. *See* Motion sickness

Seatbelts
    concussions, 235
    trauma, 870, 872
Sebaceous cysts, 248
Sebaceous glands, 19, 20
Seborrheic dermatitis, 774
Sebum, 19, 20
Secondary amenorrhea, 568
Secondary brain tumors, 146
Secondary infections, 217
Secondary osteoporosis, 636
Secondary progressive multiple sclerosis,
    599
Second degree burns, 165-166
    See also Burns
Sedatives, 234
Seeing Eye, The, Inc., 143
Seeing eye dogs, 141
Seizures, 747-751
    acute intermittent porphyria, 686
    autism, 109-110
    epilepsy, 342-343
    febrile convulsions, 357, 749
    porphyria, 586
Selective serotonin reuptake inhibitors,
    269
Self-Consciousness (Updike), 705
Self-esteem and depression, 265
Self-help for attention deficit hyperac-
    tivity disorder, 106-107
Self-inflicted injuries, 597
Semicircular canals, *255,* 312
Senile dementia.*See* Alzheimer's disease
Sennert, Daniel, 735
Senses and autism, 111
Sensorineural hearing loss, 256, 257-
    258
Sensory cortex, 814
Sensory nerve receptors, *771*
Separation anxiety disorder, 75, 574
Septicemia, 120, 495
Septicemic plague, 670
Septic shock, 759, 871
Serotonin, 74
    autism, 109, 112
    depressive disorders, 268
Severe combined immunodeficiency
    disease (SCID), 469-470, 471

Severe retardation, 577
Sewage, 649
    See also Environmental factors in
      disease; Water supply
Sex hormones, 395-396
    See also Estrogen; Testosterone
Sex-linked genetic traits, 378-379
    birth defects, 127
    genetic disorders, 380
    immunodeficiency, 469
    muscular dystrophy, 605
Sexual abuse, 596
Sexual development, 396
Sexual intercourse, 27
Sexually transmitted diseases (STDs),
    751-756
    chlamydial trachomatis, 198
    gonorrhea, 390-393
    hepatitis, 444
    herpes, 450-451
    pelvic inflammatory disease
      (PID), 654
    urethritis, nonspecific (NSU),
      889
    urinary tract infections, 891
    See also AIDS; HIV (Human
      immunodeficiency virus)
SGR4KIDS, 858
Shakespeare, William, 780
Shape Up America!, 630
Shastid, Thomas Hall, 63
Shelley, Mary, 263
"Shell shock," 690
Shingles, 195, 756-757
    herpes, 451
    skin conditions, 774
Shin splints. *See* Sprains; Strains
Shock, 758-760, 871-872
Shoes
    bunions, 164
    flat feet, 363
    ingrown toenails, 490
Short-term relief medications, 94
Shoulder tendinitis, 718
Shunts, 459, 795
Sicily, 886
Sick building syndrome, 339
Sickle-cell anemia, 66, 127, 760-764

causing immunodeficiency, 469
    genetic disorders, 381
    hemolytic jaundice, 495
Sickle Cell Association, 69
Sickle-Cell Disease Association of
    America, Inc., 764
Sick sinus syndrome, 309
Side effects of medications, 105
    See also Medications
Sideroblastic anemia, 65
SIDS. *See* Sudden infant death syn-
    drome
SIDS Alliance, 829
Sierra Leone, 201, 515
Sigmoid colon, 294
Sigmoidoscope/Sigmoidoscopy, 232
    colorectal polyps, 685
    diverticulitis, 295
Signed Exact English, 790
Sign language, 790
Signs of disease, 8
"Silent killers" (aneurysms), 69, 462
Silent Spring (Carson), 336
Silicosis, 338, 672, 673
    See also Pneumoconiosis
Silver amalgam, 187
Simon, Carly, 791
Simple fracture, 157
Simple partial seizures, 750
Singapore, 201
Sin Nombre virus, 410
Sinoastrial node, 308
Sinuses
    and colds, 217
    headaches, 413
    nasal polyps, 685
    nosebleeds, 621
    osteomyelitis, 634
    sinusitis, 764-766
Sitz baths, 440
SIV (simian immunodeficiency syn-
    drome), 31
Sjögren's syndrome, 226
Sjögren's Syndrome Foundation, 227
Skeletal dysplasia, 397
Skeletal system, 557
    See also Bones
Skin

allergies, 45
anatomy, *771*
body defenses, 475
burns, 165-167
cancer, 171, 766-770
cells, *20*
disorders, 771-776
lupus, 539
Lyme disease, 543, 544
measles, 558
psoriasis, 705-707
scabies, 732-734
superficial fungal infections, 366-
    367
tests for allergies, 92
tests for tuberculosis, 878
vitiligo, 902-904
Slang and flat feet, 363
Sleep apnea, 776-777
    obesity, 625
    sleep disorders, 779
    tonsillectomy, 861
Sleeping
    disorders of, 778-782
    and mental disorders, 574
    sleeplessness, 491-492
    sleepwalking, 781
    sudden infant death syndrome
    (SIDS), 829
SleepNet, 777
Sleepovers, 122
Slipped disk, 782-784
Small cell lung cancer, 535
Small intestine, 87, *482*
    See also Digestive system
Smallpox, 6, 7, 784-788
Smoke-Free Kids and Soccer, 858
Smokeless tobacco, 856
    See also Tobacco-related diseases
Smoking, 172, 825, 854-859
    asthma, 96
    birth defects, 128
    bladder cancer, 135
    bronchitis, 160-161
    cataracts, 185
    causing halitosis, 409
    emphysema, 325-329
    headaches, 413

    heart disease, 419
    hypertension, 462, 465
    laryngitis, 513, 514
    Legionnaires' disease, 521
    lung cancer, 534, 535-536
    mouth cancer, 592, 594
    osteoporosis, 638
    phlebitis, 664
    pneumonia, 676
    premature birth, 695
    Raynaud's disease, 715, 716
    secondary osteoporosis, 636
    strokes, 817
Snails, 736
Snake bites, 133-134
    See also Bites
Snoring, 776-777
Snow, John, 201
Social drinking, 37
Social phobia, 665, 666
Social Security Act of 1935, 142
Sodium, 426, 464
    See also Salt
Sodium salicylate, 722
Solvents, 824
Somalia, 201
Sonograms, 9, 70
    hepatitis, 446
    kidney stones, 506
    See also Ultrasound
Sophie's Choice (Styron), 262
Sore throats, 806
Sound waves, 256
South Africa, 201
South America, 194
    leprosy, 522
    parasitic infections, 649
    plague, 669
    rabies, 709
    schistosomiasis, 736
    typhoid fever, 884
    yellow fever, 910
    See also Latin America
South American blastomycosis, 368
Southern California Orthopedic
    Institute, 745
Spain, 302, 489
Spanish flu, 487

Index

Index

Index

Index

Index

heat-related injuries, 433
"Water on the brain," 458
Water supply contamination
    cholera, 201
    cryptosporidiosis, 245
    cyclosporiasis, 245, 246
    giardiasis, 386, 387
    parasitic infections, 649
    viral infections, 901
Weaning babies, 286
"Wear and tear" arthritis, 81
Weather, 218-222
Weight-Control Information Network,
    629
Weight-for-height tables, 626-627
Weight-loss programs, 627-629
Weight problems, 273, 623-630
    See also Obesity
Weight training, 627
Weilenmayer, Erik, 390
WE Magazine, 648
Wens, 248
Wernicke's aphasia, 791
Wernicke's area of the brain, 789, 814
West Africa, 508
Western equine encephalitis, 330
West Nile encephalitis, 331
Wet beriberi, 287
Wet gangrene, 374
Wheal, skin conditions, 774
Wheelchairs, 646
Wheezing, 91
When Someone in Your Family Has
    Cancer, 177
Whiplash injuries, 841
Whipple, George Hoyt, 63
Whipworms, 649
White blood cells, 17, 28, 525
    See also Blood
White-footed mice, 410
Whiteheads, 19, *20*
Who, The (musical group), 255
Whooping cough, 906-907
Wigs, 407
Wilbur, Cornelia, 595
Wild animals, 914
    See also Rabies; Zoonoses
Wilder, Laura Ingalls, 221

Williams, Tennessee, 672
Willis, Bruce, 791
Willis, Thomas, 91
Willow bark, 722
Wilms, Max, 499
Wilms' tumor, 499
Wilson, Wade, 275
Wilson, Woodrow, 306
Wilson's disease, 8, 208
Wind-chill factor, 220
Windpipe, 850
    See also Trachea
Wiskott-Aldrich syndrome, 471
Withdrawal, emotional, 688-689
Withdrawal from alcohol, 38
    See also Alcohol consumption
Woodward, Joseph J., 158
Word origins
    chemistry, 4
    diabetes, 280
    emia, 280
    glyk, 28
    Latin, 571
    leukemia, 526
    menstrual terms, 571
    muscular dystrophy, 607
    pyro, 358
World Foundation of Hemophilia, 438
World Health Assembly, 785
World Health Organization, 13
    alcoholism, 38
    anemia, 63
    cancer, 172, 173, 177
    Chagas' disease, 194
    cholera, 203
    dengue fever, 261, 262
    dietary deficiencies, 291
    diphtheria, 294
    ebola fever, 320
    elephantiasis, 323
    encephalitis, 331
    environmental diseases, 340
    genetic disorders, 383
    heart disease, 420
    hepatitis, 447
    HIV (human immunodeficiency
    virus), 34
    infections, 477

    Lassa fever, 516
    leprosy, 524
    malaria, 555
    measles, 559, 561
    meningitis, 564
    mumps, 604
    parasitic infections, 650
    poliomyelitis, 684
    radiation, 714
    schistosomiasis, 737, 738
    sexually transmitted diseases
    (STDs), 755
    smallpox, 784-785, 786, 788
    strokes, 813
    substance abuse, 821
    trachoma, 140
    tuberculosis, 877, 880
    typhoid fever, 885
    worms, 908
    yellow fever, 913
    zoonoses, 915
"World Journey of Hope '99," 213
World War I, 222
    gangrene, 374
    influenza epidemic, 489
World War II, 347
    atomic bomb, 713
    cancer medication, 549
    scarlet fever, 735
    typhus, 886
Worms, 908
    See also under specific names of
    worms
Worrying. *See* Anxiety
Wright, Wilbur, 884
Wrinkles, 773, 774
Wrists, carpal tunnel syndrome, 181-
    182
Wuchereria bancrofti, 321

X

X chromosomes, 110, 378-379
    hemophilia, 434, 435
    mental retardation, 577
    muscular dystrophy, 605
    sex-linked disorders, 127, 380
    Turner syndrome, 881
    See also Chromosomes